DIRECTING THE
D·O·C·U·M·E·N·T·A·R·Y

SECOND EDITION

DIRECTING THE
D·O·C·U·M·E·N·T·A·R·Y
SECOND EDITION

Michael Rabiger

Focal Press
Boston   London

Focal Press is an imprint of Butterworth–Heinemann.

Library of Congress Cataloging-in-Publication Data

Rabiger, Michael.
    Directing the documentary / Michael Rabiger.—2nd
ed.
      p.   cm.
    Includes bibliographical references and index.
    ISBN 0-240-80126-1 (pbk. : alk. paper)
    1. Documentary films—Production and direction.
    I. Title.
PN1995.9.D6R33   1992
070.1'8—dc20   91-30084
                                      CIP

British Library Cataloguing in Publication Data

Rabiger, Michael
   Directing the documentary.—2nd ed
   I. Title
   070.18

   ISBN 0-240-80126-1

Butterworth–Heinemann
80 Montvale Avenue
Stoneham, MA 02180

10 9 8 7 6 5 4 3 2 1

Printed in the United States of America

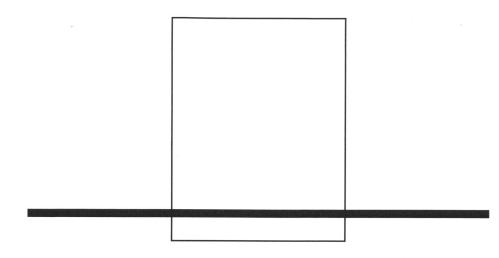

For

The Hooydonk Family
Jack Knight
Bill Lewthwaite
Brian Lewis
Richard Cawston
and
Columbia College

Without their trust and support,
this book could not have been written.

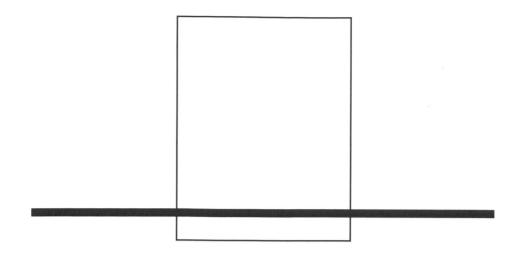

C·O·N·T·E·N·T·S

PART V   PROJECTS: LEARNING BASIC SHOOTING
TECHNIQUES

PART VI   PRODUCTION

PART VII   PROJECTS: DEVELOPING SKILLS AS A
DIRECTOR

PART VIII   POSTPRODUCTION

PART IX   PROJECTS: DEVELOPING SKILLS AS
AN EDITOR

PART X   AESTHETICS AND AUTHORSHIP

PART XI   CAREER TRACK

PART XII   APPENDIXES, GLOSSARY, AND ANNOTATED BIBLIOGRAPHY

P·R·E·F·A·C·E

To my keen satisfaction, the first edition of this book, though written primarily for the beginner, was taken up enthusiastically by film industry professionals. They said it was the first time they had seen the whole process properly described, including how it feels.

This edition, like the first, is for anyone wanting an integrated approach to screen directing. The job is more than simply captaining a crew and instructing an editor for it includes aspects—technical, intellectual, and emotional—that comprise all the holistic and collaborative skills of screen authorship. Plenty has been written about the history and aesthetics of documentary and plenty more about film and video technology, but strangely little exists on the vital craft of directing. This book attempts to remedy that situation by sharing with the reader an approach that comes out of a long background in filmmaking and nearly two decades of teaching. To lend color and background, I have occasionally used anecdotes from my own filmmaking experience.

In teaching how to use the screen as a medium of inquiry and self-expression, the book provides all that the aspiring filmmaker needs to rise from beginning to advanced levels of competency. Getting there will demand conceptual and technical understanding and lots of production practice. For the sake of clarity, I have divided the book into chapters that deal separately with concepts, techniques, and projects. In reality, ideas and their execution are, of course, inseparable. Some of this work is unavoidably complex, but I have emphasized authorship issues, keeping technicalities and theory to a working minimum. I believe people learn to use media tools very rapidly once they have something to say and a good way to say it.

Recognizing that many are experiential learners and, like myself, temperamentally unsuited to absorbing masses of untried information, I have planned the book to accommodate two very different kinds of user. The first wants a thorough conceptual preparation before venturing into production work. For this individual, each phase of the preparatory and conceptual chapters culminates in a series of graduated projects that put emerging screen authorship skills enjoyably to the test. The second user is the pragmatist who learns best by doing. If this is you, jump right into the projects and use the rest of the book as a problem-solving resource when solid issues take shape.

This edition expands on the first in a number of ways. There is more about project development and the all-important proposal process, more about documentary language and method, and more about documentary's relationship to fiction. In addition, there are many more hands-on projects, and of course, many new films are discussed. To better integrate practice and theory, I have repositioned the projects. Instead of being secluded at the end of the book, they are now strategically positioned to signal how much a director's evolution depends totally on wide experience in production. Especially valuable, and appearing at the end of the three production-oriented phases as before, are the checklists. Using these in the field can save you from many a calamity.

To me at least, documentary practice has a growing relevance to breaking down the ossification apparent in mainstream screen fiction. From making documentaries, a director learns how to search out the authentic and behavioral both in life and in actors, to improvise, and to value the open-endedness of spontaneity. Daring to encourage the impromptu is a major resource when it comes to working with actors and a script.

In the last five years, a flood of fine documentaries has appeared, usually made by independents of whom a substantial number are women. Some break significant new ground in documentary language and voice, so I have outlined some exciting and long overdue changes taking shape.

With fresh approaches and new causes to champion, the independent documentary is stirring public interest and has even appeared in cinema runs. To quicken the momentum, new and miniature video equipment has come on the market. Its superb recording quality and modest cost will surely give the documentary a shot of adrenalin by further enfranchising precisely the low-budget independent for whom this book is intended.

My special thanks go to Peter Attipetty, Camilla Calamandrei, Dr. Judd Chesler, Michael Ciesla, Dan Dinello, Dennis Keeling, Nancy Mattei, Cezar Pawlowski, and Bill Yancey for help with the text; thanks also to Dirk Matthews and Milos Stehlik for pictures and pictorial sources. I owe a great debt of gratitude to Columbia College students who are too many to name. By enthusiastically tackling the program at our Documentary Center, they showed me how to make most of the improvements that appear in this edition.

DIRECTING THE
D·O·C·U·M·E·N·T·A·R·Y
SECOND EDITION

P·A·R·T I

INTRODUCTION, HISTORY, AND FUTURE

C·H·A·P·T·E·R 1

INTRODUCTION

FILM OR VIDEO?

This book may be used with confidence by either film or videotape users since the conceptual processes are common to both. At the risk of aggravating purists, I have followed convention and termed a work in either medium "a film." The expression, still widely used even for work entirely produced in video, suggests we wish to separate the traditional article from the more ephemeral music and experimental video products.

I have assumed, purely on economic grounds, that the reader who embarks on the wonderful adventure of experimenting with the documentary image will do so using videotape. With even the simplest equipment, extensive and fascinating study is immediately possible. The advantages of videotape are that consumer-level equipment is widely available, and rehearsal of skills and reuse of tape allow an evolution in one's approach. Very importantly, one can shoot large amounts of footage at very low stock cost and duplicate "prints" cheaply and easily. Unlike working with film, no processing laboratory is necessary to see one's material so there is no delay in assessing results. You can learn so quickly from your mistakes and omissions that there is even time on occasion to rectify them.

I personally care very little whether I work in film or tape. I get a superior image on film, but I have to worry constantly about the amount of stock I am consuming. Film equipment may be smaller, more portable, and more reliable than VT, but the "camcorder" concept—camera and cassette recorder all in one instrument—is a truly revolutionary recording instrument, particularly the new high band 8mm video technology, that allows for truly minimal one-person filmmaking (see Figure 1–1). Film is more cumbersome to edit, but it allows easy lengthening or shortening of either picture or sound components.

Although the disadvantages of videotape to the creative process only begin to impinge on the filmmaker who has reached quite an advanced level, videotape editing does have one huge drawback. Because it involves selectively transferring scenes onto one uncut piece of tape, one's edited version is accumulated in a linear fashion. It means you can't go back and shorten or lengthen one scene without retransferring everything that follows. In practice, there are sometimes ways to wriggle out of this straitjacket, but the overall hindrance remains, even when one uses a computer to rebuild the successful remainder of an edited version.

For reasons of economy and morale, I advise beginners against shooting documentary on film until they have performed extensively and successfully in videotape. At the time of this writing, you can get a 30-minute video film in 3/4-inch format on the screen for $400 in tape costs, while the 16mm film equivalent (negative purchase, developing, work-printing, release printing, sound-processing charges) would cost at least $8000. While other factors enter any calculation professionals make over which medium to use, the salient fact for the novice is that the same problems and faults will show up regardless of the medium chosen. The reality is that one avenue of learning is 20 times as expensive as the other. A word of caution, though: Broadcast-quality videomaking is presently as expensive as is shooting film because the equipment necessary, particularly in editing onwards, is exquisitely complex and costly.

This book, however, is mainly about the concepts and methodology behind directing any documentary, and although I implore the reader to learn his ABCs using tape, everything I shall describe applies equally to film or videotape production. Actually, much of the information applies equally well to other non-

A   B

FIGURE 1–1 ───

(A) High band 8mm camcorder with hi-fi sound, high resolution picture, and integral time coding. (B) High band 8mm camcorder with three hi-fi sound channels, digital time base correction, noise reduction, and many special effects. Most importantly, sound level can be manually controlled. (Sony Corporation)

fiction forms such as industrial, nature, travelogue, and educational films. Some of what I discuss even applies to fiction filmmaking since both factual and fictional forms operate out of a common fund of techniques, use a common language understood by audiences, and rely on similar dramatic organizational principles for their effectiveness.

WHAT IS A DOCUMENTARY?

A documentary film can be either a controlled and premeditated essay or something lyrical and impressionistic. It can articulate its meaning primarily through words, images, or human behavior. There seem almost no limits to its possibilities, but at its best, the documentary film reflects a fascination with, and a profound respect for, actuality. It is the very opposite of escapist entertainment, being committed to the richness and ambiguity of life as it really is.

But what does *life as it really is* mean? To the literally minded, reality is what we can see, measure, and agree upon. For the wealthy TV network or funding agency safeguarding itself against lawsuits, the documentary must contain only what can be defended in a court of law. Not surprisingly, these organizations are much readier to produce informational films or carefully controlled journalism than they are true documentary, which includes an element of social criticism and implies an individual rather than a corporate point of view.

With "reality" should be included not just the externally visible material world but also the interior worlds of those being filmed. Writers have long been able to shift the reader's attention between these familiar dimensions and many include the storyteller's perceptions as part of the narrative. Though film has yet to develop the same freedoms, memorable films of all kinds present their characters and events from an identifiable, authorial identity. Hitchcock, Godard, Bergman, Wertmuller, and Altman in fiction and Rouch, Wiseman, Kopple, and the Maysles brothers in documentary each have their recognizable concerns and style—their own particular and characteristic points of view on the human comedy.

What distinguishes the modern documentary is that it shows events and authorial reactions *as they happen* so there is the same feeling of spontaneity and adaptation that we experience in the heightened moments of our own lives.

Take, for example, Nicholas Broomfield and Joan Churchill's *Soldier Girls* (1981). The film does not just show how the American army sets about training its women soldiers, it shows a great range of formal and informal moments, including scenes of sadistic training methods and systematic humiliation that are all the more disquieting when applied by men to women. There is a central paradox that the film deliberately avoids confronting until late: Because warfare is brutal and unfair, a caring instructor cannot kindly train soldiers to survive no matter whether the trainees are men or women. Because this argument fails to cover all that we see, many larger questions about military traditions and mentality remain after the film ends—just as its makers intended.

To see *Soldier Girls* is to experience what moved or disturbed Broomfield and Churchill themselves. The film never tells one how to feel or what to think, instead it jolts the viewer into a series of disturbing realizations by letting one witness all the contradictory and provocative evidence they themselves saw. Scenes of warm barrack-room camaraderie are contrasted with desperate route marches or drill sessions in which senior whites humiliate junior blacks and Hispanics— purportedly for their own good. A white woman makes a touching plea to a black woman who wants to give up in despair; later the white woman is promoted and begins berating her former companions. A black noncommissioned officer (NCO) exhorts a black female private not to collapse during a forced march; a tough drill sergeant confesses that his battle experience has left him with no human emotions except the desire to save others from suffering and dying as the undertrained American rookies did in Vietnam, and so on. The film shares the complexity of its impressions and through its camerawork and editing implies even the rhythm, reflexes, and speculation of its makers.

A good modern film not only shows the familiar in an unfamiliar way but it also gives us everything we need to function at a heightened level of awareness. Because a modern documentary is a topic unfolding as a story, it simultaneously implies an intelligence grappling with the events' meaning. The documentary is both subject and seer and event and reactions to event, and juxtaposes like and unlike just as in life one mentally compares two events to decide what they signify. The humor and pathos are those found by the makers, and the whole is arranged by them to reproduce the spirit of the experience they gained while making it.

It is important to stress that because most films are made collaboratively, this sensibility usually does not arise out of the director alone but from several like-minded individuals. In turn, the film is often appreciated by another collective—the audience. In every way, film is a truly social art form.

Because much that gets shown as documentary is either second rate or not really documentary at all, the form has acquired the unfortunate image of being a "problem" genre through which do-gooders berate society for its failings. The true documentary is concerned neither with hand wringing nor with the promotion of a product or service. It is not even primarily concerned with objectively measurable facts. For example, a factual film about the way workers manufacture razor blades would be an industrial, but a film that shows the effect upon the workers of repetitive, precision manufacturing and *that invites the spectator to draw socially critical conclusions* can only be called a documentary however well it might also relay the physical process of manufacturing.

The documentary exists to scrutinize critically the organization of human life and to promote individual, humane values. The very best films are, as you might imagine, models of disciplined passion.

Of the various nonfiction film forms—travel, industrial, nature, or educational—the documentary is by far the most significant as a force for change in society, and it is thus the most demanding to make. Everyone has seen a documentary, yet few have any idea of the conceptual and production processes that lie behind the apparently effortless presentation of "real-life" events. Although a documentary has to show what is actual, achieving spontaneity on the screen is not the real challenge. I shall of course address this problem, but it is the issues of ethical, moral, and dramatic balance that are the most demanding for any screen author.

THE ISSUE OF OBJECTIVITY

People frequently assume documentaries are 'objective' because factual television so often presents opposing points of view. Adversarial balance, runs the argument, ensures a fair, unbiased view of the events and personalities in question. In the 1930s this kind of hands-off treatment led to reputable British newspapers reporting the news coming out of Hitler's Germany as something inconsequential—a squabble between communists and fascists whipped up by "Red troublemakers." With hindsight we see that no commentator could possibly be either "fair" or responsible about the Nazis without taking sides over specific issues, without in fact *interpreting* events.

This emphasis on equipoise is a strategy originally devised by journalists as a safe passage through a minefield of dangers and responsibilities. One, ever present in the collective mind of any institution, is to avoid ever being proved wrong since that brings discredit and even lawsuits. From this point of view, it is only commonsense to camouflage all opinion as that of others and to make the writing conform to a standard, faceless style.

Another equally important responsibility, when so much in human life remains ambiguous, is simply toward being fair. If, for example, you were telling the story of a malpractice accusation against a surgeon, it would be mere prudence not only to give proper coverage to allegations from both sides but also to check and crosscheck everything that can be independently verified. This is a tradition followed by good journalists and successful detectives everywhere.

Few of the situations that interest the documentarian are elemental and clear cut, but the temptation to render them so is an ever-present danger. Nettie Wild's *A Rustling of Leaves* (1990), a courageous and sympathetic account of the populist guerrilla movement in the Philippines, leaves one guiltily skeptical throughout. Wild's political commitment has led her to showing heroic left-wing peasants in a struggle against bad right-wing thugs. This is probably true, but anyone with a grain of political savvy knows that when the most honorable resistance movement has been fighting for a while, both sides inevitably commit atrocities. Thereafter the waters become muddy indeed.

Fairness here means dealing not only with the protagonists' declared principles but also with the ugly and paradoxical aspects of liberation through violence. To be sure Wild tries to do this—showing, for instance, the trial and execution by guerrillas of a youthful informant—but one has no way of knowing if the trial is generally representative or whether a considerably quicker practice takes place when no camera is around.

So a film should not only be accurate and truthful; it must also be perceived as such. This may mean indicating whether something is widely true or instead is a sincere but subjective perception. Dealing with audience assumptions means anticipating the film's impact every step of the way and knowing when audience misgivings require something special from the film's discourse. The more intricate the issues, the more difficult it will be to strike a balance between the inevitable simplification on the one hand and fidelity to the complexity of human life on the other.

Penetrating yet fairminded exposure of a subject's issues is often called "objectivity" and lumped together with the "balanced" fence sitting that so often passes as news reporting. Worse yet, the artful ways that news and documentary practitioners have disguised their own biases have beguiled the public into thinking that the documentary form is itself objective.

Unfortunately nothing could be further from the fact. The alluring notion that a camera can ever record anything objectively begins to disintegrate the moment one confronts a few practical considerations.

What, for instance is an "objective" camera position—since the camera must be placed somewhere? How does one "objectively" decide when to turn the camera on and off? And when one views the resulting material, how does one measure which parts most represent "objective truth," and should therefore be used?

These are all editorial decisions that are inextricably bound up with film's need to compress lengthy, diffuse events into a relatively brief and meaningful essence. Quite simply, filmmaking is a series of highly significant choices—of what to shoot, how to shoot it, and what to use in the end.

If your film is to be perceived as fair, balanced, and objective, you will need a broad factual grasp of your subject, material that is persuasive and self-evidently reliable, and *the courage and insight to make interpretive judgments about its use.*

Practically every such decision involves an ethical choice, many of them disquieting and some involving sleepless nights. Whatever your intentions, the medium itself plays a very big part in the message for one is showing to an audience not the events themselves but rather an artful representation with its own inherent logic, dynamics, and emphases.

THE DIRECTOR'S CRAFT

Like so many craftspeople, most film/video directors operate out of a process of gut-recognition that is really a process of logic so internalized that it works more by reflex than by conscious deduction. They recognize what "works" and what will be effective. Of course, this is maddeningly inaccessible to the novice and seems almost calculated to shut him out. Even professional crew members routinely nurture quite wrong or distorted ideas of the directorial process especially the stages before and after shooting. Many a director has been half-jokingly accused of making decisions in some remote and arty compartment of his being. This may be just another outgrowth of the division our society draws between art and technology. If so, it is a cultural apartheid especially damaging to documentary film crews, whose special responsibility is toward wholeness of vision.

Directing is not a mystical process; if a director at work appears inscrutable, it is unlikely to be an affectation. It simply means that a strenuous inner process commands most of his energies. No film—indeed no artwork—emerges except by a series of more or less conscious and responsible decisions. A film depicting any human process—whether it is a tennis game, or a court case, or a revolution—must present not merely a passive record but also an active and persuasive account. Although cinematography appears to place the viewer in direct contact with the subject, it is apparent when one examines the issue closely that *the audience has been led by its viewing experience to expect every aspect of every shot to carry meaning*. Thus the conventions of the cinema thrust the director every step of the way into the role of active interpreter.

A "CONTRACT" WITH THE AUDIENCE

How a filmmaker engages with the audience often proceeds from deep and unexamined assumptions about who "other people" really are and how one relates to them. These assumptions, often unconsciously inherited from a lifetime stock of indiscriminate film viewing, in turn affect the choice of cinematic language and how well the film introduces its own scope and perspective.

There are different levels of respect for the audience's intelligence. Whichever level is used can be regarded as part of an invisible contract a communicator implies to the audience. The advertiser or propagandist, wanting only to condition the audience, produces only the evidence that supports his predetermined conclusions. He will often use humor or sensation to coerce his passive audience into paying attention.

Moving up the scale of respect, there is the "binary" communicator I mentioned earlier who gives "equal coverage to both sides" in any controversy—as if issues only ever have two sides. This kind of filmmaking, by suggesting that the world is full of matched opponents, tells us there is nothing we need do except stay tuned. Here too the audience is considered a passive force to be informed and entertained.

At a higher level still is the filmmaker who aims not at conditioning or diverting an audience but at sharing a human dilemma in all its complexity. Ira Wohl's *Best Boy* (1979) is about an elderly couple uneasily yielding up their mentally handicapped son to an institution in preparation for when they can no longer care for him (Figure 1–2). Delicately but perceptibly the film touches on all the regrets, pain, and failures that seem connected with the son's position as a handicapped member of the family.

A film like this does not set out to sell or convert, but rather to co-opt one's mind and emotions while one is watching a series of events fraught with meaning and ambiguity. It involves us in making difficult judgments about motive and responsibility and makes us into colleagues in an honest, sensitive quest for goodness and truth. Here the audience is actively engaged, never patronized or manipulated.

Auspiciously or otherwise, each film signals how it intends to treat its audience, what it will deal with, and under what general premise. I think of this as "the contract" struck with the audience. The best films, like good storytellers, usually put forward their contract in the first moments and generate an enjoyable prospect of suspense and promise.

THE INDIVIDUAL AND THE MEDIA

"It is the function of all art," said T.S. Elliot, "to give us some perception of an order in life, by imposing an order on it." Zola said, "A work of art is a corner

FIGURE 1–2

Best Boy by Ira Wohl. Pearl must let her "best boy" Philly leave home to enter a supportive institution. (Ira Wohl)

of Nature seen through a temperament." Evident in both these attitudes is the idea that taking an integrated and critical point of view is the prerogative of the individual, whose decisions come out of his or her temperament and conscience.

But documentary makers rely almost wholly on television to show their work. The notion that truth may reside in the vision of an individual more powerfully than it does in the consensus of the boardroom is a prickly issue for television executives, suspended as they are in the web of myth generated by our merchantile democracy. The dissenting individual, though safe to honor as a historical hero, too often must struggle unendingly to get his personal, critical voice on television. Corporations by their very nature are committed to audience figures and profits; they influence programming by paternalistically subtracting what may offend a sector of the audience, the sponsor, or the various self-appointed guardians of public morals.

Yet—another paradox—it has been either enlightened corporations or embattled individuals inside them who have taken the principle of free speech in a democracy seriously enough to keep the democracy alive. Today, the diversification of television consumption, through cable and videotape facilities—with production equipment for the latter becoming smaller, better, and cheaper—makes possible video presentations that were formerly prohibitively difficult and expensive.

Because television distribution is evolving toward the diversity seen in book publication, there will be a growing need for screen authorship on a much wider scale. Lowered production costs and an increased outlet should logically mean increased freedom for the individual voice—the kind of freedom presently available in the print media. Such a broadening of the means of expression is at the heart of any truly democratic and healthy society.

WHY YOU AND I MATTER

For anyone who wants to help create a mirror of contemporary life, filmmaking is a wonderful and fulfilling medium. To me, the value of the documentary process is that it affirms the importance of imagination and empathy while simultaneously probing the depths of real life for its meanings. It is a learning process that makes one feel truly alive. Part of its reward for me is the knowledge that, unlike the generations of ordinary people before me, I shall not pass silently out of life taking my human testimony with me. It is astonishing and tragic that we, the common people, know virtually nothing firsthand about the thought and aspirations of our ancestors. Apart from their songs and tales they left nothing because they owned nothing and could leave no personal record. Their history, practically the only one we have, was instead written for them by their masters.

Documentary filmmaking now allows the common man not only to publicly argue his case but also to leave a highly sophisticated record of his mind, surroundings, and vision. I like to think that future historians will find the documentarian's record of man and woman no less important than those of the chroniclers and diarists of old.

C·H·A·P·T·E·R 2

A BRIEF AND FUNCTIONAL HISTORY OF THE DOCUMENTARY

In a book of this kind it is not practical to take more than just a brief look at the documentary's background, and even this makes no claim to historical or geographical balance. Instead I have made a somewhat personal and selective account to serve as a backdrop to the rest of this book.

ON FILM LANGUAGE

All art forms enable us vicariously to experience other realities than our own and thus to connect emotionally with lives, actions, and issues that would otherwise remain alien. Exposed to unfamiliar ideas and experiences, we find ourselves reacting within a new context and are led to develop new attitudes. For instance, though the facts of World War II are unchanged, our perspective remains in flux so that even the monolithic image of Nazi Germany is undergoing a reevaluation; 40 years afterward, we are beginning to see works like Wolfgang Petersen's *Das Boot* and Werner Herzog's *Signs of Life,* which affirm isolated strands of humanness in the Third Reich.

Filmed action, like the "facts" of history, achieves much of its meaning from the mood of the times and from the interpretative structure imposed by the film's makers. Even at a cellular level, two film shots placed together form a suggestive juxtaposition that would be quite different if their order were reversed. Relativity and comparison are thus the very heart and soul of film language.

Unlike literature, which can easily place the reader in the past or in the future, film holds the spectator in a constantly advancing present tense. Even a flashback quickly becomes its own ongoing present. Because of the way literature is experienced, it is a contemplative medium. Reading is a reflective and intellectual activity in which the reader, at his own pace and alone, shares the mental and emotional processes of either the author or his characters. Film, on the other hand, is a dynamic experiencing in which cause and effect are inferred by the spectator *while the events are happening.*

This is not to imply that literature is any less powerful, but simply to assert the existential insistency with which the film medium grasps the spectator's mind. Because of film's density and subtlety, and because the spectator seldom wants to stop, slow, or repeat any part of the show, he is less likely to fully appreciate the means by which he has been persuaded or the extent of his own emotional subjugation.

Film language and its effects are a comparatively recent study because film is such a recent form compared to the other arts, and the language itself is still in vivid evolution.

AUTHORSHIP AND FACTUAL FOOTAGE

The nonfiction cinema existed for more than two decades before the documentary form was invented and named in the 1920s. Indeed, the very first moving pictures transfixed for the world's wonderment such everyday events as workers leaving a factory, a baby's meal, a train arriving to disgorge its passengers, a rowing boat going out to sea. There is something very poignant about these earliest recorded moments of daily life for they are the human family's first home movies.

The fledgling cinema quickly expanded its subject matter. From its beginnings as an optical trick producing lifelike illusions, it naturally followed audience taste in the direction of vaudeville, music hall and popular theater. Thus early cinema fiction includes staged comedy, historic reenactment, magic illusions, farce, and melodrama. The camera did, however, continue to gather factual footage for newsreels, always very popular. During World War I, vast amounts of footage shot of all phases of the hostilities became an important medium of communication between wartime governments and their civilian populations. Of all the early factual footage, that of World War I must be the most familiar to us today.

The question arises, are these newsreels documentary films? Plainly the newsreels are documentary material, but as individual episodes they lack the identify of a true documentary film because each is so episodic and disjointed. Instead the footage is event-centered, but the events' relationship and meaning lie somewhere else in the overall tapestry of the war. At our remove in time, the film footage and its subtitles betray a jingoistic and naive posturing, with "our side" as heroes and "the enemy" as a malevolent and inhuman machine.

Newsreels were only one contribution to the public knowledge of that war, awareness also molded by newspaper and government reports, letters, eyewitness accounts, fiction, poetry, and photography. Historians, repossessing that silent footage, have since reworked it to present altered perspectives of World War I, perspectives formed with the benefit of hindsight of course but also formed from a political and social consciousness different from the received opinion of the period. Still more interpretations of that war will be formulated as the process of evaluation and debate continues, and identical footage may support radically different contentions.

Emerging here is the idea that *truth is a matter of relativity*. As more information becomes available, as new researchers who are uncommitted to 1914–1918 viewpoints look at the complex pattern of actions and events, they propose new relationships and more broadly embracing explanations.

So not only a sound track is missing from those early film documents of the Great War, but also the kind of interpretive vision already to be found in a contemporary fictional work like *Birth of a Nation* (1915) flawed though Griffith's vision is with Southern racist attitudes. But for the fiction film, superb examples existed in fictional literature. A filmmaker looking for a treatment of war could, for instance, pick up Tolstoy's *War and Peace*. It uses the historical novel form to subvert those contemporary historical attitudes that assumed the overriding influence of kings, generals, and ambassadors during the Napoleonic wars. Tolstoy knew from his own experience as a soldier at Sebastopol that wild rumors, inadequate equipment or even popular assumptions about the enemy could put an army to flight just as easily as could any act of leadership. He did not need to alter any of the facts of the French invasion of Russia; he simply viewed them from within the ranks of the ordinary Russian people instead of from an elitist historical vantage. Tolstoy's largeness of view, his compassion for the ordinary landowner and the humble foot soldier and for the precious coherence of family life as well as for the more abstract idea of Russia herself, help us see not just those wars but all war as a tragic human phenomenon to be avoided at almost any cost.

Early films of actuality lacked any of this vision and failed to organize their materials into the kind of embracing statement about human life already becoming common in the fiction cinema. If one looks for the factual counterpart to documentary cinema's heritage in literature, there is no obvious form or body of work. Persuasive factual reporting was previously delivered through government reports, specialist literature, or the newspapers of which only the latter reached ordinary people.

But even journalism was not much of a model, for it either took a detached, factual stance or it expressed subjective opinion through literary method, using graphics only to enliven columns of print. Mayhew's *London Labour and the London Poor* (published 1851–1962) is much nearer the documentary form and uses interview methods that at least allow his subjects to speak with their own words and ideas (Figure 2–1). But the book is quite passive in its presentation of a whole interconnecting web of injustices in contemporary society.

Possibly painting or caricature are the documentary's true antecedents, and its values and concerns are to be seen in the work of artists like Bruegel, Hogarth, Goya, Daumier, and Toulouse-Lautrec. Their way of depicting actuality, from an individual and emotionally committed perspective, helped show the way for the documentary film, that unblinking eye on the terrible beauty of the twentieth century.

FIGURE 2–1

Henry Mayhew interviewed London's poor. (Illustration from Mayhew's *London Labour and the London Poor*.)

THE INVENTION OF THE DOCUMENTARY FILM

The spirit of documentary is perhaps to be found first in Russia with the Kino-Eye of Dziga Vertov and his group. A young poet and film editor, he produced educational newsreels that were a vital part of the struggle for allegiance during the Russian Revolution. He came to believe passionately in the value of real life captured by the camera and in keeping with the spirit of the time, to abhor the stylized and artificial fictional presentation of life by the bourgeois cinema. He served as a leading theorist during the Soviet Union's period of great inventiveness in the cinema in the 1920s.

The term *documentary* is said to have been coined by John Grierson while he was reviewing Flaherty's *Moana* in 1926. Flaherty, an American whose earlier *Nanook of the North* is acknowledged as documentary's seminal work, began shooting his ethnographic record of an Eskimo family in 1915 (Figure 2–2). While he was editing his footage in Toronto, he inadvertently set fire to his 30,000 feet of negative and had to set about gathering funds to reshoot everything.

Owing to the constraints of a hand-cranked camera, insensitive film stock requiring artificial light, and appalling weather conditions, Flaherty had to ask his subjects to do their normal activities in special ways and at special times. Because of Nanook's liking for Flaherty and because he knew he was helping to place on record a vanishing way of life, Nanook and his family both provided and influenced the contents, enabling the filmmaker to shoot his "acted" film like a fictional story about a battle with the elements (Figure 2–2 and 2–3).

After knowing them so long, Flaherty's relationship with his "actors" was so natural that they could quite unself-consciously continue their lives before his camera, allowing the results to look convincingly natural. The film's participants and the lives they were leading were so inarguably authentic that the film transcended mere acted representation. In addition, Flaherty's unsentimental vision of Eskimo daily life elicits the larger theme of man in a struggle for survival.

At first distributors refused to accept that *Nanook* might have any interest for the public, but they were quite wrong for it drew large crowds. Yet while audiences lined up to see the film Flaherty eventually managed to put on, its subject died on a hunting trip in the Arctic. One cannot imagine a more ironic endorsement of the truth in Flaherty's vision.

However, with *Man of Aran* (1934) and other films made later in his career, Flaherty came under fire from Grierson, Rotha and others for being more interested in creating lyrical archetypes than in observing the true, politically determined conditions of his subjects' lives. Not only did he cast his own ideal family

FIGURE 2–2

Nanook warming his son's hands from *Nanook of the North*. (The Museum of Modern Art/Film Stills Archive.)

from assorted islanders, but he carefully avoided showing the big house of the absentee landlord largely responsible for the islanders' deprivations.

But from *Nanook* onwards, the factual cinema began showing real life in a way that went beyond the fragmented presentation of news footage. By turning events into a story, the documentary interpreted its subject in a way that implied social cause and effect. Grierson, who was to pilot the British documentary movement, later described the documentary form as the "creative treatment of actuality." In the development of national cinemas that was to come, American documentaries often followed Flaherty's example by showing the struggle between man and nature. Paradoxically it was Pare Lorentz's films made for the U.S. government—*The Plow That Broke the Plains* (1936) and *The River* (1937)—that showed rather too explicitly the connection between government policy and ecological disaster (Figures 2–4 and 2–5). Their success as indictments ensured that American documentary makers were soon turned loose to work without government funding.

In Britain, after the ravages of World War I, Grierson's self-proclaimed mandate as he worked for the British Government in the late 1920s was: "[S]omehow we had to make peace exciting, if we were to prevent wars. Simple notion that it is—that has been my propaganda ever since—to make peace exciting." Grierson endorsed Brecht's saying that "art is not a mirror held up to reality, but a hammer with which to shape it." The people who collected around him were

FIGURE 2–3

From *Nanook of the North*. A family to feed. (The Museum of Modern Art/Film Stills Archive.)

FIGURE 2–4

The Plow That Broke the Plains. (The Museum of Modern Art/Film Stills Archive.)

socialists committed to the idea of community and communal strength. The British documentary school's real achievement was to reveal the dignity in ordinary people and their work. *Night Mail* (1936) and *Coal Face* (1936) recruited some of the brightest artistic talents, like composer Benjamin Britten and poet W.H. Auden, to assist in producing works that have since become famous as a celebration of the rhythms and associations of humble work.

A few years later, with the onset of World War II, Humphrey Jennings emerged as the poet of the British screen. His *Listen to Britain* (1942) and *Fires Were Started* (1943) neither preach nor idealize; instead through innumerable vignettes of ordinary people adapting to the duress of war, he produced a moving but unsentimental character portrait of Britain itself.

In Russia of the 1920s, with a revolution scarcely completed, the new gov-

FIGURE 2–5

The River. (The Museum of Modern Art/Film Stills Archive.)

ernment found itself responsible for a huge nation of peoples who neither read
nor understood each other's languages. Silent film offered the hope of a universal
language with which the citizens of the new Soviet republic could examine the
diversity, history, and pressing problems of their nation with optimism. Because
the government wanted the cinema to be both realistic and inspirational and to
get away from the falseness and escapism of Western commercial cinema, a great
deal of thought went into codifying the cinema's function. One of the outcomes
was a heightened awareness of the possibilities of editing, and another result was
Dziga Vertov's early articulation of what he called Kino-Eye, a cinema to record
life without imposing on it. It was the precursor of the modern Direct Cinema
movement about which more discussion will come later.

Vertov's *Man With The Movie Camera* (1929) is an exuberant record of the
camera's capability to move, to capture life in the streets, and even to be reflexively aware of itself. He believed that by compiling a rapid and ever-changing
montage of shots, life itself would emerge free of any point of view but that of
the all-seeing camera. For all his intention of producing an egoless film, the
chaotic profusion of imagery, the humor, and the catalogue of events and characters could only be Vertov's.

Sergei Eisenstein, the grey eminence of the Soviet cinema, never made a
documentary, but his historical reenactments, most notably *Strike* (1924) and
The Battleship Potemkin (1925) have a quality of documentary realism in their
presentation of recent Russian history.

European documentaries of the 1920s and 1930s, coming from societies neither recently settled like America nor torn by revolution like Russia, tended to reflect more the onset of urban problems. In cities many centuries old, containing increasingly dense, poverty-stricken populations, filmmakers like Joris Ivens, Alberto Cavalcanti, and Walter Ruttmann produced experimental films since labeled "City Symphonies" (Figure 2–6). Making films in France, Holland, Belgium, and Germany, their films were characterized by inventive, impressionistic shooting and editing. One is struck by the romantic feel these films show for the busy rhythms of daily life and for the stress of living in poor, cramped quarters. The paradox is that, in spite of hardship, the ordinary people in their worn and dirty surroundings show the vitality and humor of their medieval ancestors whose hands originally built the environment. It is as though Brueghel has returned with a camera.

Luis Buñuel in his *Land Without Bread* (1932) showed the appalling poverty and suffering in a remote village on the Spanish border with Portugal. In its eloquent and impassioned way, the film leaves the spectator seething with anger at a social system too lethargic and wrapped in tradition to bother with such obscure citizens.

The Nazis more than any other power group realized the unlimited potency of film in a generation addicted to the cinema. In addition to propaganda films using carefully picked actors to show Aryan supremacy and the superiority of Hitler's policies, the regime produced two epics so accomplished in the compo-

FIGURE 2–6

Berlin: Symphony of a City. (The Museum of Modern Art/Film Stills Archive.)

sitional and musical elements of film that they undeniably belong with the greatest documentaries of all time. Leni Riefenstahl's *Olympia* (1938) built the 1936 Olympic games into a paean to the physical being of athletes and, by association, to the health of the Weimar Republic. Along with Riefenstahl's *Triumph of the Will* (1937), this film is regarded as a pinnacle in the exploitation of the nonfiction cinema's potential (Figure 2–7).

What is perhaps sinister in this valuation is that *Triumph of the Will* has also been acknowledged as the greatest advertising film ever made. Its apparent subject was the 1934 Nazi Congress in Nuremberg, but its true purpose was to mythicize Hitler and show him as the god of the German people. It is an abiding discomfort to film historians that great cinema art should eulogize such a monstrous figure as Adolf Hitler, but Riefenstahl's work serves as a valuable reminder that records of reality require a wise and responsible interpreter if art is to be on the side of the angels.

World War II, which immolated half of Europe, was a time of prodigious factual filming. Most documentaries were government sponsored and focused upon the consequences of massive warfare: the destruction of cities, homelessness, the plight of the millions of refugees as well as the lives of the soldiers, sailors, and airmen who fought for their countries. Ironically it was the Nazis'

FIGURE 2–7

Hitler massed rally in *Triumph of the Will*. (The Museum of Modern Art/Film Stills Archive.)

own film records that contributed such damning evidence to Alain Resnais's *Night and Fog* (1955), possibly the single most powerful documentary ever made about man's capacity for destroying his kin (Figure 2–8).

NEW TECHNOLOGY LEADS TO ADVANCES IN FORM

The documentary film remained tethered to the limitations of its clumsy technology well into the 1950s when bulky cameras and huge, lumbering sound recorders were all that was available to filmmakers. Though location sync sound was possible, the dictates of available equipment turned documentary participants into stilted actors. One has only to see a late Flaherty film like *Louisiana Story* (1948) to sense the subjugation of content and form to a crude technology. Even Jennings' excellent *Fires Were Started* (1943) is so self-consciously arranged and shot that one has to remind oneself after dialogue sequences that the people and the scenes of wartime London ablaze are news footage.

Simply put, life was too often being staged for the camera and too seldom being caught as it happened. But this was to change with some technological advances. One was magnetic tape recording, another the Eclair self-blimped (mechanically quiet) camera that made hand-held sync filming a reality. Its magazine

FIGURE 2–8

Resnais's impassioned plea for humane watchfulness in *Night and Fog*. (Films Inc.)

design also allowed quick reloading with only a few seconds "down time" during magazine changes.

Yet another advance came from Ricky Leacock and the Robert Drew group at Time Inc. in New York. They solved the problem of recording sync without having to link tape recorder and camera by constricting wires.

These improvements transformed every phase of location filming by the beginning of the 1960s—from news gathering and documentary to improvised dramatic production. The result was a revolution in the relationship of the camera to the subject. Now truly mobile and flexible, the camera and recorder became observers adapting to life as it unfolded. A handheld unit could be operated by two people and follow wherever the action might lead. The camera became an active observer, and this showed on the screen in the immediacy and unpredictability of the new cinema form.

DIRECT CINEMA AND *CINÉMA VÉRITÉ*

Two very different philosophies evolved concerning how to handle the newly mobile camera. In America, the Maysles brothers, Fred Wiseman, and others favored an observational approach that became known as "direct cinema." The object was to intrude as little as possible in order to capture the spontaneity and uninhibited flow of live events. The emphasis was on shooting informally without special lighting or evident preparations and waiting on the sidelines for events of significance to take shape.

Proponents of direct cinema claim a certain purity for the method, but unless the camera is actually hidden—at best an ethically dubious practice—participants are usually aware of its presence and modify their behavior accordingly. The integrity of the observation is thus more illusory than actual. The appearance is sustained by editing out material where this awareness becomes apparent. Certainly this makes the audience feel like privileged observers, but the authenticity of what they see is distinctly questionable. Direct cinema works best when ongoing events consume the attention of participants, and it works less well as the camera gains visibility and priority.

Cinéma vérité originated with Jean Rouch in France who learned from his ethnographic experience in Africa that making a documentary record of a way of life was itself an important relationship. Like Flaherty with Nanook, Rouch found that authorship could legitimately be shared between participants and filmmaker.

Permitting and even encouraging interaction between subject and director, *cinéma vérité* legitimized the camera's presence and gave a director the role of catalyst for what took place on the screen. Most importantly it authorized the director to initiate characteristic events and to prospect for privileged moments rather than to await them passively.

Eric Barnouw in his excellent *Documentary: A History of the Non-Fiction Film* (London: Oxford University Press, 1974) sums up the differences.

The direct cinema documentarist took his camera to a situation of tension and waited hopefully for a crisis; the Rouch version of *cinéma vérité* tried to precip-

FIGURE 2–9

Flaherty shooting silent footage for *Louisiana Story*. Sound was impractical on location. (The Museum of Modern Art/Film Stills Archive.)

itate one. The direct cinema artist aspired to invisibility; the Rouch *cinéma vérité* artist was often an avowed participant. The direct cinema artist played the role of uninvolved bystander; the *cinéma vérité* artist espoused that of provocateur.

Direct cinema found its truth in events available to the camera. *Cinéma vérité* was committed to a paradox: that artificial circumstances could bring hidden truth to the surface.

Since both approaches capitalized on the spontaneous, neither could be scripted. Freed from the tyranny of the pedestrian blueprint, film editors were liberated to begin a new era of the film language that involved building in a freer, more intuitive form, using counterpointed voice tracks and flexuous, impressionistic cutting. In time, these poetic advances were adopted by the narrative film.

Because the *cinéma vérité* practitioner willingly affects the reality she films and the direct cinema proponent does so unwillingly, the two approaches really have far more in common practically than they do theoretically. The ideal of exalted fidelity to actuality evaporates all the more quickly when one examines the implications of editing which routinely brings together on the screen what in life is separated by time and space.

Like the fiction film, the documentary is plainly channeled through a well-defined, human point of view for all its appearance of objectivity and verisimil-

FIGURE 2–10

Albert and David Maysles—a complete film unit ready to go. (Wofgang Volz.)

itude. In the end, it summons, as best it can, the spirit of things rather than the letter, and is all the more exciting because of this.

It is the audience and the audience's knowledge of life that finally confer the imprimatur of "truthful" to any film. This too is subjective and requires emotional and experiential judgments.

In the United States, actor John Cassavetes used the new portable equipment to shoot his first film, a fiction piece that capitalizes on the power of Method dramatic improvisation. *Shadows* (1959) was grittily shot and hard to hear but undeniably powerful in its spontaneity. The intrepid Albert and David Maysles (Figure 2–10), who had cobbled their own equipment together, produced *Salesman* (1969), which follows a band of hard-nosed Bible salesmen on a sales drive in Florida. Methodically and unflinchingly it shows how American salesmen are put on a rack of success and to what limits these salesmen go in order to meet company-dictated quotas. It also proves how accurately Willy Loman in *Death of a Salesman* epitomizes the dilemma of the American corporate male. Few works expose the operating costs of the American dream with more deadly wit.

The Maysles brothers' *Gimme Shelter* (1970) followed the Rolling Stones to their gigantic outdoor concert at Altamont, California. The film shows the mean, dangerous side of the 1960s counterculture and culminates with the murder by Hell's Angels of a troublemaker in the crowd. Many camera crews were deployed, and the film continually cuts from position to position in the swollen, restless crowd.

A fine French film benefiting from the new mobility was Pierre Schoendoerffer's *The Anderson Platoon* (1967) (Figure 2–11). Schoendoerffer was originally a French army cameraman. He and his crew risked their lives to follow a platoon of GIs in Vietnam led by a black lieutenant. We accompany the Anderson platoon for many days, experiencing what it is like to grapple with an invisible enemy, to fight without real purpose or direction, and to be wounded or die far from home. The film honors the ordinary soldier without ever romanticizing war; compassionately it watches and listens, moving on the ground and in the air with the depleted patrol. Making frequent use of music, the film achieves the eloquence of a folk ballad.

Another filmmaker whose art developed out of mobility is the American Fred Wiseman. Originally a teacher of law, he was moved to make a film about an institution to which he normally brought his class. The result was *The Titicut Follies* (1967), which shows life among the inmates of Bridgewater State Hospital in Massachusetts, an institution for the criminally insane. It is a violently disturbing, haunting film that shows scenes of casual cruelty one thought must have vanished with the eighteenth century. The staff, unaware of the way they looked to the outside world, allowed Wiseman to shoot a huge amount of footage, which he accomplished using minimal equipment and no special lighting. The film caused a furor and was immediately banned by Massachusetts state legislators from showing in Massachusetts.

FIGURE 2–11

The Anderson Platoon, a ballad of an unwinnable war. (Films Inc.)

A more retrospective study, Marcel Ophuls's magnificently subtle analysis of the spread of fascist collaboration in France during World War II, *The Sorrow and the Pity* (1970), helped to open discussion on an era of shame for the French. In the United States, Peter Davis's *Hearts and Minds* (1974) did a similarly excellent, hard-hitting job of examining the roots of American involvement in Vietnam.

Cinematographer Haskell Wexler has been involved with documentaries since the 1960s. He covered the 1965 March on Washington with *The Bus* (1965), filmed a personal journey through North Vietnam in *Introduction to the Enemy* (1974), and shot footage for Joseph Strick's *Interviews with My Lai Veterans* (1971). He used his experience as a camera operator to develop a fiction film, *Medium Cool* (1969) set among actual events during the 1968 Democratic Convention riots in Chicago. It portrays a news cinematographer jerked out of the cocoon of his craft to a growing political awareness. The film crystallizes the unease Americans were feeling at the violence, both inside and outside the country, being perpetrated by their government in the name of democracy.

Another fine American documentary is Barbara Kopple's *Harlan County, USA* (1976), which follows the development of a Kentucky miners' strike, and shows that the bad old days of company intimidation and violence are still with us (Figure 2–12). In the finest tradition of the genre, Kopple shows us the close-knit ties and stoic humor of this exploited community. Surely no film has more

FIGURE 2–12

Harlan County, USA, showing real-life violence in the making. (Krypton International Corp.)

graphically spelled out the ugly side of capitalism or the moral right of working
people to protect themselves from it.

THE DOCUMENTARY AND TELEVISION

In the 1960s, increased camera mobility was matched by improvements in color-
stock sensitivity. Shooting in color increased the price of filmmaking, and the
stock budget remained a large impediment to documentary production. By this
time, television had bitten deeply into cinema box-office figures, and the documentary had migrated from the cinemas to the home screen. Always potentially
embarrassing to its patron, the documentary now had to exist by permission of
giant television networks, always susceptible to commercial, political, and moral
pressure groups. Even the BBC with its relatively liberal and independent reputation, drew the line at broadcasting *Warrendale* (1967), a Canadian film about
a controversial treatment center for disturbed adolescents (Figure 2–13). Likewise, Peter Watkins' chilling *The War Game* (1965), a BBC drama founded on
facts known from the firebombing of Dresden and made to show the effect of a
nuclear attack on London, has waited 20 years to be broadcast (Figure 2–14).
It is hard to see this kind of censorship as anything but the most blatant paternalism.

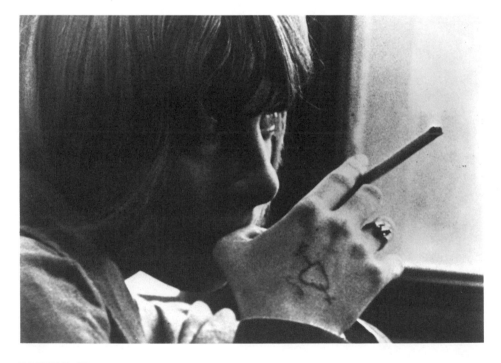

FIGURE 2–13

Disturbed children on the razor's edge from *Warrendale*. (The Museum of Modern Art/
Film Stills Archive.)

FIGURE 2–14

The War Game is a frightening view of nuclear disaster kept from the public. (Films Inc.)

For better or for worse, the ever-insecure documentary maker had become dependent on the approval and good will of the television companies for survival. On the whole, documentaries are a minority interest; they tend to concentrate on problems and areas of concern. They are awkward for an entertainment system to absorb since their length and content are best determined by an individual's judgment. They are quite often slow, make demands on the audience's concentration, and are thought to be "unentertaining." They garner low ratings, and from the position of the anxious television executive, they are dispensable.

The documentary is, however, a vitally dramatic form of factual argument. In a pluralistic society committed to principles of free speech, it plainly has a vital role to play in forming public opinion. But as the documentary makes no profits from advertisers, its makers must depend for its continued existence on enlightened individuals and enlightened corporate policy.

TECHNOLOGY: MORE WALLS COME TUMBLING DOWN

The spread of cable television and the ubiquitous video rental store offer the possibility of some fascinating changes. The familiar network editorial control that gives the viewer so little real choice must eventually give way to some diversity although difficulties of funding threaten to concentrate ownership of cable companies in the hands of large companies all over again. No one can foretell the effects of these great changes until the dust settles.

The videodisc and interactive video, in which a computerized operation allows the user to choose a path through the available material, offers all sorts of instructional and entertainment possibilities. In addition, the television industry is getting ready to upgrade standards for picture sharpness and sound fidelity as high definition television.

Again no one knows what relationships will exist among television, the computer, entertainment, and work in the future. With all these changes, the film/video industry seems set to follow the flexible, venturesome publishing operation long the norm in the music recording industry. All that can be said with confidence is that the electronics industry is evolving products of enormous potential for the workplace and the home faster than the average person can even follow in the newspapers and journals.

Not only are distribution cartels breaking down, but the huge cost of video filming seems likely to become obsolete. A new generation of video cameras is appearing in which the camera and sound recorder are hardly larger than the videocassette that takes the recording. Several hours of color sync recording can now be made on a cassette costing no more than a hot meal. Just as 16mm film superseded 35mm as the medium for television filming, so tape formats are shrinking in size and cost. The monster television camera and its associated cables, recorder, monitors, and truckloads of test gear and engineers are destined to be replaced by miniaturized digital instrumentation capable of high-quality color and sound recording. Higher resolution, large screens, and high-fidelity sound will transform society's forum for ideas and entertainment.

At the moment, high-band 8mm (Hi8) videorecording is making available for the first time an impressive video quality in pint-sized instruments—and at modest prices. Camcorders smaller than their VHS cousins are challenging 3/4" U-matic recording for quality and far exceeding it in sound fidelity (see Figure 1–1). The first desktop Hi8 editing machine is not only affordable, but contains everything for time-code controlled, frame accurate cuts, and has slow motion, freeze frame, and basic titling—all in a box no bigger than a personal computer (see Figure 2–15).

Developments in technology always herald innovations in form. One-person, broadcast-quality video filmmaking is now upon us. What Ross McElwee did with difficulty and at great expense in his delightful *Sherman's March* (1989)— that is, filming unaided a series of serendipitous encounters—can now happen as readily as a writer uses a tape recorder. Not only can the filmmaker record with little fuss, she can go home and edit as informally as one might write at a word processor. The consequences for new forms of film authorship are exciting. Admirers of the brilliant Chris Marker, for example, can build upon the diary form used in his intensely personal essay films. A filmmaker can document a journey or reunion and reflect on film about its impact and meaning. An adoptee in search of her biological parents can now record every major step in this most fundamental and moving of all journeys and share the frustrations and revelations of self-discovery.

Soon the ordinary person may use the screen with almost the same freedom a writer uses paper in a typewriter. As everyone knows, there is more to writing

FIGURE 2–15

Hi8 editing rig: All you need in a package the size of a desktop computer. (Sony Corporation.)

than paper, but undeniably it is the cheapness of paper that makes a writer's evolution possible. Evolution for filmmakers has never been easy. The medium is a hard one to use competently. Previously only the lucky, the aggressive, or the privileged have been allowed to use it. Just as cheap magnetic recording facilities unlocked the door to impoverished musicians in the 1960s, so access to video facilities is democratizing the hands at the controls. There is little reason why the competent video film should not soon reach a selective and fair-sized audience as the medium's hunger for product grows.

THE DOCUMENTARY'S FUTURE

This brief survey of the documentary's history—little more than a personal impression of its highlights—is meant to show that the documentary is as much, if not more, a medium for the individual, committed voice as is the fiction film. The necessary crew is small and getting smaller, and the approach is intimate while accommodating a balance of structured preparation and existential spontaneity. *A documentary is the sum of relationships during a period of shared action and living, a composition made from the sparks generated during a meeting of hearts and minds.*

Documentary makers have an ardent respect for the integrity of the actual, for the primacy of the truth in the lives of real people both great and small. The documentary maker's mission is not to change or evade destiny but rather to embrace its substance, to speak passionately of the lessons of history and the choices yet open toward making a humane and generous society. Experimenting and learning about this mission is becoming daily more possible as improved consumer equipment puts the necessary technology into the ordinary person's hands.

We are presently seeing an awakened public interest in actuality films, from "infotainment," cop shows, and popular shows that exploit home movie clips all the way to the work of the serious independent filmmaker. PBS (Public Broadcasting Service) in its *POV* series has begun showing work by independents on a variety of controversial subjects, and three American works (*Sherman's March* (1989), *The Thin Blue Line* (1989), and *Roger and Me* (1989) have all made it to the cinemas. Wonder of wonders, the audience choice movie for the 1989 Chicago International Film Festival was a documentary, *Roger and Me*.

The popularity of these films lies partly in their fresh language and innovative forms—about which I will comment in later—but there is also a movement toward what may be called the ordinary person's "voice." It is particularly strong and pertinent in rewriting history, as "Yesterday's Witness" showed in England. This series, said to be the world's first television oral history series, ran to over 100 episodes. History is seldom written by those outside the establishment. Though the person in the street has been the subject of documentary since the form's inception, only recently has she become the author.

As electronic publishing becomes more extensive and more responsive to minority interests, there is every reason to expect an increased demand for the personal film about actuality. There will also be a need for imaginative and committed authorship. For the medium needs not only new products but also new approaches and new voices.

P·A·R·T I·I

PREPRODUCTION

C·H·A·P·T·E·R 3

THE PREPARATION BEFORE SHOOTING

The preproduction period of any film is that which covers all the decisions and arrangements prior to shooting. For a documentary, this includes choosing a subject; doing the research; assembling a crew; choosing what equipment will be necessary; and deciding the method, details, and timetable of shooting.

The depth of thought you invest at this time and the extent to which you foresee problems and obstacles go very far indeed to ensure a successful shoot; more important, this preparation largely determines if the movie will be a coherent entity. Directing a documentary, contrary to the impression of instant "auteurism," is less a process of spontaneous inquiry than one guided by conclusions reached during research. In other words, the shoot may largely be collecting "evidence" for underlying patterns and relationships identified earlier.

There is a good reason why even seasoned filmmakers seldom rely on spontaneous inspiration, expressed very succinctly by Werner Herzog after a show of his work. Questioned about "the intellectual challenge during shooting," he replied caustically that "filmmaking is athletic, not aesthetic." In no uncertain terms, he proceeded to tell his startled questioner that most filming is so grueling that rarefied thought is an impossibility.

François Truffaut makes a similar point in his autobiographical movie *Day for Night*. It is about a director whose film runs into a typical thicket of problems and compromises. The director, played by Truffaut himself, says at one point that he always starts shooting convinced the film will be superb, but halfway into the schedule all he hopes for is to be able to finish. My own fantasy, which returns at least once in every shoot, is to escape further filming by miraculously turning into the owner of a rural grocery.

CHOOSING A SUBJECT

When you start the search for a good subject, you should ask yourself some searching questions if you want to avoid the common pitfalls. Possibly the most important question is, "Do I *really* want to make a film about this?" The question may seem silly until one sees how many beginners unerringly choose subject areas in which they have little direct knowledge and no emotional investment.

It should be said loud and clear that making a documentary is a long, slow process, and one must be prepared for one's initial enthusiasm to dim over the long haul. I cannot stress too strongly how important it is to wed yourself to more than a passing attraction.

Why do people take on subjects in which they later lose interest? To answer this one need only glance at the family television. Insidiously it has conditioned us so that, presented with the opportunity to make some kind of screen statement, we instinctively reproduce what we are used to seeing. For most, a "documentary" is one of those worthy, boring little reports shown Sunday mornings to satisfy the station licensing requirement for socially responsible programming. If it lacks vitality and makes us want to switch channels, it is because of a lack of any critical edge. Instead one is presented with a closed, approving view that discourages the audience from making any judgments of its own. This is the essence of propaganda, and a training film is just a training film, no matter how much one approves of the subject.

To avoid the temptation to be merely worthy, you must dig as deeply into your own makeup as you would if you were choosing a new country of residence. Here are some questions to try asking:

1. Is there an area in which I am already knowledgeable and even opinionated?
2. Do I feel a strong and emotional connection to it—more so than to any other practicable subject?
3. Can I do justice to the subject?
4. Do I have a drive to learn more about this subject?

You can see that these questions are framed to gauge one's true level of commitment. The wish to *learn* (question 4) is a very good indicator of one's ability to sustain interest and energy. You should also be careful not to bite off more than you can chew—a very common mistake. Simple economics will prevent you having access to many resources open to large companies. For example, a biographical study of a movie actor would be impossible without corporate backing because the actor's appearances all take place in heavily copyrighted works.

Another instance of inaccessibility might be the choice of a particular institution as one's subject. Institutions are usually extremely wary of uncertified individuals who might dig up, or manufacture, damaging evidence. To make a film about the police or the army, for instance, would be virtually impossible without very high-level approval. Even a local animal shelter may be hedged around with politics and suspicions.

Indeed most institutions make poor subjects because they run very much as anyone would expect, so a film merely confirms what common sense would suggest.

What I am suggesting very strongly is that you narrow your sights and deal with a manageable subject area. No awards are given for failed good intentions, so treat yourself kindly and only take on something that matches your capabilities and budget.

Not for a moment need this confine you to small or insignificant issues. For instance, if you do not have access to the combat footage and archival material to make a compilation film about the roots of the Vietnam War, there are always other approaches open to the inventive. For instance, you may find that the man who sells newspapers on a neighborhood street corner is a Vietnam veteran with a fascinating and representative experience and that he has a network of friends who, among them, have many snapshots, home movie film, and mementos. You may well have the makings of an Everyman tale that tells of the ordinary man's experience of fighting for one's country.

Ingenuity and a willingness to reject the obvious will help you locate good subjects. Many documentary makers are omnivorous readers of newspapers and periodicals and hoard clippings of anything that seems promising. Merely reading over your clipping file can start you thinking. Be aware that one's first and immediate ideas for a subject will nearly always be those everyone else has already had, so to avoid clichés ask yourself:

5. What is this subject's underlying significance to me?
6. What can I find that's unusual and interesting about it?
7. Where is its specialness really visible?
8. How narrowly (and therefore how deeply) can I focus my film's attention?
9. What can I *show*?

Confronting the personal impact of a subject, instead of trying to see it from the audience's point of view, can often take one in new and exciting directions—though it can take one out of the subject altogether on occasion. Making a conscious effort to discover and reveal the unexpected and the unusual is also vital if one is to produce a stimulating film, and this involves narrowly defining what you really want to show, and what you want to avoid. You might, for the sake of argument, want to make a film about inner-city life. But to encompass the whole subject is clearly both impossible and ill-advised. Trying to stretch one's attention in too many directions will only lead to poorly supported generalizations, which the viewer will reject. On the other hand, profiling a particular cafe from dawn to midnight might say a very great deal and in very specific terms.

Think small. Think local. There are many good films to be made within a mile or two of where you live. Most people do not think of exploiting their own "turf." Think small and local, and, to begin with, think short too. Try out your beginning skills on fragments, or you risk being overwhelmed and discouraged.

USING THE MEDIUM

Documentaries exist not just to act on us intellectually but also to create a change in the way we feel about something. The veteran BBC producer Stephen Peet believes that the best documentaries do this by delivering an emotional shock. Documentaries, therefore, have to be aimed at the heart not just the head.

One can, for example, know as a fact that women's musical compositions are seldom played and that virtually none conduct orchestras yet have no special feelings about this—after all, the world abounds with worse injustices. It takes the film *Antonia* (1974) by Jill Godmillow and Judy Collins to change all that. The film draws us into liking and identifying with Antonia Brico, who had all the qualifications to conduct, all except one: she was not a man. Although this is only one person's heartbreak, I have ever since scanned each new orchestra to see if the roles are still as unbalanced.

Using the documentary form well means producing not just facts and opinions, vital though they may be, but also showing the polarizing evidence that will make a strong impact. Question 9 "What can I show?" is the key to developing this aspect.

Since film portrays people and situations by externals, by what can be *seen in action;* participants describing past events or inner feelings make less impact than when we see them actually living through the experience itself. Doing is more interesting, more inherently credible, than talking about doing. Sometimes, of course, there is no alternative, but behavior, action, and interaction are always the preferred way of showing life.

A tough test of one's research is to pretend you are making a silent film. Do you have the material to tell a story without speech? This expectation emphasizes using the camera instead of the microphone. It reveals immediately if your project will be cinematic or journalistic. The literary starts with words and reaches for images to illustrate them as the journalist uses photographs to enliven text. A journalistic conception of *Nanook of the North* might base the film on a narration or interview and use small parts of the action as cutaway illustration—clearly a travesty because it demotes an observed experience in all its mystery and suspense to the status of slide lecture.

The documentarian, however, looks for ideas already manifest and symbolized in living reality. When the search is successful and the action of a scene imparts a clear, strong feeling, little or no corroboration through words is necessary.

Another benefit from a visual rather than verbal design is that good cinematography and good action help create a series of strong moods. When they are effective, this predisposes viewers to enter the movie wholeheartedly and opens them to the film's more abstract values. Once a film is freed from the tyranny of the interview-with-illustrations it can become more sensual, more lyrical, and more sensitive to atmospheres and lighting and to small but significant details that build up the strong aura of subjectivity that is for the viewer inseparable from personally felt experience.

An additional way to plan a series of moods through your film is to deliberately design a sound composition. The best materials will usually be found in the locations where you shoot. Using indigenous or other added, authentic sound you can build up a layered and effective sound track. Much of a film's power to enter the imagination lies not in the visuals but in the use of sound. Music, properly used, can give focus and dimension to the inner lives of the characters or make an authorial comment.

A good place to practice sound design is at an outdoor event like a street market, which usually has a profusion of voices, sounds, and music played over radios or speaker systems. Spend some time concentrating on what you hear as if you were a blind person trying to "see" through sound, and make an inventory of what to record for a sound montage.

RESEARCH AND PREPARATION OVERVIEW

No two people research alike, but there are some common steps that follow choosing a subject. After looking at generalities, we will apply them to an example and see what happens in practice. You will see that research methods are decided as much by the exigencies of the subject as they are by the researcher.

From the start, the researcher must give priority to practicalities—that is, one must recognize whether one really has a film here, be realistic and admit the difficulties, and most importantly realize what film can be made to emerge from the available material since that is all one truly has to work with. While you are researching, write on the back of your hand: "Films can only be made from what can be photographed, not from good intentions."

Often you will be forced by circumstances to take the recommended steps in a different order, or several at the same time. Often one hits an impediment and must turn elsewhere so as not to waste time. Because progress in one area changes what has been decided in another, you must constantly readjust the whole—very frustrating until you get used to it.

1. *Define hypothetical approach* to subject (see Hypothesis section of Documentary Project Proposal Helper below). You will often return to this step.

2. *List the action sequences,* and decide how far they alone would go toward making an interesting and coherent silent film.

3. *Check reality.* Make a preliminary feasibility survey by deciding if what you want to film is accessible, whether the people concerned are likely to be amenable and interested, and whether you can expect the requisite permissions. Add up the foreseeable costs, and face the financial reality involved. Make a reality check more than once during research.

4. *Check written resources.* Study what has been published about your subject and develop a list of basic points that your film must make. Magazines, newspapers, journals, fiction can be useful repositories of ideas and observations, showing what to look for and what to avoid. You may also want to look at films on the same subject, depending on how vulnerable you feel to their influence.

5. *Do the legwork.* Become familiar with the enclosed world that you want to film. Get to know the people and the places, and become thoroughly familiar

with their rhythms and routines. Hanging out with people over a length of time is often the most valuable thing you can do. Make a private list of what is normal, and what you notice is atypical. Decide who are the possible protagonists and what life role each acts in the play you are beginning to perceive. Get multiple perspectives from each qualified person on every other person, especially when there are ambiguities.

6. *Develop trust.* Make yourself and (selectively) your purpose known to those you may want to film. Keep this to generalizations because you do not want to tie yourself down. But you do need to create trust in your motives and interest in your project.

7. *Develop a working hypothesis.* Carefully review step 1, your approach to the subject. It will have changed considerably by now. The more completely you can define your thematic purpose, the easier it will be to know what to shoot.

8. *Preinterview.* Under the guise of preliminary research, do audio or video preinterviews of those you want to consider for filming. Ask no searching questions—keep them for the time of actual shooting. It is important to put people on record and to hear and see how they come across. If audio tracks are good quality, you may use them later as voice over.

9. *Make final draft proposal revision.* Even if you have nobody to please but yourself, working over all the considerations prior to shooting will be invaluable preparation.

10. *Write a treatment.* This is optional, and consists of writing the film you see in your head after developing the research. A treatment is probably a necessity if you are applying for a grant. See the section on "The Treatment" below.

11. *Obtain permissions.* Approach those you wish to film and secure a promise of their time and involvement. If you intend to shoot in special locations, secure written permissions beforehand.

12. *Secure crew.*

13. *Make a shooting schedule* and thoroughly develop plans to deal with foreseeable difficulties.

14. *Make a budget.*

15. *Plan shooting style* and special strategies to secure the film you envision.

16. *Do trial shooting* to work out communications and assumptions with a new crew.

THE DOCUMENTARY PROPOSAL

Writing a proposal helps raise the organizational and thematic analysis developed during research to its ultimate clarity. You will find this of tremendous help while you are shooting because it prepares you to genuinely direct the film to say something rather than to hope this will somehow emerge on its own.

A good proposal also allows you to place a persuasive statement of intention before others so you can solicit support from crew or money sources. While a proposal presents the film as a series of categories, the treatment is a narrative version of what is intended to come from the screen. Both are written to convince the reader that you can make a film of impact and significance. For either, it always brings the proposal alive if you incorporate pithy quotations using your characters' own words.

The proposal should show you can fulfill the conditions of documentary itself. That is, all documentaries should tell a good story; true documentary does not relay value-neutral information like a textbook, it aims to give a personal, critical perspective on some aspect of the human condition. To dramatize human truths both large and small, the documentary usually depends on the traditional dramatic ingredients of characters, exposition, suspense, building tension and conflict between opposing forces, confrontation, climax, and resolution. So the proposal must try to demonstrate how these expectations of the form are to be met.

The categories below are like the pigeonholes in a mail sorting office. A well-researched film will have something substantial and different in each pigeonhole. The questions in the proposal form below are designed to help you discover what is needed in each category. If you find you are putting the same answer under more than one head, go on to another draft and decide where that material really belongs. If the proposal is to be succinct, free of redundancy, and easy to assimilate, there will no duplication between sections.

Documentary Project Proposal Helper

Working title _____

Director _____   Camera _____

Sound _____   Editor _____

Others: _____ (role) _____ (role)

1. WORKING HYPOTHESIS and INTERPRETATION. What are *your* persuasions about the world you are going to show in your film, the main "statement" that you want to emerge out of the film's dialectics? Write a hypothesis statement incorporating this wording:

   In life I believe that
   My film will show this in action by exploring (situation)
   The main conflict is between   and
   Ultimately I want the audience to feel
   and to understand that

2. TOPIC. Write a concise paragraph about:

   a.   Your film's *subject* (person, group, environment, social issue, and so on)

   b.   The necessary *background information* the audience must have to understand and to be interested in the enclosed world you intend to present. Be sure to show how this information will emerge.

3. ACTION SEQUENCES. Write a brief paragraph for each intended sequence that shows an activity. (A sequence is usually delineated by being in one location, one chunk of time, or an assembly of materials to show one topic.) Incorporate the following:

   a. What the activity is and what conflicts it evidences

   b. A metaphor to explain its subtextual meaning

   c. The expected structure of events

   d. What the sequence should contribute to the whole film and to the hypothesis

   e. What facts the audience must gather from watching it

   f. What key, emblematic imagery you hope to capture

4. MAIN CHARACTERS. Write a brief paragraph about each of your main characters. For each include:

   a. Who (name, relationship to others in film, and so on)

   b. Where (where does this person belong in your scheme of things?)

   c. What (what is this character's role, what makes the character(s) interesting, worthy of special attention, and significant? what is this character trying to do or to get?)

5. CONFLICT. What is at issue in this film? Consider:

   a. Who wants what of whom?

   b. What conflicting principles do the characters each stand for?

   c. Does your film put different principles in opposition (of opinion, of view, of vision, and so forth)?

   d. How will we see one force finally meet with the other? (the "confrontation," very important)

   e. What range of possible developments do you see emerging from this confrontation?

6. AUDIENCE BIASES. To make a documentary means not only using conflicting "evidence" to put forward your subject's dialectics, it also means knowing what stereotypes or expectations carried by your audience your film must deliberately set out to alter.

   a. Biases (may be positive or negative)

   b. What alternative views, facts, or ideas does audience need to understand?

   c. What evidence will you show to get the audience to see those different truths?

7. TO-CAMERA INTERVIEWS. For each interview, list:

   a. Name, role in life, metaphoric role in film's dramatic structure

   b. Main elements your interview will seek to establish

8. STRUCTURE. Write a brief paragraph on how you hope to structure that your film. When you are doing this, consider:

   a. How you will handle the progression of time in the film

b. How and at what point information important to story development will appear

c. What you intend as the climactic sequence and where this should go

d. How this relates to other sequences in terms of the action rising toward the film's projected "crisis" or emotional apex and the falling action after it.

e. Sequences or interviews you intend to use as parallel storytelling

9. FORM AND STYLE. Any special considerations in shooting or editing style that might further your film's content. Here you might comment on narration, lighting, camera handling, type and amount of intercutting, juxtaposition of scenes, parallel storytelling, and the like.

10. RESOLUTION. Write a brief paragraph about how you imagine your film will end and what you would like the ending to accomplish for the audience. Comparing any intended ending with the film's beginning also exposes what it must accomplish as a story to get there. The ending is your last word to the audience and has a disproportionate influence on what the film will mean.

11. BUDGET. (Appended to proposal)

12. LOGISTICS. Briefly address any obvious problems of feasibility, practicality, and so on.

THE TREATMENT

Using the information worked up in the proposal draft, restructure your presentation into treatment form, writing a narrative description in the present tense that is confined to what would be seen and heard from the screen with a new paragraph for each sequence. Write so the reader can see and hear the film you have in your head as a result of researching. Do not be afraid to use language that elicits the emotional responses you expect your film to evoke in your audience.

A treatment does not include any philosophy or directorial intentions—so take care to confine yourself to what an audience would get from the screen.

A SAMPLE SUBJECT FOR DISCUSSION

Let us assume that you have chosen to make a film about a local school band. You want to go further than merely showing how the band rehearses or how it absorbs new members since that would merely illustrate what common sense alone would expect. Your purpose is to try and lay bare the fanaticism and quasi-military discipline underlying the band's success.

Before shooting anything, you will need to find out whether such an idea is feasible. This is one of the prime purposes of research. By the way, if you have to produce a film in a given time, it is a good idea to pursue the fundamentals of *several* possible ideas from the outset. Projects have a nasty habit of folding up. Permission to shoot might be a stumbling block, but sometimes one loses all conviction during research that any really meaningful film is possible. The chances of recognizing this in time are always much improved if you have alternatives on standby.

We are going to pursue the possibilities of this school band through the various stages of preproduction. Researching means initially surveying the general area to see if it is promising and to begin a "shopping list" of possible sequences. To do this you must start visiting for informal chats.

RESEARCH RELATIONSHIPS

As a researcher, be purposely tentative when you explain to people the project you have in mind. Only outline it in rather general terms so you can feel your way and also signify that you are open to influence.

In order to get to the bandmaster in our hypothetical school, you would start with the school principal, saying that you live nearby and have had thoughts on making a video film about the school's marching band. In all probability, the principal will be delighted and will tell the bandmaster to expect you. When you go to see the bandmaster, approval of your project is already implied because the signal has come from the top. In dealing with any kind of institutional structure, it is usually best to work from the top downward.

When you first make a research visit, take a notebook and nothing else. Present yourself in a friendly, respectful way. You are there to learn from experts; that is your role, and that is what you should project. It is a truthful presentation of your purpose (though not the whole truth perhaps), and it is a role to which most people respond wholeheartedly. At this point you really do not know what your future film might contain, nor do you have more than the vaguest notion of what it will really be about. It is therefore not only prudent but also truthful to keep your options open and to parry questions with a request for *their* ideas.

Your position as a researcher should be one of extremely wakeful passivity, watching and listening and correlating what you receive. In my experience, even the innately suspicious individual is intrigued by a moviemaker's interest and presented with consistently open interest will usually lower any barriers. This almost always takes an investment of time on your part, but keep in mind that *documentaries are only as good as the relationships that permit them to be made.* Few relationships of trust are achieved quickly so you should expect to proceed at your subject's own speed. This may mean you spend days, weeks, or even months getting to know your subjects and letting them come to trust you. This approach will work with just about everyone except those who have decided they have something to fear from your attention.

TWO RESEARCH STRATEGIES

There is a useful way to elicit opinions that still does not commit you to any particular point of view. In essence, you play the part of the "student of life" and sometimes that of devil's advocate. Instead of saying to the bandmaster, "I think you are tough and inflexible toward those kids," you probe in a more general and depersonalized way, no matter what your convictions may be, saying, "Some of the people I've spoken to say you are pretty definite about what you want. Do you find there's opposition to this?" And perhaps later, you might hazard something like: "Your experience has probably shown you that kids need to be shown a strong sense of direction?" Without committing yourself to agreement, you have shown that you appreciate the bandmaster's convictions. Most people assume incorrectly that because you can accurately describe their convictions you share them. While this is sometimes true, it is more likely to be a convenient misunderstanding and one which it would be unproductive to correct.

It is, I think, worth delving a little deeper into why the student-of-life approach finds such ready acceptance. Initially you will probably feel yourself trying to fake a confident, relaxed interest that you are too anxious to really feel. Do not worry; this is researcher's stage fright, and it always seems to accompany the initial stages of a new project even for old hands. Yet you will be amazed at how readily your presence, and your right to ask all sorts of questions, is usually accepted. And then you will be passed eagerly on from person to person. Have you stumbled upon exceptionally cooperative people? Probably not. Rather you have stumbled upon a useful facet of human nature.

I have come to believe that most people privately consider they are living in rather undeserved obscurity and that nobody properly recognizes their achievements or their true worth. When someone comes along wielding the tools of publicity—the pen, microphone, or camera—it is flattering, and it offers the fulfillment of a deep-seated yearning. In addition, there are more people than you would imagine with a philanthropic desire to tell the world a few truths it should know. All this, I think, helps explain why people may receive you with surprising enthusiasm and respond gratefully to the recognition your attention seems to confer.

With this comes an obligation on your part to act responsibly and to treat the lives you enter with care. It is not unusual to leave the scene of a documentary with the feeling that your participants have not only given you dinner but also have shared something profoundly personal with you and your camera. You are left with a strong sense of obligation not just to "the truth," which is an abstract thing, but also to the individuals who gave you something of themselves. You may even feel this toward those whom you don't much like and with whom you find little agreement. Making a documentary often poses unexpectedly pressing problems of moral obligation.

I cannot stress too forcefully one cardinal rule during the research period. *Never even hint you will film any particular scene or any particular person unless you are absolutely certain you are going to.* Most people are longing to be interviewed or filmed working, no matter how cool they are on the outside. If you don't commit yourself, you will avoid disappointing people and making them feel you have rejected them. This is why you must stress the tentative and uncertain aspects of your research as long as you possibly can. You may yet have to shoot certain scenes or interviews, just to keep someone important happy. Diplomacy of this kind costs time and money and is to be avoided.

Another cardinal rule: *Never say you will show footage to participants, either cut or uncut, if you think there is the remotest possibility that pressure will be brought on you to make undesirable changes.* Participants in a film, whether documentary or fiction, are generally appalled by their own appearance and mannerisms and thus are the worst people to help you make judgments about balance and content.

A reporter does not have to show his notebook to anyone before the article comes out in the newspaper, and you should likewise avoid actions that lead to loss of editorial control. This is ultimately in your participants' interest as well as your own since their initial shock and embarrassment usually changes later to pleasure and self-acceptance when an assembly of people is approving.

DECIDING THE ACTION AND CASTING THE PLAYERS

I mentioned earlier that you should start making shopping lists of possible sequences. In the hypothetical band project you have begun researching, you would spend time at the school getting to know the band's personalities and routine. You would start listing the possible action sequences as:

Band auditioning

Band practicing

Band marching

Playing in practice

Special performances

Social activities between members either before or after sessions

Social activities between members in between times

Like a fiction movie, you have been finding locations and pieces of action. Now you need to set about "casting players." You should begin making private, confidential notes on outstanding individuals. What kind of people are they? What does each represent in the whole? One may be the clown, another might be the diplomat, another the uncertain kid who is uncomfortable with the band's militarism but values being a member too much to leave. There may be senior kids who act as "policemen" and enforcers of the band's discipline. There may be a few eccentrics whose presence is tolerated because their playing outweighs their oddities.

THE VALUE OF ASSIGNING METAPHORICAL ROLES

It is extremely helpful that you find not just a functional description for each of your characters, but a *metaphorical* characterization too. All this, of course, is for your private use and not to be divulged to your subjects who might think you were mocking them in some way. By producing a metaphorical vision of the group and their situation, you are compelling yourself to define each person's underlying and unacknowledged role. Fred Wiseman's *Hospital* (1969) makes us think of Purgatory, where souls are rescued or sent onward. The image is so prevalent and so sustained, one realizes that through the force of his own vision he has made us see a New York emergency room as an embodiment of classical mythology. Before our eyes the doctors, nurses, policemen, and patients become players in a renewed version of legend.

It is your job as documentarian and artist to do more than simply show reality. That tends to be value-neutral and banal. You want your film to reveal that there is more to your subject than anyone would expect. You want to demonstrate that it contains the characters, passions, atmospheres, and human struggle that underlie any proper tale. The key lies in seeing your characters not with the scientific eye of a sociologist but as a poet or dramatist, alive to the recurring constants of myth and legend in everyday human life.

As you try to assign metaphorical roles to the participants (for example, king, queen, jester, prophet of doom, diplomatic troubleshooter, sentry, earth mother), it becomes apparent that, like any established group, they have unknowingly set up a microcosmic society with its own roles, rules, values, and sanctions.

Let us imagine that the band begins to look like a militaristic, patriotic, and authoritarian microcosm. It seems to be saying a lot about the ideology and background from which most of the teachers and students come. You now think it would be good to supplement the band activities, which confusingly suggest the values both of collaboration and dictatorship, with interviews. These you hope will give your audience access to the way the students and their teachers think. From chatting with people and from getting many different points of view, you come to realize which individuals are most deeply representative of the conflicting ideals you want to make visible. Certainly the bandmaster is a charismatic figure, whose power is accepted by most as a beneficial imposition. You talk to key instrumentalists and to other teachers, and you cross-check your own impressions by asking them each for their view of the others.

THE PREINTERVIEW AND HOW PEOPLE ALTER IN FRONT OF THE CAMERA

During research, you will not only investigate the subject, you will also need to test the behavior of possible participants as they go on record. Someone with an unsuppressed yearning to "be famous" (which is what people associate with film and television cameras) may come across poorly, show off, or perhaps clam up from sheer nervousness. This could derail your shooting.

At a subsequent research visit, take along an audio cassette recorder to record your conversation. Informal audio interviews like this can be used later as voice-over (if you take care to record well and avoid letting voices overlap). They strongly indicate who will give you the most in a manner least distorted by character hang-ups and who, on the other hand, cannot or will not deliver when he goes on record.

I always ask permission before turning my machine on. When I begin recording, nearly everyone is self conscious and a bit constrained. The best people will speak freely and with feeling, but others will not. When they are faced with a microphone, some people become monosyllabic or show an accentuated tendency to digress or to qualify everything they begin to say. Still others have a monotonous voice or an expressionless affect that has the unfortunate effect of negating whatever they say or do on screen. Even the voice quality itself matters greatly. Henry Kissinger's harsh voice, for example, may be a major factor in his unpopularity.

Once you have made a recording, take it away and just *listen*. Sometimes an interesting and likeable person simply does not record well. His voice may be flat or uncongenial, or he does not construct verbal pictures in a logical, communicative way. For some reason, this is hard to see until you are out of the person's presence and can listen with relative objectivity. Recognizing what does or does not work at this early stage will save time, money, and heartache later. Often, of course, a recording simply augments what you already knew: This person is a delight to hear, and you are sure you want to use him.

Your priorities have emerged by now, and the key participants—each representing different and probably opposed aspects in your underlying framework—have become a fairly easy choice.

DEVELOPING THE FILM'S THEMATIC STRUCTURE

Let us suppose for argument's sake you become convinced that the band is really a viable analogue for an aspect of your country's political structure with its charismatic father figure at the helm. This analogy is by no means farfetched. *Hearts and Minds* repeatedly uses scenes of American sports and the competitive team spirit atmosphere they engender as a parallel to the values expressed by proponents of the Vietnam War. The makers were advocating the idea, through the implied comparison, that a sports mentality can condition men to think of an international ideological conflict in the tragically misleading terms of "our team" and "their team." Only later did the young GIs begin to question what "playing for the team" really meant. By such conditioning and metaphors, the film implies, do we prepare ourselves to send our sons to suffer and die. Finding metaphors so alive and vibrant is the job of the documentarian who wants to draw attention to the underlying and invisible structures in society.

DOUBLE CHECKING ONE'S FINDINGS

During research, it is important to talk to as many people as possible and to collect as many relevant viewpoints as you can. One's initial judgments are often based upon brief and sometimes unrepresentative exposure, so testing one's assumptions against the impressions of people whose lives make them expert witnesses is a way of sifting out as much reliable information as possible.

It is fascinating to realize how people, especially highly visible people, are frequently perceived quite differently according to who you question. Partisan viewpoints and biases are inevitable, but you need to know what they are based upon. Cross checking people's impressions of your major "characters' enables you to avoid superficial judgments and allows you to build into your film the richness and diversity underlying the web of tensions binding any group of people.

By this time, you have become almost overwhelmingly knowledgeable about the people and practices that surround the school's marching band. You must first withdraw to decide your priorities, for if you were to shoot now, you would have no clear direction.

DEVELOPING THE WORKING HYPOTHESIS

Whatever your initial motives were for looking into the marching band, they must now be reviewed in the light of your much more extended exposure. My earlier comments about documentary make it apparent, I think, that, *if a film is to qualify as a documentary, it must imply a critical attitude toward some aspect of society*. It has been aptly said in Richardson's *Literature and Film* that "literature has the problem of making the significant somehow visible, while film often finds itself trying to make the visible significant." This is overwhelmingly true of documentary where there is often an oversupply of verisimilitude and a shortage of interesting underlying meanings. It is not enough to merely *show* something: we must also ensure that its *significance is implied*. How is this achieved?

Most of what we find significant in issues as well as in individuals lies in the fact that there is some kind of conflict at work. The conflict may be between people of different opinions, different convictions, or different ambitions. It may, like Nanook's, be between the individual and his surroundings, or it may be between the parts of an individual torn internally between classes or generations of people, between races or nations. It may even be between the parts of an individual torn internally between conflicting desires.

Jean-Luc Godard once said, while he was rejecting psychological formulas as a means of creating screen characters, that in real life we never gain possession of some magic psychological key to another's thoughts and feelings. Everything we learn is suggestive and fragmentary and is pieced together from that person's external behavior alone. Godard's chosen method to reveal personality was, he said, to concentrate on a person's contradictions because these showed most clearly what was unresolved and therefore most active in a person's inner life.

In the same way, if an honest documentary is to show the ambiguities and contradictions of its characters and situations, it must zero in on "unfinished business" and on those aspects of its subject truly in flux.

In our example, we have imagined going in to research an alarmingly militaristic high school band. But now a snag crops up. You find that, though the bandmaster is an authoritarian of the worst kind, a lot of the kids like him. Even more confounding to your principles is that, in spite of disagreeing with all his ideas, you find yourself liking him too.

What do you do? Give up? Surely you have stumbled upon a truly interesting subject, all the more so because you yourself have contradictory, ambivalent feelings toward him and toward the situation that he has projected around himself.

For your own clarity, you now need to define the focus, the underlying and implicit concept of your film. This definition should almost certainly not be shared with anyone outside your crew, but it is absolutely vital in determining any shooting to come.

A helpful example comes to mind from a feature film. You may have seen *Orchestra Rehearsal,* a ribald Fellini movie about an orchestra that rebels against its conductor and slides into anarchy. The film is one the surface a comedy, but it uses the orchestra as a metaphor for our complex, interdependent, and of necessity highly disciplined society. The conductor functions as the leader, but his role only works to everyone's advantage when all the instrumentalists co-operate and accept his authority. When a number of individuals begin to assert their autonomy, the music becomes first flawed and discordant and then completely chaotic. Even the opera house, under attack by unseen enemies, begins to fall down. Eventually out of sheer discomfort the orchestra reforms itself and returns to fulfilling its best potential.

The film demonstrates how an allegory can be implied by a group of musicians, and helps us see that a band with its bandmaster might be a rather potent metaphor for a political unit like a tribe or a nation. In fact, our band movie in dealing with charisma and authority could quite easily be turned into a parable about power and prevailing ideology.

Some people whose persuasions are perhaps toward the social sciences will undoubtedly feel uneasy here, and say, "But that's manipulation!" To them I would answer that the documentary does not exist just as a tool of social science, postulating the existence of such-and-such a phenomenon and reinforcing its arguments with a table of facts and figures. Rather its purpose is artistic, to share a way of seeing. The documentary is at its most effective when it gives us a heightened, subtly argued vision of something formerly banal and unmeaningful, now revealed as charged with significance.

An example is Fred Wiseman's *Hospital,* referred to earlier, where we see some patients who will be saved and some who will be damned, but there will never be an end to the distressed who enter the hospital's doors and never, seemingly, enough medical heroism to staunch the flow. This is an unforgettable film not only because of its subject matter, but also because it releases the power of an archetype that all of us unconsciously carry with us.

So what meaning, what thematic structure are we finding in our band situation? Let us imagine that you have unwittingly discovered what you never believed existed: that there is such a thing as a benevolent despot and that he is valued and valuable even though all his "subjects" see themselves in stereotyped terms of rugged individualism. Here then is a wonderful allegory for a "free" society that consents to march in lockstep in order to achieve supremacy and that enthusiastically submits to a form of leadership the very antithesis of its democratic and individualist ideals.

Let us say this is the kernel of your idea, the paradox you have discovered below the surface, what you "see." Now all your sequences, your activities, your interviews, and the discussions you ask the kids to have between themselves for the camera must create the contradictory parts of this central vision. It is a complex vision, and ultimately a nonjudgmental one that sensitively reflects not what you expected to find but what was actually there, existing in the face of all logic and belief.

Although I invented this example, I have myself experienced a very similar kind of conversion while making a film many years ago on a lordly estate in England. My film (*A Remnant of a Feudal Society,* BBC "Yesterday's Witness" series) does, I am told, reflect my inability to reconcile the contradictory nature of the estate, which operated in a quite feudal way down until modern times. For some of the survivors the estate was remembered nostalgically as a place of security and order—plenty of hard work but a great spirit of community. For others the regime was to some degree imprisoning, demeaning, and overdemanding. Not one person had clear, simple feelings, for all of them had differing experiences and had come to tentative, qualified conclusions if they had come to conclusions at all. The only predictable element was that the people in the upper part of the social scale remembered the old days more pleasurably than did those at the bottom though all valued the sense of safety and continuity the place formerly had.

Before going to the estate, I had expected people who served a feudal master to be united in their condemnation, for this was the rather monolithic course of history described in my schoolbooks. The real thing turned out to be much more human, much more complex and interesting, and showed me why my history books even then seemed simplistic and dull.

THE WORKING HYPOTHESIS AS A NECESSITY

It is axiomatic that one cannot start any kind of journey without first choosing a direction and having a purpose. In documentary making, it is my opinion that at the outset any kind of hypothetical explanation, even a prejudice, provides a better starting point than does the emotional vacuity that accompanies opinion-lessness. Had I not begun my feudal estate film with strongly felt opinions, I doubt whether my vision of the place would ever have developed as it did. Instead the film could have been a tedious little exercise in nostalgia in which old retainers remember the old days.

Always write out *the minimum your film must express* so you can ensure this at the very least is fulfilled during shooting. When this hypothesis, this underlying message, has been defined and when the supporting facts to be elicited from participants have also been defined, you are freed during shooting from the gremlin whispering in your ear, "Do you really have a film here?" In fact with thorough and focused preparation, the basic film is sure, barring accidents.

It is from this kind of solid base that you can find yourself able to see further and able to supplement or modify your original vision. Even with the pressures of shooting, it is quite straightforward to keep the hypothesis in mind as the measurement of everything you film. Indeed when one is committed to a working hypothesis, it is invariably extended and enriched during the shooting into something far beyond the original minimum requirement for an interesting film.

One gruesome fact about research must be stated emphatically: If you do not decide in advance what your film's hypothesis is to be, you will not find it during shooting. *A documentary only becomes a true inquiry when it starts from having something to say.* If you go shooting in the expectation of finding that "something to say" during the shoot, all your energies will be burnt up keeping the crew busy and trying to deceive everyone that you know why you are there. When you arrive in the editing room, the material will have no focus and therefore no vision. All this emphasizes how vital it is to crystallize research down into specific, practical, concrete resolutions. For this reason, it is a dead giveaway each time one reads a vague documentary proposal beginning, "This film will be an enquiry into . . ." I read on with the sinking feeling that I am being asked to support acrobats who think one can improvise a first performance.

THE NEED FOR DEVELOPMENT, CONFLICT, AND ENSURING CONFRONTATION

One ingredient essential to any documentary is the evidence of growth or change. Many documentaries fail by dwelling on what is essentially a static situation. One way to avoid this, if logistics permit, is to film over a period of time so that change is built in. One film that capitalizes magnificently on the passage of time is Michael Apted's *28 Up* (1986), which revisits a group of children at 7-year intervals from the age of 7 to 28. Because so many eerily fulfill their 7-year-old ideas about education, career, and marriage, the film is haunting and raises important questions about how and when people make the choices that so deeply affect personal destiny.

Unfortunately most documentaries have to be shot in a restricted period, and many leave the viewer with the disgruntled sense of having wasted time over something that never developed.

The best way to ensure development in your film is to search out where change is happening. This may be *physical movement* (for example, new house, new job, journey) or *movement in time* (change of season for farmer, growth in child, retrospective of painter's work), or it may be *psychological development* (ex-prisoner adjusts to freedom, teenager gets first paying job, adult illiterate learns to read).

Another way to give your film a feeling of development is to make sure that it deals with conflict in one form or another and that the conflict is followed through sufficient stages to achieve a sense of movement. This conflict might be within one character (a mother takes her child for his first day at school), between two characters (two social scientists have conflicting theories of criminality), between a character and the environment (an African farmer survives a drought from day to day), or thousands of other combinations.

As much as anything, achieving this is a matter of sensitivity to people and their issues. When you demand of yourself the questions, what is this person trying to *do?* what does he *want?* you are already defining that person in terms of movement and will. Because there is no movement without opposition, you are also led to the next question, what or who is keeping this person from getting what he wants? The elements of struggle, contest, and will are at the heart of drama in every medium including documentary. A documentary without some struggle for movement is likely to be just a catalogue of episodes.

In your marching band film you might build in several sorts of development. One might be to follow the development of a young contender from among those who audition to enter the band. Another might be to make sure the shooting period covers some big competitive event that puts everyone under special stress. Yet another might be after graduation when a senior goes from being a big man at school to a nobody in search of a job. Metaphorically speaking, you have encompassed a cycle of birth, life, and death in the band's ongoing existence.

Once you have defined a conflict, it will remain an abstract concept unless you take care to show it in action on screen. Be sure, therefore, that you orchestrate a *confrontation* between the opposing elements in your movie. If an instrumentalist has to pass a stringent test, be sure to shoot its key elements. If a young man must find a job, be sure to shoot him interviewing for one. It is always better to show struggle than to talk about it.

In many circumstances you may have to ensure that "the confrontation" happens; you might, for instance, arrange for two players with opposing views of the band to slug it out verbally in front of the camera. If the key issue in a film about a shelter for the homeless is whether such strict adherence to the rules by inmates is necessary, be sure to film clashes between inmates and those in charge. It may be necessary to ask either staff or inmates to initiate a typical episode if none happen spontaneously. Here you are using a degree of artifice in order to do justice to the spirit of your subject. This is a good example of the catalyst function that a *cinéma vérité* director would employ and a direct cinema exponent would abhor.

THE DRAMATIC CURVE

What documentary materials will be is not easy to foresee. Applying the traditional dramatic curve (Figure 3–1) to one's ideas, however, is useful during research and outstandingly useful as an analytic tool during editing, which is really a second chance to direct.

The dramatic curve concept postulates that a story develops through conflict to an apex or "crisis" after which there is change and resolution—not, let me say quickly, necessarily a peaceful one. In Broomfield's and Churchill's *Soldier*

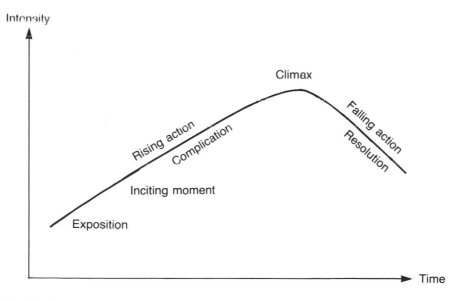

FIGURE 3–1

Dramatic curve. Variations of this apply to most narrative art, including documentary films. The same curve can also be useful in analyzing a single scene.

Girls (1981), the crisis is probably the point at which Private Johnson, after a series of increasingly stressful conflicts with authority, leaves the army dishonorably but in a spirit of relieved gaiety. The film's resolution after this major character leaves the stage is to examine in more detail what is required to train soldiers to survive battle conditions.

In the Maysles brothers' *Salesman* (1969), spectators usually point to the apex as being when the salesman, Paul Brennan, who has been falling steadily behind the pack like a wounded animal, inadvertently scuttles a colleague's sale. In the film's coda, one feels his partners distancing themselves as if they are deserting a dying man, and the film leaves Paul staring offscreen into a void.

If one understands the idea of the apex or crisis, the rest of the dramatic convention arranges itself naturally in stages before and after the peak of the curve:

1. The *introduction or exposition* lays out some of the characters and what their situation is and gives other necessary factual information about time, place, period, and so on. Since modern drama often lacks a captive audience, it cannot afford to delay major committing action, so the main conflict, or struggle between opposing forces, will probably be delineated early in what I think of as the documentarian's "contract." Signaling the scope and focus of the film to come, it aims at securing the audience's interest for the duration.

2. The *inciting moment* is whatever sets in motion the opposition of interests. In the army, basic training is a battle between the homogenizing goals of the army and the individualism of the recruit. The army aims to break down individual identity and replace it with a psyche trained to unthinkingly obey. In *Soldier Girls* the inciting moment is when Sergeant Abing sees Private Johnson smirking after he has rebuked her. This signals the onset of a long and unequal struggle between them. Because it is a white male imposing his will on a black female, there are disquieting overtones of slavery being reenacted.

3. *Rising action* or *complication* usually shows the basic conflicts repeatedly played out with variety, surprise, suspense, and escalating connotations. In *Soldier Girls,* the army's expression of will and the misfits' expression of cowed resistance are repeatedly raised a notch to a more serious and offensive level. Seeing protagonists and antagonists engaged in such a revealing struggle, we come to understand the motivations, goals, and background of each and may even be led to choose sides.

4. The *climax* or apex of the curve is where the final *confrontation* leads to irreversible change as was described earlier.

5. The *resolution* or *falling action* is what the piece establishes as a consequence afterward. This includes not only what happens to the characters but also what interpretation is suggested for the whole by the choice of last scene or scenes. In documentary as in other story forms, one can change the emphasis of a whole film depending on where and how the audience leaves the characters.

Few documentaries fall neatly into this shape, but a number of memorable ones do. The formula was invented by the Greeks, and is used with awful fervor in Hollywood. Many scriptwriting manuals go further and add alarmingly rigid prescriptions that may call for "plot points" on particular pages. Documentary, thank goodness, is too wayward a form to attract this kind of control fever, but the need for documentary to be dramatically satisfying remains inescapable. An important element here is suspense. As Wilkie Collins, the father of the mystery novel, said: "Make them laugh, make them cry, but make them wait." This applies fully to the documentary.

What is fascinating is that, under examination, the successful individual scene reveals itself as a drama in microcosm, following the same curve of pressures that build to a climax then release into a new situation. As a documentary director you will often see a spontaneous scene get so far, spin its wheels, and refuse to go anywhere. Then, perhaps with some side coaching from the director, the characters lock onto an issue and struggle over it until one gives in. This fulcrum point of change, called in the theatre a *beat*, is the basic unit of any scene containing dramatic interchange. Even montages with no people such as those in Lorentz's *The River* (1937) follow the same expressive curve.

The cycle of build and confrontation, that leads to a major realization or change of consciousness in one character may be repeated several times in a single scene. Recognizing what is happening, one knows what portions of a documentary scene to use. And whether one knows the terminology or simply the effect in life by instinct, recognizing how and when this dramatic breathing action takes place is really the major empowerment to direct films.

FACTS AND NARRATION

Before you begin shooting, you can often predict the need for some narration to get your film rolling and to link successive blocks of material. It is not good practice to rely on narration, however, so keep an ongoing list of facts vital to an audience's understanding of the material such as names, places, ages, dates, times, the sequence of main events, relationships, and so on. This is information that must emerge from the film in one form or another if the film is to make sense to a first-time audience. Part of your task as a director will be to make sure all of this material is adequately drawn out of the participants. You should evoke more than one version and from multiple persons. If you thus cover all your bases, it may be possible to evade altogether writing and recording narration and let the images and characters supply vital information as it is needed.

RESEARCH PARTNERSHIP

An ideal way to research is in partnership with a second person, perhaps a key member of the crew. Film's strength is that it is made collaboratively, and you will appreciate how much richer your perceptions and ideas can become when you exchange them with a like-minded partner. Another benefit is that one often needs moral support in penetrating new places and in breaking down prejudicial attitudes. It is possible then for both partners to be relatively relaxed, and the naturalness visible between the two of you often seems to be a reassuring signal, carrying over in your participant's attitude to the camera.

A further benefit of working in partnership is that it is useful to see if your intuitive feelings are shared, particularly those of foreboding. So often what is significant is received only on the edge of one's consciousness, and so you are inclined to overlook what may later turn out to have been an early warning. If this seems negative, there is a positive: The edge of your consciousness may pick up clues and hints that lead to greater things. And in this area too a partner can provide the vital endorsement.

SETTING UP THE SHOOT: LOGISTICS AND THE SCHEDULE

Estimating how much time it will take to shoot certain scenes is something that really only comes with experience. In general, careful work takes much longer than you imagine possible. You should probably only schedule two or at most three sequences in a day's work unless you are using available light and have good reason to anticipate that what you want is straightforward. Even a simple interview, lasting 20 minutes on tape, may take an overall three hours to accomplish. You should allow quite a lot of time for transport between locations, for tearing down equipment in the old location, and for setting it all up again in the new. A new unit is usually a lot slower than the same unit 10 days later.

A 30-minute documentary can take between three and eight working days to shoot, depending on (a) amount of travel, (b) amount of large lighting setups, and (c) the complexity and the amount of randomness inherent in the subject matter. For instance, if you are shooting in a schoolyard and want to film a confrontation between boys during break, you may have to hang around for days. On the other hand if you simply want to film the postman delivering a particular letter, you can organize things so it hardly takes more than 10 minutes.

Avoid the tendency to schedule optimistically by making best-case and worst-case estimates, and alloting something in between.

One luxury the independent filmmaker has that is usually only allowed the nature photographer is the freedom to shoot over a long period. Most documentaries have trouble showing any real development, and this stems from the economics of filmmaking in a commercial world where it is uneconomic to reassemble a crew at, say, six-month intervals for a period of two years. Yet it is precisely this kind of long observation that is likely to capture real changes in people's lives.

Whether you are shooting in a spun-out or in a compact way, make up a model schedule in advance and show it to all concerned for comment. Well in advance, *make sure everyone has a copy of a typed schedule.* Time spent planning and time spent informing people of the plans is time, money, and morale saved later. Poorly informed people tend to wait passively for instructions and to take no initiative in troubleshooting.

Always try to include in a schedule a phone contact number for each location. It is maddening to be short a crew member and to be incapacitated through lack of the information he could phone through. Whenever several people are meant to converge on an arranged place at an arranged time, you can expect someone to get lost or to have car trouble. The contact number allows messages to get through, even for two people in transit to contact each other. A schedule should also list special equipment or special personnel required in particular locations and give clear navigational instructions to help get everything there. Distributing photocopies of a map can save hours of precious time.

THE PERSONAL RELEASE FORM

The personal release form is a document in which the signatory releases to you the right to make public use of the material you have shot. You will not normally have to contend with legal problems unless you allow people to nurture the (not unknown) fantasy that you are going to make a lot of money selling their footage. No one ever got rich making documentaries, and you should lose no time correcting contrary notions.

Have personal release forms (see Appendix B) ready for participants to sign immediately after their filming is complete. No signature is valid without the $1 minimum legal payment, which you solemnly hand over as symbolic payment. The signed release is a form of consent that gives you copyright over the image and words of the participant. Since it is clearly impractical to get releases from, say, all the people in a street shot, one usually gets signed releases from speaking participants. Naturally judgment must be used here: The release is to prevent those you have filmed from going back on a purely verbal agreement or deciding at the eleventh hour that they do not want to appear in your film. So forestall any problems over getting permission to use the footage later by always obtaining the signed release. Minors cannot sign legal forms themselves and will need the clearance of a parent or guardian.

PERMISSION TO FILM AT LOCATION FACILITIES

While personal releases are signed *after* the performance has just been given, location permission must be secured *before* you start shooting. Strictly speaking, you should obtain *written* permission to shoot inside private buildings and in public transportation, parks, stadiums, and so on. Anything unrestrictedly open to public view (such as the street, markets, public meetings) may be filmed without asking anyone's permission. Events on private property would have to be cleared by the owner unless you care to risk being taken to court for invasion of privacy. This very rarely happens unless you or your company seem worth suing.

Most cities have restrictions on filming in the street. In practice it means you are supposed to get police permission and perhaps pay for a cop to wave away troublesome bystanders ("rubbernecks") or to control traffic. Technically if you abandon a hand-held technique and put up the tripod, you are deemed to have crossed over from news gathering to the big time, but there is seldom anyone around who cares as long as you don't tie up traffic. Documentary makers often shoot first and ask questions afterward, knowing that the combination of ideals and poverty will probably lead to an irritable dismissal if someone official starts asking questions. I should say emphatically that this solution runs all sorts of risks in nondemocratic countries where cameras are often and correctly regarded as engines of subversion.

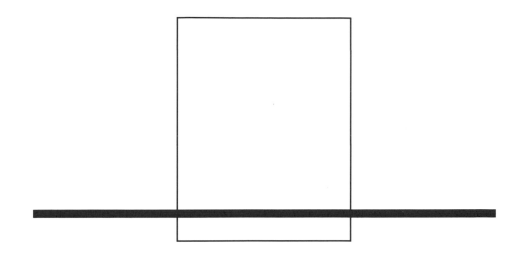

C·H·A·P·T·E·R 4

DEVELOPING A CREW

USING PEOPLE WITH EXPERIENCE

I have deliberately titled this "developing" instead of "choosing" a crew because even if experienced crew members are available, you should do some experimental shooting with them. Of course, you will want to verify that equipment is functioning, but you will also want to be sure you understand each other. A brief and unambiguous language of communication is always important, but if you are "grabbing" material, or shooting *cinéma vérité*, quick and positive exchanges of information become vital. In this shooting situation, camera-position changes are usually made rapidly and in response to the situation being filmed. There is no possibility for rehearsal, so a wide margin exists for misunderstanding between director and crew.

Even in relatively controlled shooting circumstances, it is regrettably usual to discover that one person's close-up is another person's medium shot. Framing, composition, speed of camera movements, and microphone positioning all come about through mutual agreement and compromise. This can only happen if the people concerned understand each other's signals and terminology. In shooting exercise footage, you will probably find wide variance of taste and skill levels as well as variations in responses, technical vocabulary, and interpretation of standard jargon.

DEVELOPING YOUR OWN CREW

Let us now suppose that you live in a place remote from centers of filmmaking and are having to start from scratch, work up your own standards, and find and train your own crew. We will assume that you have access to a videotape rig comprised of a camera, recorder, microphone, and a monitor. How many and what kinds of people will you need? What are their responsibilities?

All of them need to appreciate—or better yet to share—your values. Before deciding to work with someone, you should inquire not only about her technical expertise and experience but also about the potential crew member's ideas and values. You might ask what she feels about the purpose of documentary films and about favorite films, books, plays, hobbies, and interests. While technical acumen is important, a person's maturity and values are more so. Technical ignorance can be remedied, but you cannot expect to make much headway with someone who dislikes your choice of subject or who openly disapproves of your approach to it.

CREW MEMBERS' TEMPERAMENTS ARE IMPORTANT!

A documentary crew is very small, three to six persons. A good crew is immensely supportive—not only of the project, but also of the individuals in front of the camera, who are usually being filmed for the first time.

When I worked for the BBC, I usually had wonderful crews, but occasionally I was assigned individuals with personality problems. Often it was only that the crew member could not keep focused on the job in hand, but more than once I was assigned someone actively subversive. Being under pressure and away from home seems to unbalance some people and bring out the most childish insecurities and jealousies. This is not easy to foresee, but such people are an appalling liability in an activity dependent for its success on good *relationships*. The crew members make a large contribution for their interest and implied approval is a vital supplement to that of the director. Conversely any crew member's detachment or disapproval will be felt personally—not only by you the director but by participants, usually in a state of heightened awareness owing to the unfamiliar work you are asking them to do.

If a potential crew member has done film or other teamwork, try to speak to people who worked with her. Filming is very intense, so work partners rapidly gain a good idea of temperamental strengths and weaknesses. You may just have to rely on your judgment as to what kind of temperament your potential crew member really has.

In all film crew positions, beware of the personality with only one working speed (usually medium slow) for everything. Faced with a need to accelerate, these people usually either slow up in confusion or, if it is a crisis, go to pieces. Beware also of people who forget or modify verbal commitments or who repeatedly fail to deliver what they promise on time. Another liability is the person who habitually overestimates her own abilities and whose attention is inclined to spread detrimentally beyond her own field of responsibility. You will be looking for realism and reliability in your crew members, people who can sustain effort and concentration for long periods, and who like what they are doing.

HAVING AREAS OF RESPONSIBILITY CLEARLY DEFINED

No crew will function well unless the members' roles and responsibilities are clearly understood and a chain of command has been established that takes into account the different circumstances (such as the absence of one member) likely to occur. For instance, in the absence of the director or when the director is occupied, the camera operator leads the crew and makes necessary decisions. Crew members should in any case be discouraged from taking any and every query to the director when perhaps the camera operator could take the load from your shoulders. A director has enough of a burden without having to decide if someone should put another coin in the parking meter.

When first working together, stick to a formal working structure in which everyone takes care of their own responsibilities and refrains from comment or action in all other areas. As people come to know and trust each other, the formality can be relaxed. If on the other hand you start out informal and discover after all that you need a tight ship, the changes will be mightily resented.

You might say that a small film crew—director, camera operator, sound recordist, grip, and production manager—also consists of prophet, visionary, scribe, strong man, and fixer. Someone will always assume the role of jester or clown for each crew develops its own set of roles and its own special dynamic. The pleasure that comes from working effectively as a group is the best intoxicant you can imagine and seems to be especially strong during times of greatest pressure. And there is no hangover the morning after. Careful selection of partners makes anything possible. A team of determined friends is unstoppable.

CREW ROLES AND RESPONSIBILITIES

I will try to assign desirable personality types and backgrounds to the different crew positions. Of course, in real life many of the best practitioners are the exceptions, but here anyway is an outline of each crew member's responsibilities and the strengths and weaknesses you can expect to find. To make the list complete, I have included a summary of the director's role as well.

DIRECTOR

The director's responsibility is for nothing less than the quality and meaning of the final film. This means that she must conduct or supervise research, assemble a crew, decide on content, schedule shooting, lead the crew, and direct participants during shooting as well as supervise the editing and finalization of the project. Frequently, because there are no fat profits in view, the documentary has no producer so the director must also assemble funding before the making of the film and hustle distribution afterwards.

A good director will have a lively, inquiring mind fascinated by the causes and effects underlying the way people live, a mind that tries to find hypothetical links and explanations. She likes people and enjoys delving into ordinary people's stories. Outwardly informal and easygoing, she is actually very methodical and organized though able to throw away prior work if she finds her assumptions have become obsolete. A good director has endless patience in stalking the truth and in doing the truth justice in cinematic terms. A director needs to be articulate and succinct and to know her own mind without being in any way dictatorial. She should know enough about each craft to speak on terms of respectful equality with any of her technicians and thus be able to understand their problems and co-opt their efforts into realizing her intentions.

If this sounds impossibly idealistic, here are some of the negative traits that make even good directors all too human. Many are obstinate, private, awkward beings who do not explain themselves very well, who change their mind, and who are disorganized and visceral. Most can be intimidated by bellicose technicians. They find difficulty in giving appropriate time and attention to both the crew and the participants, and often tend to desert one for the other. During shooting, sensory overload catapults many into a Woody Allen condition of acute doubt and anxiety in which all choice becomes painful effort. Some cannot bear to deflect from their original intentions and appear to crew members like an obsessive captain who insists on sinking at the wheel of an imaginary ship.

Directing frequently changes perfectly normal people into manic-depressives who suffer extremes of hope and despair in pursuit of the Holy Grail. If that is not enough of a puzzle to crew members, the director's mental state often generates superhuman energy and endurance that test crew members' patience to the limit.

The truth is, I suppose, that directing an improvisation from life, which must then crystallize life itself, is a heady business. The person responsible for coordinating the efforts that go into doing this successfully is living existentially; that is, fully and completely in the moment. Living existentially has also been defined as living each moment as if it were your last, and directing a movie usually ensures that this happens whether you like it or not. This is especially true after an initial success: Thereafter you face failure and artistic/professional death every step of the way. Just as mountaineers say they truly feel the value of life only when they are dangling over a precipice, so the film director feels completely alive as she experiences the dread and exhilaration of the cinematic chase. Like stage fright for actors, this is a devil that never really goes away.

But, then, isn't the portent of any worthwhile experience that it makes you rather afraid?

CAMERA OPERATOR

In the minimal crew, the camera operator is responsible for ordering the camera equipment and videotape recorder, for testing and adjusting that equipment where necessary, and for being thoroughly conversant with its working principles. No important work should ever be done without running tests as early as possible in order to forestall Murphy's Law (that is, anything that can go wrong will go wrong). The camera operator is also responsible for lighting arrangements, for scouting locations to confirm electricity supplies, and for supervising the setting up of the lighting instruments.

The camera operator is also responsible for the handling of the camera, which means she takes an active role in deciding camera positioning (in collaboration with the director), and physically controls the camera movements such as panning, tilting, zooming in/out, and dollying. (Technical terms are explained in the glossary.)

The camera operator should of course be image-conscious, preferably with a track record in photography and fine art. Out of this you should hope for a sense of composition and design, and an eye for the sociologically telling details found in people's surroundings. It is also an advantage if your candidate picks up on the kind of behavioral nuances that tell so much about character. In documentary camerawork, which is sometimes "grab-shooting," it must often be the camera operator who decides moment to moment what to shoot. While the director sees *content* happening in front of (sometimes behind) the camera, the operator sees the action in its framed, cinematic form. The director may redirect the camera to a different area, but much of the time only the operator knows exactly what is being recorded so the director must be able to place considerable reliance upon the operator's discrimination.

For this reason a camera operator needs to be decisive and dexterous. Depending on the weight of the equipment, she may also need to be robust. Keeping a 20-pound camera up on your shoulder for an 8-hour day is not for the delicate nor is loading equipment boxes in and out of vehicles. The job is dirty, grueling, and at times intoxicatingly wonderful. The best camera people seem to be low-key individuals who don't ruffle easily in crises. They are practical and inventive and like improvising solutions to intransigent logistical, lighting, or electrical problems. What you hope to find is a perfectionist who will still try to get the best and simplest solution when time is short.

Rather alarmingly, quite a number of experienced camera personnel will isolate themselves in the mechanics of their craft at the expense of the director's deeper quest for themes and meanings. One such replied to a question of mine with: "I'm just here to make pretty pictures." He might have added, "and not get involved."

While it can be troublesome to have frustrated directors in one's crew, it can be disastrous to find you have a crew of isolated operatives. The best crew members comprehend both the details and the totality of a project and can see how to make the best contribution to it. This is why a narrow "tech" education is simply not good enough.

GAFFER

The gaffer is an expert in rigging and maintaining lighting equipment, and who knows how to split lighting loads in order to make them run off light-duty household supplies without starting fires or plunging the whole street into darkness. Good gaffers carry a bewildering assortment of clamps, gadgets, and small tools. Resourceful by nature, they sometimes emerge as mainstays of the unit when others get discouraged or defeated. During a night shooting sequence in England, I once saw a boy stumble behind the lights and hurt his knee. Because he had been told he must be silent while we were shooting, he doubled over and clutched his knee in mute agony. The kindly electrician (as the gaffer is called in Britain) swooped silently out of the gloom and cradled him in his arms until the shot was finished.

Because the gaffer is usually the only person unemployed when the camera is running, he may be the only person with a whole and unobstructed view of the action. Directors in doubt therefore sometimes find themselves discreetly asking how the gaffer felt about a certain piece of action.

Gaffers are usually chosen by the person responsible for lighting (cinematographer or videographer), and the two will often work together regularly. An experienced gaffer gets to know a cinematographer's lighting style and preferences, and can even arrive ahead of a unit doing exteriors to prelight. Teams who have worked together for a long time even dispense with a need for much spoken language.

SOUND RECORDIST

In an inexperienced crew the unfailing casualty seems to be sound quality. It would appear that capturing clear, clean, and consistent sound is either deceptively demanding or that sound recording lacks the glamour to induce people to try. Probably both are true. Another obstacle is that even quite expensive video recorders have a propensity for picking up every known electrical interference, allied to a sound quality that would disgrace even one of the humbler cassette recorders. Radical improvements have arrived in the shape of frequency modulation (FM) and pulse code modulation (PCM) recording, each producing true high fidelity recording, but many older machines will survive to bring hot tears of rage to the low-budget filmmaker.

It is the sound recordist's responsibility to check equipment in advance and to solve malfunction problems as they arise. The sound recordist therefore needs to have patience, a good ear, and the maturity to be low man on the totem pole. For in an interior setup, lighting and camera position are determined first, and the sound recordist is expected to somehow position the mikes without them being seen and without causing shadows and still achieve first-rate sound quality. A shoot therefore turns into a series of aggravating compromises that the sound person is all too inclined to take personally. A significant number of professionals turn into frustrated people inhabiting a world in which "good standards" are routinely trampled. Again it is the disconnected craftsperson rather than the whole filmmaker who cannot see the necessity and priority of compromise.

Because the sound recordist should listen not to words but to *sound quality*, it is immensely useful to have someone who has specialized in music and who can listen analytically to a track and actually hear the kind of buzz, rumble, or edginess that the novice will unconsciously screen out. The art of recording has very little to do with recorders and everything to do with the selection and placement of mikes and *being able to hear the difference*. There is no independent assessment possible apart from the discerning ear. Only musical interests and, better still, musical training seem to instill this critical faculty. Sound recording is considered easy and unglamorous among the uninitiated and is often left uncritically to anyone who says she can do it. But badly recorded sound disconnects the audience even more fatally than does a poor story. Most student films, if you close your eyes, sound like studies of characters talking through mashed potatoes in a labyrinth of echo-y bathrooms.

The sound recordist is often kept inactive for long periods and then suddenly expected to "fix up the mike" in short order. It helps to have the kind of mind that habitually makes contingency plans. The less satisfactory recordist is the one who only begins to think when her setup time comes, and who then, and only then, asks for a lighting change.

A lot of documentary work is done with a mobile unit. The recordist has to keep the mike on the edge of the camera's field of view and as close to the sound source as possible, without casting shadows or letting the mike creep into frame. With a camera handheld and on the move, this takes quite a bit of skill and agile, quiet footwork.

GRIP

A grip's responsibility is to fetch and carry. She also has the highly skilled and coordinated job of moving the camera support to precisely worked out positions when the camera takes mobile shots. It follows that grips should be strong, practical, organized, and willing. On the minimal crew, they will help to rig lighting or sound equipment. They will probably turn on and off the videotape deck, and they may leave the crew to fetch or deliver while shooting is in progress. A skilled grip knows something about everyone's job and in an emergency can do limited duty for another crew member.

PRODUCTION MANAGER (PM)

The PM is probably a luxury on a minimal crew, but there are many people whose business background equips them to do this job surpassingly well. The PM takes care of all the arrangements for the shoot. These might include finding overnight accommodations, booking rented equipment to the specifications of camera and sound people, making up a shooting schedule (with the director), making travel arrangements, and locating restaurants near the shoot. The PM will watch cash flow (if there is one!) and have contingency plans in case bad weather stymies exterior shooting. She will progress-chase and prepare the way in advance. All of this lightens the load on the director for whom these things are an unnecessary and counterproductive burden.

It is hardly necessary to say that the good PM is organized, a compulsive list-keeper, socially adept and businesslike, and able to scan and correlate a number of activities. She must be able to juggle priorities; make decisions involving time, effort, and money; and be the kind of person who is unintimidated by officialdom.

EQUIPMENT SELECTION: DRAWING UP A WANT LIST

In a book of this kind it is not possible to give many details about what equipment is desirable. If you own or are borrowing equipment, you will in any case have to work within its capacities. There are, however, some broad recommendations.

Sit down as a group and brainstorm over what you think you need. Make lists and do not forget to take basic tools with you. It is very rare that some piece of equipment does not need corrective surgery on the job.

Plan to shoot as simply as possible, aiming for straightforward solutions rather than elaborate ones. Any decisions about the style of the movie—how it looks, how it is shot, how it conveys its content to the audience—are best developed organically from the nature of the subject. The best solutions to problems are usually elegantly simple. Insecure technicians sometimes try to forestall problems by insisting on a need for the "proper" equipment, which usually means the best and most expensive. This can be a costly gesture to neurosis because initially you will be trying to conquer basic conceptual and control difficulties and will have little use for the sophistication of advanced equipment. You should make it your business to learn as much as you can about all the technical functions in the shoot so you and your PM can decide what outlay is truly justified. Some extra items turn out to be life savers, but many more cost money and are never used.

Remember it is human ingenuity, not just equipment that makes good films.

Read all equipment manuals carefully; there is always vital and overlooked information there. At the end of this book, there is a bibliography that can lead you to much more detailed information on the techniques of lighting, sound recording, and so on.

Do not be discouraged if your camera has every known design defect. There is no camera without handicaps and no film ever made without equipment problems. Indeed the first chapter of film history, so rich in creative advances in the medium, was after all shot with hand-cranked cameras made out of wood and brass.

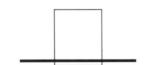

PREPRODUCTION SUMMARY

During preproduction, remember that:

Preparation is the key to coherent moviemaking.

Documentary making is long and slow; be ready for enthusiasm to dim.

You need to find subjects in which you can make a personal, emotional, long-term investment.

Behavior, action, and interaction best show how people live.

Documentaries are only as good as the relationships that permit them to be made (this applies to crew as well as participants).

Most people blossom when given lights, camera, and a sympathetic hearing.

You must act responsibly and treat the lives you enter with care.

You will face moral dilemmas in which the greater good is often pitted against a sense of obligation to an individual.

You should avoid situations where you may be expected to give up editorial control.

You must know in advance of shooting what you want to say through the film.

It is not a documentary unless it makes the audience want to weigh evidence and make judgments about human values.

A documentary shares a way of seeing and evokes feelings.

You must be ready to supplement or modify your original vision.

No plans lead to no film; the pressures of shooting will prevent radical inquiry.

Research is useless unless it is focused into specific plans for shots, sequences, or questions. Generalization is the enemy of art!

Good documentary, like any good drama, shows people in some kind of struggle and shows change and development. Development is often missing in documentaries, and this makes them feel static and pointless.

You need to find ways to bring conflicting values into on-screen confrontation with each other.

In preproduction, do not:

Bite off more than you can chew.

Set out to make a film that merely confirms what anyone would expect of the subject.

Stretch your resources too thin or your subject too wide.

Be put off by participants' initial reservations and hesitancy. Keep explaining, and see what happens.

Force people into situations or attitudes that are not theirs.

Tell anyone you are filming anything until it is 100 percent sure.

Promise to show footage if by doing so you lose editorial freedom.

Allow yourself to act as if you are begging favors, especially with officials. Make requests sound natural and rightful, and you will often get the moon.

When searching for a subject:

Make a habit of maintaining several project ideas on the back burner.

Read avidly about what is going on, and keep a subject notebook and clipping file.

Reject the obvious subject and the obvious treatment.

Only take on something that matches your capabilities and budget.

Make a conscious effort to discover and reveal the unexpected.

Define what you want to avoid as well as what you want to show.

Think small, think local, think short. Do something contained and in-depth.

When researching a particular subject:

Expect researcher's stage fright.

Take a research partner with you, and exchange impressions afterward.

Be purposely tentative and general when you explain your project.

Be friendly and respectful, and signify that you are there to learn.

Make a prioritized shopping list of possible participants.

Make a shopping list of sequences, and define what each might contribute.

Keep your options open and make no impulsive commitments.

When you have found a subject, ask yourself:

Do I *really* want to make a film about this subject?

In what other subjects am I already knowledgeable and opinionated?

Do I feel a strong and emotional connection to this subject, more so than any other practicable one?

Am I equipped to do justice to this subject?

Do I have a drive to learn more about this subject?

What is this subject's *real* significance to *me?*

What is unusual and interesting about it?

Where is its specialness really visible?

How narrowly and deeply can I focus my film's attention?

What can I *show?*

What recent films am I competing with?

What can I reveal that will be novel to most of the audience?

What are my prejudices that I must be careful to examine?

What are the facts an audience must know in order to follow my film?

Who is in possession of those facts? How can I get more than one version?

What change and development can my film expect to show?

When talking with possible participants:

Assume the right to be uncommonly curious and questioning.

If they ask about your ideas, try to turn the conversation so you learn theirs.

Go at the participant's speed, or you will damage trust and spontaneity.

Use a "student of life" attitude to encourage the participant to see herself in an instructional role.

Use the "devil's advocate" role to tread in risky areas without implicating yourself.

Watch, listen, and correlate what you take in with what else you know.

Use networking: Ask to be passed on to the next person. It always helps to have been personally referred.

Evoke each person's private view of the others as a crosscheck.

Do some informal, nonaggressive audio interviews to see if being "on record" hinders participants' spontaneity.

When deciding what and how to shoot:

Define what each participant's function is in life.

Define what each might represent or contribute as a character in your film.

Give each character and situation a metaphorical role.

Define what each sequence should contribute to the whole.

Define what microcosm your subject is and what macrocosm it represents.

Define what conflicts are at the heart of your drama and how to show them in confrontation on the screen.

When defining the working hypothesis:

What is the minimum your film absolutely must be able to say?

What are the conflicts you want to show?

What are the contradictions in the people and their situations?

What is each person's "unfinished business"?

When scheduling:

Schedule loosely, especially to begin with. Other people need food and rest!

Place least demanding work first.

Discuss scheduling in advance with those affected.

List special equipment or special requirements on the schedule.

Take into account travel time.

Make sure there are phone contact numbers in case anyone gets lost or delayed.

Give a typed schedule to crew and participants ahead of time.

Give clear navigational directions, plus map photocopies to drivers.

Obtain location clearances well in advance.

Have personal release forms and fees ready for shoot.

P·A·R·T I·I·I

PROJECTS: LEARNING TO SEE WITH A MOVIEMAKER'S EYE

I·N·T·R·O·D·U·C·T·I·O·N

Many people find conceptual theory either uncongenial or too abstract to absorb without some ongoing practical application. Those who wish may jump in cheerfully at this point where the things to do begin.

The discovery projects that follow may be undertaken alone, as part of a group, or as the basis for coursework in a college or university. They are structured not just by complexity but also as a sequence building the skills needed to aim at a professional level of competency. If you sometimes lack expert guidance (and who doesn't!), don't be discouraged when a project seems to be of excessive depth. They are designed to go a long way for those who want it. Do what you are able to do, and move on to new ground, which is what practicing filmmakers do anyway. It is in the nature of things that one always encounters unsolved problems again, and what made no sense in the book previously will look different and relevant once you have some experience.

I have not specified what kind of films to study, because almost all the work in this part can be done using either documentary or feature (that is, fiction) films. Features are more widely available and make a very good study subject. Their makers can control more aspects of filmmaking and thus use film language more fully than can documentary makers whose approach must be tempered by respect for the actual. Fancy lighting, smooth and complicated camera movements, clever transitions, tight "story line" are all rarities in the documentary, which draws its strength from the fact that its action is unpremeditated. Since film language is universal to all forms, it makes sense to learn screen grammar from the most consistently accomplished vehicle.

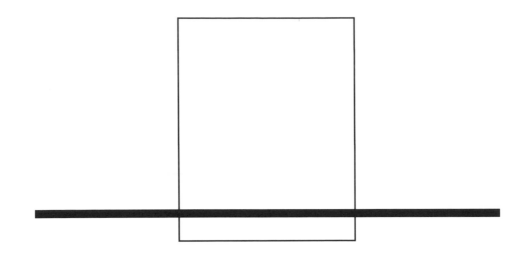

P·R·O·J·E·C·T 1

PICTURE COMPOSITION ANALYSIS

Equipment required: Video player, preferably with freeze-frame and variable-speed scan functions. Note that four-head players have better scan and freeze-frame capability than do two-head ones, which usually break up a static picture unrecognizably. Your monitor set can be a domestic television receiver, but it is best to connect VCR sound (usually labeled "Line out") to the AUX input (or "Line in") socket of a stereo. Reproduction is better, and you are less likely to get an almighty hiss each time you stop the player. A slide projector and/or an overhead projector is useful but not indispensable.

Object: To study how the eye reacts to a static composition and also to consider its reaction to dynamic composition in order to compose visual elements more consciously.

Study materials: Visually interesting sequences from a favorite movie on video-tape though an Eisenstein movie would be really useful. A book of figurative painting reproductions (best used under an overhead projector so you have a big image to scan) or, better, a dozen or more 35mm art slides, also projected as large images. Slides of Impressionist paintings are ideal, but the more eclectic your collection is, the better.

ANALYSIS FORMAT

I haven't found a need for any formal way of logging one's reactions, though if you are working alone, notes or sketches would be a good way of reinforcing the meaning of what you discover. Unfortunately, help from books on composition is not easily gained as many texts make the whole business seem intimidating and formulaic. The novice will often come away feeling there must be rules. In my experience, such rules prevent seeing instead of encouraging it. My stress is therefore not only upon trusting your eye to see what is really there, but also upon using your own nonspecialist vocabulary to describe it.

A stimulating and highly productive way to investigate composition is to do it with several other people. What follows is therefore written for a study group, but there is no reason why it can't be undertaken solo if circumstances so dictate.

STRATEGY FOR STUDY

If you're working with a group, you will need to explain what is wanted more or less as follows:

I'll put a picture up on the screen. Notice what point your eye is drawn to in the composition first, and after that, remember the course it takes as you examine the rest of the picture. After the image has been on the screen for about 30 seconds, I'll ask one person to describe the sequence of movements his eye followed. No special jargon is required, since your responses arise out of the specifics of each picture. Please avoid the temptation to try to find a story in the picture, or to guess what the picture is "about," even if it suggests a story. This project is aimed solely at discovering how each person's visual perception actually worked.

Each time you project a still frame, pick a new person to comment. Not everyone's eye responds the same way, and there will be some interesting discussion about the variations. There is usually a good deal of agreement, however, so people are led to formulate ideas about visual reflexes and about those components of compositions that the eye finds attractive and engrossing. Encourage your group to extract some guidelines from this experience after they have seen enough pictures.

I usually show both good and bad photos after the group has formed some ideas and some confidence from paintings. Photos are less obviously controlled and manipulated, and photography in general tends to be accepted less critically because the artistic choice is less evident. This is a good way to discover just how much control goes into a photograph that on the face of it seems to be just a straight record. You can graduate to more abstract images, even to completely abstract ones, and find a lot of pleasure in seeing the same principles at work. Many people, relieved of the burden of deciding a picture's subject, can begin to enjoy a Kandinsky, a Mondrian, or a Pollock for itself without fuming over whether it's "really art."

STATIC COMPOSITION

Here are some questions to help you formulate ways of seeing more critically. They can be applied after seeing a number of paintings or photos, or you could direct the group's attention to each question's area as it becomes relevant.

1. After your eye has taken in the whole, review its starting point. Why did it go to that point in the picture? (Common reasons are that it was the brightest point in composition, the darkest place in an otherwise light composition, a single area of an arresting color, or a significant junction of lines creating a focal point.)

2. When your eye moved away from its point of first attraction, what did it follow? (Commonly lines, perhaps actual ones like the line of a fence or an outstretched arm, or inferred lines such as the sightline from one character who is looking at another. Sometimes the eye simply moves to another significant area in the composition, going from one organized area to another and jumping across the intervening "disorganization.")

3. How much movement did your eye make before returning to its starting point?

4. What specifically drew your eye to each new place?

5. If you trace an imaginary line over the painting, following the route your eye took, what shape do you have? (Sometimes a circular pattern, sometimes a triangle or ellipse, but maybe many shapes. Any shape at all can point out an alternative organization that helps to see beyond the wretched and dominating idea that "every picture tells a story.")

6. Are there any places in your line that seem specially charged with energy? (Often these are sightlines such as between a Virgin's eyes and her baby's, between a guitarist's and his hand on the strings, or between two field workers, one of whom is facing away.)

7. How would you characterize the compositional movement (geometrical, repetitive textures, swirling, falling inwards, symmetrically divided down the middle, flowing diagonally, and so forth)? Making a translation from one medium to another—in this case from the visual to the verbal—always helps one discover what is truly there.

8. What parts, if any, do the following play in a particular picture:
   a. Repetition
   b. Parallels
   c. Convergence
   d. Divergence
   e. Curves
   f. Straight lines
   g. Strong verticals
   h. Strong horizontals
   i. Strong diagonals
   j. Textures
   k. Nonnaturalistic coloring
   l. Light and shade
   m. Human figures

9. How is depth suggested? (This is an ever-present problem for the camera operator who is liable unless he was trained otherwise to place his human subjects against a flat background and shoot. Unless there is something angling away from the foreground to suggest a receding space, the screen is like a painter's canvas and looks very much what it is—two dimensional.)

10. How are the individuality and mood of the human subjects expressed? (This is commonly through facial expression and body language, of course. But more interesting are the juxtapositions the painter has chosen of person to person, of person to surroundings, and of people inside a total design. The message here for documentary makers is that you control a sort of chicken and egg situation; the framing is arranged—so far as is legitimate—according to an interpretation of the subject's underlying identity. Yet that composition plays a considerable part at an unconscious level in defining the subject to the spectator. The good camera operator is the man or woman who *sees in terms of relatedness* and uses that vision responsibly to further the ends of the film.)

11. How is space arranged on either side of a human subject particularly in portraits? (Usually in profiles there is more space in front of the person than there is behind him, as if in response to our need to see what the person sees.)

12. How much headroom is given above a person, particularly in a close-up? (Sometimes the edge of frame cuts off the top of a head or does not show a head at all in a group shot.)

13. How often and how deliberately are people and objects placed at the margins of the picture so you have to imagine what is cut off? (This raises the question of using a restricted frame in such a way that the viewer's imagination supplies what is beyond the edges of the picture.)

VISUAL RHYTHM

I have stressed the idea of an immediate, instinctual response to the organization of an image because, unless shots are held to an unusual length, this is how an audience must deal with each new shot in a film. Unlike the response to a photograph or painting, which can be leisurely and thoughtful, the filmgoer must interpret within an unremitting and preordained forward movement in time. It is like reading a poster from a moving bus; if the words and images cannot be assimilated in the given time, the message goes past without being understood. If the bus is crawling in a traffic jam, however, you have time to see it to excess and to become critical, even rejecting, of the poster.

This analogy dramatizes the fact that there is *an optimum duration for each shot to stay on the screen* according to its content (or "message") and the complexity of its form (how much work the viewer must do to interpret the message from the presentation). That duration is also affected by an invisible third factor, that of expectation. For the audience will either work fast at interpreting each new image or slowly, depending on how much time they were given for immediately previous shots.

This principle in which a shot's duration is determined by content, form, and inherited expectation is called *visual rhythm*. As you would expect from such a musical term, a filmmaker can either relax or intensify a visual rhythm, just as a musician can. There are consequences in this for both the rate of cutting and the tempo of camera movements.

Ideal films for the study of composition and visual rhythm are those by the Russian Sergei Eisenstein, whose origins as a theater designer made him very aware of the impact upon an audience of musical and visual design. His sketch-books show how carefully he designed everything in each shot, down to the costumes.

Designer's sketches and the comic strip are perhaps the progenitors of the *story board* much used by ad agencies and the more conservative elements in the film industry to lock down what each new frame will convey. I find the wish to exert such total control over the vagaries of the creative process at once admirable and somewhat totalitarian. As in its political counterpart, there may be a price to pay for what it takes to get the trains running on time. Needless to say, there is no real place for story boarding in documentary, which derives much of its power and authenticity from accommodating the spontaneous.

DYNAMIC COMPOSITION

When you look at moving images instead of still ones, more principles are at work. If the components of a composition move, it is called a dynamic composition and a new problem emerges for a balanced composition can become disturbingly unbalanced if someone moves across frame or leaves the frame altogether. Even the movement of a figure's head in foreground may posit a new sightline, which in turn demands a compositional rebalancing. A zoom in from a static camera position, for instance, almost always demands reframing since compositionally there is a drastic change even though the subject is the same.

To study this, use a visually interesting film sequence. A chase scene makes a good subject. You will find the slow-scan facility on your VCR (if it has one) very useful. See how many of the following aspects you can find.

1. Reframing because the subject moved. (Look for a variety of camera adjustments.)
2. Reframing because something/someone left the frame
3. Reframing in anticipation of something/someone entering frame
4. A change in the point of focus to move attention from background to foreground or vice versa. (This changes the texture of significant areas of the composition.)
5. How many kinds of movement within an otherwise static composition can you find? (Across frame, diagonally, from background to foreground, from foreground to background, up frame, down frame, and so on.)
6. How much does one feel identified with each kind of subject movement? (This is a tricky one, but in general, the nearer one is to the axis of a movement, the more subjective is one's sense of involvement.)

7. How quickly does the camera adjust to a figure who gets up and moves to another place in frame? (Usually subject movement and the camera's compositional change are synchronous. The camera move becomes clumsy if it either anticipates or lags behind the movement.)

8. How often are the camera or the characters blocked (that is, choreographed) in such a way as to isolate one character? What is the dramatic justification for zeroing in on one character in this way?

9. How often are camera and/or characters blocked so as to bring two characters back into frame?

10. How often is composition more or less angled along sightlines, and how often are sightlines across a screen? (Here there is often a shifting of point of view from subjective to objective.)

11. What does the change of angle and change of composition make you feel toward the characters? (More involved or more objective.)

12. Find a dynamic composition that forcefully suggests depth. (An obvious one is where the camera is next to a railroad line as a train rushes up and past.)

13. How many shots can you find where camera position is altered to include more or different background detail in order to comment upon or counterpoint foreground subject?

INTERNAL AND EXTERNAL COMPOSITION

What we have seen so far has been composition within, and therefore internal to, each shot. But there is another form of compositional relationship. It is the momentary relationship between an outgoing shot and the next or incoming shot. This is called external composition, and it is a hidden part of film language—hidden because we are unaware that it influences our judgments and expectations.

An example might be: The point where a character exits frame in shot A leads the spectator's eye at the cutting point to the very place in shot B where an assassin will emerge from a large and restless crowd. In this example the eye is conducted to the right place in a busy composition.

Another example of external composition might be the framing of two complementary close shots in which two characters have an intense conversation. The compositions are similar but symmetrically opposed (see Figure P1–1).

Other aspects will emerge if you apply the questions below to your sequences under review. Using the slow-scan facility will help you more easily see the compositional relationships at the cutting point. Try finding for yourself the aspects of internal and external composition that follow.

1. Ask yourself where your point of concentration at the end of the shot was. (You can trace where your eye goes by moving your finger around the face of the monitor. Your last point in the outgoing shot is where your eye enters the composition of the incoming shot. An interesting point here is that the length the shot is held determines how far the average eye gets in exploring the shot, so shot length can influence external composition.)

FIGURE P1–1

Complementary compositions in which external composition principles call for balance and symmetry.

2. Ask yourself what kinds of symmetry there are between complementary shots (shots designed to be intercut).

3. Ask yourself what the relationship is between two different-sized shots of the same subject that are designed to be cut together. (This is a revealing question; the inexperienced camera operator will often produce medium shots and close shots of the same scene that cut together poorly because proportions and compositional placing of the subject are incompatible.)

4. Examine a match cut very slowly and see if there is any overlap. (Especially where there is relatively fast action, *a match cut to look smooth needs two or three frames of the action repeated on the incoming shot.* This is because the eye does not register the first two or three frames of any new image. We can think of this as an in-built perceptual lag, and the only way to cut to music on the beat is to make the cuts two or three frames before the actual beat point. Even some professional editors do not know this and are satisfied with cutting to the literal beat point.)

5. See if you can find visual comparisons in external composition that make their own nonliteral point (cut from a pair of eyes to car headlights approaching at night, from dockside crane to man feeding birds with arm outstretched, and the like.)

COMPOSITION, FORM, AND FUNCTION

If form is the manner in which content is presented, visual composition is not just embellishment but also a vital element in communication. While it interests the eye and even delights it, *good composition is an organizing force that exists to visually dramatize relationships and to project ideas.* Superior composition not only makes the subject (or "content") accessible, it also heightens the viewer's perceptions and stimulates his imaginative involvement, just as language does when used by a good poet.

My own persuasion is that one should first involve oneself with a subject and then find an appropriate form in which to best communicate that subject. Another way of working, which comes from being primarily interested in language rather than subject, is to decide on a form and then look for an appropriate subject. The difference is one of purpose and temperament.

While this project has been devoted to pictorial composition, it would be an omission not to point out that a film's sound track is also a composition and one critically important to a film's overall impact. The study of sound is included in Project 2, "Editing Analysis."

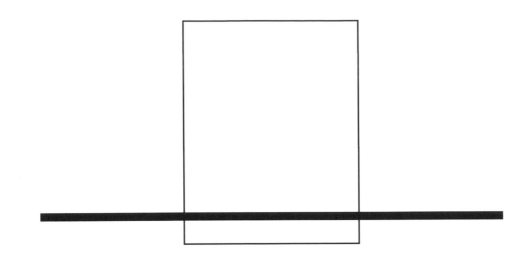

P·R·O·J·E·C·T 2

EDITING ANALYSIS

Equipment required: Video player as in Project 1. Your monitor set can be a domestic television set, but connect VCR sound to line input of a stereo (usually labeled AUX) for better reproduction and for silence instead of system hiss during stop periods.

Object: To produce a detailed analysis of a portion of film using standard abbreviations and terminology; to analyze the way a film is constructed; to learn the conventions of film language so they can be used with confidence.

Study materials: Few documentaries are yet available on tape at accessible prices. Those that are tend to be World War II compilation films (that is, compiled from archive footage) with heavy use of narration to bind together otherwise unrelated material. While this kind of material is useful for studying how narration is written and placed, it tells nothing about modern editing techniques. These only emerged after the early 1960s when mobile equipment began producing "grabbed" material with a dynamic lending itself to more imaginative interpretation in the cutting room. One way to avail yourself of modern material is to watch the television listings and to record off the air anything that promises to be a good, up-to-date documentary.

    As with the composition project earlier, a superb editing education can be gained from analyzing part of an imaginatively shot fiction film. The language of film is essentially the same in both factual and fictional modes, but the language is apt to be more freely and deliberately used in fiction because the makers have a greater degree of control over what and how they film.

    Making a documentary, however, places a greater requirement on finding a structure for the whole during the editing stage because there is no hard and fast blueprint in the beginning. Individual scenes are constructed—even contrived—out of available material, which may not cut together all that elegantly. Though the spontaneity and realism of *cinéma vérité* shooting is still tempered with the storytelling devices that accompany a concern for style and cinematic elegance, the documentary-maker's hands are often tied by concern for the integrity of actuality so there are many compromises. To study the full range of editing expression, one must therefore study the fictional form.

A well-made feature film with a wealth of editing techniques is Nicolas Roeg's *Don't Look Now* (1973). An adaptation of a Daphne du Maurier short story, the film is set in Venice and imaginatively exploits its exotic location. The narrative style is admirably compact and allusive, relying heavily on editing to telescope events into a brief montage of essential moments. Roeg's background is in camerawork so not only does he value the visual above the spoken but also his composition and camera use are masterly. The film also has a dense and highly evocative sound track. The narrative, which develops out of the trauma a couple suffer at the loss of their child, moves freely backward and forward in time, and this is particularly evident in the love-making scene.

Another feature film I would recommend for study is Carroll Ballard's *The Black Stallion* (1979). Ballard was originally a documentary maker and makes use of documentary shooting methods. The scene on the island where the boy first tames the horse is superbly lyrical filmmaking. Ballard's rapport with the boy who played the central character shows in the way his camera studies the fleeting changes in the boy's face and in the physicality of the whole movie. One only has to see the same boy actor under another director in the sequel *(The Black Stallion Returns)* to comprehend the breadth of Ballard's real contribution.

For an adaptation of a classic Ambrose Bierce short story there is Robert Enrico's *Occurrence at Owl Creek Bridge* (1962), which tells its complex story with virtually no dialogue and uses the camera with great intelligence. The film is specially useful for the way it uses rhythms and sound effects, for its creative distortion of time, and for its agile camera with many matching angles, each contributing a piece of revelation to the whole.

FIRST VIEWING

Whatever film you choose, *first see the whole film without stopping,* and then see it a second time before you attempt any analysis. Write down any strong feelings the film evoked in you, paying no attention to order. Note from memory the sequences that sparked those feelings. You may have an additional sequence or two that intrigued you as a piece of virtuoso storytelling. Note these down too, but whatever you study in detail should be something that stirred you at an emotional rather than at a merely intellectual level.

ANALYSIS FORMAT

Before you go ahead and analyze one of your chosen sequences, you may need to review standard film terminology (see Glossary) so your findings can be laid out on paper in a form any filmmaker can understand. What you write down is going to be displayed in split-page format, where all visuals are placed in the left half of the page, and all sound occupies the right half (see Figure P2–1).

You will need to make a number of shot-by-shot passes through your chosen sequence, dealing with one or two aspects of the content and form at a time. Your "script" should be written with wide line spacing on numerous sheets of paper so you can insert additional information on subsequent passes.

It is better to do a short sequence (say two minutes) very thoroughly than to do a long one superficially since your object is to extract the maximum information about an interesting passage of film language. Some of your notes, say on the mood a shot evokes, will not fit into the script format, which must primarily be concerned with *what can be seen and heard*. Keep notes on what

Action	Sound
F/I L.S. FARMHOUSE, EXT, DAY	Birdsong, Music
	Ted's V/O: "The agent said it's now or never. We've got to make our minds up."
Cut to MS Farmhouse, burned out barn in B/G	
	Karen's V/O: "But I thought you said that whole business was being put off! When we last talked about it, you said. . . ."
Cut to KITCHEN, INT, DAY 2S Ted & Karen	
	Ted: "It doesn't matter what I said. Everything's changed."
CU Karen, worried, shocked	
CU Ted, bitter then compassionate	Ted: "We're not to blame. You know that."
MS Karen moves L-R to stove	K: "Everything's changed?"
MS Ted moves slightly after her	T: "There's a buyer . . . someone's interested." (Music fades out)
Karen turns sharply to face him	K: "Ted, Ted! What are you telling me?"
BCU Ted, eyes waver & drop	K: "You told me . . . (dog begins barking) . . . you promised me . . .
Cut to O/S on to Karen	you said you'd never let the lawyer
Cut to O/S on to Ted	swindle us out of this place. You said
Cut to OTHER SIDE KITCHEN DOOR	
Anna, 4, clutching Raggedy Ann doll, looking frightened.	K., V/O: nothing like that could possibly happen. (Pause. Crying.) That's what you said. And I believed you. . . ."

FIGURE P2–1

Example of split-page format script.

the viewer *feels* as a separate entity. First you should deal with the picture and dialogue, shot by shot and word by word, as they relate to each other. The initial split-page script might look like Figure P2–1.

Once this basic information is on paper, you can turn to such things as shot transitions, internal and external composition of shots, screen direction, camera movements, opticals, sound effects, and the use of music.

MAKING AND USING A FLOOR PLAN

In the case of a sequence containing a dialogue exchange, make a floor plan sketch (see Figure P2–2) to help determine what the room or location looked like in its entirety, how the characters moved around, and how the camera was placed to show this. Knowledge of this kind can help you decide where to place your camera later when you start shooting.

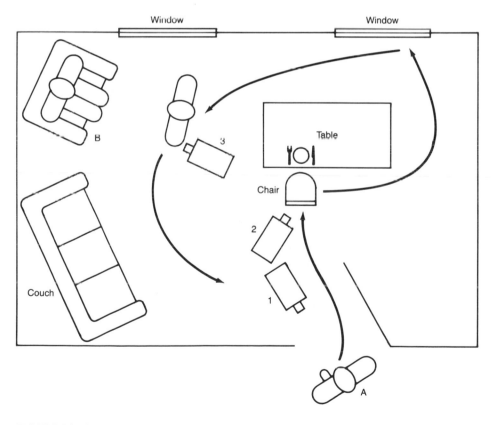

FIGURE P2–2

Floor plan: Shows entry and movement of Character A within a room in relation to the seated Character B. The three numbered camera positions cover all of the action.

STRATEGY FOR STUDY

Your split-page log should contain action-side descriptions of each shot and its action as well as sound-side notes detailing the content and positioning of dialogue, music start/stopping points, and featured sound effects (that is, more than mere accompaniment).

The scrutiny of a film sequence proceeds by categories. I have listed them below in a logical order for inquiry, but do not hesitate to reorder my list if another works better for you. To avoid overloading yourself, concentrate on a few of the given aspects at a time. To get the most out of this project, you should find at least one example of everything so you understand the concept at work. If you find yourself overwhelmed, do only what is rewarding and interesting and return later when your perspective has been refreshed.

FIRST IMPRESSIONS

What was the progression of feeling you had, watching the sequence? It is important to learn to read *from* film rather than read *into* it. Film is a complex and deceptive medium; like a glib and clever acquaintance, it can if it is allowed to make you uneasy about your perceptions and inclined to accept too easily what "should" be seen or "should" be felt. It is therefore important to recognize what you did feel and to connect your impressions with what can actually be seen and heard in the film. For instance, the beginning of *Occurrence at Owl Creek,* where Civil War soldiers are making some sort of ritual preparation at a distance, makes a disturbingly contradictory impression of forest beauty mingled with a lurking sense of menace. Careful reexamination of the film reveals that the camera is constantly sliding sideways, peering through a screen of tree trunks. Much of the scene's menace comes not from the scene's content but from its form, from the prowling, stealthy manner in which the events are revealed to us. In effect, we become voyeurs.

DEFINITION AND STATISTICS

What determines the beginning and end points of the sequence? Is its span determined, for instance, by being at one location or by representing a continuous segment of time? Is the sequence determined by a particular mood or by the stages of a process?

How long is the sequence in minutes and seconds?

How many picture cuts does the sequence contain? The duration of each shot and how often the camera angle is changed are aspects of a director's style but are also just as likely to be derived from the sequence's content. Try to decide whether the content or its treatment is determining the number of cuts.

USE OF CAMERA

What motivates each camera movement? Does the camera follow the movement of a character, or does it lay out a landscape or a scene geography for the audience? Is the camera move one that goes closer and intensifies our relationship with someone or something, or does the camera move away from someone or something so we see more objectively? Does the camera reveal significant information by moving? Is the move really a reframing to accommodate a rearrangement of characters or is the move a reaction, panning to a new speaker, for instance?

When is the camera used subjectively? When do we directly experience a character's point of view? Are there special signs that the camera is seeing subjectively (for example, an unsteady handheld camera for a running man's point of view)? What is the dramatic justification? (For instance, imagine we see a hot, delirious man in the desert in MLS. He walks for a while and then slumps down near some cactus. We cut to a scorpion sliding forward near his foot. We cut to a CS of his face, oblivious of the danger, then his expression suddenly changes. Cut to a subjective shot, in which the scorpion, seen from his eyeline, moves into the shadow of his knee. Obviously sharing his eyeline has been reserved for a crucial moment when we will most identify with his feelings of panic.

Are there changes of camera height? To accommodate subject matter (for example, to look down into a barrel)? To make you see in a certain way (for example, to look up from child's point of view at a stern teacher's face)?

USE OF SOUND

What are the sound perspectives used? Does the sound complement camera position (near mike for close shots, far from mike for longer shots—replicating camera perspective) or counterpoint camera perspective? (Altman films are fond of giving us the intimate conversation of two characters distantly traversing a large landscape.) Is the sound uniformly intimate (as with a narration or with voiceover and "thought voices" that function as a character's interior monologue)?

How are particular sound effects used? Is sound used to build atmosphere and mood, for punctuation, or to motivate a cut (next sequence's sound rises until we cut to it)? Is sound used as a narrative device (horn honks so woman gets up and goes to window where she discovers sister is making a surprise visit), or to build, sustain, or defuse tension? Does sound provide rhythm? (Meal prepared in a montage of brief shots to the rhythmic sound of a man splitting logs with the last shot being man and woman sitting down to a meal.)

EDITING

What motivates each cut? Is there an action match to carry the cut, or is there a compositional relationship between the two shots that makes the cut interesting and worthwhile? Is there a movement relationship (for example, cut from car moving L–R to boat moving L–R) that carries the cut or does someone or something leave the frame (making us want to see a new frame)? Does someone or something fill the frame, blanking it out, and permitting a cut to another frame, which starts blanked and then clears? Does someone or something enter frame and demand closer attention, or are we cutting to follow someone's eyeline, to see what they see? Is there a sound, or a line, that demands that we see the source? Are we cutting to show the effect on a listener and what defines the "right" moment to cut; or are we cutting to a speaker at a particular moment that is visually revealing, and if so, what defines that moment? If the cut intensifies our attention, what justifies that? If the cut relaxes and objectifies our attention, what justifies that? Is the cut to a parallel activity (something going on simultaneously), or is there some sort of comparison or irony being set up by the juxtaposition? Are we cutting to a rhythm—say of music? Or perhaps of the cadences of speech?

What is the relationship of words to images? Does what is shown illustrate what is said? Is there a difference and therefore a counterpoint between what is shown and what is heard, or is there a meaningful contradiction between what is said and what is shown? Does what is said come from another time frame (for example, a memory of one of the characters or a comment on something in the past)? Is there a point at which words are used to move us forward or backward in time? (Can you pinpoint a "change of tense" in the film's grammar? This might be done visually, as in the old cliché of autumn leaves falling after we have seen summer scenes.)

What is the impact of the first strong word on each new image? Does it clarify the new image, or does it give it a particular emphasis or interpretation? Is the effect expected (satisfying perhaps) or unexpected (maybe a shock)? Is there a deliberate contradiction?

Where and how is music used? How is it initiated (often when characters or story begin some kind of motion)? What does the music suggest by its texture, instrumentation, and so forth? How is it finished (often when characters or story arrive at new location)? What comment is it making (ironic, sympathetic, lyrical, or revealing the inner state of a character or situation)? From what other sound does it emerge at its start, and into what other sound does it merge at its close? Sound dissolves like these are each called a *segue* (pronounced "seg-way").

POINT OF VIEW AND BLOCKING

Blocking is the theatrical term meaning the way the actors and camera are moved in relation to the set. Point of view means more than just literally whose eyeline the audience shares: *Point of view refers to whose reality the viewer most identifies with at any given time.* This turns out to be a much more complicated and interesting issue than it first seems, for a film, like a novel, can present a main point of view (probably through a "point of view character"), or it can present multiple, conflicting, points of view. The author's statement is largely through the handling of point of view, yet the work's appearances can be deceptive unless you look very carefully. A good example in literature would be Thomas Hardy's *Tess of the d'Urbervilles*. The novel reads almost like a history with the author looking down on his heroine moving through the phases of her life in a changing landscape. Yet the experience of reading the novel is not one of distanced compassion like the tone of Hardy's writing. Instead readers experience the kind of trembling indignation one feels when violence has been done to a much loved friend. There are tricks of language at work here: Hardy was a poet as well as a novelist, and if one looks really closely at his use of language, something interesting and significant emerges. You find that, in the most discreet way imaginable, Hardy makes the reader share Tess's subjective, emotional perspective most of the time.

Interestingly this skillful use of words, which has its counterpart in a film-maker's use of film language, was not very evident in Roman Polanski's film version of *Tess* (1980). Although the camera keeps a cool distance, discreetly observing like Hardy's eye while telling the tale, one never feels the same involvement with the injustice of Tess's situation. Instead one experiences it more as an onlooker denied the chance to offer sensible solutions. The fault is hard to pin down; had the emphasis in directing been different, had Nastassja Kinski's playing had more resonance, our point of view might have been different too. And even here, opinions about the success or failure of the film to engage our sympathies are not united. Some viewers were moved, some were not. Some inside the film, some outside it. So the eye of the beholder plays its part too.

Point of view in storytelling changes: Although overall Tess's experience is the focus of the book, we get momentary insights into those of a range of other characters, whose limitations and misperceptions shape the central figure's perceptions and destiny.

In film terms, then, we may momentarily share the villain's point of view at the time he faces destruction or a man in the street's perspective of a parade containing our central character. This multiplicity of viewpoints helps to give richness and variety and to indicate a full spectrum of human characteristics in secondary figures, who nevertheless make up the human environment for the central character or characters.

Sometimes there is one central character like Travis Bickle in Scorsese's *Taxi Driver* (1976). There may be a couple whose relationship is at issue as in Woody Allen's *Annie Hall* (1977). Successive scenes may be devoted to establishing alternate characters' dilemmas and conflicts. Altman's *Nashville* (1975) has nearly two dozen central characters, and the film's focus is the idea of the music town being their point of convergence and confrontation with change. We find the characters are part of a pattern, and the pattern itself is surely an authorial point of view expressing ideas about the way people influence their own destiny.

Here are some practical ways of digging into a sequence to establish how it is structuring the way we see and react to the characters. A word of caution, though. Point of view is a complex notion that can only be confidently specified by considering the aims and tone of the whole work. Taking a magnifying glass to one sequence is therefore a way of verifying your overall hypothesis. The way the camera is used, the frequency with which one character's feelings are revealed, the amount of development she goes through, the vibrancy of the acting, all play a part in enlisting our sympathy and interest.

To whom is the dialogue or narration addressed? From one character to another or to herself (thinking aloud, reading a diary or letter)? Is dialogue or narration addressed to the audience (narration, interview, prepared statement)?

How many camera positions were used?

Using your floor-plan, show basic camera positions and label them A, B, C, and so on.

Show camera dollying movements with dotted lines leading to new position.

Mark shots in your log with the appropriate A, B, C camera angles.

Notice how camera stays to one side of subject-to-subject axis (an imaginary line one avoids crossing) to keep characters facing in same screen direction from shot to shot. When this principle is broken, it is called "crossing the line." The effect is disorienting for the audience.

How often is the camera close to the crucial axis between characters?

How often does the camera *subjectively* share a character's eyeline?

When and why does it take an *objective* stance to the situation (either a distanced viewpoint or one independent of eyelines)?

Character blocking: How did the characters/camera move in the scene? To the location and camera movement sketch you have made, add dotted lines to show the characters' movements (called blocking). You can use different colors for clarity.

What point(s) of view did the "author" engage us in?

Whose story is this sequence if you go by gut reaction?

Taking into account the angles on each character, whose POV were you led to sympathize with?

How many viewpoints did you share? (Some may have been momentary or fragmentary.)

Are the audience's sympathies structured by camera and editing? Or are they molded independently, perhaps by acting or the situation itself?

P·R·O·J·E·C·T 3

LIGHTING ANALYSIS

Equipment required: VCR as in the previous project. You will find it helpful when you are studying lighting to turn down the color control of your monitor so that initially you are seeing a black-and-white picture. It is very important to adjust the monitor's brightness and contrast controls so the greatest range of gray tones are visible between video white and video black. Unless you adjust the controls for optimum performance, you simply will not see all that is present.

Object: To produce an elementary analysis of common lighting situations found in both fiction and nonfiction films in order to better understand what goes into creating a lighting mood.

Study materials: Same as in the previous project only this time it will be an advantage to search out particular lighting situations rather than sequences of special dramatic appeal. It is not unlikely, of course, that the same sequences will fulfill both purposes.

LIGHTING TERMINOLOGY

Here the task is to recognize different types and combinations of lighting situations in order to become familiar with the look and effect of each and to be able to name them with the appropriate standard terminology. Unless you are specifically interested in color, it helps on many occasions to see just *light* by turning down the color control on your monitor so you see a black-and-white picture. Here is some basic terminology:

High-key picture is a shot that looks bright overall with small areas of shadow.

In Figure P3–1, the shot is exterior day, but the interior of a supermarket might also be high key.

Low-key picture is a shot that looks overall dark with few highlight areas. These are often interiors or night shots, but in Figure P3–2, we have a backlit day interior that ends up being low key.

Graduated tonality shots would have neither very bright highlights nor deep shadow but would instead consist mainly of an even range of midtones if they were viewed without color. This might be a rainy landscape or a woodland scene, as in Figure P3–3. Here an overcast sky is diffusing the lighting source, and the disorganized light rays scatter into every possible shadow area so there are neither highlights nor deep shadow.

High-contrast picture shots may be lit either high key or low key, but there is a big difference in illumination level between highlight and shadow area. This would be as true for a candlelit scene as it is for Figure P3–1. Figure P3–4 is a clearer example of a high contrast scene because there is a much more obvious area of shadow.

Low-contrast picture shots can either be high- or low-key but with shadow area illumination not far from highlight levels. The country post office scene in Figure P3–5 and the woodland scene in P3–3 are both low contrast.

Hard lighting describes light quality and can be any light source that creates hard-edged shadows (for example, sun, studio spotlight, candle flame). The barn scene in Figure P3–4 with its sharply defined shadow is lit by hard sunlight.

FIGURE P3–1

A lighting style illustrated here, in a *high-key* image.

A *low-key* image is shown in this example of a lighting style.

FIGURE P3–3

A *graduated-tonality* image is shown here, illustrating lighting from diffused source.

FIGURE P3—4

A *high-contrast* image, showing a big difference in illumination levels.

Soft lighting describes light quality from any light source that creates soft-edged shadows (for example, fluorescent tubes, sunlight reflecting off matte-finish wall, light from overcast sky, studio soft light). Figures P3–3 and P3–5 are both illuminated by soft light and lack any defined shadows.

Key light is not necessarily an artificial source for it can be the sun. It is a light source that creates intended shadows in the shot, and these shadows in turn reveal the angle and position of the supposed source light. In Figure P3–4 the key light is coming from above and to the right of the camera as revealed by the line of shadow. This of course indicates time of day.

Fill light is the light source used to raise illumination in shadow areas. For interiors, it will probably be soft light thrown from the direction of the camera to avoid creating additional visible shadows. Fill light, especially in exteriors, is often provided from matte white reflectors. In Figure P3–2, the girl would not

FIGURE P3–5 ───

A *low-contrast* image contains little range between levels of illumination.

be visible unless some fill light was being thrown from the direction of the camera.

Back light is a light source shining on the subject from behind and often from above as well. A favorite technique is to put a rim of light around a subject's head and shoulders to create a separation between her and the background. You can see this in Figure P3–2, where the girl's arm and shoulder are separated from the background by a rim of backlight. Although Figure P3–6 is high key, the key light comes from above and behind so the boy is backlit. This gives texture to his hair and makes him stand out from his background.

Practical is any light source that appears in frame as part of the scene (for example, table lamp, overhead fluorescent). The elderly couple in Figure P3–7 not only have practicals in frame (the candles) but are lit by them. Each candle tends to fill the shadows cast by the others so the overall effect is not as hard as the light normally associated with a candle flame's point light source.

LIGHTING SETUPS

Here the illuminations are of the same model lit in various ways. The effect and the mood in each portrait vary greatly as a result. In the diagrams, I have only shown key and fill lights, but most of the portraits contain other sources, including backlight, which is shown separately. In floor-plan diagrams such as

Back-lit image can also be a high key picture but with the light source behind the subject.

FIGURE P3–7

A *practical* is any lighting source that appears in frame no matter whether it is a functional source.

these, one cannot show the *height* of the shadow-producing light sources, only the *angle of throw* relative to the *camera-to-subject axis*. Heights can be inferred from the areas of highlight and their converse shadow patterns.

Frontally lit setups have the key light close to camera/subject axis so shadows are thrown backward out of the camera's view. You can see a small shadow from the blouse collar on the subject's neck. Notice how flat and lacking in dimensionality this shot is in comparison to the others. (Figures P3–8.)

Broad-lit setups have key light to the side so a broad area of the subject's face and body is highlighted. If you compare this shot to the previous one, you will see how skimming the key across the subject reveals her features, neck contours, and the folds in the blouse. We have pockets of deep shadow, especially in the eye socket, but these could be reduced by increasing the amount of soft fill light. (Figures P3–9.)

Narrow-lit setups have the key light to the side of the subject and maybe even beyond so that only a narrow portion of the woman's face is receiving highlighting. The majority of her face is in shadow. This portion of the model is lit by fill. Measuring light reflected in the highlight area and comparing it to that being reflected from the fill area gives the *lighting ratio*. It is important to remember when you are taking measurements that fill light reaches the highlight area but not vice versa so you can only take accurate readings with all the lights on. (Figures P3–10.)

Back-lit setups have the key light coming from above and behind the subject, picking out body outline and putting highlights in hair and profile. Some additional fill would make this an acceptable lighting setup for an interview. If you examine P3–9 and P3–10, you will see that backlight is a component in each, helping to suggest depth and roundness. Figure P3–8 is so flat because it lacks both shadow and highlights. Some back light would put highlights around the edges and give it the sparkle and depth of the other portraits. (Figures P3–11.)

Silhouette lighting has the subject reflecting no light at all and shows up only as an outline against raw light. This lighting is sometimes used in documentaries when the subject's identity is being withheld. (Figures P3–12.)

STRATEGY FOR STUDY

Locate two or three sequences with quite different lighting moods and, using the definitions above, classify them as follows:

a.	Style:	High key/low key/graduated tonality?
b.	Contrast:	High or low contrast?
c.	Scene:	Intended to look like natural light or artificial lighting?
d.	Setup:	Frontal/broad/narrow/back-lighting setup?
e.	Angles:	High/low angle of key light?
f.	Quality:	Hard/soft edges to shadows?
g.	Source:	Source in scene is intended to be ....
h.	Practicals:	Practicals in the scene are ....
i.	Time:	Day for day, night for night, dusk for night, day for night?
j.	Mood:	Mood conveyed by lighting is ....

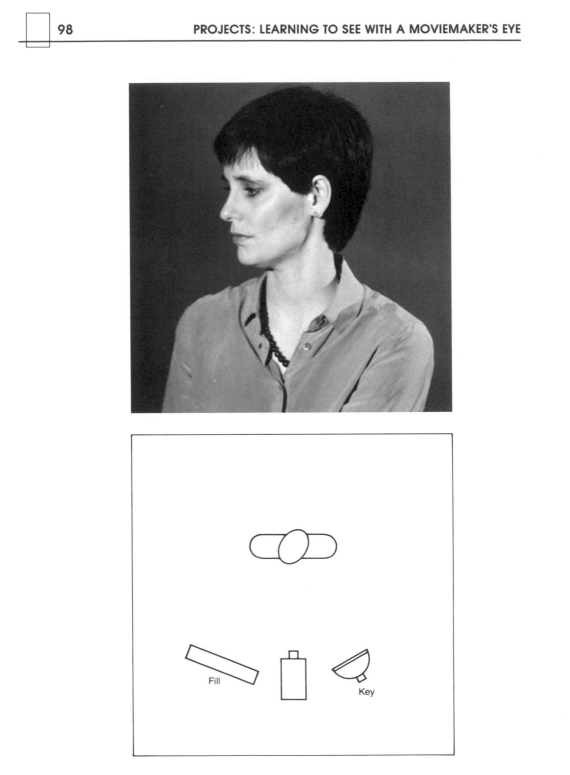

FIGURE P3–8

Frontal lighting example with setup diagram. (Dirk Matthews.)

FIGURE P3–9

Broad lighting example with setup diagram. (Dirk Matthews.)

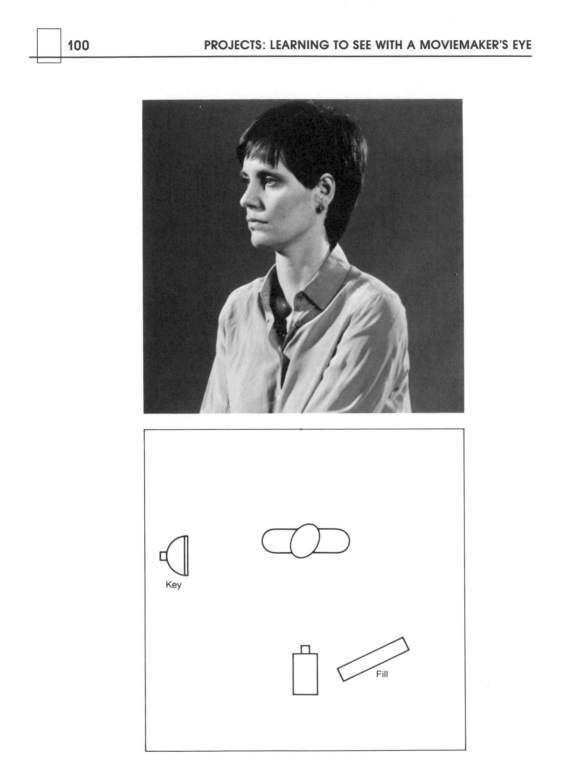

FIGURE P3–10

Narrow lighting example with setup diagram. (Dirk Matthews.)

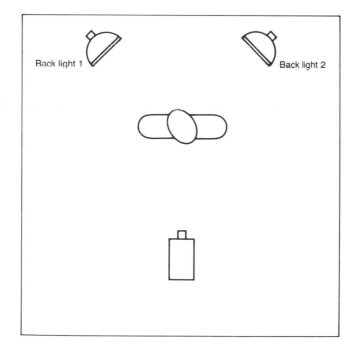

FIGURE P3–11

Back lighting example with setup diagram. (Dirk Matthews.)

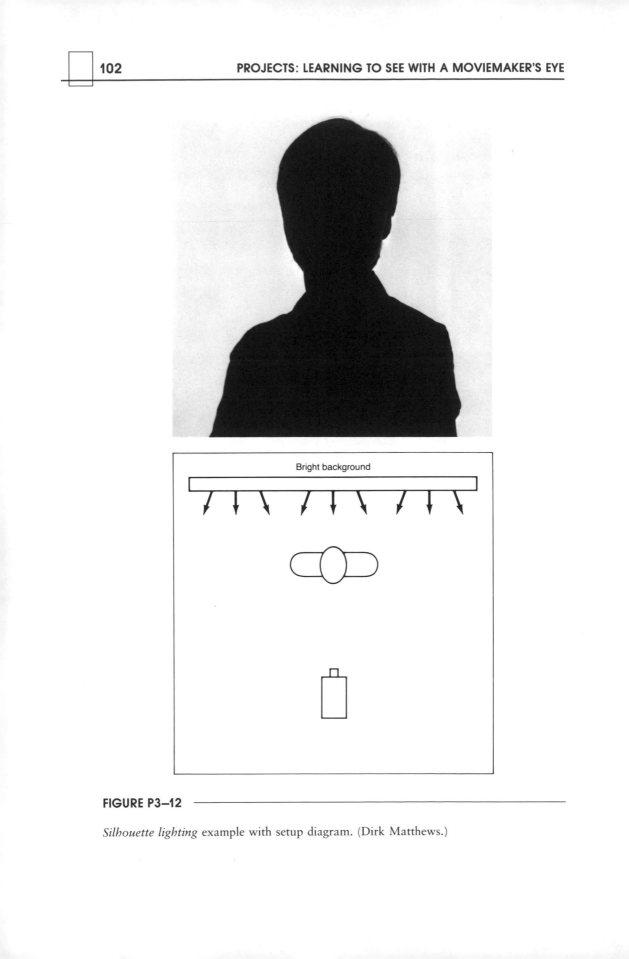

FIGURE P3–12

Silhouette lighting example with setup diagram. (Dirk Matthews.)

After you have analyzed several different sequences, see if you can spot patterns emerging that suggest how cinematographers set about translating the emotional associations of the location and situation through lighting. I think you will also see that predominant colors have a good deal to do with a scene's effect on the viewer. For instance, Antonioni color films, particularly *The Red Desert* (1964), and Kubrick's *A Clockwork Orange* (1971) show a highly conscious use of color and design. Polanski's *Tess* (1980) follows Hardy's novel in associating either red or white with the heroine, assigned to indicate her status between purity and ruin on the Victorian scale of sexuality.

Two classic, superbly lit black-and-white films are Welles's *Citizen Kane* (1941) with cinematography by the revolutionary Gregg Toland and Jean Cocteau's *Beauty and the Beast* (1946) whose lighting Henri Alekan modeled after Dutch painting, especially its interiors. Also fascinatingly lit is Louis Malle's *Pretty Baby* (1978), a film set in 1917 New Orleans; it was lit by the great Sven Nykvist, Bergman's cinematographer, who once said that his own sense of achievement over the years was in learning to work effectively with simpler and simpler lighting setups.

Tips on lighting practice follow in Part IV, Chapter 6, "About Lighting," which deals with lighting rudiments from the point of view of the low-budget documentary maker.

P·A·R·T I·V

TECHNICAL BASICS
BEFORE SHOOTING

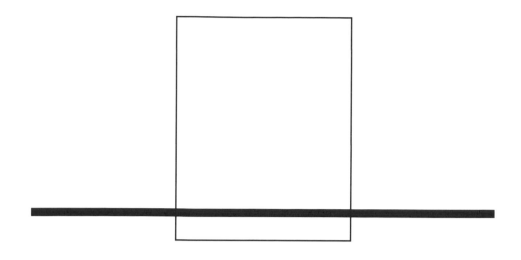

C·H·A·P·T·E·R 5

EQUIPMENT SELECTION

CAMERA BODY

Since you are almost certainly going to handhold, you will need a camera that has a viewfinder on the side and is balanced to sit on the operator's shoulder (Figure 5–1). Some videotape (VT) cameras have the finder at the back of the camera, 8mm home-movie-camera style. These often have a pistol grip, which makes them hard to hold because you cannot steady the camera against your head and shoulder. To add insult to injury, pistol-grip cameras usually mount on a tripod poorly.

LENS

You should take a look at the lens specifications. The range of the zoom lens is expressed in millimeters from shortest to longest focal length—for example, 15—60mm. If the lower number (or "wide-angle" end of the zoom lens) is lower than 15mm, you are in luck. Nine or 10mm is especially useful, because it gives your camera a wide angle of acceptance, which in turn allows you to cover a decent area in a small room. You are also, at this focal length, freed up from the necessity of doing a lot of focus adjustment. If the focal length at the wide-angle end of the lens is greater than 15mm (say 18—25mm), it is going to present problems. You will be unable to shoot very effectively in tight surroundings, you will have problems achieving a steady handheld picture, and staying in focus in low-light situations will be difficult. Test shoots will reveal what limitations you must work within to do acceptable work. Supplementary lenses are widely available that alter a zoom's entire range, but picture definition may suffer, particularly at the edges and in low-light situations.

FIGURE 5–1

Typical camera layout. (Sony Corporation)

Check to see if your camera has an interchangeable lens. Some will accept a C-mount (or standard 16mm) film lens. You can rent a 10mm lens quite reasonably; it is wide enough to provide a steady handheld image to take in a reasonable-sized image in confined quarters, but not wide enough to introduce the fairground distortions characteristic of wider lenses. It allows you to go anywhere at almost any time.

A real curse of the low-priced consumer camera is the electric or power zoom lens, which generally has one slow speed and may emit an enthusiastic whining noise every time you change image size. You should check to see if the zoom feature can be used manually. Likewise, see if automatic focus can be disengaged so the camera is not hunting for focus every time the picture composition changes.

EXPOSURE CONTROL

Examine your camera's lens and controls to see if the lens aperture (or f-stop) can be manually controlled. Your camera may not have a manual exposure control, which means that the image will go wild if a lady in a white dress walks across your frame during a street shot. This happens because automatic exposure circuits react slavishly to brightness changes with no regard for picture content. A manual control allows the user a degree of control vital to many kinds of lighting situations. For many reasons, non-disengageable automated controls are not favored by professional users.

COLOR BALANCE AND PICTURE GAIN

The least expensive VT cameras sometimes lack rather important features such as a white balance control or independent color controls. The white balance allows you to electronically adjust the color rendition to reproduce white as white under different kinds of light sources (daylight, tungsten-filament bulbs, and fluorescent light sources all have different "color temperatures"). A useful feature is a white balance memory, which holds on to the desired white balance even when the camera power is disconnected. Many cameras will need to be rebalanced every time you switch back on. Before you attempt to white balance (done by framing up a piece of white paper under the relevant light source), you should place the camera's filters at the appropriate setting—usually a choice between exterior, interior/tungsten and interior/fluorescent. Independent color controls are then useful for fine tuning, but they also allow you to do moody stuff—blue at night, cold greenish prison scenes, and so on. The ultimate reference in all color work is that flesh tones should look natural.

A useful feature found on some cameras is a picture gain control. It allows you to shoot an enhanced image in low-light situations. Usually there is an increase in "picture noise" and graininess. A back-light control is supposed to alter exposure to deal with a subject whose major illumination is coming toward the camera and is thus back lit. Many cameras in the low price range perform rather poorly in low light, however, so you are always well advised to keep your choice of subject within the performance range of your equipment.

POWER SUPPLIES

Consumer equipment is usually designed to run off 110-volt AC current. The more convenient equipment intended for location shooting runs off batteries that can be recharged. The charger often doubles as a power converter so you can run the whole outfit from an AC wall outlet. Batteries commonly do not run the equipment for very long especially if they are incorrectly charged after use. Be pessimistic about how many and what kind of batteries you would need for any extended exterior location. Manufacturers' literature usually errs on the side of optimism. One solution is to rent a battery belt, which has a much larger capacity than a battery pack and may power a recorder and camera for a whole shooting day without the need to recharge. All rechargeable batteries are inclined to be slow chargers—6 to 10 hours being normal. Never allow rechargeable batteries to become completely exhausted, but use each Nicad battery to the limit before recharging or you will shorten the battery's "memory."

CAMERA SUPPORT SYSTEMS

Here there is not much comfort for the underbudgeted film maker. The inexpensive tripod and tilt head is a miserable piece of equipment indeed. For static shots it is adequate, but as soon as you try to pan or tilt, your wobbly movements will reveal why heavy tripods and hydraulically damped tilt heads are preferred. A wide-angle lens will minimize a lot of camera movement problems though.

For a dolly, an excellent solution is a wheelchair. For exteriors, sit in the back of a station wagon or rope yourself securely on to the hood and handhold the camera with a wide lens. For tracking shots with sync sound (dialogue, for instance), use a light car with partially deflated tires as a dolly, and get several people to push it. That way engine noise will not drown your dialogue. A well-practiced, well-coordinated human being also makes an excellent camera support.

SOUND EQUIPMENT

Here we arrive at the area of commonest neglect. One should start by investing in a good pair of headphones. Get the kind that enclose the whole ear and so exclude outside noise. Next shun camera-mounted mikes at all cost as they pick up camera-handling noise transmitted through the camera body. Use the mike in a rubber shock-absorbing mount on a short "fish-pole" (a light, extendable aluminum boom). This mount allows the mike to be held forward of the camera but out of shot, either above, below, or to one side of the shot perimeter. You can improvise a fish-pole using an extending aluminum paint-roller handle from a paint store. Be careful to buy one that will not rattle in use.

Good low-cost mikes of the electret family are small and perform well. You will need a foam plastic windscreen for outdoor work where air currents will rattle the mike's diaphragm. Omnidirectional mikes usually give the most pleasing voice reproduction, but they pick up a lot of sound reflected by surrounding surfaces. A directional mike (often called a cardioid because of its heart-shaped pickup pattern) helps to cut down on reverberant sound and background noise but is not a magic solution. Using mikes intelligently is a highly specialized skill requiring considerable theoretical knowledge and the ability *to hear the difference.*

A very useful type of mike is the lavalier (or chest) mike, which is small and worn under a subject's upper clothing. These are excellent for achieving good intelligibility in noisy surroundings. One mike per speaker is required, and a small mixer is necessary unless your recorder has multiple-channel sound. Your subject's mobility is limited by the mike cable, hidden in clothing and emerging from a pants leg or skirt bottom. One of the funnier sights is seeing people who have forgotten they've wired get to the end of a cable. Radio mikes are theoretically wonderful but frequently pull in taxi and radio frequency (RF) interference in urban areas.

The mike operator rather than the recordist (deck operator) should wear the "cans" (slang for headphones) so she can assess the effect of the current mike positioning. Make sure you have backup cables, for breakdowns most commonly occur in cables and connectors, which are inexpensive to duplicate. Electret mikes need batteries: be sure to carry spares.

VIDEOCASSETTE RECORDERS AND CAMCORDERS

There are so many of these that comment has to be rather general. Try to use a videocassette recorder (VCR) with manual sound-recording-level control so pauses during speech don't get absurdly amplified by the automatic level control hunting for a signal. Check your machine with long cables (mike and camera) for RF interference (radio stations and other such noise), and check that it has a good level of headphone sound output. A digital counter is a time saver—and a time counter is even better as readings remain consistent from one machine to another. If you are using a multiple speed machine, use the speed that runs the cassette through fastest if you want superior picture quality.

MONITORS

Your VCR will need to produce an RF (radio frequency) output if you must monitor from a domestic television set. Much better results are obtainable by using a specialized video color monitor linked at the video signal stage rather than using a signal that has gone through two lots of additional RF circuitry. Some sort of monitor on location is indispensable. The more portable and the truer its color the better since it may be your only guarantee of color fidelity while shooting and the only check on the framing shown in the camera viewfinder. Almost all monitor sets as well as domestic television sets have abysmal sound quality. Videorecorders are made with a sound output (line out) that on playback can be fed into any stereo set (line in or AUX input). The improvement in sound quality is dramatic.

LIGHTING INSTRUMENTS

This entire book could be written about lighting alone. A considerable amount of quite acceptable interior work can be done using only a 1000–2000-watt softlight (also expressed as 1–2Kw, "Kw" standing for kilowatts) (Figure 5–2). It needs to be four to six square feet of illuminating area. This might mean that a spotlight's output was diffused by silk or fiberglass, or that you used a luminaire (jargon for lighting fixture) with recessed bulbs and a very large, white-painted reflector. Either way the effect is the same: Because the light is coming from a broad area, it throws very soft-edged shadows—shadows that are perhaps so soft they are not noticeable. Hence the terms *hard light* and *soft light*, which refer to the hardness or softness of any shadows cast.

If you want to cast the kind of hard light associated with sunlight or any other source that makes hard-edged shadows, you will need to carry focusing lamps or spotlights (Figures 5–3, 5–4). Open-face quartz lamps are relatively light and inexpensive (Figure 5–5). One warning: Never touch the bulbs as the oil in your skin will bake into the quartz envelope and cause it to discolor or even explode when it is next turned on. For interior work, you should use studio lamps (with a color temperature of 3200° Kelvin or K) to standardize color rendition and avoid mixing their light with daylight (approximately 5600° K) or with other light sources such as fluorescent lighting.

Movie lights are power-hungry, consuming 500–1000 watts each. A decent softlight will require 2Kw (2 kilowatts, or 2,000 watts). Since 1000 watts is equivalent to 9.5 amps when you are working from 110 volts, it follows that one cannot expect a 15A standard household circuit to power a 2K lamp—one must search for a 20A power circuit. To calculate power consumption in *amps* (rate of flow), add your desired *watts* (amount of energy consumption) and divide it by the *volts* (pressure) of the supply voltage. We can represent the common calculations as formulas:

FIGURE 5—2 ————————————

A 2k Softlight. The bulbs are recessed so that light is diffused by the white reflector. (Mole Richardson Co.)

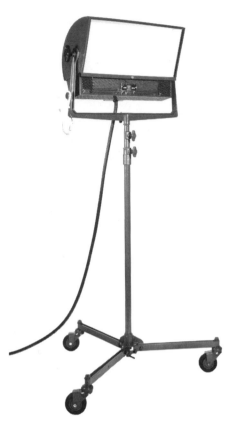

FIGURE 5—3 ————————————

Handy small spot: The fresnel lens produces hard light. (Mole Richardson Co.)

FIGURE 5—4

Larger spotlight. The stand allows the lamp to be rigged high or low and to be wheeled rapidly into position. (Mole Richardson Co.)

FIGURE 5—5

Lightweight open-face quartz kit. Barn-doors on lamps permit lighting spread to be restricted. (Lowel-Light Mfg.)

To calculate amperage (A):	A = W divided by V
To calculate wattage (W):	W = A multiplied by V
To calculate voltage (V):	V = W divided by A

Rather high current requirements must be kept in mind when you scout locations for electrical supply, and you must be extremely careful not to tap into a 220-volt supply by mistake. You also should plan to have extension cables so you can take each light's supply from a differently fused source and thus spread the load. The amount and type of lighting you will need depends on such things as size and reflectivity of the space to be lit, how much available light there is, and what kind of lighting setup you are aiming for.

Lighting is highly specialized, but there are simple and basic setups outlined in Chapter 6 that can get you through a lot, especially if you are shooting in color. Black-and-white lighting demands more skill if the viewer is to have a sense of dimension, space, and textures. Color can separate different tones by hue so less elaborate lighting is necessary for an acceptable result.

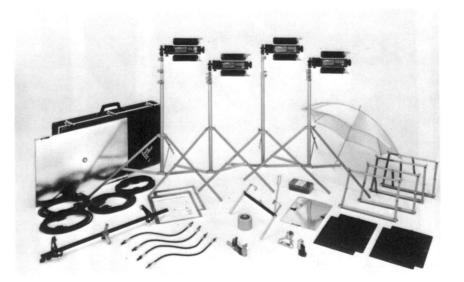

FIGURE 18—6

A lighting kit with great flexibility. The reflective silver umbrella converts an open-face (hard) light into a soft-light source. The frames carry diffusion material or gels. (Lowel-Light Mfg.)

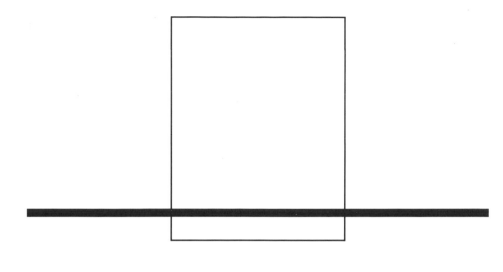

C·H·A·P·T·E·R 6

ABOUT LIGHTING

Any comprehensive lighting instruction for film or videotape is far beyond the scope of this book, but here are some basic points that most people will find helpful. Videotape has the immense advantage over film that the success or otherwise of a lighting setup is immediately apparent from the monitor.

WHEN YOU NEED IT

Lighting is usually necessary because there is not enough light to get an exposure or because there is so little that a very wide lens aperture is necessary. This in turn demands very precise focusing on objects that may be in movement. Adding light allows the cameraperson to work at a smaller lens aperture, have a greater depth of field, and suffer less acute focusing problems.

Another reason lighting becomes necessary is that no film stock or videotape camera behaves remotely like the human eye, which effortlessly evens out disparate illumination levels and color-temperature inequities. Image-recording systems simply record within their capacities what is scientifically present, something the human eye has got far beyond.

You will need lighting when you cannot get a minimum exposure, when you have too little light to give a working depth of field, and when you have very contrasty available light that creates very "hot" (bright) highlights and deep shadow, and you may need lighting to overcome a problem of mixed color-temperature sources.

CONTRAST AND COLOR-TEMPERATURE PROBLEMS

Because of film and videotape limitations, it is often necessary to lower contrast between shadow and highlight areas. You do this by raising shadow light levels to reduce the disparity between the highest and the lowest illumination levels in the picture. Using "fill light" to fill and therefore boost shadow levels is a way of reducing the lighting ratio or ratio of shadow to highlight illumination. This makes the range of brightnesses acceptable within the limited capacity of the recording medium so that on the screen one sees the contrasty picture one wanted with highlighted areas and deep shadow both containing detail that would have been lost had the picture been taken without lighting adjustments. Fill light may come from a lighting instrument, or it may be provided by a bounce-card (reflector made of white card).

Currently film stocks reproduce detail over a wider brightness range than does videorecording, which tends to perform best in brightly lit, low-contrast situations and poorly in contrasty low-key setups. This is particularly true of inexpensive cameras.

Another problem with any form of color shooting is that daylight and artificial lights have different color biases, a problem that must be addressed if flesh tones are to look human rather than Martian. The eye effortlessly compensates for the biases in light source and sees a white object as white whether the light illuminating it is sunlight, tungsten-bulb light, or the light from a fluorescent tube. But film stock either has to be specially chosen or the camera lens correctly filtered in order to render white as white. Electronic cameras have adjustments that allow you to find an optimal color rendition. This is called "white balancing" and is a simple, routine operation. While an electronic camera can be balanced for *one* color-temperature source, there is nothing it can do to balance an uneven mixture.

WORKING WITH LIGHT SOURCES
OF DIFFERENT COLOR TEMPERATURES

Imagine an interior setup lit by available daylight. You need to raise exposure in the shadow, but of course problems of color consistency arise when one tries to boost a setup lit with blue-biased daylight by adding orange-biased tungsten light. For if the color camera is adjusted to render daylight (5400° K) as "white" light, the light coming from a movie tungsten light (3200° K) will, by comparison, cast a noticeably orange hue. A domestic bulb (approximately 2800° K instead of 3200° K) will look even more orange, if there is one in the shot, because its color temperature is lower still.

If we try to solve the problem by filtering the camera for the 3200° K light generated by movie lighting, the daylight-illuminated highlights will now look very blue. In close-ups, these unnatural lighting effects are particularly noticeable as we tend to base our judgments on how natural flesh tones look. Thus it is usually necessary when mixing light sources to use a color-conversion gel over one or more of the light sources in order to bring its color-temperature output in line with the majority lighting. Though you solve the imbalance, you lose about 50 percent of the light's output by filtering, so you may need twice as much light. If you expect to meet this problem, see the Annotated Bibliography at the back of this book for specialized literature.

Even an apparently simple interior lighting setup can become very complex as the inexperienced cinematographer looks for solutions to inherent problems such as having too-high contrast, burnt-out walls, multiple shadows, and/or mike shadows, to mention just a few of the common ones.

ADDING TO A BASE AND USING A KEY LIGHT

Luckily if you are working in color, you can get away with a fairly simple and reliable solution to lit interiors. Called "adding to a base," it simply means that you provide enough ambient light for an exposure, and to this base quantity of light you then add some modeling by way of a key light. This base light can most easily be made by bouncing light off white walls and ceilings, thus casting a comparatively shadowless overall illumination. If there are no white walls, light can be bounced off white card or diffused through spun glass or any other diffusion material that will not discolor with heat.

The lighting from bounced light alone will probably be rather flat and dull, especially in longer shots, so you can add some key light. The key light should look as if it is coming from the scene's source light so it must come from a logical direction. For a bedroom scene, you might have the key light apparently coming from a bedside lamp so your key would have to be mounted low and out of frame. For a warehouse scene in which light comes from a bare overhead bulb, the key would have to come from above. In a laboratory scene where the source is a light-table, the key would have to strike the subject from a low angle, and so on.

You can cheat substantially on the angle of the key for artistic effect and to minimize shadow problems, provided you do not depart too blatantly from what seems likely and possible.

Any lamps that appear in the picture are called "practicals" but are not usually a functioning part of the lighting. They are adjusted for light output; enough to register as a light, but not enough to burn out that portion of the picture. If a practical looks too orange, use a photoflood, but be careful of the heat it generates. Cut a practical's output by putting a neutral-density filter or layers of paper around the inside of its shade.

DEFINING SHADOWS: HARD AND SOFT LIGHT

The key light not only provides highlights but also throws a shadow, and it is mainly by a scene's shadow pattern that the observer infers time of day, lighting mood, and so on. This means that your base or fill light must be a soft, diffuse light that creates minimal shadows.

Here we run up against some jargon that is indispensable in conversations deciding lighting and lighting style: hard and soft light. Hard light, you will recall from the "Lighting Terminology" discussion in Part III, Project 3, "Lighting Analysis," is light that creates *hard-edged shadows* while soft light is light that creates *soft-edged shadows* or even no shadows at all.

Note that "hard" and "soft" have nothing to do with strength of illumination. Thus in spite of its dimness, a candle flame is a hard-light source because it creates hard shadows. Hard light tends to come from a small-area light source or from one effectively small through being distant (like the sun) or because it is fitted with a lens (like a spotlight). Light rays coming from the sun are relatively organized and parallel to each other and thus project a shadow image of impeding objects; candles in a grouping will only cast a relatively soft light, with each candle tending to fill in shadows from the others.

Soft light tends to come from a large-area source that sends out disorganized rays of light incapable of projecting clean-cut shadows. A fluorescent tube is such a source, and is specially favored in everyday use as a shadowless working light. The most bountiful source of soft light when you are shooting exteriors is an overcast sky. This is why one sees huge lights being used on feature shoots during daylight shots; available light is too soft to produce adequate shadow patterns so it must be augmented with a local hard source.

KEY LIGHT DIRECTION AND BACKLIGHTING

Folklore about taking photos "with your back to the sun" tends to make us think automatically that light must fall on the subject from the camera direction. But since this ensures a minimum of shadow area, it tends to remove evidence of the subject's third dimension—depth. Actually some of the most interesting lighting effects are created when the angle of throw of the key is to the side of the subject or even relatively behind it (see Part III, Project 3, "Lighting Analysis," for pictorial examples).

Backlighting creates a rim of light that helps to separate the subject from the background. Achieving this separation is especially necessary in black-and-white but less so in color where the colors themselves help to define and separate the different planes of the subject.

Key light can come from an open-face quartz lamp, suitably backed off, or like the fill, it too can be somewhat diffused to soften unsuitably hard shadows. Using multiple key lights is a skilled business and without a lot of care can lead to that trademark of amateur lighting, ugly and unrealistic multiple shadows.

TESTS: HOW MUCH IS ENOUGH?

For shooting videotape or film, you will need three or more quartz lamps of at least 750 watts of power each. Quartz bulbs have a relatively long life (upward of 25 hours compared to 7 for a photoflood). They are small enough to provide fairly hard light and remain a stable color temperature through their life. A certain amount can be done with photofloods, but they lose both light output and color temperature relatively rapidly and in general just are not powerful or directional enough to solve more than a purely local problem.

I must emphasize that three or four kilowatts of lighting goes nowhere in a large space or for that matter in a smaller room painted a dark tone. The only way to know about lighting is to shoot tests. If you are hiring camera equipment and want to know ahead of time what your lighting will look like, an excellent way of spotting inequities is to shoot 35mm color slides (tungsten balanced) on a fairly fast slide stock (say 125 ASA at 1/50-second shutter speed). You can later project them and study in depth what your deficiencies or triumphs look like. Many people use a Polaroid camera, which gives an immediate idea of lighting, but instant-camera stock can lead to misleading results.

Avoid lighting and electrical failures by having a lighting rehearsal beforehand. Check out where high-consumption, intermittent appliances such as refrigerators and air conditioners are supplied from since their load kicking in during shooting may cause circuit overload. Long, demoralizing delays are the norm when people take chances that everything will work without prior planning and tests.

AVOIDING THE OVER-BRIGHT BACKGROUND

One truly aggravating problem when you shoot in small light-colored or white spaces is the amount of light thrown back by the walls. The on-screen result is a set of characters moving around as dark outlines against a blinding white background. The video image is especially vulnerable because the automatic-exposure circuitry adjusts for the majority of the image, letting the actual subjects go relatively dark. Color quality and definition all suffer, and this is why family video often seems to document a colony of orange hominids living in a glacier.

The solution to "hot" walls is to angle and barn-door your sources to keep light off the background walls and instead to raise the illumination level of the foreground subject. Ideally one should try to shoot in spaces with dark or book-covered walls, which absorb instead of reflect light.

To hold down background light level yet keep illumination high in the foreground, keep participants away from the background wall. This means "cheating" chairs, tables, and sofas several feet forward. It should not look unnatural on screen, and it helps in another way; with light coming primarily from above and characters away from walls, their shadows are thrown lower and thus largely disappear from sight. To move speaking participants away from a sound-reflective surface also means improved sound quality.

REACTIONS TO LIGHTING

People should be given a chance to get used to unusual amounts of light pouring down on them, particularly in their own homes. More than anything else, the discomfort caused by injudicious lighting serves to inhibit the nervous. The lights create a good deal of heat, and when windows have to be kept closed to reduce noise from outside, interior shooting can become unpleasantly tropical. Participants who sweat noticeably may need to be dulled down with a skin-tone powder to prevent glistening highlights. This is the only makeup ever used in documentary. Unless makeup is applied skillfully, it tends to look dreadful, and there really is no need for it apart from dealing with perspiration problems. Use a removable dulling spray (from an art supply store) for objects producing over-bright reflections, such as chrome chairs or glass tables. We found a rather torrid but serviceable makeshift in *Secret*™ spray deodorant.

C·H·A·P·T·E·R 7

AVOIDING PROBLEMS

LOGS AND BUDGET CONTROL

When you shoot a documentary or a fiction project on film, logs for both film and sound are imperative (see Appendix B for "Shooting Log" form). They serve various functions; one is to know in what sound tape or roll of camera original a particular shot or interview can be found. Should the lab or the cameraperson want to examine a particular camera original or video original after seeing a work print, the log allows quick access. It also allows for tracing which piece of equipment was responsible for any anomalies.

Another and important function of a log is that it enables you to keep a running total of how much stock has been consumed and therefore how nearly the production is running to budget. It is a common mistake for beginners to make an overall assessment of the stock requirement for the total shooting and then to put it out of mind until dwindling reserves direct everyone's attention to approaching famine. This results in liberal coverage for early material and insufficient coverage for later material.

Keeping a running total not just of stock used but of all vital expenditures helps the low-budget filmmaker to use precious resources intelligently and according to a rational set of priorities. The production manager rather than the director is in the best position to carry this out.

Budget monitoring is really a facet of the original cost projection. With a detailed cost projection, one can keep a running total to compare against the projected budget (see Appendix B for "Budget"). This warns of impending economies, and it teaches what changes to make in future.

WHERE VIDEOTAPE DIFFERS

Videotape is, of course, relatively cheap compared to film stock, but its very cheapness and accessibility encourage one to shoot promiscuously and without keeping track. This is a pity: Sound and picture are all on one tape so a log is easily maintained. Usually a contents description (tape roll number, date, location, activity, personnel, digital counter reading) is enough to assist a quick replay during the shooting period. Another and highly detailed log will be made at the start of postproduction.

Keep logs and records simple on location. The more elaborate your bureaucracy, the most likely it is to be abandoned when the pressure is on, leaving you with incomplete records that are as much of a handicap as no records at all.

SHOOTING RATIO

Shooting ratio is a way of expressing the ratio of material shot to material finally used on the screen. It is quite usual for a half-hour film to emerge from six hours of shooting. This would be a ratio of 12:1. A commonly asked question is, what is a normal ratio for a documentary? I usually answer, "How long is a piece of string?" It all depends on what you are tying up.

For example, my film about Alexandra Tolstoy and her relationship with her parents (*Tolstoy Remembered by his Daughter,* "Yesterday's Witness" series, BBC) was shot in about three hours. It consisted of one long interview, which I afterwards slugged with many still photos, 1910 news film, and shots of documents. The shooting ratio was about 5:1. It was as low as this because I kept my questioning to clearly defined areas (see list of questions in Appendix A), and since Madame Tolstoy was herself a writer, her replies came as beautifully succinct paragraphs.

Another example is a film I made about a London girl making her first trip abroad to work in a Parisian family (*Au Pair to Paris,* "Faces of Paris" series, BBC). As a result of leaving home, she had a heightened sensitivity both to her home environment and to the new surroundings in a Paris suburb. To reproduce this, I shot a great deal of visual material that could be used lyrically and impressionistically. This film came in at about 20:1.

The films of Fred Wiseman, usually 90 minutes long, may be culled from perhaps 70 hours of film (46:1). The high ratio is a result of aiming for a long screen time with its need for large themes and plenty of action material to sustain a complexity and development over such a long haul. The high ratio also stems from Wiseman's strict policy of nonintervention, which prevents him from polarizing or influencing the events he films or even from providing any narrated guidance in the finished product.

The only way to predict an adequate shooting ratio is to take each sequence and rate it for its contents. If you are shooting in a kindergarten and you want to catch certain kinds of unusual but highly significant behavior by the children, you might have a 60:1 ratio. An interview with the principal, on the other hand, might be confined to very specific comments and come in at 3:1 because she is very knowledgeable and very much to the point in everything she does. A good practice is to project smallest and largest figures for each sequence so you can modify as necessary how you predict the necessary ratio.

When you add all you expect to shoot and divide it by your intended screen time, you have an intended shooting ratio. During the shoot someone can monitor actual consumption and predict what needs to be done to come in on target.

EQUIPMENT BREAKDOWNS

Many equipment failures can be traced to inadequate checkout procedures in the first place. However "good" a rental house may be, no matter how "well" someone maintains a piece of rented equipment, nothing should leave its place of origin without a thorough inspection and a *working test*. Batteries for cameras, recorders, and mikes are frequent culprits. Rechargeable batteries are picky about how much and how often they are put on charge, and hire houses may unknowingly issue defective units. Try to run off a power line using an AC power supply (also called a "battery eliminator") whenever possible.

Parts that wear out, such as lamp elements, belts, and plugs, should have backup spares on hand. Wiring of all sorts is vulnerable especially at its entry point to plugs and sockets. The crew should carry electrical and mechanical first-aid equipment to carry out spot repairs.

Equipment failures sometimes jeopardize a project to such a degree that it is economical to hire or otherwise procure replacements in double-quick time. One way of preparing for this situation is to keep an emergency aid list for the area (or country) in which you will be working. This cuts down time lost in getting information. Not long ago I had a camera cable for a new Hitachi camera die on me while I was on location in Baltimore. No cable existed in all Baltimore, but I had my $15 test meter and soldering equipment. With these modest tools, I was able to trace the problem to a particular wire lurking inside a particular plug and to reconnect it.

If you prepare for the worst, you are seldom disappointed.

HUMAN BREAKDOWNS

Human breakdowns are not unknown, but any technician who walks off a shoot will find out that the word goes around, and no one will ever use him again. Volunteer labor, on the other hand, can be highly unreliable owing to the idea "If I'm doing you a favor, I'll come if I feel like it." Volunteers need to be drawn from that special and dying breed who honor commitments to the letter.

A more usual form of human breakdown is that of error or omission especially as people get tired. A good schedule and carefully made requirement checklists help to minimize these (see summaries provided at the end of Parts II, VI, and VIII). Sometimes when lines of responsibility are not carefully drawn or are misinterpreted, a duty will be carried out by two people or worse by neither.

A real disaster is when a participant withdraws or fails to appreciate how carefully synchronized your operation is when you plan something. Sometimes people act as if it is nothing to put off shooting for a couple of days, offering only that maddeningly evasive explanation, "Something has come up."

You should stress how important your arrangements are when you are setting up shooting times. Even then, people drop out. I once had a couple of artists back out on me three days before I was due to start shooting in Paris. I had read about a sculptor on the plane on the way over and was lucky enough to be able to make him the subject in time for the crew's scheduled arrival. What I did not know was that my new subject spent a good part of each day wandering by some migratory instinct from one favorite haunt to another. He had little concept of time, nor did he always remember where he promised to meet us. We played a lot of pinball, waiting. I was convinced that the film would be so awful that I would never get another to direct. This conviction I have since discovered is with most directors most of time. It is an occupational hazard like dogs are to postmen.

KEEP ALTERNATIVES UP YOUR SLEEVE

Given the ever-present possibility of technical and human difficulties, it is prudent to keep alternatives in mind in case you have to make a substitution. Exteriors that rely on a certain kind of weather should be scheduled early with interiors on standby as alternative cover. It is unwise to shoot crucial sequences, those that decide the viability of the film as a whole, at a late point in the schedule. Build the foundation of your house before you buy the furniture.

Likewise when something "cannot" be done, scan the explanation very carefully before you accept that it really is so. Filming always seems to depend on the coordination of several things. Many people assume that if one aspect is unfavorable, the intention cannot be carried out. Often it takes a less linear mind to see that changing two of the other aspects now makes the original intention once again viable. I have seen a student fiction crew try to solve a lighting problem by moving the camera or by moving a light or two. If neither of these works, the cinematographer is apt to announce that the scene needs to be relit. Actually a change of camera height or reblocking the actors might do the trick, but it takes experience and quirky, nonlinear imagination to find the answer.

P·A·R·T V

PROJECTS: LEARNING BASIC SHOOTING TECHNIQUES

I·N·T·R·O·D·U·C·T·I·O·N

Just as the strength of a chain lies in its weakest link, so your ability to use the medium effectively rests in how well you master basic documentary and film-making techniques. The projects in this book start simple and become increasingly sophisticated. Carrying them out will equip you with a range of invaluable new skills and awarenesses. Ahead in Part VII "Projects: Developing Skills as a Director," there are assignments that demand conceptual and authorial skills, but here in Part V, your work will focus on gaining the prerequisite control over the tools and basic techniques. The sound experiments can often be combined with camera handling assignments.

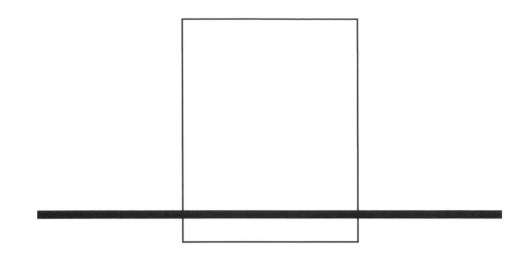

P·R·O·J·E·C·T 4

SOUND EXPERIMENTS

The object is to familiarize yourself and your ear with the basic necessities for successful voice recording. Some outline of theory is unavoidable. For the sake of this discussion, let us imagine a voice recording taking place in a room within hearing of an office and busy traffic.

All sound recordings have four basic components:

1. Signal (desired recording subject, in this case a speaker).
2. Ambience (background sound inherent to the location, which might include traffic, a distant typewriter, voices).
3. Reverberation (sound waves that continue to rebound around the room by bouncing off sound-reflectant surfaces. These muddy the clarity of the new signal by adding in the still-decaying reverberations of the old).
4. Noise (hiss or interference inherent to sound systems often amplified with each generation of sound transfer and which might include hum or radio frequency [RF] interference).

The recordist judges a voice recording according to:

> How well the signal is separated from ambience
> How much reverberation is mixing with the signal
> How much noise there is

Intrusions on the desired signal are considered as a comparison or ratio. A high ratio of signal to ambient sound is desirable because it yields more intelligible speech. A low signal to ambience ratio threatens intelligibility and puts undue strain on the audience. The golden rule is always to place a mike as close to the source (the speaker) as possible. In film, this ideal is compromised by the need to hide the mike or to allow one's subjects the freedom to move.

The location recordist generally works with two main types of microphone, each reception pattern having its uses and drawbacks.

Omnidirectional. Usually giving slightly better fidelity, it picks up sound equally from all directions, and is useful for covering spontaneous group conversations. The omnidirectional's big drawback is that it cannot help you separate ambient sound from signal. Lavalier (chest) mikes are "omnis."

Directional. This type, often called cardioid for its heart-shaped pickup pattern, suppresses or "discriminates" against sound coming from off axis. During a shoot in a noisy street location, for instance, this can make a critical difference to intelligibility and audience comfort. Superdirectional mikes do not bring sound "nearer" or make it inherently louder; they simply discriminate even more against off-axis sound but at some cost to fidelity.

Producing good sound means learning to hear the differences between common kinds of sound coverage and to recognize the effect of an environment. These experiments will help develop your ear and your analytic ability. Although you will probably shoot and edit on videotape, try listening at least once to the edited versions with your eyes closed. Editing your results is important as many sound inequities do not show up until juxtaposing makes them glaringly apparent.

VOICE RECORDING, INTERIOR

Use a fairly large, minimally furnished room. Shoot a seated person who reads in a constant voice but who never holds the text so it gets between mouth and microphone. Use a basic videorecorder or camcorder setup with headphones, equipped if possible with both directional and omnidirectional mikes.

1. *Ambience.* Set up a wide shot about 12 feet from a seated person. Station a radio near the camera playing music as a source of constant ambient sound. Using either an omni or directional mike near the camera; listen through monitor headphones; and set the radio sound level so it makes the reader difficult but not impossible to understand. Neither moving nor changing the voice and radio, now shoot 15 seconds each of wide shot, medium shot, and BCU, using an appropriately changed mike position for each. Edit the three shots together for a dramatic illustration at the cutting points of how the signal to ambience ratio changes as the mike approaches the speaker.

2. *Sound perspective and reverberation.* Repeat the experiment without the radio playing. Shoot wide-angle and close-up shots with appropriate mike positions, then reverse the logic by shooting a close-up picture with a wide-shot mike position, and wide shot using close-shot sound. Edit the resulting footage together in different permutations. You will see that changing the mike positioning itself produces a sound perspective change and that close-

shot sound is acceptable over a wide shot but not vice versa. Notice the hollow and "boxy" sound quality of the wide shot. Its recording contains a considerable admixture of reverberant sound compared with that of the closeup.

3. *Microphone axis.* Take a continuous medium shot of your reader with the mike in shot directly before the speaker at about four feet distance. During a continuous reading, point a directional mike on axis (directly at speaker's mouth) for 10 seconds, then rotate it smoothly and silently to a position 90° from axis, hold this position for 10 seconds, then rotate it a further 90° so it now points at the camera and away from the speaker. Hold this for a further 10 seconds. View/listen to rushes, then make an edited version that shows only the three static mike positions. Again it is when sound is cut together that one really hears the changes. Notice as the mike leaves the axis, how the voice quality becomes thinner and the reverberant component increases.

4. *Speaker axis.* Speech, in particular the all-important consonants, comes out of a person's mouth directionally. Shoot a medium-close shot of the reader, taking 10 seconds of speech with a mike (preferably omnidirectional) hand-held two feet in front of the person's face. Be careful not to introduce any handling noise. Keeping the mike at the same distance, circle around to the side, holding steady there for 10 seconds. Finish by circling to the rear of the speaker, again holding for 10 seconds. View/listen to rushes, then edit the three positions together for an illustration of what happens to a voice's quality when the mike moves progressively away from the speaker's axis. Compare consonant clarity and fidelity of other shots with the best (on-axis) recording, and note any changes in ratio of signal to reverberant sound.

VOICE RECORDING, EXTERIOR

5. *Perspective.* In a quiet open space, use a directional or omnidirectional hand mike to shoot a speaker first in close, then wide, shot (camera about 20 feet distant). Edit back and forth between the two shots for an illustration of sound perspective changes that this time lack reverberant sound.

6. *Signal to ambience ratio and camera distance.* Shoot in the open near some constant source of outdoor ambient sound such as a highway, fountain, or school playground. Using a directional hand mike, shoot a minute of interview with camera and mike pointing toward the ambient sound's source and the speaker's back to it. Then turn the action around and shoot a minute with the mike's axis away from the sound's source. Intercut the two tracks several times. Because there is virtually no reverberant sound, the mike's degree of discrimination will be readily apparent at the cuts.

7. *Signal to ambience: Mike choice.* In the same noisy exterior setup, shoot an additional section for the interview in (6) above using a lavalier mike. Intercut CS sound from (6) with lavalier sound to discover the differences between the two forms of mike coverage. Discuss the ratios of signal to ambience in your coverage.

P·R·O·J·E·C·T 5

CAMERA HANDLING

Documentary camerawork divides into two different categories, each serving a different purpose.

Tripod. Camerawork done from a tripod allows smooth movements, controlled transitions from one subject to another, and stable closeups at the telephoto end of the zoom lens. A tripod-mounted camera conveys the kind of cool, assured view familiar from studio television and feature films and is associated with an invulnerable, omniscient point of view. Usually used in controllable circumstances, it goes with careful, elegant lighting. Invaluable for interviews, the tripod-mounted camera is virtually immobile and handicapped when it comes to covering spontaneous events. Either a moving subject must be covered with multiple cameras, or the action must be interrupted to allow moving the single camera to a new position. This limits coverage to subjects that can be made subservient to the needs of the camera.

Handheld. The *cinéma vérité* handheld camera is usually on the operator's shoulder so that it can pan or track with the subject at will. During a protest march this could allow one to follow a single demonstrator throughout a day or alternatively to cover the main elements—speaker, marshals, police, contingents of demonstrators—that make up the event's totality. When events move with any speed the operator must make on-the-spot decisions about subject framing, camera moves, and showing either action or reaction. Under more controlled circumstances these decisions would be handled by the director and editor so the *cinéma vérité* operator assumes more responsibilities. The operator's challenge is to minimize the jerkiness and indecision of the human being supporting the camera. To reduce unsteadiness, keep your lens on wide angle, and physically move close to or distant from the subject for close or wide shots.

From here onward, each project is accompanied by italicized criteria that can be rated to indicate your degree of success. I use the following scale of agreement.

Outstandingly so   = 5
Considerably so   = 4
Acceptably so   = 3
Somewhat so   = 2
Slightly so   = 1
Not so   = 0

Over a number of assignments, your pattern of strengths and weaknesses will emerge. I rate students' work only after they have rated each other's because assessing someone else's work also contributes to developing a quick, experienced eye in the field.

TRIPOD INTERVIEW, ONE SUBJECT

Read the section on interviewing. Place the interviewer's head right under the lens, so the interviewee appears to address the viewer. For approximately four minutes of screen time, shoot an interview lasting five minutes on a seated subject using three image sizes:

Wide shot (top of head down to knees)

Medium shot (head and top of shoulders)

Big close-up (forehead to chin)

A lavalier mike is ideal for this setup. Arrange a touch signal between the interviewer and the camera operator to indicate angle changes. The interviewee must not overlap the interviewer because the interviewer's voice is going to be cut out. If overlap happens, get the interviewee to repeat the reply without overlap. Suggested subject: Someone who had a major influence on your life. Edit using Project 11 guidelines:

Composition proportions match on cuts between angles

Subject position matches between angles

Zooming and recomposing happen simultaneously and smoothly

Editing maintains natural rhythm of speaker's speech

Interviewer's voice successfully eliminated

Interview successfully (re)structured to develop meaningfully

Tends to use wide shot for new subject matter

Tends to cover moments of intensity in BCU
Interviewee is at ease
Interview has impact and intensity throughout
Good sound and no mike visible

TRIPOD COVERAGE OF THREE-PERSON CONVERSATION

Here the camera must pan, recompose, and choose the appropriate shot size, which may include one, two, or three persons. How you group participants will affect how natural they feel and look. Shoot *plenty* of safety cutaways on each person listening to each of the others. A director will often let the conversation run past completion while covertly signaling the operator to shoot vital cutaway closeups. Find a mike position out of frame that will cover all three speakers equally, or use a fishpole that can pan the mike just above or below the frame (watch out for telltale mike shadows). Shoot eight minutes for four minutes screen length. Suggested subject: The rewards and difficulties of artistic collaboration. Edit using Project 12 guidelines:

Composition proportions appropriate from angle to angle
Zooming and recomposing happen simultaneously and smoothly
Cuts maintain rhythm of speaker's speech patterns
Cutaways used successfully to eliminate some camera transitions
Director's voice successfully eliminated
Conversation successfully (re)structured to develop meaningfully
Tends to use wide shot for new subject matter
Tends to cover moments of intensity in BCU
Participants are at ease
Conversation has impact and intensity throughout
Good sound and no mike visible

HANDHELD TRACKING ON STATIC SUBJECT

Using the wide-angle end of your zoom, make a slow walking track at 45° to a brick wall at three feet distance. The bricks should slide past neither bobbing up and down nor swaying nearer to and further from camera. To track smoothly, make the camera into a solid part of your head and shoulders, walk with legs a little bent so you can glide, and make your footsteps fall in a straight line to eliminate swaying. As you walk, draw your feet over the ground surface. This helps transfer your weight smoothly from foot to foot without a pounding motion and permits your sliding foot to encounter obstacles or irregularities in time to accommodate them.

Camera stays upright
Maintains 45° to wall
Maintains three ft distance
Camera does not bob or sway

HANDHELD TRACKING FORWARD ON MOVING SUBJECT

Walk behind a stranger in the street, staying about eight feet distant and at 45° to the person's axis. Keep your subject steady and appropriately composed in the frame. Feature the background meaningfully. Have something pleasant to say in explanation if your subject becomes aware of you!

Camera "in sync" with subject
Stays at appropriate closeness
Subject steady in frame
Composition adapts to subject changes
Background meaningful and interesting

HANDHELD TRACKING BACKWARD WITH MOVING SUBJECT

Arrange for a subject to walk facing you. The camera operator walks backward, guided through a light touch by an assistant for safety's sake. Frame the subject in a wide shot, and hold that shot for about 15 seconds, then by letting the subject gain on you, hold the same amount of medium shot, and do the same again to produce a big closeup. Now try the same thing, shooting at an angle of about 30° to her axis. Experiment with the framing, angle to axis, and background to find the most acceptable shot. Remember to include lead space (more space ahead of a moving subject than there is behind it) in the composition. You may need to give your subject mental work so she can forget the camera. In editing, cut together WS and MCU, being careful to preserve the walker's footstep rhythm. Notice what combination of subject size, angle, and background seem to produce the smoothest shot.

Person relaxed and unselfconscious
Camera glides as if on wheels
WS well framed
MS well framed
BCU well composed
B/Gs used effectively
The two cuts look natural

HANDHELD COVERAGE OF COMPLEX ACTION

This will require a lot of practice, and at times you will need to keep your nonviewfinder eye open to see where you are going. Using both eyes for different purposes is a chameleon skill that one acquires. Start inside building, your subject walking toward you. Pan round to follow her through a door into the open air. Overtake the subject so we see subject's face as she walks toward a car. Then let subject overtake you so you are again following as the subject moves toward the driver's side of a four-door car. Keeping the driver framed, open the rear passenger-side door with your free hand, and slide into the car as the driver gets in. By shooting over the car roof and sinking the camera as you both get in, you can completely avoid showing your own door opening and closing. Hold on the driver as the car starts, then pan forward to show the road ahead. Hold for 15 seconds. If you cannot use an onboard video camera mike, shoot silent. Edit using Project 13 guidelines:

> *Good framing throughout shot*
> *Solves getting out of house door*
> *Shows person's face as she walks*
> *Solves getting into car*
> *On driver as car gathers speed*
> *Pans to straight ahead*
> *Camera steady throughout*
> *Camera moves in sync with events*
> *Compositions appropriate*
> *Sound is OK (no expletives, bumps, crashes etc.)*

"DAY-IN-THE-LIFE" MONTAGE THAT CREATES MOOD

Using camerawork, lighting, and sound indigenous to your location (but no superimposed music), make a four-minute film that compresses into shorthand form the feel and mood of a location over a time span. Subjects might include a bird feeder, a train or bus station, a family or restaurant kitchen, a street market, or a construction site. Any locale with a cyclical life is potentially a good subject. Spend some time just listening; you will be amazed how many sounds there are to choose from. For editing tips see Project 14:

> *Develops strong mood*
> *Camera observation shows interestingly typical events*
> *Camera also shows the unexpected*
> *Lighting is interesting*
> *Sound track is varied and interesting in its own right*

Sound track is layered

Sequence builds from beginning to climax then winds down

Film develops the location's indigenous character or characters

Has strong sense of visual rhythm

Has strong sense of aural rhythm

Has sense of humor or other authorial trait

There are more assignments in Part VII "Projects: Developing Skills as a Director" and Part IX "Projects: Developing Skills as an Editor."

P·A·R·T V·I

PRODUCTION

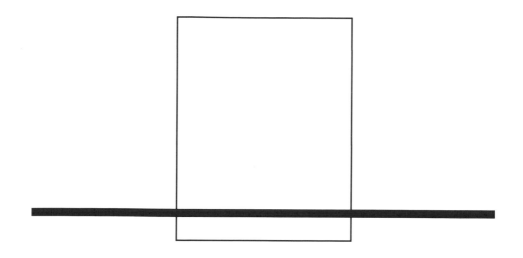

C·H·A·P·T·E·R 8

INTERVIEWING

WHY INTERVIEWING MATTERS

Interviewing is at the heart of documentary filmmaking—even though you may not be making a "talking head" film. Here I mean not only eliciting factual information but also getting at deeper truths. For to interview is to face another human being; it is to probe, to listen, to respond through further questioning, and to assist in the expression of a life. Considered as an extended, trusting exchange, the research interview is plainly the foundation for most documentaries. And later when the resulting film itself tells someone's story well, when it builds through exposition and specific emotional detail to a satisfying climax so that we have the sensation of seeing into a human soul, it is almost certainly because a skilled and empathic interviewer (that is, director) drew out what we see. Subtly or otherwise, the interviewer *directed* the participant, provided him with either the necessary guidance or the necessary resistance to help make a soul visible.

This is where we touch the duality of documentary. Interviewing, like the documentary relationship itself, can create a liberating arena for discovery and growth, or it can become an exploitative intrusion. This is also true for all human relationships. A friendship, for example, can be kept safely limited, or it can by mutual agreement be steered into areas of risk. The more there is at risk, the greater is the potential for growth—and for damage. No gain without pain, they say.

In documentary filmmaking, the relationship is seldom as equal as it is between friends. The director comes in with many advantages hoping to be given access to another person's life—indeed, he has no film without such access. So there is an obligation to be sensitive yet also assertive. Often the documentarian aspires to set up a partnership like the "poet as witness" that Seamus Heaney describes in his discussion of World War I poets. To Heaney, Wilfrid Owen and others represent "poetry's solidarity with the doomed, the deprived, the victimized, the underprivileged."[1] But Heaney might equally be speaking of the committed documentarian when he continues, "The witness is any figure in whom the truth-telling urge and the compulsion to identify with the oppressed becomes necessarily integral with the act of writing itself."[2]

Interviewing is a form of displaced authorship and a means of guiding others into eloquence, particularly those unused to speaking about their innermost lives. Because a good, edited interview should have all the ingredients of a successful oral tale, one can learn much about one's directorial skills from doing one. Even when all the questions have been removed, the interviewer's power as a catalyst, selector, and organizer remains written all over the screen. By critically examining one's performance, a true measure of one's strengths and weaknesses as a director is always available. Invariably one discovers blinds spots and artificiality in one's behavior as one gropes for a style of interviewing that is truly one's own.

WHO INTERVIEWS

Some documentary units include a researcher whose job is not only to dig up facts but also to locate and even choose the participants. Inevitably she makes an important contribution to the identity of the film. Some directors rely quite heavily on the experience and intuition of their researchers. Such a situation of shared control usually arises out of a long working relationship that has established trust in the researcher's judgment.

During the researcher's initial visits, he should refrain from pressing interesting questions to a conclusion so that important and unexplored areas will only be opened up when the camera is present. But when shooting is to begin, the question arises as to who is better equipped to conduct the interviewing; the researcher or the director? Of the two, each has possible advantages. If the researcher does the interviewing, she is continuing the relationship begun during the research period. This continuity might be crucial in putting a hesitant participant at ease. If instead the director conducts the questioning, the interview may be more spontaneous since the subject is addressing a fresh listener instead of repeating herself to the researcher.

In fact, a researcher/director team often decides who does the interviewing on an ad hoc basis according to which combination is likely to be most productive. Sometimes more bizarre arrangements are necessary to put a subject at ease. I made a film with Dr. Spock (*Dr. Spock: "We're Sliding Towards Destruction,"* "One Pair of Eyes" series, BBC) and found that though I had done all the research, the to-camera interview I was conducting with him was stiff and unnat-

---

1. Seamus Heaney, *The Government of the Tongue* (London: Faber, 1988), p. xvi.
2. Ibid.

ural compared to his usual manner. We stopped the camera and talked about it. He admitted that he was used to talking to women and would feel more comfortable explaining himself to a woman. I placed Rosalie Worthington, our production assistant, in my position under the camera lens. Though I was asking the questions, Dr. Spock addressed himself to Rosalie and his manner became more relaxed and spontaneous.

TYPES OF SITUATIONS

Interview situations can be set up almost anywhere, but it is important when planning to think of their likely effect on the interviewee. There are settings in which the interviewee is more at ease such as at home, in the workplace, or at a friend's. Here you are likely to get the more intimate and individual response because the interviewee feels expansive. There are public places like the streets, parks, or the beach where the interviewee, again affected by the environment, is likely to have more of a sense of being one of many. Then there are unusual settings such as a battlefield or the scene of an accident or of a demonstration, in which the speaker feels in a dramatic juxtaposition with events outside his control.

In all these situations where people speak their thoughts spontaneously on camera, each set of surroundings evokes a different "self" in the interviewee and makes him resonate a little differently. What is subsequently emphasized or revealed is not entirely unpredictable, but by using common sense and imagination and by taking into account the significance the person probably attaches to being filmed, the interviewer can guess the contribution different settings are likely to make and choose accordingly.

We are all—interviewers included—very much affected by our surroundings and tend to lower barriers (or erect them) according to our sense of circumstance. Filming may dignify a situation or render it embarrassingly public; it may offer a hot line to the world's ear, be the confessional box, or be just good conversation with a friend. Which situation an interviewee feels himself in depends on both environment and the way the filmmaker presents his purpose. It is vital, however, that you be empathetically sensitive to how your subject is feeling if you are to make a real connection. Remember, *a documentary film is largely the sum of a set of relationships:* The unseen relationships are at least as influential as those visible on screen.

Another practical factor in shooting interviews is the effect someone off-camera may have on an interviewee. If you are interviewing a gentle old woman whose peppery husband is always correcting her, it is wise to have the husband otherwise occupied and out of the room while she tells you her story. On the other hand, the relationship between two people may be an important and visible aspect of who they are and what they represent. I once shot an interview of a farm manager and his wife with the two of them together (*A Remnant of a Feudal Society,* "Yesterday's Witness" series, BBC). She continued to interrupt and modify everything he said, and this, apart from being funny, drew attention to the modified, idealized nature of her account.

Interviewing is not therefore only one-to-one. A married couple may separately be inarticulate through shyness yet prod each other into talking very well. Friends or workmates can likewise provide a sense of mutual support. But inhibitions may just as easily be released through mutual antipathy so interviewing two people who disagree can be a most productive strategy. One may even interview a whole group, and here you have two options: One is to "recognize" each new speaker from among those who want to speak, and the other is to encourage them to begin speaking to each other. Really interviewing is just a way of eliciting spoken thoughts and feelings, so if this can better take place between participants, you should not hesitate to abandon your interviewer's role.

Usually when you start talking to a few people in a public place—say at a factory gate—others gather to listen and will spontaneously join in. Unless the interviewer asserts himself, it will turn into a spirited conversation or dispute among those present—depending of course on how controversial the topic was in the first place. The interviewer is now on the sidelines but may step in at any time with a question or even a request, such as, "Could the lady in the red jacket talk a bit about the union's attitude toward safety precautions?" And talk she will.

There is one very useful technique often used with street interviews. Called vox pop (short for *vox populi,* meaning "voice of the people"), it consists of asking a number of people the same few questions, and then stringing the replies together in a rapid sequence. It is very useful for demonstrating a diversity of opinion in a range of people. Conversely the technique can be used to show homogeneity of opinion.

Sections of vox pop are favored as lively relief from something rather sober and intense, such as an expository section explaining a complicated political development. They can also function as a legitimate parallel action to which you can resort in times of need. In the film about Dr. Spock mentioned above, I had to compress the salient points of his 3-hour peace speeches into about 12 minutes. I did it by setting up a dialectical counterpoint between Dr. Spock at the podium and the ubiquitous man in the street. Each gave piquancy to the other so a virtue came out of necessity.

PREPARATION AND BASIC SKILLS

Whoever does the interviewing, the same basic skills are needed. First and foremost, the interviewer needs to be prepared. This confirms how vital it is to define a focus for the entire film in advance of any shooting. With that minimum outcome and fundamental *purpose* behind the directing of the film defined, you should have a clear expectation of what each interviewee will contribute. I am not suggesting you prepare any kind of script or even anticipate specific statements. Anything so confined would thrust a participant into an acting role, which, however authentic the message, would have a rehearsed flavor. Such a departure from spontaneity would be sensed by the audience as a manipulation distorting the simplicity of truth. Some documentary makers intrude unnecessarily on their interviewees; perhaps it is out of anxiety to be in control. At any rate, the participant feels a heightened sense of requirement and tries to fulfill it.

The results are a pervasive staginess and self-consciousness that devalue the whole film.

During the interview, you should maintain eye contact with your subject, and give visual (NOT verbal!) feedback while the interview goes on. Nodding, smiling, looking puzzled, and signifying agreement or doubt are all forms of feedback that can be relayed through your expression. They sustain the interviewee in what might otherwise feel like a situation of egocentric monologue.

SETTING PEOPLE AT EASE

Research, I have argued, is to reveal more or less what a person has to contribute after which the interviewer's task is to respectfully and sympathetically set the interviewee talking.

To put the interviewee at ease and yet prevent the interview from digressing unprofitably, it is a good practice to describe in generalities the subject areas you are interested in and thus by implication to alert the participant to areas that do not interest you. You also need to prepare the interviewee for your occasional interruption or redirection so I usually say something like, "This is a documentary and we always shoot a lot more than we use. So if you get mixed up or say something wrong, don't worry because we can always edit it out. Also, if I feel we're getting away from the subject, I may rudely interrupt if that's all right with you."

No one has ever objected; indeed, people seem reassured that I take responsibility for the overall direction of our conversation. This approach unfailingly reduces the pressure people feel. I augment this further by making my first question slow and relaxed. This way I demonstrate that my shooting expectations are nothing like the manic brightness people usually see in television interviews. By my manner I am signaling that I expect no change of self-presentation just because a camera is rolling.

To obtain spontaneity, you must first be natural yourself about asking questions. It is you who sets the tone for the interview; if you are formal or uptight, your interviewee will be more so. Because I believe it is important not to bury one's face in a page of notes, I prepare a list of questions short enough to go on an index card. These I keep on my knee. Having them there is a "security blanket" that releases me simply to have a conversation. I'm free to really *listen*, knowing I can always glance down if my mind goes blank. Most of the time the act of preparing the questions ensures that you naturally and informally cover all your intended ground. Before concluding the interview you should of course double check that you really did cover everything you intended. I often end with, "Is there anything you want to say, anything we forgot to cover?" This gives final control to the participant.

FRAMING QUESTIONS

Before an interview, carefully formulate your questions so they are direct and specific. Speak each question out loud and by listening to your own voice, deliberately try to interpret the question "wrongly." Sometimes you find your question has another interpretation, and you will want to alter it so only the intended understanding is possible.

Focused questions are vital if you want to direct rather than follow your interviewee. Inexperienced interviewers often use general questions like "What is the most exciting experience you've ever had?" This signals that the interviewer is devoid of preparation or focus and is casting a big, shapeless net. Another common pitfall is the long, rambling question with so many qualifiers that it ends up as a shapeless catalogue of concerns. The confused interviewee only answers what he remembers, usually the last thing said.

Know what you want, use simple, conversational English, and deal with one issue at a time. A question like, "You have some strong feelings about the fears suffered by latchkey kids?" will work well because it points the interviewee at a vital experience already mentioned during research and signals your interest in how he *feels*.

There is nothing wrong with signifying your interest in an exact area. In fact there is everything right in this practice since it gives clear and encouraging guidance. It should not, on the other hand, be confused with the leading question, which seeks to manipulate the interviewee into a particular response rather than to indicate a particular *area* of interest.

A sample list of questions appears in Appendix A.

GUIDELINES FOR EFFECTIVE INTERVIEWING

There are a number of straightforward techniques that will help you to maintain focus and intensity. One should plan an interview so that questions produce responses covering specific areas. One should maintain eye contact at all costs. One should give direction to the interview and not give undue control to the interviewee who probably does not want it anyway.

One method of steering an interview is to summarize briefly what you have so far understood and ask the participant to continue. This reassures the interviewee of her progress to date and gives clear permission to go on. A polite way to redirect someone is to say, "Can we return to . . ." and name the topic for which you would like amplification. Yet another way is to repeat particular words the interviewee has used in a questioning tone as encouragement to further explore them.

The interviewer needs to listen for leads, that is, for hints of further material—especially where strong feelings may be involved—that need following up. You might say, "I thought you probably have strong feelings about . . ." and you give a name to what you detected. Most people are grateful for your discernment and encouragement. If your interviewee goes silent, respect the silence and wait for him to go on. If he needs encouragement, try repeating his last words in a questioning tone. Stay with an important subject until you feel it is exhausted. Never settle for generalities; always ask for an example or a story to illustrate the point. If you do not know what the interviewee meant, press for clarification. Remember that your audience has no prior knowledge so you must get a comprehensive description. A large part of your job is to *listen as if hearing it for the first time* so you can elicit whatever response a first-time audience would need.

Interviewing should be exploration that leads to understanding. One should keep exploring until one reaches complete understanding oneself—factual and emotional understanding.

Do not be afraid of interviewing people in crisis. For them, the truly satisfying exchange leads to a sense of release which, if it is at all strong, is something that you and your audience will feel too.

Excellent examples of formal interviewing can be seen in Connie Field's *The Life and Times of Rosie the Riveter* (1980) and Erroll Morris' *The Thin Blue Line* (1988). Very informal interviewing can be found in Ira Wohl's *Best Boy* (1979) where it produces what looks like spontaneous conversation. Here Philly's family members, principally his mother, pour out their hearts.

When a person speaks from the heart, particularly for the first time, it can be magical. Here, speech *is* the action. Conversely when an interviewee speaks routinely and without a sense of discovery, the result on the screen can sever our connection with the film. Talking head films must be intense and tell a good story, or they can become hypnotically boring.

We will look at these fundamentals in greater detail.

PREPARATIONS TO EDIT OUT THE INTERVIEWER'S VOICE

If you have placed the interviewer offscreen and intend to edit out her questions, you will need to prepare interviewees by telling them that information in each question needs to be included in the answer. Many people will look puzzled so you will have to give an example: "Say I ask, 'When did you first arrive in America?,' you might answer '1959,' but the answer '1959' wouldn't stand on its own, so I'd be forced to include my question. However, if you said, 'I arrived in the United States in 1959,' that's a whole and complete statement."

In spite of an explanation like this, many people repeatedly forget to make a whole statement out of their answers, so you will have to listen carefully to the beginning of each answer. Sometimes one feeds an interviewee the appropriate opening words to clarify by example what one needs, such as, "Try beginning, 'I arrived in America. . . .' "

Another interviewer's hazard is the monosyllabic answer.

Q: "I understand you weren't entirely satisfied when you moved into this apartment?"
A: "Yep."

This of course is the interviewer's nightmare—someone who can't or won't talk. Try pressing for specifics: "Would you tell me what you remember?" If the person doesn't respond to this kind of verbal prodding, it is probably wise to abandon your attempt. He may be stonewalling or may simply not be a talker.

THE IN-DEPTH INTERVIEW

There is a good general rule for interviewing: Start with factual questions and keep the more intimate or emotionally loaded material for later when the interviewee has become more comfortable with the situation. If there is a delicate area you want to open up, there are a couple of ways it can be done. One is to use the devil's advocate approach; for instance, "Some people would say there's nothing special or frightening for a kid in getting home a couple of hours before his mother." The interviewee is being invited to discharge his feelings against all those too lacking in imagination or curiosity to have discovered what a latchkey kid's experience is really like.

Another way to initiate a sensitive topic is to first invite generalized, impersonal comment. For instance, you are almost certain that the woman you are interviewing has a suppressed anger because she ended up nursing a chronically ill mother instead of getting married. You may want to ask, "Didn't your love for your mother turn to resentment over the years, after you saw your fiancé marry someone else?" But instinct warns you that this is too brutally direct. Instead start more generally and at a safe distance: "Our society seems to expect daughters more than sons to make sacrifices for their parents, doesn't it?" She has the choice of stopping at an impersonal opinion as an observer of life or of getting closer and closer to describing the injustice that has spoiled her life.

To encourage this, when she ventures her opinions, simply ask for an example. By mutual and unspoken agreement, you steer toward the poignant testimony both you and she want to put on record. You frame her situation as one of the world's sad injustices that overcome people who are not warned, rather than inviting her to display her sense of personal victimization. The distinction is an important one since many people who are too proud or too realistic to complain will break self-imposed restraints if they feel they can save someone else from the same experience.

The secret to good interviewing is really to *listen* and always to press for specifics and examples. Simple rejoinders like "How?," "Why was that?," and "What did that make you feel?" are the keys that release the sentient human being from an apparently detached observer. Sometimes it helps to ask the interviewee to take his time and only speak when he can see things in his mind's eye. Often this elicits a new and better kind of telling.

People often recount the same events in more than one way. When you first pose an unexpected question, your interviewee will search and struggle to explain. This can have a very attractive quality of spontaneity. However, if this kind of battle is directed toward, say, getting a few facts in order, it can be very frustrating to watch. Sensing this, an interviewee will often of his own accord repeat the explanation in a much more orderly and rapid form. If this does not happen, and you have any doubts about the utility of the version just recorded, you should ask, "Maybe you'd just like to go over that last explanation again as there were one or two stumbles." People are usually grateful for such assistance and the result is that you equip yourself with useful alternative versions. In editing later, you may even be able to combine the best of both.

PUSHING BOUNDARIES

Most interviews deal first with what is familiar and comfortable and only then steer the interviewee toward places to which she has never been before. A memorable interview encourages the interviewee to step over some emotionally significant threshold—either large or small. For the audience to see a person in change is part of the emotional shock I mentioned earlier—something we all seek in dramatic art. It might be leading a woman to examine the contradictions in her account of her mother and seeing her realize that she despises someone she believed she loved. Or it might be a man admitting to himself that he was unequal to a job in which he suffered a humiliating demotion. In both examples, the interviewee *is living out something important for the very first time*. The suspense as this major "beat" takes place is electrifying.

There are other strange moments in interviewing when one senses there is more to tell, but the person is unsure whether to risk telling it. A gentle "And?" or simply "Yes, go on" signals that you know there is more and that you support him in continuing. After this, do not be afraid to remain silent. *The expectant silence is the interviewer's most powerful encouragement to go deeper.* When it is used appropriately, it provides a memorable and telling moment on the screen when the interviewee is visibly grappling with a vital issue. The inexperienced or insensitive interviewer often fails to realize that a silence is full of "action" for the viewer, and construing it as a failure to "keep the interview going," comes crashing in upon every reply with a new question, oblivious to all the missed opportunities left dangling. The real cause of the problem is *not listening properly*. If you use the "security blanket" trick of keeping written questions on hand, you will be released to really listen to your subject and maintain eye contact. Remember that the material will be edited and that you are really not taking chances with silence and waiting.

THE RIGHT ORDER FOR QUESTIONS

Do not worry about the order of questions in relation to your intended film. Later you can reorganize the replies any way you want. The only logical order for an interview is the order that makes sense to the interviewee. Facts are safe while opinions or feelings require more trust and a more relaxed state of mind. Thus you keep the most demanding material for the end when your subject has become used to the situation and is even enjoying it.

In my documentary with Alexandra Tolstoy, the most controversial of Leo Tolstoy's many children, I knew from my reading beforehand that she was his twelfth child and that in childhood she had found out she was unwanted. I began to see that this grievous knowledge had affected not only her youth but also her adult life. Nervous of offending or hurting her, I delayed this my most vital questioning to the end (see Appendix A for the actual questions I asked, noting how each is specific), hoping I would be able to touch on it. Her reply patently came from the heart. But in the film I used this section fairly early since here she acknowledges contradictory feelings about her parents that illuminate everything else she says about herself. In my naiveté, I hardly supposed that an old lady of 86 could still feel the pains of childhood so deeply, but what really emerges in the end leads to a deeper understanding of her strengths.

Many of the really impressive passages in interviews come about because of a moment of truth when the interviewer unexpectedly leads the subject into confronting a painful or unacknowledged aspect of the subject's life. At such moments, it is like watching a mountaineer climb a challenging rock face. We witness not only the danger of the climb but also watch with solicitude and admiration the climber's commitment.

BELIEVING IN ONE'S AUTHORITY

It takes observation and empathy on the part of the interviewer rather than any mystic powers to spot these areas of unfinished business in another person's life. Indeed it is far easier to see the shape and thrust of another's actions than it is to see those of one's own. Anyone who has ever read a mystery novel knows how to gather and collate the clues about patterns, personality and motives. Many novice directors are too hesitant about their own role, however, to act on their ideas and intuitions for fear of rebuff. Remember that the mere intention of making a record—as a writer or as a filmmaker—empowers one to be assertive and demanding. Most people unquestioningly accept your role as a seeker after truth and will collaborate to a degree that is surprising and on occasion very moving.

If you, the fledgling director, doubt your importance and your authority to do what you are doing, remember that the person in the street probably doubts his importance and authority even more. To ask him to become part of your record, even on your terms, is not only flattering but also confirms that his existence is significant.

All this indicates that the filmmaker is not only allowed but even expected to make incursions into people's lives, all in the name of recordmaking. Beginners find this hard to believe and even harder to act on. At first one asks favors with an almost grotesque sense of apology and obligation. It is always a pleasant surprise to find how often you are welcomed and assisted open-heartedly. While you should treat people's openness with great responsibility, you should also resist having your editorial decisions forged out of a multiplicity of obligations. Sometimes this is very hard.

INTERVIEWER AND CAMERA PLACEMENT

There are two approaches to camera placement when you are filming interviews, each reflecting a quite different philosophy of the interviewer's function. You can distinguish which approach is being used by looking at the interview on screen. One approach (Figure 8–1) has the interviewee answering an interviewer who sits with his head just below the camera lens. This makes the interviewee appear to be looking directly into the camera. In the other approach (Figure 8–

FIGURE 8–1

Placement of interviewer affects subject's eye-line: With the interviewer's head immediately under the camera lens, the subject talks directly to the viewer.

2), the interviewer sits to one side of the camera and out of frame, which makes the interviewee look off-camera at an unseen interlocutor.

These two approaches have a subconscious effect on the audience. My preference is to edit out the interviewer altogether, leaving the audience in a face-to-face relationship with my interviewee. This means I organize my shooting so my subject speaks into the camera (as in Figure 8–1). I see my interviewing as a means of asking questions the audience would like to have answered. Thus I interview on behalf of the audience and function as a catalyst. Once the interviewee is talking, my presence as the listening party is irrelevant to the audience and even a distraction.

In order to clear away traces of my input from the process, I sit on something low with my head just under the camera lens. Although the interviewee is talking to me, it looks as if he is talking directly to the camera (that is, the audience). When my voice is edited out, the audience is left in direct relationship to the person on the screen.

As soon as you sit to either side of the camera (as in Figure 8–2), your interviewee appears to be talking to an off-screen presence, whether the interviewer's voice survives into the finished film or not. The farther away from the camera/subject axis the interviewer is, the more acute is the impression. Some filmmakers like this on the grounds that it acknowledges there is an interviewer even when his voice is no longer present. When one questions the logic of this, the answer usually is that it is more honest to acknowledge the filmmaking process. My private thought is that some people who make films really want to be in them. Television journalists have no such ambiguity; when they interview,

FIGURE 8–2

With the interviewer to the side of the camera, the subject is evidently talking to someone offscreen.

they expect to be in picture. Appearing on screen is their career. If you use off-axis interviewing, be careful to vary the side from which you interview, or all of your interviewees will monotonously face the same way.

A further possibility, then, is to have the interviewer oncamera. Unless the interviewer is an active participant, it seems redundant to see the occasional question being asked and to cut away to a nodding listener once in a while. British editors refer maliciously to these reaction shots as "noddies." Reaction shots or "cutaways" are regularly used in news shows, but one must remember that "reporters" are really the networks' attempt at building audience identification with familiar figures in order to create loyalty to a particular channel. Of course, there is an element of fiction in all this since news gathering and news editing are carried out by an unseen team that deploys reporters and newsreaders as the actor/performers they really are.

The most valid situation for the questioner to appear on camera is one in which there is a confrontation of some sort. Here the questioner's reactions become a highly relevant component of the exchange. One has only to recall the Watergate hearings to become convinced that some situations demand both questions and answers if their full significance is to emerge.

My own conclusion is that the more indirect the spectator's relationship is with the characters on the screen the more passive and detached he feels. Looking at it from the spectator's point of view, someone who speaks directly to you stimulates you to formulate your own ideas more than does a person plainly talking to someone else. Since watching a film is an inherently passive occupation anyway, I think filmmakers should mobilize the viewer's sense of involvement as much as possible if the viewer is to watch in an emotionally active and critical frame of mind.

One problem that arises in any filmed interview is how to shoot it so it can be abbreviated in editing. Shooting the whole interview in a one-size shot and then bridging the different sections together leads to the jump cut (Figure 8–3). In practical terms, this means that our subject's face suddenly changes expres-

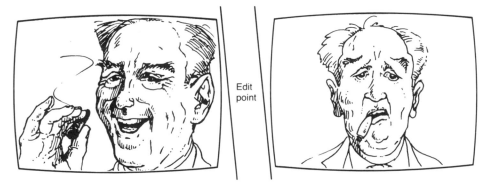

FIGURE 8–3

A jump cut: When footage is removed from a static camera angle, the image may jump at the cut.

sion, and his head is suddenly in a slightly different position. This almost certainly draws unwelcome attention to one's technique. You can cut away to a "noddie" of the interviewer, but they usually make the poor interviewer look inane.

There may be something else more relevant to which you can cut away. For instance, if the interviewee is talking about the Dust Bowl, you might cut away to some of the classic photos showing the arid farms and hungry faces of the period. You could indeed show a sequence of photos that develop independently and tell their own story in parallel. To do this, you would probably restructure the interview somewhat and resort to the speaker's face at moments of special animation.

This technique, in which two ongoing stories are intercut, is called parallel cutting, and it is immensely useful because it allows the restructuring and telescoping in time of not just one but of both story elements.

Documentarians therefore *always try to cover each issue in several ways* to allow for this. A political demonstration, for instance, would primarily be covered by footage showing the march beginning, close shots of faces and banners, the police lines, the arrests, and so on. But it should also be covered through interviewing participants and perhaps the police chief. There would thus be a multiplicity of attitudes available on the purpose of the march and a number of faces to intercut (and thus abbreviate) the stages of the march footage. Two vital purposes are thus served: Multiple and conflicting viewpoints can be evoked, and the materials can be focused into a brief screen time. Erroll Morris in *The Thin Blue Line* (1988) shoots his interviews in one unvarying shot size, but constantly cuts away to reconstructions that evoke the time, mood, or "facts" being recalled by the speaker. The result is usually to heighten the subjective quality of the account, drawing one into the speaker's world of memory and perception.

This leaves one situation still unsolved. Suppose you want to shoot an interview for which there is no valid cutaway and still achieve abbreviation and restructuring without resorting to the pernicious jumpcut. How can it be done?

If during the interview the camera operator uses the zoom lens to unobtrusively change the image size, the conventions of the screen allow you to subsequently edit segments together, provided (a) there is a bold change of image size, either larger or smaller, and (b) the apparent flow of the subject matter remains uninterrupted by the cut. Because of the bold change of image size between the two frames in Figure 8–4, minor mismatches will go unnoticed by the audience, especially because *the eye does not register the first three frames of a new image.*

When I am interviewing, I ensure changes of image size during the interview by agreeing with my operator on three standard image sizes for the particular shot we are doing. While I am interviewing, I signal changes, using taps on different parts of her foot.

Typically this will be: a wide shot, used to cover each question; a medium shot, used after answer has got under way; and a close shot, used for anything particularly intense or revealing.

I alternate between medium and close range until there is a change of topic when I again signal for a wide shot. One place to change image size is when a speaker shows signs of repeating herself. The repeat version is usually more

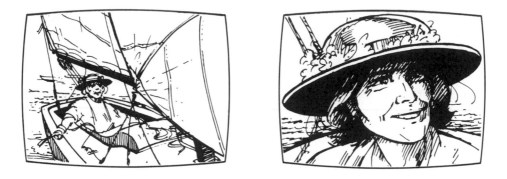

FIGURE 8–4 ──

A match cut: By a bold change in image size, two shots can be edited together if the images match.

succinct and may with advantage be intercut with the first version for brevity where it is desirable.

This size-changing technique accomplishes three important ends. It allows the interview to be watched for longer stretches on screen because the camera movement at salient points, intensifying and relaxing its scrutiny, answers the unconscious need of the spectator for variation. It facilitates repositioning the parts of an interview into a linear structure, and it allows for selective abbreviation. One vital consequence of abbreviation is that it allows one to eliminate the interviewer's questions.

Additional notes on camera placement appear in the next chapter, "Directing Participants."

CONCLUDING THE INTERVIEW

At the end of an interview, always ask participant if there is anything she wishes to add. Then cut the camera and thank the interviewee, making a point of acknowledging whatever was successful about the exchange. Keep everyone in place so the recordist can shoot a minute of quiet atmosphere (also called *buzz track, presence,* or *room-tone*). Later the editor will use this to fill out spaces in the track, for without the correct "presence," the background atmosphere to the recording would either change or go dead, either way drawing attention to itself. When everyone rises to start dismantling equipment, give each participant a sum of money (often the minimum $1) and the *personal release form,* so you have signed permission to use the material publicly.

Very occasionally it happens that one wants to conclude an interview because the interviewee is—for whatever reason—hopelessly unsatisfactory. Every film director has at some time run without film in the camera in order to escape the situation without hurting the participant's feelings. With videotape, one can always subsequently record over unusable material. Sometimes to satisfy people in the street who want the unit to "take a picture of my store," the crew will, upon a prearranged signal, solemnly go through the actions of taking a shot without actually turning the recorder on. It is a small price to make a complete stranger happy.

C·H·A·P·T·E·R 9

DIRECTING PARTICIPANTS

IN SEARCH OF NATURALNESS

A common question people ask of documentarians is, "How do you get people to look so natural?" Of course, one is tempted to shake one's head sagely and say something about many years of apprenticeship learning professional secrets. Actually naturalness is much easier to achieve than is a satisfactory dramatic structure.

Interviewing is one way of giving direction in a documentary, but if it is overused, it leads to a "talking head" film. With an oral history film where there is nothing but survivors left to photograph, this may be the only film possible. Most directors, however, are at pains to show people active in their own settings, doing what they normally do. In part, this is to spare the audience from the hypnotic intensity of being spoken to for long periods, but it is important to remember that we judge a person's character and motivations from what she does and how she does it, more than from anything she might say. Words, after all, can be adapted to the situation so we place inherently greater trust in how a person behaves.

In practice then, one might deliberately film a person at home dealing with some banalities of family life, at work instructing an employee, and in the neighborhood bar playing pool with cronies. Each "typical" situation must, if it is to earn its place in the movie, make behavioral revelations about the subject and her milieu. This all sounds easier than it really is since an important condition of normality for anyone is that she not feel unduly watched. If our subject feels she is under critical scrutiny, her whole sense of feeling normal may become uncentered. I once filmed in a glass door factory, and one of the workers, who had spent years passing frames through the same machine, completely lost the facility as soon as we turned the camera on. Self-consciousness caused the poor worker to begin thinking about her actions instead of just doing them, and to her consternation the frames began to jam or miss the jet of rubber solution.

THE MIND-BODY CONNECTION

The Russian dramatic theorist Konstantin Stanislavski understood very well the connection for an actor between the mind and the body. He argued that there is no inner state without an outward manifestation and that, if an actor becomes self-conscious instead of maintaining "focus" (experiencing the thoughts and emotions of her character), she visibly loses conviction in everything she says and does. Far from being peculiar to acting, this principle actually underlies everyone's sense of normality. In everyday life, we carry on our actions and relationships from a wellspring of assumptions about who we are and how we appear to the world. These assumptions are seldom queried except under exceptional circumstances when, suddenly made self-aware, we cease to function harmoniously and normally.

The implications are major to the documentary maker whose aim is to capture and interpret real life. Attacks of introspection on the part of one's subject can suddenly introduce unforeseen problems. The factory-worker at first felt confusion, and lost automatic harmony with her machine. There was not a lot I could do except reassure her that this quite often happens. We simply waited until, after profuse apologies, she managed for a few rounds to resume something like her old, unthinking rhythm. It was a striking example of the mind's activity impeding the body's habitual function because she suddenly felt she must "act."

There are useful clues for dealing with this situation to be found in drama techniques. Stanislavski stressed that an actor who is to perform realistically must have her attention fully occupied with the thoughts and actions of the character she is playing. Both the director and the actor must provide the actor with plenty of "work" in the role. Any opportunity for unstructured thought will permit the ever-anxious mind to make a self-conscious assessment of the way she thinks she must appear to critical observers. This of course is disabling and leads to "loss of focus." Insecurity of all kinds, even fear of losing focus, can lead to a loss of focus. In a moment, a realistic character disintegrates into a beleaguered actor. This may not be immediately apparent to the nonspecialist, but the actor feels totally exposed unless she has learned to deal with the situation.

Likewise, unaccustomed self-awareness can stultify many a documentary participant's normal exuberance. The key to directing people who are "only playing themselves" is the same as that in drama: Make sure they have plenty to do. If you ask a mother and daughter to let you film them washing the dishes at night, they may be visibly conscious of the camera until you ask them to pick a normal topic of conversation. They start to discuss their plans for the next day and now have so much familiar physical and mental activity to keep going that they become oblivious of the camera.

If there is an atmosphere of trust and a justification for filming, people will take part with complete equanimity. If on the other hand someone feels that you are trying to make her do or be something she isn't, she will become uncomfortable and even uncooperative.

Something I found one should never say is, "Just be yourself." It seems to set people worrying: What did he really mean? How does he see me? And which me does he really want? It is much better to relate your wishes through asking the participant to do something rather than to try to be something. Ask what they usually *do*. If conversation is appropriate, ask what they usually talk about, and pick a combination that relates to your planned film. As before in interviewing, tell them not to worry about any mistakes as you expect to edit the material down a great deal. Very important is to ask them *not to look at the camera* but to simply ignore the crew's presence. This prevents them from falling into the trap of "playing to the audience." The crew can help in this by concentrating on their jobs and giving no facial or verbal feedback.

So, by using common sense and some ingenuity, you can achieve a naturalistic appearance fairly easily; you simply ask people to busy themselves with what they usually do. What this turns out to be, if you have chosen interesting people, is usually very revealing. An oppressive middle-aged couple, for example, may fall into a recurring argument about what kind of food to buy the dog tomorrow.

Another situation in which you can expect your subjects to be revealingly natural is when you film them doing something that has more significance for them than does being filmed. Start filming children playing the latest video game, and they will quickly forget about everything except the space monster. I once filmed old miners recalling the bitter days of the 1926 General Strike in England, and because I took them to the mine in question, I was able to let the camera come within a couple of feet of their faces as they talked among themselves. They seemed to lose all concern over being filmed.

Such a situation is like drama improvisation; actors will frequently have no memory of a roving camera's presence because they were too involved in the "improv" to even notice it. With the miners, the situation was similarly intense; the events were their lives' finest moment and embodied the deepest and most provocative issues in their community's history. Our camera's attention gave a special gravity and meaning, so their involvement was extremely emotional, leaving no attention to spare for what they might look like to us and to the world beyond our camera.

SELF-IMAGE AND SELF-CONSCIOUSNESS

The easiest people to work with are always those oblivious to their effect on others. When old people and small children are so wonderfully natural, it is because there is no internal censor at work. You can imagine now who is going to present difficulties. People who are compulsively careful of their appearance or who have many nervous mannerisms are unlikely to be at peace in front of a camera. During a street interview I once had a lady completely lose focus. I was puzzled as to what had happened until, in midsentence, she began to remove the hair net she had just realized she was still wearing. The more "proper" a person feels she must look for the record, the less flexible, impulsive, and communicative that person is likely to be.

But care and circumspection were this lady's stamp, so the action was also wonderfully representative. Her friends, seeing the film, would smile in recognition. What is interesting is that the camera did not make her behave uncharacteristically.

People often ask, doesn't the presence of the camera change people? The correct answer, I believe, is that it changes the degree of a person's behavior just as all observation does, but it does not change a person's nature or make her act out of character. Indeed the intensity of making a statement to a camera sometimes draws on depths unknown to the person's closest friends and relatives. When the human craving for recognition is at last satisfied, the floodgates may open disconcertingly wide.

WHY YOUR MOTIVES FOR FILMING MATTER

Ultimately, your camera can only plumb the more profound depths of people's lives if they sense that you and your crew personally accept, like, and value them. If a documentary film is really a record of relationships, the key to success is in what takes place before the camera is ever switched on. For this reason I avoid subjects for which I do not expect to feel interest and understanding. I once embarked on a film about Sir Oswald Mosley and his 1930s British Union of Fascists (*The Battle of Cable Street,* "Yesterday's Witness" series, BBC). We set about tracing people who would admit to being followers, and in the end I interviewed Mosley himself. I was apprehensive not only about the violence that surrounded those people but also about the disgust I felt for their values. A part of me, I suppose, was afraid to deal with what I considered the ultimate in evil.

It turned out that Hannah Arendt's phrase about the banality of evil fitted the situation better than any of my imaginings. The British upholders of the ideology that sent 11 million people to their extermination were shockingly ordinary; no horns or cloven feet to be seen. They made a specious kind of sense and were anxious to present their case. The stance the researcher (Jane Oliver) and I took was simply that of younger people wishing to learn history from its protagonists.

During the lengthy editing period, I found myself both repelled and keenly interested in Mosley. Somehow he merited a very special attention because he was an urbane, upper-class member of the establishment who had egocentrically distorted everything remotely connected with himself. I wanted to present faithfully his version of the 1936 events, yet show what a hollow self-delusion his version was. The film was successful in juxtaposing violently opposed opinions. Yet it contrived to satisfy the Left (who opposed the freedom Mosley was given to organize racial hatred), and it pleased Mosley himself, because he had expected to have his own account distorted.

Part of creating trust is explaining plausibly why you want to shoot a particular scene. Organizations, especially those on the political Left, are much more likely to be paranoid than are individuals. Even so, you are unlikely to be asked for further explanations, and people with nothing to hide almost always are only too happy to help. You can get a taxi driver to chat to the camera while he cruises looking for a fare because it is so natural and unexceptional an activity for him. You may discreetly film a woman in the intimacy of her morning bath because it was in this very bath she once made the momentous decision to visit Egypt. You can film a man feeding his dog and talking to it because he believes you too feel this is a special part of a special life.

OBSTACLES: HABITS OF BEING

Certain jobs attract a certain kind of person, and some jobs seem to generate mannerisms and self-awarenesses that are a liability in filmmaking unless of course it is these very characteristics you want to show. Many officials, afraid of offending superiors and unused to public statement, make the most excruciatingly boring and self-conscious contributions. On camera, lecturers and politicians are inclined to address invisible multitudes instead of talking one-to-one as they did with you during research.

One must keep in mind that unfamiliar circumstances cause people to fall back on habit, and many ingrained habits of behavior are hard or even impossible to change.

When the participant's conception of her relationship to the camera must be altered, it is wise to try to guess what is habit and what is only a misperception about filming. The latter you can probably correct. For instance, the person who seems to be addressing a large audience can sometimes be redirected by simply saying, "There is only one person, me, listening to you. Talk only to me." Another common mistake is the idea that one must project the voice. A little playback may correct this if the person cannot respond to direction. People are often shocked, however, when they first see themselves on the screen so showing an unsatisfactory "performance" should be a last resort and should be done privately and supportively.

Sometimes you will get someone whose concept of a film appearance is taken from commercials and who valiantly tries to project *Personality*. The important thing to remember is that this is still true to the individual's character and assumptions; if you are making a film about mothers who send their children to learn acting for commercials, you could hardly ask for anything more revealing. A person's response to being filmed may or may not be appropriate, but some thought beforehand can often prepare you for what's likely. Choosing participants is "casting" as much as it would be for a fiction film.

COMPROMISES FOR THE CAMERA

When you are shooting action sequences, you may need to ask people to slow down their movements down since movement in general, once it has a frame round it, looks perhaps 20 to 30 percent faster. There is also the fact that even the camera operator's fanciest footwork cannot keep a hand framed and in focus if its owner moves it around too fast. Such a compromise on behalf of technology raises the question of how much you are willing to intrude on behalf of a visually and choreographically accomplished result. Certainly the ethnographer will want to intrude as little as possible into the life she purports to be capturing, and all true documentarians have some of the ethnographer in them.

But as Godard perceived, if you start out making a documentary, you are driven toward fictional techniques, and if conversely you make fiction films, you will be compelled in the direction of documentary. Even in a well-rehearsed drama, there is always an element of improvisation and inventiveness that places the camera in the position of documenting a "happening."

If you are shooting outdoors, especially in a public place or where there are crowds, do not be afraid to penetrate areas where you normally would not go. The camera is your license to record and will allow you to cross police lines, go to the front of a crowd, or push between two people looking in a shop window. In western countries, the camera's right to do this is accepted as part of the freedom of the press. Of course, this is a cultural assumption not made every-where. A colleague of mine went to film in Nigeria and learned (through being stoned) that taking a person's image without asking is regarded there as theft.

MAINTAINING SCREEN DIRECTION

Camera placement is one of the few areas where a little ignorance can produce catastrophic results. A little knowledge of theory on the part of director and camera operator can avoid all this. Because film presents the pieces of an artfully fragmented world, an audience member is constantly assembling an image of the whole in her mind for each succeeding location. Four partial angles of individuals in a room conjure up an idea of the entire room and the positions of its occu-pants. If the director is to avoid confusing the audience, she must obey certain rules to maintain a sense of geographical consistency.

Let us imagine you are shooting a parade (as in Part VII, Project 10, "Cov-ering an Event or Process"). You must decide ahead of time (based on back-ground or lighting factors) from which side of the parade you intend to shoot. By shooting from only one side, everyone will march across the screen in the same direction, say screen left to screen right. If halfway through you hop through the parade and start filming from the opposite side, however, on the screen your parade will suddenly start marching in the reverse direction, screen right to screen left. Intercutting this material will create complete confusion for the viewer. Is this a counterdemonstration marching from another direction to clash? Is this another wing, marching away toward another destination?

We are dealing with the idea of *staying one side of an axis or invisible line.* You can draw an axis between two people having a conversation as illustrated in Figure 9–1. As long as your camera stays to *one side of that line*, the character in black will always look left to right, and the character in white will always be looking right to left across the screen. Three different camera angles are shown in Figure 9–1: B is a two shot, and A and C are over-shoulder shots. Look at the resulting frames: You can intercut each with either of the others.

If, however, instead of taking up position C, the camera crosses the imagi-nary line to film from position D, we have a problem. Compare frame D to its complementary shots. The character in black is now facing the same direction across the screen as is the character in white. This makes no sense!

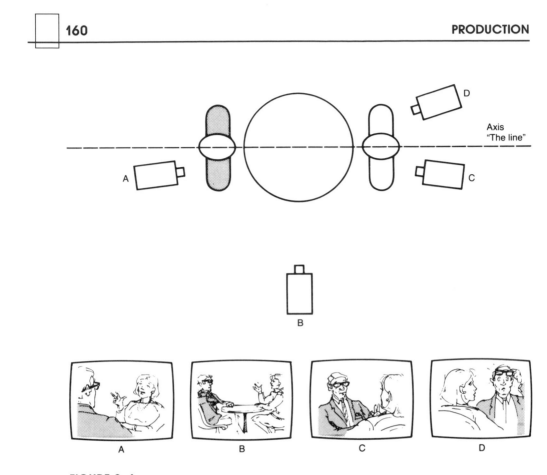

FIGURE 9–1 ――

"Crossing the line": The three images produced from camera positions A, B, and C all intercut because the characters maintain their screen directions. Position D, however, produces a composition that reverses the characters' eyelines and would not intercut with the other angles. Position D has crossed the invisible line between the characters.

This is an example of the cardinal filmmaking sin called "crossing the line."

In this best of all possible worlds, there are of course no sins without redemption. In fact, you *can* cross the line halfway through the conversation, but you would have to dolly the camera sideways during the shot from position B to position D so the audience sees the camera *moving to the new position* on the other side of the imaginary line. From here onward, all new angles must be shot from the new side of the line to preserve the revised logic of screen direction in which both characters now face the other way.

In a situation like a parade where you have people and objects on the move, you can structure certain shots to show a change of direction on screen. Figure 9–2 shows that the parade, formerly marching right to left, has turned a corner and is from now on marching left to right. By taking the precaution of including several such shots in a day's shooting, you can shoot from either side of the

FIGURE 9–2

Changing screen direction: The procession starting right to left changes to left to right all in the one shot. A useful shot to keep in reserve because, in showing a change of direction, it allows you to shoot from both sides of the axis and still cut together into a logical flow.

parade and know in advance that it can be made to cut together into a logical flow.

Of course, when people in a confined space have the freedom to move around during a scene, they themselves may regroup to face in new screen directions during the scene. This means that early and late material may not be easily intercut as one so needs when restructuring a scene to make a more logical development. Cutting away to reaction shots will help especially if the person's eyeline indicates movement going on offscreen. Remember therefore to cover yourself with these useful cutaway shots.

MOTIVATION FOR CAMERA POSITIONING AND CAMERA MOVEMENT

Making recommendations for using the camera is difficult because every location has its own nature to be revealed and its own inherent limitations. These are usually physical; windows or pillars in an interior that restrict shooting to one direction or an incongruity to be avoided in an exterior. A genuine settler's log cabin might have to be framed low in order to avoid seeing over the ancient trees an ominous revolving sausage that proclaims the neighborhood hotdog emporium. Such pragmatic limitations shape film art to a degree undreamed of by film critics. Making films and especially making documentaries is a serendipitous activity in which plans must often be jettisoned and energy redirected to accommodate the unforeseen.

Once while I was making a film about sabotage to a train during the 1926 General Strike in England (*The Cramlington Train Wreckers*, "Yesterday's Witness" series, BBC), an express derailed at high speed the night prior to interviewing a survivor of the 1926 incident. (Figure 9–3) In eerie mimicry of history, it happened within a mile of the 1926 event so we altered our plans, filming the wreckage to bring home the destruction the saboteurs had courted by their demonstration.

For the rigid, linear personality, this constant adaptation to the unexpected may be unacceptably frustrating, but for others it represents a challenge to their inventiveness and insight. Nonetheless you have to make plans, and sometimes things even go according to intention.

The first step in filming any scene is to determine what it must establish and what it could contribute to the planned film. As always, list these so nothing

FIGURE 9–3

Be ready to adapt to the unexpected—here a train wreck at the site while filming *The Cramlington Train-Wreckers*.

gets overlooked in the heat of battle. If, for instance, you are shooting in a laboratory, showing the lab's general layout is necessary, also that six people work there, that there are three kinds of equipment and four experiments going on, and that one experiment is dangerous and is being handled with extreme care. You also want less tangibly to show that the people who work there are dedicated and even heroic. This is your bottom line; you know you cannot leave without shots that establish these things.

Then, treating the camera as an observing consciousness, you must imagine in detail *how you want the scene to be experienced.* If you are shooting a boozy wedding, it would make no sense to limit the camera to carefully placed tripod shots. Better for the camera to adopt a guest's point of view; by going handheld and peering into circles of chattering people, it can legitimately bump into raucous revellers, ask questions of the principals, and even join in the dancing.

If instead you were to shoot in a courtroom with its elaborate ritualized performances, the placing and amount of coverage by the camera would be different and should not be unsteady and mobile.

No matter what the shooting situation, always ask: Whose point of view is the audience mostly sharing? Where does the majority of the telling action lie? In the courtroom, for example, does it lie with the judge or the plaintiff, the prosecutor or the jury?

Camera positioning can change a piece of action's statement. Isolating two people in close shots, for instance, and intercutting them will have a very different feel than cutting will between two over-shoulder shots. In the single shots, the observer is always alone with one of the contenders, but in the overshoulder shots their relationship in space and time is shown, not manufactured in editing, and the viewer constantly sees one in relation to the other. This is not some arcane mystery; the guide to the audience response always lies within the realm of common experience and common sense.

Another camera positioning issue lies in deciding how the background is to comment on the foreground. If one participant is in a wheelchair, and the shot contains a window with a vista of people in the street, the composition will unobtrusively highlight her immobility and the fact that she is denied certain aspects of life.

Looking down on the subject, looking up at the subject, or looking at it between the bars of a railing can all suggest different ways of seeing—and therefore of experiencing—the action that is the subject of the scene. The camera simply cannot be a passive recorder but must be made into a conscious instrument of disclosure. Though this sense of revelation can be manufactured through a blowhard editorial juxtaposition of shots, the same thing can be achieved more subtly and convincingly if a multileveled observation is built into the shooting itself.

Exploiting the location as a meaningful environment, being responsive to the actions and sightlines of participants in a scene can create a vivid and spontaneous sense of the scene's hidden dynamics unfolding. It is the difference between sharing the consciousness of someone intelligent and intuitive who picks up the underlying tensions and potential of events as opposed to sharing that of someone dull whose eye swivels automatically to whatever moves.

How best to shoot one's movie is best answered by intensively and critically studying how others have shot theirs. Film study projects in Part III can help you define a director's specific choices and intentions.

HANDHELD OR TRIPOD-MOUNTED CAMERA?

A tripod-mounted camera can zoom in to hold a steady close shot without physically "crowding" the person filmed. It cannot move to a new or better vantage, however, when the action calls for adaptation. The handheld camera gives this mobility but at the price of a certain unsteadiness. This may be the only solution when you cannot predict the action or know only that it will take place somewhere in a given area.

The two kinds of camera-presence—one studied, composed, and controlled and the other mobile, spontaneous, and physically reactive to change—give quite a different sense of involvement, imply quite different relationships to the action, and contribute significant differences to the film's storytelling "voice."

The tripod-mounted camera always "sees" from the same point in space no matter which direction the camera pans or tilts. Even when zooming in, the perspective remains the same, reiterating how much the observation is rooted to an assigned place. This feeling would be appropriate for a courtroom, because the positions of judge, jury, witness box, audience are all symbolic and preordained by seating. As no court would tolerate a wandering audience member, it is logical that the camera/observer also be fixed.

The handheld camera is an intelligence on legs. Because the close end of the zoom is impractical, the camera must be moved through space to change a long shot to a close shot, and the changes of perspective alone make this physical relocation apparent. During a handheld conversation the camera may change position and image size to produce all the shots one would expect in an edited version—long shot, medium two-shots, complementary over-shoulder shots, big closeups. Covering a spontaneous event with a well-balanced succession of such shots is a rare skill that calls for the sensibility of editor, director, and camera operator in one person.

Something special emerges from successful handheld coverage: it gives the audience the feeling of a spontaneous, uncut event unfolding, and complements this with the sense of a discriminating intelligence at work. This astute, comprehensive point of view is common in fiction filmmaking, but in handheld documentary, it is manifestly a daring improvization, something unfolding on the run. Good camerawork becomes an issue of acute concentration and acute sensitivity to underlying issues. Surely this is why the veteran Hollywood cinematographer Haskell Wexler calls documentary "real filmmaking."

USING SOCIAL TIMES AND BREAKS

Giving reassuring and appreciative comments to participants, either between questions or during a reloading break, can provide the kind of supportive approval that matters so much to any performer's confidence.

During the shooting period, spend time outside the actual shooting with your participants. It is a mistake to retreat from the intensity of your participants to the understanding company of the crew, however exhausted you may be. Without imposing, try to keep everyone together during meals or rest periods. Frequently while lunching or downing a beer with your participants, you will learn something that significantly adds to or changes your conceptions. The process of filmmaking itself generates many levels of new awareness and shakes out many memories and associations. It also applies a kind of shared intensity and sense of adventure that can bind crew and participants together. If conserved and encouraged, this sense of excitement about the shared project can so awaken everyone's awareness that a more profound fellowship and communication develops.

This can have an important effect on the crew too, for an aware and involved crew will act as an antenna, alerting you to things said or done beyond your knowledge. While we were making the film about Dr. Spock on his peace rallies, my sound recordist, Roger Turner, picked up a radio broadcast calling for demonstrators at a Christian prowar rally. As a result, we changed our plans and went to Trenton, New Jersey, where we filmed proponents of the Vietnam War in full cry.

At the end of a day's shoot, make a point of thanking both crew and participants personally and be especially careful to see that all furniture has been replaced exactly as it was when the crew arrived. This attention to the details of someone else's home will signify in the most practical way your concern and appreciation. It also helps ensure that you will be welcome if you want to return. Initial reluctance to accept a film crew's presence often comes from people hearing a horror story about another crew that was inconsiderate.

LIMITS TO THE FORM

There are no rules in this young art form, only decisions about where you will draw lines and how you will remain consistent to the contract you have set up with your audience. Part X, "Aesthetics and Authorship" gives an extended analysis of the relationship between form and content and discusses the narrative styles available as options.

Documentary film can include acted reconstructions of events long before living memory; it can include docudrama, a controversial form of reenactment mixing actors and real people, and it can include reenactment of previous events by the protagonists themselves. Ruth First, imprisoned in South Africa, acted her own story in reconstructed surroundings and with actors playing the parts of guards and interrogators. Is this documentary? I frankly don't know.

A predictable topic when documentary makers get together over a beer is always what is or is not documentary. Allegiance to fact is fundamental, but Grierson's "the creative treatment of actuality" has yet, in my opinion, to be surpassed as an all-purpose, all-embracing definition.

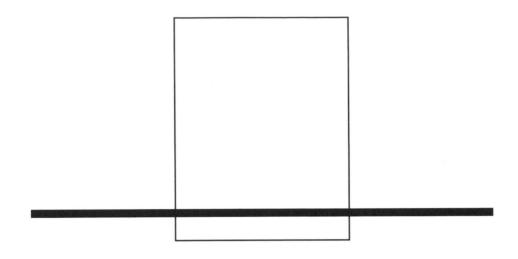

C·H·A·P·T·E·R 1·0

DIRECTING THE CREW

SCHEDULING AND COMMUNICATION

There are two major aspects to directing a crew: One concerns the moment-to-moment briefing and feedback during the shoot, the other determines how well each crew member is made aware of the larger dimension to which his work contributes. This awareness in turn allows him, if he is able, to make a creative contribution beyond the technical requirements of his own specialty, be it lighting, operating, or sound recording.

Day-to-day direction should begin from a solid, typed schedule with typed and distributed updates in cases of change. You should include travel directions and a location contact phone number in case of emergency. *Everything of possible importance should be written down* since location shooting is no time to make discoveries about people's powers of recall.

Good scheduling gets the right people armed with the right equipment to the right place at the right time. Once there, you should add any qualifiers to advance instructions and reiterate what is especially important at this particular location. You might want a store location to look shadowy and fusty, or you might want to emphasize the squalor of a trailer park. Confirm the first setup, so the crew can get the recording and lighting equipment ready. From this point you will be busy preparing the participants. A clear working relationship with the camera operator should allow this person to direct the crew so that you are not called on to decide a myriad of minor details.

Because the director alone is always fully involved, you are the last to notice mere bodily inconveniences like hunger, cold, and fatigue. If you want a happy crew, keep to an eight-hour working day, and have meals and coffee breaks built predictably into the schedule. A flask of coffee and packets of sandwiches produced at the right moment can work miracles on a weary crew's morale.

Beginners tend to expect more shooting than possible in a given time; after a few days of grueling slog, work will get sloppy, and costly mistakes will become inevitable. A crew in this condition of fatigue becomes resentful and hypercritical. It is better to underschedule than to overschedule; underworked people are always ready to shorten a given schedule by working longer, but an overworked crew will probably come near mutiny at the idea of an extra two hours. If you treat crew members reasonably, they usually rise to genuine crises with great selflessness.

You should make every effort to be a role model of professionalism yourself if you expect professional reliability in your crew. It is better to be formal about the chain of responsibility at first. After repeated proof of a person's trustworthiness, you can relax the traditional structure as appropriate.

On long shoots, crews need time off. When I first directed, I learned in an aside from my producer, Brian Lewis, that, if you go on location to a distant place, you had better schedule time for the crew to go shopping. Each crew member has a tourist tucked up inside who cannot bear to leave without presents and souvenirs. It proved excellent advice.

MAINTAINING COMMUNICATION

The director of a film, the leader of the enterprise, has a special responsibility toward the crew members if they are to avoid battle fatigue over the long haul. The members must be informed of the pattern of the intended filming, and while filming is going on, they must be kept abreast of developments and encouraged during breaks to debate the pros and cons of the production to date. One usually learns something useful from listening.

Novice directors may be shocked at the lack of all-around observation by such key crew members as the camera operator and the sound recordist. The reason is simple: A good operator is wholly concentrated on composition, lighting, shadows, framing, and camera movements. Only to a minor degree can he be aware of intellectual content. For the diligent sound recordist, actual words are less important than voice quality, unwanted noise or echo, and the balance of sound levels.

Crew members have their work cut out monitoring a restricted area of *quality* and can only be peripherally aware of developments in subject matter. The requirement that each tend a particular vegetable patch, however, brings obliviousness toward the garden as a whole unless the director invests energy in connecting the crew periodically to the project as a conceptual entity. With the best will in the world, crews do not always appreciate your efforts. But if you are trying to develop a farsighted crew, you will need to take pains to involve and without condescension acclimatize the crew to thinking in both local and global terms.

Because it takes special effort for a crew member to consider the work in hand from an authorial standpoint, crew feedback should never go unacknowledged even when it is embarrassingly off target. A wise director makes mental adjustment for any skewed comments and valuations crew members make since doing a crew job well makes a comprehensive view impossible.

MONITORING AND INSTRUCTING

Each time you start shooting, allow a minimum of 10 seconds of equipment run-up time before you say "Action" to your participants. Video editing equipment needs a preroll period of 5 to 10 seconds before each editing in point. A good piece of action immediately following a camera start may be unusable because no edit preroll is possible. Another reason for run-up is that you may have color and picture instability problems until the mechanical and electronic coordinations have settled down.

Before and after shooting, always look through the camera to check that what you expect and what is being shot are the same thing. This is of paramount importance when film is being used; it is too late to correct misunderstandings when you are watching the rushes two days later.

When directing action material, make a practice of standing next to the camera so you see as nearly as possible what it sees. Relay camera directions in a whisper into the operator's ear, making sure, of course, that your voice will not spoil a recording. You will need to be brief and specific: "Go to John in medium shot," "Pull back to a wide shot of all three," or "If he goes into the kitchen again, walk with him and follow what he does."

Your sound recordist will adapt to the action and to what the camera is doing but will probably shoot you meaningful glances now and then. Listening for quality, he will grow agitated at the approach of a plane or the rumble of a refrigerator that has turned itself on in the next room. Because he wears headphones, he will have no idea of the direction from which the interference is coming and will begin to look around in alarm. He may draw his finger across his throat (industry sign for "cut") so that you find yourself being wordlessly beseeched to call "cut!"

You have to make a decision. The stress on you is considerable for you are supposed to be keenly aware of ongoing content while resolving, through glances or hand signals, problems of sound, shadows, people who have done the unexpected, or pets who have escaped temporary bondage. At such times the director suffers a sensory overload in her effort to accommodate all the shifting factors.

While you still have everyone assembled, cast your mind back over the events you have filmed and specify some cutaways to use as inserts in the event that you want to shorten or cross-cut segments. For instance, during an interview with a carpenter in his workshop, I noticed that he folded and unfolded his rule as he spoke. We afterward did a close shot and its use in the final film enabled me to bridge together two separate sections of the interview and also to visually explain the clicking noise coming from offscreen. Many times you will use eyeline shifts to "motivate" cutaways. For instance, if someone says it is getting late and looks up, you would shoot an insert of the clock. If he looks moodily out of a window, you would do a cutaway of his POV. Frequently someone will show a picture, refer to an object in the room, or point offscreen at someone, and in each case he directs our attention to a legitimate cutaway.

Sometimes the cutaway will reflect an authorial attitude: For instance, in the kitchen of a neglected old woman, the tap drips incessantly. You film a close shot of it because it symbolizes a longstanding neglect that goes with your subject as do the dusty, yellowing photographs on the shelf. These are cutaway shots that deliberately draw the viewer's eye to significant detail.

When you are shooting more than one person, be sure to shoot listening or watching close-up shots of each individual. These are worth their weight in gold to the editor. Never leave a scene, interior or exterior, without shooting a presence track (audio background filler shot with same mike position, same recording level, and with everyone keeping silent and still for two minutes—also called buzz track or room tone).

NEGATIVE ATTITUDES IN THE PROFESSION

Interestingly the situation for the film crew is almost the exact opposite of that of the participants. While the participants need a sense of purpose and work on which to focus, the crew has ready-made work, which can insulate them from the responsibility to a larger purpose. Too often, seasoned crew members bury themselves in technical or "company" concerns and by their attitudes, remarks, or lack of involvement signify a disconnection from the real point of making the film.

This is not malice, but an exigency of the job. Unfortunately, working regularly for a corporation can turn an ordinary person into a production-line operative. Because corporations are steered by competition and the profit motive, the crew member begins to feel like a foot soldier shunted cynically from pillar to post. Even the excitement of going to distant places wears off. Seriously jaded crews rate director and production solely by the level of hotels and restaurants to which they are taken. The terminally institutionalized know both company and union rules backwards, and are hardly aware of individual filmmaking efforts. They will lay down tools on the stroke of the clock and revel in computing overtime payments to the penny.

I do not mean to detract from the achievements of the craft unions in protecting their members from the gross exploitation that has bedeviled film technicians since the dawn of the industry. There were, and still are, huge profits to be made in entertainment, and it is absolutely right that the men and women who create the product should share in the rewards. However, rules and restrictions become the refuge for the third-rate operative mentality whose presence is a dead weight in any small, tight-knit operation.

The origins of the situation are complex and instructive, and they reflect those culturally divided factions in our society not often called on to work together. I am referring again to the division between conceptual and technical workers. At BBC television studios, you could usually spot at a distance who was "engineering" rather than "production" by how formally they dressed. The stereotype of the engineer was a reticent male whose mission in life was to "maintain standards," meaning technical standards, which he saw as constantly in danger of erosion by a bunch of arty university types called producers. From the production point of view, the engineers, essential to solve problems and to deploy a technical labyrinth, were too often dismissed as narrow and conservative technocrats unwilling to bend to human values.

The problem begins with the aptitudes and education (in the broadest sense) of the individual. Many film and television makers are inadequately or narrowly educated and as a result have built a multitude of defenses around themselves. Directors disassociate themselves from the technical problems of their sound and camera people and draw ill-informed and emotional conclusions; sound and camera personnel remain within tightly drawn compartments of technical operation and avoid acknowledging to any real degree the conceptual problems inherent in direction. Only film schools—those that teach responsibly and in adequate depth—are turning out filmmakers with the kind of integrating education so lacking in previous generations. This book is of course intended for them, but it is also extended appreciatively to all those who presently feel trapped in the role of technician and who would like to direct films themselves.

WORKING ATMOSPHERE

Shooting should take place in as calm an atmosphere as possible. If there is disagreement or dissension among the crew, it should be kept scrupulously away from the participants. For them, a calm, respectful atmosphere is a necessity. The transition into shooting should hide the excitement and tension you may feel and should instead be an extension of previous times of serious, focused attention. The crew should be able to convey any warning messages or questions discreetly through signs. For instance, the recordist may hold up three fingers to indicate stealthily to the director that there are only three minutes of tape left. It is important that, in potentially divisive situations, only the director gives out information or makes decisions. The crew should preserve outward unity at all costs, and should as a matter of professionalism make no comment or observation that might publicly undermine the authority of the director.

Filmmaking, although collaborative, cannot efficiently be a democratic process. A crew used to working together can be very informal with one another, but there must be lines of responsibility respected on all sides if the unit is not to look foolish and discordant. The prime reason for the breakdown of many student film projects is that each individual privately considers himself more competent to lead than the person actually directing. When difficulties arise, each person bestows well meant but contradictory advice on the director. Such disunity of purpose soon generates alarm and despondency within the whole unit.

THE PROBLEM OF HAVING AUTHORITY

For almost every beginning director, the most pressing fear is of not being considered competent or authoritative. For authority is not something a person can just assume especially under hostile scrutiny. The director must therefore choose colleagues carefully and, once in a collaborative relationship, work to reduce the misunderstandings and compartmentalizations that will, if they remain unchecked, grow like barnacles on any enterprise. The director needs to understand the concerns and problems of his technicians and at the same time make every practical effort to include the crew in the conceptual considerations of the film. This in turn invites suggestions that may not be practical or desirable. Unless everyone understands from the outset that only a director can decide ultimately what goes into a film, the director's openness may be misconstrued as an invitation to make the film by a committee process.

Obviously the balance between authority and true collaboration is a delicate one, but it will not be a problem with the reasonably sophisticated person who finds his function in the unit fulfilling. Not all groups of people behave so maturely and responsibly. Sometimes there are odd chemistries, and one must be alert to the fact that groups react to the pressure and intensity of filmmaking in unpredictable though always revealing ways. The director is at the center of all this but cannot necessarily control what goes on. Simultaneously the information center and a sort of parental figure, the director is likely to be found wanting in both areas.

That said, most who choose to work in documentary are fine, dedicated people. It is unwise to try to fool them or to make claims beyond your knowledge. Having authority really means being respected; it means having the humility to ask for help or advice when you genuinely need it.

A good way of developing a mutual understanding is to see films together and discuss them and to analyze rushes of your own project. Often television crews often never see their own material except on the air, after it has been edited, and are thus routinely denied the chance to learn from their own mistakes. Some indeed act as if they were devoid of weaknesses or fault, and these are in reality the individuals least secure in their craft. Ideally the crew should be present at salient points during postproduction, when the growth and internal complexity of the film come under intense scrutiny. It is here, if anywhere, that the comprehensiveness of the director's task is most likely to show, here that crew members will understand the contribution they have made and come to understand your work and achievements.

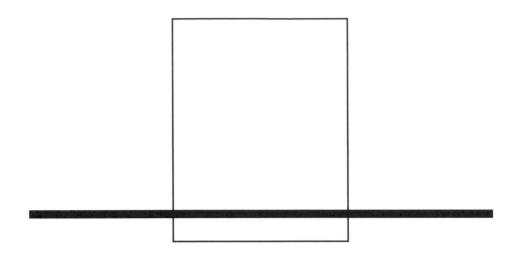

C·H·A·P·T·E·R 1·1

AUTHORSHIP

SCRIPTING

Some readers may be looking in perplexity for information on how to write a script. But if a modern documentary is an improvisation fashioned from real-life materials, trying to write a detailed script would rob the result of spontaneity by forcing participants into the role of actors.

There are, however, types of film for which a preplanned relationship between words and images is legitimate. The compilation film, made up from library or other available footage and achieving its continuity and meaning through narration, voice-over, and music, can be planned out on paper beforehand by using the split page script format shown in Figure P2–1. Much favored by news, scientific, corporate, industrial, and educational sponsors who have little use for the more individual, artistic process, the script approach gives a highly detailed, if misleadingly final, idea of what a film will be. The weakness is that it shows goals rather than what the material's idiosyncrasies support. Any good editor will confirm that one reaches objectives only after experimenting with the sound and picture materials themselves.

Because much factual film exists primarily to convey information, scripting can be useful and timesaving. But whenever, as in Ken Burns' *Civil War* series (1990), there is an emotional significance arising from the interplay of given words and images, you will always need to be sensitive in the editing room to the actual impact from the screen, to be ready to make a myriad of significant adjustments.

In the conventional live-action documentary, the nearest we get to scripting is to list intended sequences and to assign to each the contribution we hope it will make. But each situation and each new participant must be individually approached to preserve and respect their autonomy. Approaching actuality is like entering a love affair. One needs hope and expectations, but planning what should happen would bring nothing new or spontaneous.

FULFILLING ONE'S INTENTIONS

The toughest demands on the director during shooting is to know if one is fulfilling one's intentions and to determine "whether one has a film." Earlier I talked about forming a working hypothesis during research to define your film's basic statement. I want to stress again that without such a commitment guiding your choice of material, without this definition influencing all aspects of your direction, you will surely be rudderless during the shoot. Some people approach shooting a first film in the same spirit as naive students tackle exams: Make good resolutions; study all night as an act of consecration; and then on the day, employ *Positive Mental Attitude* to encourage miracles. This is magic thinking—and magic thinking creates neither rain nor documentary films. That carefully wrought definition of intent is *vital!*

Here is a sample of intention for an imaginary film about a likable, impulsive

Scene	Intended Meaning
Hans at shop counter, afternoon.	Last normal day of business.
Hans descending stairs from apartment, morning.	Morning, a new day.
Hans in greasy spoon restaurant eating breakfast.	Listless, sad, unresponsive to friends.
He arrives at shop, walks through.	Change of routine, ominous.
Stands high above his silent workshop; begins to tour the metal shop, picks up one or two items.	Making his last rites.
Drawer with photographs emptied.	Collecting, sifting his past.
Other clearing out, ending shots.	" " " "
Shock cut to auction: Hans stands impassively as machine after machine is auctioned.	Hans stoic, numb, betrays no feeling.
Check being signed.	The price of his life's work.
Torn papers in waste bin.	Break with the past.
Subjective shot, walking into building with "Mayo Clinic" sign.	Feeling what it is like to enter as a frightened, sick person.
Voice-over: Receptionist greeting him, telling him his room is ready, etc.	

FIGURE 11–1

Example of split-page format script.

engineer I knew who lost the battle against cancer. An overall statement would say, "These scenes must establish this German immigrant engineer's decision to sell all he has worked for and jettison his whole life in order to try to buy back his health and future."

The engineer's name was Hans, and he lived above his electric-motor shop. In the back was a workshop of staggering size and untidiness, containing many large metalworking and electrical machines. From visiting with him, a documentary director would make up a shopping list of shots and sequences annotated with their intended meaning to the audience as can be seen in Figure 11–1.

These are typical notes a director makes based on what she knows Hans intends to do. The list shows not just shots she expects to shoot, but also an indication of the feeling and information desired from each and the impact the various brief scenes should have on the audience both factually and emotionally as the story is built up.

MEASURING PROGRESS

Keep your intentions clear and keep them handy in list form so you can make running checks. Keep nothing in your head that can be dumped onto a piece of paper. When you have defined what story points must be made and have nailed down what you need from each sequence, you are directing from a plan of campaign: At each juncture, you may now assess whether you have won or lost the individual battles. This is the hard part because one is usually underwhelmed by what one sees take place in front of the camera.

Seeing the rushes later usually shows that a great deal more is present on film than one saw at the time, but during the shoot, one generally suffers a gnawing doubt just when one is supposed to be feeling "creative." This, of course, is not an emotion one dares to share with anybody.

DIGGING BELOW THE SURFACE

My example of intentions for the film about Hans looks rather rigid and locked down. The list is only a safety net, not a sacred text so it is in no sense a script. It would remind me what to look for, what to expect, how to get a decent range of material on the subject. It is a resource and must not be a straitjacket.

Look for the "subtext" in each situation—the real meaning lying below the surface hidden from the casual observer. Many times there are hints of something else imminent, something hanging in the balance. You need to be alert and ready to back your instincts. Just leaving the camera running may tip the balance and make it happen. A few words of side-coaching from you might steer the scene toward the confrontation you strongly sense wants to happen. Side-coaching means you interpolate at a dead moment in the scene a verbal suggestion or instruction, such as "Richard, try asking her what she really means."

If your instinct is right, the real magic happens, and the genie comes out of the bottle. You can best grasp after the genie by looking beyond the surface realism of the scene and asking yourself: What life roles are these people playing?

What dramatic characters do they remind me of? What human truth is being played out here? What metaphor sums up what is happening here?

These rather metaphysical questions help to make you conscious of the larger event in progress. In my example above, one sees Hans selling his life's collection of tools and getting rid of a lot of nostalgic memorabilia before entering a hospital. Sad but necessary, one thinks. But to stop there is to miss the point. For the man is actually doing something both daring and desperate: He is betting his shirt on one last convulsive gamble. The destruction of his past is a consecration, an offering to the gods in which he says, "If I let go everything I've ever loved, will you let me live a little longer as a reward?" Here we are no longer seeing a man go through the steps of the inevitable, we see him unconsciously bargaining with the devil clutching at his coattails. He has become a latter-day Faust.

In directing, the enemy is one's passive, gullible habit of accepting life "as is." Try to acquire the artist's habit of refusing to accept life's superficial surface. Instead treat it as a deception, a facade to be peeled away by those few who insist on deeper meanings. Treat each event you will be filming as a scene behind which hides a profoundly significant meaning that must be extracted.

Trying to do this forces one to think in terms of juxtaposition, irony, and comparison. This is creating as you go, instead of just being a recorder. Never forget that you are working in a highly allusive medium and that your audience is attuned by decades of film history to expect metaphorical and metaphysical overtones. You must work overtime with your imagination to look beyond surface normality and see the poetry in the raw material of life—most particularly because the camera itself deals with externals and surface banality.

How does one move a film beyond the literalness of recorded realism? Perhaps the most potent way is by juxtaposing materials, assembling them into a provocative antiphony. Look for the dialectics in your subject and make sure they are well-evidenced. By dialectics, I mean the opposing polarities of opinion and will that set person against person, movement against movement, idea against idea, and the parts of a person against herself. These are the spars—pressures and tensions, often insoluble and irresolvable—that stand like bridge construction in a fog of banality.

COVER IMPORTANT ASPECTS MORE THAN ONE WAY

Be doubting, and cover your backside. If you have vital points to make, make sure they are made several ways so you can choose the best. I once made a film about men who were conscientious objectors in World War I (*Prisoners of Conscience,* "Yesterday's Witness" series, BBC), and I wanted to find one man whose story could stand as an analogue for all of them. But it was a movement without leaders and a movement that even downplayed its own heroism. I also found no one person with more than fragments of the total experience. So I ended up doing detailed interviews with some 20 men and women to profile the movement and its underground support. In the rushes, no individual prevailed so I gave equal voice to all as Robert Altman did with the characters in *Nashville* (1975). Because I shot several accounts of many incidents, I was able to choose the best, as well as combine them. It was a gamble that came off because the texture of voices, faces, and photographs was a simple and very appropriate form for a leaderless, self-effacing movement.

CONCESSIONS AND RISK

Authorship means at a certain point giving up your control to some amorphous but vibrant sense of "truth." This process is usually manifest in the editing room, when an assembled piece begins insistently to make its own demands, and dictate to you, its creator, what it wants its final form to be. Any scrupulous parent will recognize this situation. One's films, like one's children, each turn out to have their own nature, imperfections, and integrity and will start wanting to make their own decisions and exist autonomously. It is a shock and a delight to see them take wing, each differently.

Similar capitulation is often required during shooting. A different truth is emerging about a certain character or a certain situation you are shooting, and you have to decide whether to ignore it or to acknowledge it and live with the consequences. Marcel Ophuls believes the documentarian must aim to deal with the unknown, and for that reason he limits his preparation so he "will be surprised." He wants to shoot something open and developing, rather than to fulfill a blueprint. This is filmmaking at its scariest and its most existential. It puts one's authority in jeopardy and threatens identity and career. But if you do not respond to those emerging, elusive truths and instead deny them, at the very least the crew will realize it and respect you less.

Committing yourself to this search for underlying truths really makes you a sort of Everyman committed to a spiritual journey. What you sense is present may always be the devil in disguise, throwing a seductive irrelevancy at you to confound you, or it may be the angel of truth, challenging you to follow its footsteps to unknown destinations.

Authorship is analyzed in greater depth in Part X "Aesthetics and Authorship." In Chapter 21, I contend that the documentarian searches the world for the free-standing counterparts to her own experience. Finding them, she is able to communicate a vision that removes the need for self-portraiture.

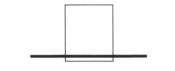

PRODUCTION SUMMARY

Before interviewing:

Rehearse questions aloud and listen to see if there is room for misunderstanding.

Decide who is best equipped (director or researcher) to interview.

Consider putting people together to talk: people in couples or in groups sometimes give you more.

Remember that antipathies and disagreements often stimulate good "talking" situations between people.

Have a clear expectation of what each interviewee can contribute to your film through prior research.

Decide the audience's relationship to interviewees, and plan on- or off-axis interviews as appropriate.

Decide if the interviewer or her voice should ever be in the film.

Focus questions carefully on issues you want discussed.

Decide what setting will most productively affect interviewee.

Remember that you must know in advance the minimum your film must say.

When interviewing:

Carry questions on index card as a "security blanket."

Make sure you have properly explained to participants *why* you are filming.

Warn interviewees that you may interrupt or redirect conversation.

Coach interviewees to include the question's information in the answer.

Review who is present and what effect they might have on interviewee(s).

Be natural and unaffected when you interview.

Listen to the beginning of each answer to be sure it stands alone without your question. Be ready to jump in and ask for a new start.

Maintain eye contact with the interviewee.

Listen not only for what you want, but for what she is *really* saying.

Give facial, but never verbal, feedback while the interviewee is talking.

Use the devil's-advocate role to represent negative attitudes in questioning.

Ask factual, nonthreatening questions first, hold back difficult or intimate matters until interviewee becomes comfortable.

Ask *always* for specifics, examples, or stories to back up any assertion that is interesting.

Get a second version if the first, though spontaneous, was clumsy or overlong.

Remain silent whenever you suspect there is something yet to be said.

Remember the camera empowers you to go further and deeper than does everyday life.

Make sure you have filmed the necessary confrontations inherent in your movie's system of issues.

When interviewing, do not:

Forget to allow camera at least 10 seconds of run-up before letting action begin.

Worry about the order of interview—it will all be cut and reorganized.

Use vague, general questions.

Ask more than one question at a time.

Overlap your voice upon an interviewee's.

Make sounds of encouragement or agreement—use facial expressions only.

Hurry on to next question or you may quash a "moment of truth."

Allow correct editorial decisions to be swayed by a sense of obligation.

Be surprised by mannerisms accompanying certain lifelong roles held by participants.

Forget to shoot presence track for each interview location.

Preparation to get proper coverage and ensure variety:

Make shopping list of sequences and shots, and *what feeling each must convey.*

Ask participants not to look at the camera.

Do not forget inserts, cutaways, and reaction shots.

Remember that vox pops are a great resource (the "person in the street" speaks).

Show people active in their own surroundings.

Each situation must be credible but also must reveal something special about the participants through their behavior.

Make sure each participant has plenty to do to avoid self-consciousness.

Expect people in unfamiliar circumstances to fall back on habit.

Shooting in general:

Decide with camera operator the size and framing of each shot.

Stand next to camera so you see more or less what it is seeing.

Whisper directions into operator's ear, or use touch signals (if the camera is on a tripod).

Try to make the camera into a conscious instrument of revelation and story-telling rather than just a passive observer.

Look through the camera often to check framing, composition, and image size.

Choose for each sequence between a steady, immobile camera (tripod) and a subjective and mobile but unsteady camera (handheld).

Decide whose point of view the camera should sympathize with moment to moment.

Decide where the center of significant action lies.

Exploit location as a meaningful environment rather than as a mere container.

Try wherever possible to create a sense of depth in the frame.

Be responsive to participants' changes of eyeline, and be ready to follow them.

After the main shooting, use participants' eyelines as guides for shooting all possible safety cutaways.

Social skills:

Give individualized positive reinforcement to participants and crew as you go.

Keep the group together during rest periods and meals so the process of relationship continues informally.

Keep to meal breaks, do not overwork people.

Thank everyone personally at the end of each day.

Replace locations exactly as you found them.

Insist that the director alone speak for the unit.

Keep dissent from the ears of participants.

Let your crew know when you need advice or help and when not.

Crew and scheduling:

Make sure there is a clear structure of responsibility for everything that may happen.

Provide the crew with a clear schedule that includes map details and phone contact numbers.

Underschedule when in doubt.

When everyone is in transit, make sure there is a phone number all can call in the event of separation or breakdown.

Be tolerant of the crew's incomplete grasp of subject development.

Keep the crew involved and aware of developments in the picture's content and themes.

Authorship:

Look for subtext in each situation, and try to make its existence evident.

Use side-coaching to impel something nascent into being.

Be aware of life roles people fall into.

Think of the dramatic characterizations each seems to have.

Create a private metaphor for each situation and activity.

Look for the dialectics in everything and therefore for the confrontations called for.

Make sure facts and vital points are covered in more than one way so you have alternatives to choose from later.

Check your shopping lists as you go to make sure you have not overlooked anything important.

P·A·R·T V·I·I

PROJECTS: DEVELOPING SKILLS AS A DIRECTOR

I•N•T•R•O•D•U•C•T•I•O•N

Like the earlier projects, these will further your technical skills, but their main purpose is to develop your grasp of authorship possibilities. Most raise far-reaching issues of skill, ethics, and control and will help you build toward that "heavy" subject you are impatient to begin. Almost certainly you can adapt these modular projects to explore singular aspects of a longer-range interest.

After shooting and before you get too far in editing, *show your movie to two or three uninvolved people, and find out how it works for an audience* even if you think you are doing well. Your right judgments will be confirmed and your miscalculations will be revealed before any work is released as "finished." After more than three decades in filmmaking, I am still learning about inconsistencies and incompleteness in my own work and about my subjective shortcomings when I alone assess that work. Nearly everyone wants to hide until they are ready to come out, but taking honest criticism on the nose and profiting by it is an inescapable part of mainstream work in an audience medium.

Learning to become a filmmaker is a chicken-and-egg business. You need information to get started, but you need practical experience before a lot of information makes sense. Please be kind to yourself, and expect progress to be studded with errors and regressions. Your initial progress will probably be rapid and gratifying, but soon you will think you are hardly developing. It is easier to become a tough film critic than a tough filmmaker; many beginners find their soaring standards boomerang and condemn their own efforts as unworthy. Keep the faith even when progress seems invisible.

For these projects I have provided a minimal conceptual preparation since most people enjoy learning through reaching for given objectives in their own way. Actually, this approach is a realistic preparation for professional life, since one often runs up against problems in the field for which there is no ready solution. However, extensive conceptual and technical help is available in the relevant sections of this book, and there's a Glossary and Index at the end. If you still can't find the answer you need, try the Select Bibliography to track it down in specialized literature.

Study the italicized criteria carefully. They contain many of the project objectives and will help you hold on to all the variables that lead to a fine piece of work. Many of these projects require editing: If you are not an experienced editor, read the postproduction sections, and use the rushes from one of these projects as materials for an editing project. The criteria for editing will help solve your project postproduction problems.

P·R·O·J·E·C·T 6

INTERVIEW IN DEPTH

The object is to direct an interview that will stand without the interviewer's questions, to evoke memories and feelings in an interviewee, to provoke him into self-examination, and to take the interviewee over some personal threshold of realization that requires effort and courage on both your parts.

Tell your interviewee in advance only that you want to ask about an event that has been pivotal in his life. Preinterview so you have a sense of what is involved and what is at stake. Concentrate on listening for the underlying issues, and be sure not to ask any probing questions until the interview proper.

Try to set up the interview in one of the person's own environments such as a place of work, kitchen, study, or whatever else seems appropriate. Try to make the setting comment on the individual. Perhaps you can revisit the site of the event itself, and this will trigger feelings and memories for your participant.

Be sure to elicit whole statements; you will want to cut out your own voice later. Respond facially but not vocally, or you will interject your voice into the interview and make it very hard to edit. Before you begin, tell the interviewee:

- Not to worry about the recording, as anything can be edited out
- That you may interrupt if he gets away from the subject or if you want more information
- That you want the question included in the answer so you can later cut out the questions

As the interviewer, you will have to listen for freestanding sentence beginnings or later face the problem of having to keep the interviewer's voice, usually unnecessary and intrusive. Most interviewees need repeated reminders about including the question in their answer.

The interviewer must listen very closely, not just for what he expects but also for the utterly unexpected subtext. Most missed opportunities happen when you were given a generalization and should have asked for an example, for specifics. But sometimes there is something major. Before leaving, prepare the ground for a return visit in case you afterward discover this is necessary. Edit using the guidelines in Project 11.

Interviewee at ease, spoke interestingly and freely

Relevant facts about the event supplied

Relevant facts about himself supplied

Gave an emotional perspective—how he felt, what the event meant in personal terms

Revealed his own change and development

Faced a substantial issue or implication for the very first time

No questions or narration are necessary to make sense of the answers

Interview structured as story with beginning, middle, and end

Climactic moment well placed

Interviewer nowhere overlapped the interviewee

The sound quality was clear and intimate in quality

High overall impact

This exercise is for honing skills at oncamera interviewing, but it is also an excellent procedure for eliciting an informal, natural-sounding narration or voice-over.

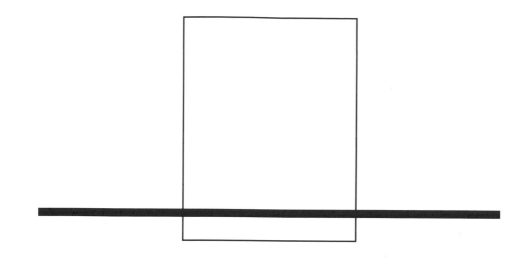

TWO-PERSON CONVERSATION WITH CONFLICT

There are several objectives here, but the main one is to find, manage, and present a human conflict. Use your ingenuity to film a conversation with conflicting viewpoints that nevertheless looks spontaneous. Because this is not "grabbed" material it needs to be elegantly shot and to have faultless sound.

First locate and preinterview two people, being careful at this stage to be nondirective. Pick a shared event in their lives about which each feels very differently and for which there are photos, movie or video footage, or other visual documentation on which they can concentrate. Note in advance what their cutaway pictures might support so you can direct their attention to particular subject matter for which visuals exist.

After research and before shooting, write up a working hypothesis, and get feedback from someone reasonably objective and critical. When you've got the best, clearest statement of intention, shoot. Because this is *cinéma vérité*, not observational cinema, you need to select actively and to enhance everything you shoot without violating credibility or your own code of ethics. You will need to set things up or even intercede *so your participants focus on what they disagree about*. Make sure they cover everything you thought significant during research. Aim to shoot a 15-minute interaction. You should:

- Do/say whatever is necessary so their interchange becomes natural.
- Make sure known differences of emotion and perception emerge strongly and be ready to intercede if they do not.

- Get them to *talk to each other* rather than to the camera.
- Contrive the setting so the frame is "packed" and interesting and so subject placement does not force awkward camera movements.
- Shoot from *one camera position only*.
- Use zoom to shoot different-sized images on each person.
- Make the camera follow the scene's psychological focus.
- Shoot a copious amount of natural reaction shots on each person.
- Cover any motivated cut-ins or cutaways after the main shooting.
- Make videotape of any pictures, 8mm film, graphics, or family video that would legitimately expand your interview's purview.
- Take care to get good sound.
- Shoot sound presence to fill sound gaps during editing.

Edit down to a 5–6 minute piece, using reaction shots and cutaways to help restructure and condense their interaction. For editing guidelines use Project 12.

Couple interesting, well chosen

Event well defined

Sharply differing perceptions

Sequence builds to a climax

Climax well placed in sequence

Resolution interesting

Sequence has natural end

Length of sequence is appropriate

People creatively placed, not just ranged on a couch

Setting creates a mood

Lighting augments mood

Compositions create depth and perspective

Camera movements are smooth and unobtrusive

Camera movements (tripod) follow psychological center of the action to reveal subtext

Compositions well framed

Framings cut together well

Imaginative, well shot cut-ins and cutaways

These used in motivated, creative way

Listener reactions used effectively

Good sound throughout

Editing rhythm smooth

Sound is checkerboarded onto two tracks

Mix is good for level and EQ

High overall impact

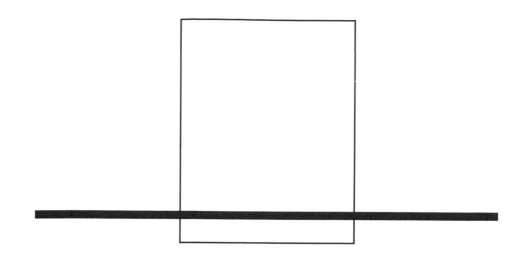

P·R·O·J·E·C·T 8

COVERING A CONVERSATION HANDHELD

Two people waiting for public transportation discuss something that interests them intensely. Using a handheld camera and *wide-angle lens only,* keep the audience at the conversation's psychological center. You will need to move the camera near or far physically to create truly different image sizes. Be sure to shoot an all-purpose "any sync" shot (an establishing shot where mouth movements are either hidden or too distant to be properly seen). This will help you get around any unforeseen cutting difficulties.

This is a direct or observational cinema assignment so, once the interchange begins, your continuously running camera must not only cover all aspects of the conversation but also respond to its changing focus and implications. The rushes should present an "edited" look that shows reactions, follows eyelines, and implies the conversation's subtext.

It helps to sketch a ground plan to figure out what angles are necessary and what cutaways can be legitimized by POVs and eyeline shifts. Remember that your people are waiting for something, and that it should be visually established. Try to include:

- BCU (big closeup) single shots
- OS (over-shoulder) 2-shots, both well framed
- Low angle shot

• Smooth, useable transitions between all shots, following speed and rhythm of exchanges. Make maximum use of the subjects' movement to motivate and carry the camera's movement. Be aware that the mike operator must follow different priorities and stay out of frame.

• Cutaways and/or reaction shots to help editing

Edit into a smooth four-minute sequence using Project 13 for editing guidelines.

Visuals set interesting mood

Participants look spontaneous and natural

Camera movements properly motivated

Compositions well framed

Compositions create depth

CUs come when speakers are most intense

OS shots well composed, complementary

Low angle shot(s) motivated

Cutaways, reactions motivated and good

Eyeline shifts exploited in cutting

Camera moves in rhythm with conversation

Why they are waiting is visually explained

Recording yields good sound

Extra cut-ins and cutaways shot and used

Distant shot ("any-sync") to aid editing

Length requirement (4-minute max) observed

Sound checkerboarded and mixed

High overall impact

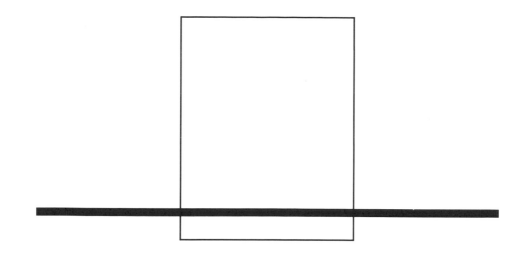

P·R·O·J·E·C·T 9

VOX POPULI STREET INTERVIEWS

Vox populi (voice of the people) is a montage technique for creating a "Greek chorus" of faces and voices that will broaden the texture of a narrowly focussed film and demonstrate where a main character belongs in relation to mass opinion. Reminding us of the richness and diversity of so-called ordinary people, it can also reinforce the idea of received truths and remind us how the individual exists fallibly within a web of prejudices and transient, societally influenced norms.

What one asks and how one asks it have a great influence on replies. Confusing, unfocussed, or unchallenging questions do not give the interviewee much to push against, but live issues presented from a provocative, devil's advocate position can release a tirade.

Because the street interview is instant rather than emerging from a relationship built over a period of time, it can be manipulated for propagandistic purposes both at the interview level and later in editing. Posing the same few questions to a range of people often yields predictable and useful results, but one sometimes meets unusual and original responses or simply finds that one's assumptions have been wrong. This in turn presents an ethical dilemma about what truths one can represent and to whom one's film will ascribe them.

This is a *cinéma vérité* project that requires you to think on your feet and have a good grasp of both technical and authorial skills. Pick a subject area in which you think the public will be searching, divided, or prejudiced. Avoid overexposed topics such as AIDS, abortion, and racism unless you feel you can expose and critique received wisdom.

Decide the main conflict you expect to emerge and write a hypothesis: *"In life I believe that. . . . To demonstrate this in action I will show that . . . The main conflict is between . . . and. . . . I want my audience to understand that . . . and to feel. . . ."*

Remember that conflicts may exist within the individual or between the individual and somebody (or something) else. Through your questioning, you will need to make your interviewees establish any factual framework necessary to understand the conflict especially as you will be editing out your questions.

Using *only four major questions,* be ready to probe the interviewee to get a satisfactory response to each. The key questions must be brief, directive, in the vernacular, and hard to misinterpret—even for people of limited intelligence. Your object is not to produce "balanced reporting" or to elicit a body of data by neutral questioning. It is first to tap into public feeling and opinion and secondly through responsible editing *to make an overall statement of your own* about the issues at stake.

Shoot your interviews in at least two locations. One person armed with clipboard acts as "catcher," stopping passers-by to ask if they will participate. You will need an interviewer/mike handler and a cameraperson. As you interview, be careful to:

- Stay informal and really listen to the subtext of the response.
- Follow up the idiosyncrasies of the person you are interviewing.
- Try to elicit responses that do not need the interviewer's questions.
- Address at least two distinct socioeconomic groups.
- Shoot without showing interviewer or microphone.
- Use backgrounds that comment on the person's identity wherever possible.
- Vary backgrounds, composition.
- Using a wide-angle lens alone, move the camera to produce varying shot sizes within the interview.
- Interview equally from either side of the camera for onscreen variety.
- Rotate group members through all roles.
- Monitor how your hypothesis is working, change it to match reality.
- With growing experience, refine and rephrase your questions or even reformulate them if it helps to sharpen the responses.

If each group member does her own edit, you will see quite different sequences emerge out of a shared experience, each expressing something of the editor. "Art," Jay Ruby has said, "contains and espouses the ideology of the artist". And, "Image makers show us their view of the world whether they mean to or not."[1] Here is the chance to see for yourself. Use Project 14 for editing guidelines.

Good subject area

Good hypothesis or premise made evident on the screen

1.　Jay Ruby, "The Ethics of Imagemaking," in *New Challenges for Documentary,* Alan Rosenthal, ed. (Berkeley: University of California Press, 1988).

Sequence makes a coherent, socially critical statement
Conflicting views, ideas, feelings well evoked
Interviewees stimulated and at ease
Different socioeconomic groups represented
Backgrounds varied and pertinent
Good framing
Good composition
Camera steady though handheld
Depth created in compositions
Variety of image sizes, angles
Entertaining, lively in pace
Good sound throughout
Edited into developmental curve of ideas
Length of cut well judged
High overall impact

P·R·O·J·E·C·T 1·0

COVERING AN EVENT OR PROCESS

If you are able to influence the speed, sequencing, or direction of the action while covering an event or human process, you are using a *cinéma vérité* approach to shooting. Essentially you ask your participants to collaborate in reproducing the appearance of authenticity by occasionally adjusting or temporarily suspending what they normally do. When you either cannot or do not want to impose this degree of control, you must use noninterventional, or "direct cinema," shooting.

This project asks you to use a direct cinema approach. You will need to research carefully to discover the event's predictable *patterns* that must be covered and to prepare a *strategy of alternatives* to cover anything that may resolve in several possible ways.

First find the event or process, and decide which people to focus on. Decide what is likely to happen, and work out how to elicit sufficient factual preparation ("exposition") in the sequence and how to reveal geographical layout. During research, note every arresting image, action, and action sequence that might be filmed. Plan to make anything of significance evident through action and behavior just as if you were shooting a silent film.

A sequence *must be planned like a complete film,* with the proverbial beginning, middle, and end just as if you were a screenwriter. Likewise each step within the sequence must also be shot with a deliberate beginning, middle, and end.

You should aim to produce a sequence of actions linked by movement, screen direction, eyelines, and common characters. Like a detective novel writer, you need to acquire the materials for rapid narrative development onscreen and its sense of movement through time. A common shooting fault is to come away with a portfolio of "photomontage" shots that fragment the event into still moments. This kind of coverage arises reactively from private, circumscribed moments of awareness that are quite appropriate to still photography where one freezes a significant moment of time but that lack narrative flow. Somewhere this operator has been taught to think in isolated symbols and lacks an embracing vision of life as an organic process with its constant resolutions and renewals. You can help avoid this by strenuously defining the development and flow of an event, and therefore its form, in advance. Be sure to cover each transition between stages, not just the resulting plateau of outcome.

Every human event contains the typical—typical people, typical actions, and typical conversation. Quintessential examples will make your audience smile in recognition. Conversely every event also contains elements that are unique, odd, and piquant. Be ready to catch them both. Prepare to show:

- What precedes the event
- How the event begins to build
- How each salient step in the pattern of development begins
- When and how each step is at its zenith
- What signals its decline
- How it resolves (ends)
- What is left after it ends
- How the next step begins
- What signals the end of the very last step

These concepts work equally well for a sequence of a man getting a haircut, a herd of cattle in a thunderstorm, or a circus visiting a small town.

Most events and processes have more than one activity going on at the same time, and *this allows you to condense events through parallel storytelling.* As though this sequence were a whole film, ask yourself before and during the shoot:

- From what direction does available light come?
- What general axis does the event follow and on which side of it should I mainly be?
- What shots could I need as neutral angles by which to link shots of differing screen direction?
- What is interestingly, amusingly characteristic and typical and must be shown?
- What is odd, unexpected, different, quirky, unique?
- Who are my main characters?
- What does each represent?
- What do I know about them that must be *shown* to my audience?
- In what situations (usually of stress) are they most likely to reveal themselves?
- What facts must I establish as part of an implied or spoken exposition?

- What parallel activities can I shoot so that, through intercutting, I can shorten and intensify all the materials?
- What interesting, characteristic or rhythmic sounds can I record to help my track become an imaginative sound play, not just ear filler?
- What vox pop, or more formal, interviews should I get to cover myself against the need for "narration" and narrative exposition?

Now define your working hypothesis as outlined in the previous project. This will shape how and what you shoot. Draw ground plans, organize the crew movements to facilitate coverage, and get any necessary permissions. Use Project 14 for editing guidelines.

Process/event develops in clear steps

Necessary factual framework supplied or implied

Setting/geography interestingly revealed

What is typical is well shown

Shows fresh and unexpected detail

Main characters emerge interestingly

Parallel action intercut effectively

Voices and/or interviews used effectively

Hypothesis evident and effective

Conflict and contradictions implied

Crisply edited

Sound is effective in all ways

Uses eyelines and axes to create other POVs

Has something to say about life

High overall impact

P·A·R·T V·I·I·I

POSTPRODUCTION

CHAPTER 17
Editing: The End Game   246

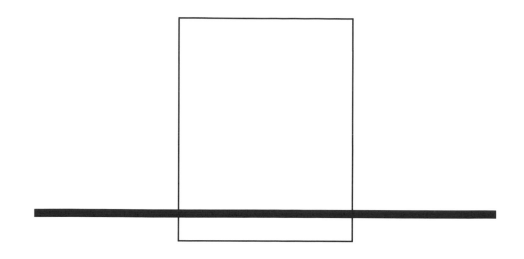

C·H·A·P·T·E·R 1·2

A POSTPRODUCTION OVERVIEW

Postproduction is the phase of film- or videomaking that transforms the shot material, or rushes, into the film that the audience sees. It is mainly handled by the editor, whose work includes: screening rushes for the director's choices and comments; getting dialogue transcripts made; logging; and making a "paper edit" (a way of planning the intended film on paper), an assembly, a rough cut, and a fine cut. The editor also supervises any narration or music recording, builds the component parts to the multitrack sound, and supervises the mixdown of these tracks into one smooth final track. Other processes, also supervised by the editor, follow the editor's main work: In film it is laboratory work to produce projection prints and in video an online, or computer assisted, postproduction process to create a final sound track and a clean, stable image suitable for broadcasting.

You can see from the list of responsibilities alone how the editor is a key figure in the creative evolution of any film. This is particularly true in documentary, where so much of a film's final structure and authorial voice emerge from the editing process itself.

THE EDITOR'S ROLE AND RESPONSIBILITIES

In a low-budget movie, the editor and director are sometimes, for economic reasons, one and the same person. An independent creative mind collaborating with the director is a great asset, however, and any description of the editor's role begins to reveal how much is lost when the director undertakes her own editing. Sometimes a director does her own editing because she wishes to preserve a unified artistic identity in her film, but I think this is impractical. Let us look at what usually happens.

The editor receives the director at a time of considerable anxiety and uncertainty; the film is shot, but has yet to emerge as anything coherent. At this time most directors, however confident they appear, are acutely aware of their material's failures, and are often suffering a sort of postnatal depression after the sustained impetus of shooting. If the editor and director do not know each other well, both will usually be formal and cautious. Both feel the editor is taking over the director's baby, and that the director carries mixed and potentially explosive emotions.

An editor needs to be patient, highly organized, willing to experiment extensively, and diplomatic about trying to get her own way. On a documentary, the editor who is given some creative leeway is really the second director since the materials supplied are often capable of many permutations and, unlike a scripted production, require a willingness to make responsible subjective judgments.

An editor's job is thus far more than simply the physical task of assembly. While the director is familiar with all the situations that produced the film, the editor, not having experienced that process, comes to the material with an unobligated and unprejudiced eye and can tell the director what possibilities truly lie in the material.

There are a number of working methods commonly employed by directors at this stage. One director might present the editor with a paper edit (an edit plan on paper) to carry out. Another might discuss what her intentions were at the time of shooting and leave the editor to find the best materials to carry out those intentions. Yet another might grill the editor to try to confirm which materials seemed strongest, what feeling each sequence carried, which had the most interesting situations and impact, and so on.

Then the editor sets to work assembling a first, raw version of the film. Most directors leave the cutting room during this period to ensure that they see what the editor produces with a fresh eye. The obsessive director tends to sit in the cutting room night and day to direct the editor's actions. Whether this is an amenable arrangement depends on the editor. Some like to be able to debate their way through the cutting procedure. Others, more independent-minded perhaps, prefer being left alone to work out the film's problems in bouts of intense concentration with their logs and machinery.

In the end, very little escapes discussion; every scene and every cut is scrutinized, questioned, weighed and balanced. The relationship is intense, and the editor is often using delicate but sustained leverage against what she senses are the prejudices and obsessions that every director develops about the material. Ralph Rosenblum's *When the Shooting Stops . . . the Cutting Begins*[1] shows just how varied and crazy editor/director relationships can be.

However relationships may be worked out, the serious director is eventually going to avail herself of the partnership of a good editor if only at first to avoid

---

1. Ralph Rosenblum, *When the Shooting Stops . . . the Cutting Begins* (New York: Penguin, 1980).

burnout. The scrutiny of the emerging work by an equal and the advocacy of alternative views, normally produces a tougher and better-balanced film than any one person can generate alone.

THE EDITING PROCESS BEGINS: VIEWING THE RUSHES

At the completion of shooting and even if the rushes have been viewed piecemeal, it is important that the crew members see their work in its entirety if everyone is to learn the maximum for the future. Screening may have to be broken up into more than one session as four hours of unedited footage is about the longest segment on which even the truly dedicated can maintain concentration.

The editor may be present at this viewing, but since the crew viewing is a retrospective and a post-mortem while the editor's viewing concerns future construction, they are probably better made into separate occasions.

At the viewing with the editor, you begin to search out and note the possibilities of the material. You are interested in what information and facts emerge, but you are also on the lookout for what might make telling juxtapositions. For example, I made a film about a famous 1936 march by the British Union of Fascists through the Jewish East End of London (*The Battle of Cable Street*, "Yesterday's Witness" series, BBC). Individuals of different political outlooks gave such utterly different accounts that the interviews cried out to be intercut if only to warn the viewer of the emotion and subjectivity vested in the issues.

A marathon viewing of rushes highlights the utter relativity of all the sequences and the issues each raises. As you view the material, note down all new thoughts about ways the material could be used. These spontaneous ideas will be a useful resource later in the process, and like important dreams they are apt to evaporate unless committed to paper on the spot.

You should also note any particular mood communicated by a sequence or interviewee. If, during the rushes viewing, you find yourself reacting to a particular individual with, "Funny, but I don't trust him," write this down because, far from being personal and isolated, the feeling is almost certainly latent in the material, a sabotaging force in whatever film you go on to make. Many gut feelings seem so logically unfounded that it is tempting to ignore or forget them; yet what triggered them remains present and potent as an experience for any first-time audience.

It is useful to have someone present who is willing to take dictated notes. Failing this, you can dictate them into a cassette recorder. Try never to relax your attention from watching the screen, as you can easily miss important points. The normal, conversational half-attention given to most television is quite inappropriate if you want to be a creator of film rather than just a consumer.

There will probably be debates over the meaning or importance of different parts of the filming, and different crew members and the editor may have opposing feelings about some of your characters and what they say. By all means take part in these and encourage them, but also listen carefully. You will get advance warning over how much or how little agreement is elicited by some of your film's contents, and you may find your own assumptions being modified.

While the director must serve her own central vision, this must not be so fixed that it cannot evolve through cross-fertilization. It is important to listen to representative reactions, to think deeply, and to examine your own persuasions at this stage. Essentially you must set aside all the intentions you ever had, purify your heart of all passions connected with the shooting, and confront the materials in a spirit of open-minded inventiveness. *Nothing outside the rushes is relevant to the film you are going to make; you must find your film in the given materials.*

RETURN TO INNOCENCE

The discipline of filmmaking requires one to return at crucial times to a state of innocence. For instance, when you are about to see a first assembly of the film, you need to purge yourself of any foreknowledge and try to see the film with the eyes of a first-time viewer. This of course is not easy. But the ability to see with the eye of an audience member is at the heart of working in an audience medium like film. Only by acquiring it can you construct a film that speaks satisfyingly to someone of your own intelligence seeing the film for the first time.

This same unobstructed, audiencelike viewing is necessary every time you run a new version. Though you use your familiarity with the source material as creatively as possible especially in solving problems, this is only one of your identities. You have to be able to change hats at each new juncture when you assess the film *and see it for itself, as a first-time audience would.* It helps to have one or two people present who have not seen the movie before; although they may never utter a word; in some mysterious way, the mere presence of newcomers enables the makers to see the film from a fresh perspective.

If, on seeing an editor's new version, you experience a resistance in yourself because it is not what you expected, screen the new version again in order to see it more acceptingly, as an audience sees it, before you make any negative pronouncements.

THE CASE FOR MAKING TRANSCRIPTS

Tedious though it may seem, transcribing every word your characters say is of inestimable value in editing. As journalists who examined the Nixon White House tape transcripts discovered, this is still not a foolproof method of determining a speaker's full meaning since *how* something is said is quite as important as *what* is said. Transcription is by no means as laborious as people fear: later it saves work and helps ensure that you miss few creative opportunities when the long editing process is done.

If you cannot endure the idea of typing a transcript of everything of any importance said in your film, there is an alternative method that is less arduous. Instead of writing down actual words, you summarize the topics covered at each stage of a discussion, filmed scene, or interview. This gives you topic categories so you may have quick access to any given subject. You make decisions during the editing process by running whole sections and deciding which parts are best.

But avoiding transcripts in this way is a "buy now, pay later" situation, for trying to make content and choice comparisons without a transcript will only be labor of a different stripe and ultimately not labor saving at all.

Aids, lists, and filing systems that make the material more accessible are the lazy person's shortcut to creative excellence. The search function of a word processor can immeasurably speed up locating particular words and phrases, too.

LOGGING THE RUSHES

In filming, every new camera start receives a new clapperboard number. The clapper is there to help the editor synchronize the separately recorded picture and sound. With videotape, picture and sound are recorded alongside each other on the same magnetic recording medium, so scene numbers (and clapperboards) are not strictly necessary. Any log, however, must later facilitate easy access to the material (see blank log in Appendix B). A log of rushes should be cumulative, giving the new timing (or digital counter number) for each new scene or for each important action or event. Descriptions should be brief and serve only to remind someone who has seen the material what to expect. For example:

00:00	WS man at tall loom.
00:30	MS same man seen through strings.
00:49	CS man's hands with shuttle.
01:07	MCS face as he works. Stops, rubs eyes.
01:41	His POV of his hands & shuttle.
02:09	CS feet on treadles (MOS).

The figures are minutes and seconds, and there are a number of standard abbreviations for shot terminology (see Glossary). It helps to draw a line between sequences and to give the sequence a heading in bold writing. Thus if I am looking for the loom sequence, I will look first for "Handicrafts," knowing the loom material was shot as part of a block of handicraft coverage.

Because the log is there to help you quickly locate material, any divisions, indexes, or color codes you devise will help the eye make selections and ultimately save time especially on a production with several hours of rushes. Murphy (of Murphy's Law) loves to lurk in filing systems. You can be sure that the shot you forgot to describe will be the very last shot you absolutely have to find. The search will inevitably be late at night, and the shot will be buried in five hours of material. Short-cut filing systems exact their own kind of payment.

SELECTING SECTIONS FOR THE FIRST ASSEMBLY

Any assembly you make will be initially constructed from long, loosely selected sections, so let us look at methodology step by step for narrowing one's choices into a workable form. Figure 12–1 is a flow chart that illustrates this.

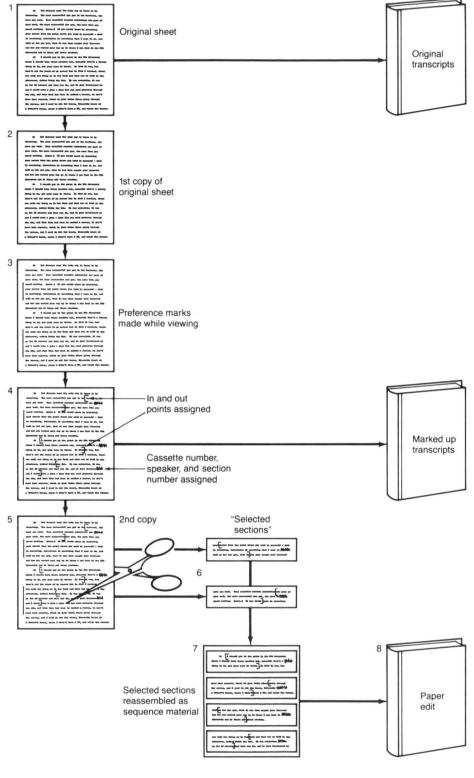

FIGURE 12–1

A flow chart illustrating the use of transcripts to make a paper edit.

Step A: Let us assume you made transcripts (1) and have made a photocopy. Place the transcripts in a binder titled *Original Transcripts,* and keep them somewhere safe. You are going to work with the photocopy (2).

Step B: On a videotape player or editing machine, rerun dialogue sections, and follow the speaker's words in the transcript photocopy (2). When you are struck by an effective section—for no matter what reason—put a line in the margin more or less against the words in question as in (3). Here you are leaving a practical record of your responses. Some will be to a story graphically told; others to some well-presented factual information; still others will be in response to an intimate or emotional moment, be it humor, warmth, anger, or regret. It is important at this stage just to *respond* and not to stop to analyze your responses. There will be a time for that later.

Step C: When you have drawn preference marks against all the sections that were striking in one way or another, study the marked photocopy and find a logical in-point and out-point, for the section, using brackets to show the start and finish of the section you hope to use (4).

In Figure 12–2, you can see that a chosen section of this interview has been bracketed at an in-point [and at an out-point]. Only by returning to the recorded material can you determine whether the verbal warm-ups at the beginning so common when people get going with a statement can be edited out as intended. Similarly, the intended out-point might need modifying if it forced you to cut away from Ted on a rising voice inflection that sounded strange and unfinished.

In the margin against the section is the cryptic identification "6/Ted/3." Decoded, this simply means "Tape cassette 6, Ted Williams, section 3." These section IDs will later prove vital because they allow you to locate the film section

---

```
Q:  What do you remember about the farmer?

Ted:  What do I....?  Oh, well, you know, [he
was all right if you kept your place.  But if
you got smart, or asked too many questions,
he'd be after you.  "Where's that wagon load of
straw?  Why ain't them cattle fed yet?"  And
then he'd say there were plenty of men walking
the streets looking for work if I didn't want
to work.  The only thing you could do was be
silent, 'cos he meant what he said.]  Now his
wife was different.  She was a nice soul, you
know what I mean?  Couldn't see how she came
to marry him in the first place....
```

margin annotation: 6/Ted/3 — Ted's descript. of Farmer Wills.

FIGURE 12–2

A section of an interview transcript marked with in-point and out-point brackets, cassette/ speaker/section ID, and margin description.

in its parent cassette, or to look up the full text of which the section is only a part. There is no set format for section identity codes, but as with all filing systems, *stick with one system for the duration of the project,* and build improvements into the next project when you can start clean.

Returning to Figure 12–1, you now have photocopies (4) with selected sections marked, their in-points, out-points and IDs, any or all of which might go into a finished film. You need to assign each section a description of its function. In the case of the example above, I would write in the margin, "Ted's descript. of Farmer Wills," as shown in Figure 12–2.

Step D: Now take these marked sheets and photocopy them—brackets, identifications and all. This new copy (5) you are going to cut into selected sections. The marked transcript photocopy (4) can now be set aside. You file its sheets in cassette order in a binder titled *Marked-Up Transcripts,* with an index at the front so you can quickly locate each character. Later, during editing, this file will be an important resource.

Step E: The photocopy of the marked-up transcripts (5) is cut up with scissors into selected sections (6), ready for sorting and grouping in pursuit of the paper edit. Because each slip is identified by subject or intended use and because it carries an ID, you not only know what it is and what it can do but you can also pick up its parent sheets, the *Marked-Up Transcripts,* and check its context in a flash should you need to.

Now you are ready to go to the next chapter, which tells you how to construct a "paper edit"—really a detailed sketch for the first assembly. The selected sections (6) will eventually be stapled to sheets of paper (7) as sequences, and the sequences will be assembled into a binder (8) holding the paper edit or plan for the first assembly of your movie.

This procedure may sound unnecessarily complicated, but believe me time spent organizing at the outset (indexes, graphics, guides, color-coding, and so on) is rewarded by disproportionate time saved later especially if the project is complex. My biggest headache came when I was hired to edit the final game in a Soccer World Cup documentary. There was 70,000 feet of 35 mm film (nearly 13 hours) shot from 17 camera positions. The only coordination was a shot of a clock at the beginning of each 1000-foot roll. I spent a week with my assistant, Robert Giles, up to our armpits in film, making a diagram of the stadium and coding each major event as it appeared in all the various angles. The game had gone into overtime due to a foul, and it was my luck to painfully establish, definitively, that *not one* of the 17 cameras was running at this decisive moment! From sports reports and with Robert's far superior grasp of the game, I set about manufacturing a facsimile of the foul using an assortment of appropriate close shots.

No one ever guessed I had faked it.

The project was an editor's nightmare. If we had not taken the time to invent and maintain a retrieval system to fit the circumstances, men in white coats would eventually have come to take us away in the legendary rubber bus.

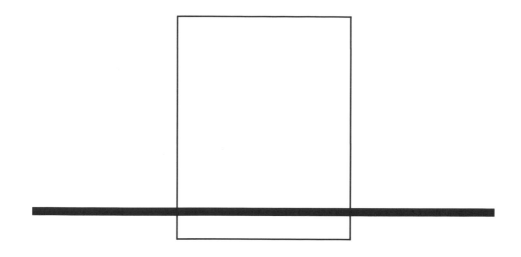

C·H·A·P·T·E·R 1·3

THE PAPER EDIT: DESIGNING A STRUCTURE

Now that the raw materials of your film are thoroughly accessible, you can make the paper edit. This phase of preparation for editing uses transcripts and shot descriptions to work out an order in which selected material can effectively be assembled.

There is a special value at this stage to manipulating paper rather than footage. Descriptions of scenes and transcripts of what people say enable one to consider content and subtext from a useful distance and to concentrate on how each segment might function. If one looks instead at the material itself, one gets caught up in the moment-to-moment action at the expense of the material's underlying potential. Making a paper edit therefore helps one concentrate on finding the *underlying structure and factual logic* that must be present to underpin any successful film.

WHY A STRUCTURE MATTERS

It may not be fully apparent what I mean by the need for a structure. Is this an audience requirement or a formality traditional among professionals? Surely, you might argue, any arrangement of film shots proceeds in a linear fashion through time, and this alone is already a structure. Experimental filmmakers of the 1960s and 1970s, in their efforts to demolish the stale and claustrophobic conventions of television and cinema, often consciously rejected conventional organization of material into a linear "story." They countered audience complaints by telling people that their expectations were conditioned to limited and familiar forms.

This was inarguably true. Around this time in literature, William Burroughs published a novel sold in a box, which the reader could arrange himself.

But in neither medium was the arbitrariness of presentation satisfying to more than the philosophically committed few: randomness seems alien to most people's expectations in both life and art. T.S. Eliot's definition of art as something that gives "some perception of an order in life, by imposing an order upon it" is thus not an isolated aesthetic judgment but the articulation of a widespread human need. Equally important but unstated is the need for these perceptions to develop and change.

If I seem to belabor the importance of a strong, clear structure, it is because I believe it is here that the documentary has a special handicap. Owing to the documentary's dependence on the spontaneity and "performance" of people who are not actors and who do not have any kind of script, many films suffer from the appearance of wandering aimlessly from topic to topic. Such a film mimics the activity of an idle mind, drifting by loose association rather than advancing purposefully toward some goal. The viewer cannot concentrate for very long unless the film begins to reveal its purposes.

In this book, I have repeatedly insisted on the need for a thematic organizing principle when selecting and priming participants and when deciding what to shoot and how to shoot it. If you are able to adhere to your goals while directing, structuring the resultant material may only be a matter of acting on the obvious. If your goals turned out to be unrealistic or were not met for some other reason, then you have a pressing need during the paper edit to try to make up lost ground.

TIME AS AN ASPECT OF STRUCTURE

Planning a structure means deciding, among other things, the handling of time. In essence, one is deciding in what order cause and effect will be shown and what dramatic advantages there may be in altering the natural or actual sequence of events.

A film about stained glass windows might have no discernible time structure in the actual footage but might benefit from arranging the examples in order of their historical dating. Alternatively this film could be structured by technical developments or by the provenance and regional idiosyncrasies of the glassmakers.

A favorite dramatic structure, common to documentaries and fiction, is to show the events of a set time period. I assisted on a BBC series called "All in a Day," which chronicled from multiple viewpoints some events taking place in a single day.

Agnes Varda's *Cleo from Five Till Seven* (1961) is a fiction work that could well be a documentary, for it is a two-hour film that follows a woman for the two hours after learning she has cancer. Pierre Schoendoerffer's documentary *Anderson Platoon* (1966) follows an American platoon in Vietnam for two weeks, and acts as a log of the events that befall them. I made a film that showed the development of an amateur dramatic production from casting through to the last performance (*Ronald Fraser: Having a Lovely Time,* "In the Limelight" series, BBC). Countless films have marked out a time span in order to show the developments that take place between, so to speak, the bookends.

Progression through time is thus one of the most important organizing features in *any* film's structure and is arguably the most important aspect of the contract struck with the audience. This idea of a contract is important because it maps out the goals and route of your film and suggests what premise the audience can expect. The contract may be spelled out in a narration, or it may be implied in the logic of the film's development. Then again, it may be implicit in the film's title or in something said or done at the outset. Consciously or unconsciously the audience needs to grasp a sense of direction and possible destination in order to accept the pleasurable inevitability of the journey.

There are any number of organizing devices for a documentary or a fiction film, and it must suffice here to give a few other examples just to indicate the diversity possible. One device is to show an event and then backtrack in time to analyze the events and interplay of forces that led up to it. Heinrich Böll's novel, *The Lost Honor of Katharina Blum* (1975), made into a feature film by Volker Schlöndorff and Margarethe Von Trotta, shows the murder and the murderer first: it then doubles back to show the concatenation of events that impel the blameless, gentle young woman to shoot the newspaper reporter.

Other kinds of structure reflect the vision dominating the way the film was made. Michael Rubbo's *Sad Song of Yellow Skin* (1970) investigates the impact of the American occupation on the Vietnamese. It uses the medium of a journey through a series of personal impressions rather like Louis Malle's in his 1968 *Phantom India* series. The film is driven more by Rubbo's contemplation than by considerations of space and time. Rather different are some of Les Blank's films about Americana, such as *Garlic Is as Good as Ten Mothers* (1980), *In Heaven There is No Beer* (1984), and *Gap Toothed Women* (1987). They are like leafing through pleasurable catalogues offering many versions of the same item and reflect Blank's anthropological leanings.

At first sight, the structure of Ross McElwee's *Sherman's March* (1986) seems determined by the succession of failing encounters he has with southern U.S. women. But lightly paralleling these are segments of McElwee's discourse on the equally fatal swathe cut by his doppelganger General Sherman during the Civil War. The filmmaker and his benighted ghost cross the country arm in arm and at the film's conclusion their journeys end—in death for Sherman and in ominous rebirth for McElwee in the shape of another new attraction.

One of the real problems for structuring a documentary is that, unless one is prepared to shoot intermittently over a period of months or even years, human change and development may have to be implied because it is very difficult or impossible to show credibly. Here Michael Apted's *28 Up* (1986) is spectacularly successful because it revisits the same children at seven-year intervals over two decades, repeatedly exploring each individual's sense of goals and destiny. Few filmmakers are lucky enough to have an enlightened employer like Britain's Granada Television so one must look for other means to show growth and change.

A BBC documentary series on which I worked, called "Breakaway," was collectively formulated to create films with built-in development. We did this by deliberately searching out individuals in transition, people intentionally making a significant change in their lives. One of my efforts concentrated on a Jewish family emigrating from London to a kibbutz in Israel near Lake Galilee (*Kibbutzniks,* "Breakaway" series, BBC). Other films in the series showed a novice entering a monastery and an old person going into a home for the elderly. Centering thus on the emotion that goes with upheaval, we set out to avoid the bugaboo of so many documentaries in which people talk about change without the viewer ever actually seeing any.

Sometimes a subject is large and diffuse and must be dealt with through examples to suggest the larger setting. A BBC series on which I worked, made as Britain was about to join the Common Market, attempted to deal with the contrasting values of Britain's nearest neighbors. Called "Faces of Paris," it set out to show aspects of the French capital by profiling some interesting citizens. Here one confronts a familiar paradox, which goes something like this: I want to show Paris, but since that is too diffuse an idea, I will concentrate on one Parisian so my film will have unity and progression. Nice idea, but how does one then choose a "typical" Parisian?

To represent the universal, one tries to find an example that is particular. But particularizing on behalf of the general tends to demonstrate how triumphantly atypical all examples turn out to be.

Making generalizations without resorting to manipulative narration can be a real problem. The camera is relentlessly literal to its surroundings: It can only ever approach the metaphysical through the physical world. Thus the ideas it conveys most readily arise from what is visible and therefore superficial, rather than from what is underlying and so much more significant. Compared to literature, film authorship is handicapped in the attempt to convey subjective insights and make compact generalizations.

Similar problems faced writers in previous centuries. One answer is to find a subject that can be viewed objectively but carries strongly metaphorical overtones. Bunyan's *Pilgrim's Progress* is on one level a journey of adventure, but it is also an allegory for man's spiritual voyage. The Maysles brothers' superb *Salesman* (1969) is a journey film that shows a group of Bible salesmen on a sales drive in Florida and during it the eclipse of Paul, the star salesman, according to the measure he and his company apply to determine success. Not only does the film show every phase of door-to-door selling—something the Maysles brothers had done themselves at one time—but it suggests most powerfully that moral compromise and personal humiliation may be the price of competing for a share in the American dream.

Another famous documentary maker has used a similarly allegorical "container" repeatedly. Fred Wiseman's favorite structure is to take an institution and treat it as a walled city, a complete and functioning microcosm of the larger society it serves. Through the emergency-room doors in *Hospital* (1970), for example, come the hurt, the frightened, the wounded, the overdosed, and the dying in search of succor. One has a powerful and growing conviction of the tragedy that haunts American cities. As a mirror of society or as a metaphor, the movie is terrifyingly effective. Yet the same "institution as walled city" idea applied in *High School* (1968) seems diffuse and directionless; the relationship between teachers and taught that Wiseman wants us to notice is too low-key and too repetitive to build a sense of development. Because his approach is nonintercessional, because he rejects narration and interviews, he seems ill-equipped to develop and intensify our scrutiny of what I presume is the key issue: whether an unexceptional American high school can possibly prepare children to participate in a democracy.

One's choice of approach and structure for a particular subject must therefore assist and make evident a development, not just in the film's material world of cause and effect but also in its thematic and interpretive stance. Defining this from a negative standpoint, we can say that a film having an interesting subject but insufficient development in theme and emotion is one that cannot fulfill its potential.

A documentarian is always a storyteller. You are looking for good stories and effective ways to tell them. Do not be fooled by the novelty of video into thinking that a storyteller's apprenticeship has changed. Your masters are in all the arts, particularly the narrative arts; you belong with both Bunyan and Buñuel, and probably with Brecht, Bergman, Breughel, and Bartók too.

ASSEMBLING THE PAPER EDIT

The paper edit is the first conceptual blueprint. To begin it you will need to design the overall structure of your film, paying most attention to the handling of time. It is best at the beginning to be somewhat conservative. If you have a film about a rural girl going to the big city to become a college student, you are well advised to first assemble a version of the film that stays faithful to the chronology of the events (as opposed to the events unfolding according to their importance, say). Afterward, when you can better see how the material plays, you might present her high school graduation, conversations with a teacher, discussions with her father, and leaving home, intercut with the development of her first semester as a college drama student. You would now have two parallel stories to tell, one in the "present" and one in the "past." It might be a serious mistake though to assume that this version can be achieved in one step. First make a safe, linear version beginning from a paper edit.

To do this you must now work with your chosen sections of the transcript as discussed in Chapter 12 (see Figures 12–1 and 12–2). These sections should be cut into slips of paper, making sure each has its code so you can rapidly turn to the parent copies in the *Marked-Up Transcripts* binder, where you can see each chosen section displayed in its original context. The selected section slips might look something like:

1/Jo/1	Graduation speech
1/Jo/2	Dinner with boyfriend's family
1/Jo/3	Conversation with English teacher
2/Jo/1	Conversation with Dad

In addition to these transcript sections you will have many pieces of action that must also be cut into the film. These are best represented as sequences rather than as individual shots, which would be too detailed and cumbersome. Each sequence can go on a separate slip of paper with a cassette location (cassette number, minutes, and seconds) thus:

1/5:30	Exterior school, cars arriving
2/9:11	Preparations at podium, Jo rehearses alone
4/17:38	Airport, Jo looking for bus

On a large table you can now begin to move the slips of paper around and try different orders and juxtapositions. Certain pieces of interview or conversational exchange belong with certain pieces of action either because the location is the same or because one comments on the other. This "comment" may be literally a spoken comment, or it may be implied by an ironic juxtaposition (of action or speech) that makes its own point in the viewer's mind.

An example would be a scene in which our student Jo has to make a graduation speech before the whole school, an obligation she feels nervous about. To make a literal comment, one would simply intercut the scene with the interview shot later in which she confesses how nervous she feels. A nonliteral comment might take the same rehearsal and intercut her mother saying how calm and confident she usually is. A visual comment might show during the rehearsal, that her hands are unsteady turning the pages of her speech and that she is flustered because the microphone is the wrong height.

What is the difference here? The literal comment complements the picture and gives us a verbal, subjective picture of Jo's thoughts and feelings. The nonliteral comment supplies us with information that in this event obviously does not apply. The effect is interesting because it supplies a counterpoint of impressions. Her mother rather enviously thinks she can handle anything, but we see the girl is under a lot of strain. Either this is a unique occasion or her mother is overrating the girl's confidence. This alerts us to scrutinize the family dynamics more carefully. The visual comment, on the other hand, gives us behavioral evidence that all is not well, that the girl is suffering. It is a privileged insight discreetly shared with the audience.

The order and juxtaposition of material will, in the final cut, have very potent consequences. The way you present and use the material is a function of your ideas about the people and the subject you are profiling and of your sense of relationship as a storyteller with your audience. In essence, you are juxtaposing *pieces of evidence* in order to stimulate the interest and involvement of the jury, your audience.

Such refined control cannot possibly be embraced in the paper edit since so much of the final effect depends on the nuances of the material as it plays on the screen. But the mobility and flexibility of the paper edit system can reveal any number of possibilities and get you thinking in an overall way about the design these individual materials could make. Do not be disturbed if your paper edit leads to the inclusion of repetitious subject matter. This is normal, for many of your decisions will only be made after repeatedly screening the material.

During this process your slips of paper have been moved about like the raw materials for a mosaic. It is useful to rule a line between sequences and divide the film into scenes and acts. This will help you see your film in terms of dramatic presentation from the start. Once a reasonably logical order for the chosen materials has been found, you can staple the slips of paper to whole, consecutively numbered sheets, which are then bound into a file called the *Paper Edit*.

From this master plan you can begin making a loose, exploratory assembly on the editing machine of chosen materials. After the assembly or even during it, your material itself will begin to suggest to you where and how to cut.

C·H·A·P·T·E·R 1·4

EDITING: THE FIRST ASSEMBLY

EQUIPMENT

Videotape equipment of all kinds is being developed and marketed so rapidly that it would be imprudent to make specific recommendations in this book. There is, however, some more general information about editing that will be of particular use to the beginner.

Few independent filmmakers edit on their own equipment because it is too expensive to purchase. Instead one either rents editing time or talks one's way into being allowed access to free facilities. Quite sophisticated and underutilized equipment may be found at small television stations or audio-visual departments in hospitals, police departments, universities, and high schools. You can also rent time from a production house (expensive!) or from a video cooperative. Cooperatives are good because they hold prices down and provide a center of activities for like-minded people.

If you can find none of the above, do not despair. It is not unusual for the owner of a commercial operation to allow someone dedicated and impoverished to use the equipment during down-time either free or for a very modest sum. A surprising number of hard-bitten media types have a soft spot for the committed novice, and many an unlikely partnership has developed from such an initial relationship.

The most common format for editing machines is the 3/4-inch U-Matic (Figure 14–1). But 1/2-inch editing has become common, and there is even a frame accurate desktop Hi 8 editing machine. If you shoot on one format and want to

FIGURE 14–1

A typical off-line (noncomputerized) video editing setup (A), and a typical film editing machine (Steenbeck Flat-bed) (B).

edit in another, you simply dub (transfer) from one to the other before editing. Though there is some quality loss from one generation to the next particularly in picture, this is a minor consideration when one is learning. Later, when you are competent to shoot material for broadcasting, you will need to research the minimum requirements for each link of the chain: camera, recorder, editing, on-line edit, time base correction, and so on. This is dauntingly technical, but there are indications that cable stations and cassette distribution are much less demanding of technical perfection than is broadcast television.

Cassette-to-cassette editing is quite simple in principle and does not take long to master. Essentially it is the progressive transfer of sections from one machine to another. You pick an out-point in material already cut and then in- and out-points for the "new" section to be added on. The rig will line up the already-recorded material and the new material at their cutting points and let you see what your choice of cut will look like. If you are satisfied and now want to do it "for real," the machine will once again back up, stop, roll forward for 5 to 10 seconds of preroll, and go into record mode at the prearranged cutting point. You see it all on the monitor: the last seconds of previously compiled material and then the new segment cut onto the old.

Figure 14–2 shows in diagrammatic form how sound is transferred from the feed deck to the recorder. I have assumed that the original tape was a two-microphone setup with each mike's output appearing on a separate track. The two tracks are adjusted for level (or volume) at the mixing board, and the mixed result is routed to the recorder. At the mixing board you send the mixed track alternately to track 1 and track 2 scene by scene in what is called checkerboard fashion. At a later stage (Figure 14–3), these individual scenes' tracks can be further mixed down, equalized (made consistent through adjustment of individual tone controls), and adjusted for level, resulting in a smooth, seamless sound mix. Figure 14–3 includes a cassette player that is feeding in a nonsync atmo-

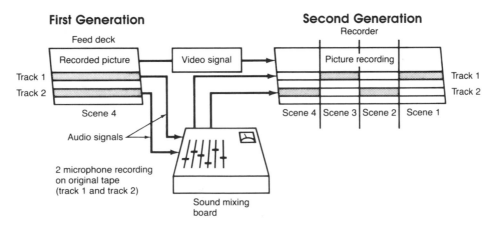

FIGURE 14–2

Assembling scenes from rushes with sound checkerboarded to facilitate sound mixing later.

sphere such as wind, traffic, or sound from a television set in an adjacent motel room.

You can see from Figure 14–3 that in each stage two tracks get combined into one. This leaves an unused track on which you can, as a separate step, record additional materials for a further mix. Each stage prior to the final mix is called a premix. The repeated mix-downs lead to a generational deterioration audible as an increased hiss level, but there are more sophisticated ways of using time-code and a multitrack recorder to keep degeneration to a minimum.

Generational losses in picture are disturbingly evident, as increasing "noise" (picture break-up) and a deterioration in color fidelity and overall sharpness. You can, however, place a sixth- (or any other) generation sound track on a second-generation picture. The last stage is risky because it involves wiping an audio track from the second-generation video (combined picture and sound) cassette and replacing it with the sixth-generation audio mix, starting from a common sync start mark. *Practice with unimportant copy tapes before you take risks with vital materials!*

Rather sophisticated equipment is needed to make picture dissolves and other electronic effects because a minimum of three replay and record machines capable of absolute synchronization is required as well as a video switcher to handle superimpositions. This raises the cost of equipment by perhaps 10 times over that of a basic rig.

Graphics and titling equipment is slowly coming within reach, especially if you already own the right kind of home computer. A down-to-earth character generator (CG) is a useful addition to the basic off-line editing rig because it allows one to create titles on black, grey, or colored backgrounds quickly or to superimpose them on live action. Not only can one put a person's identity as a

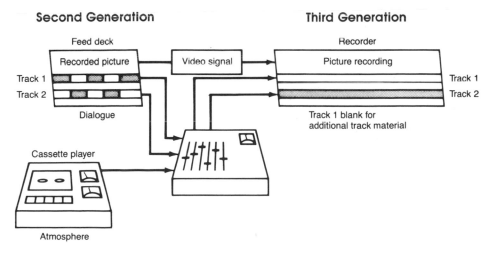

FIGURE 14–3

Premixing tracks 1 and 2 down to one leaves an unused track on the new recording where track 3 may now be laid. A cassette player is contributing a nonsync atmosphere track.

title under her image at the beginning of an interview but also linguistic barriers disappear when foreign language footage can be quickly and easily subtitled.

It is nevertheless quite possible to make a professional film with none of these optical embellishments. Having access to basic editing alone need not restrain your creative development in any significant way.

TIME CODE: ON-LINE AND OFF-LINE EDITING

Time coding is a process that gives every frame of video its own digital identification—an invisible version of the bar code familiar from groceries. Formerly available only in professional video equipment, it is now appearing in the consumer/professional, or "prosumer," equipment too. Time code allows computerized postproduction equipment to locate a single frame with total accuracy or to provide a reference system for running several video and audio machines in interlock sync.

Time code is either laid down on a separate address track while you are recording or is retrospectively applied in postproduction to an address or unused sound track. It is vital if using the latter—common with 3/4" video—to examine each camera original cassette throughout to check that nothing valuable will be forever lost in that channel by overdubbing time code.

From the time-coded camera original is made a window dub. This is a copy with a burned-in window displaying each frame's coding (see Figure 14–4). The edit is made from window dubs—partly to protect the camera original from heavy use and partly because all copies of the window dub, no matter how degraded their image, will carry the time code display. Regardless of how complicated the editing process becomes, the time code—like the legendary ball of string—allows one to return safely to the point of origin, the camera original.

Because on-line editing is expensive and complicated, a simplified type of setup is widely used for the creative part of editing, called an off-line rig. It is little more than a programmable transfer setup. Because older or less expensive machines do not read time code, their edits are only accurate to within a few frames. If you preview a cut before making it, accuracy deteriorates further—maddening if you are trying to cut between two words in a sentence. Newer equipment, including the Hi 8 desktop editor (see Figure 2–15), operates from time code and is frame accurate every time.

Once a fine cut is achieved, a clean copy of the entire edit will be reconstructed from the camera original. The process works much like a film lab conforming the negative to the workprint using film edge numbers. Video postproduction consists of taking an off-line fine cut, the log or edit decision list (EDL), and camera original cassettes to a postproduction house. Here, using a computerized rig and working from a log of time code in- and out-points, specialists make a pristine replica of your bleary and battered fine-cut. The process includes audio sweetening, adjusting the video signal components to broadcast standards, and making color corrections. Most importantly, the process includes electronic restabilization of the image made jittery through mechanical replay and rerecording. This is done using a time-base corrector (TBC), a device that

FIGURE 14–4

A video image displaying time code with cassette number, hours, minutes, seconds, and frame counter.

takes in each frame as it emerges in time, whether slightly ahead or behind schedule, and releases it to the recorder with phenomenal accuracy in time. Such precision is unnecessary in most video replay equipment, which is deliberately made tolerant, but becomes vital when a signal must be dispersed over a nationwide system of interlocked transmitters.

Video production allows a high shooting ratio at little extra cost, but because electronic postproduction is labor- and equipment-intensive, broadcast quality is often as expensive per screen minute as it would be shooting good old low-tech film on a tight ratio. Few real documentaries allow one to work with the tight control possible in fiction filmmaking so the ability to shoot speculatively and at length usually forces the independent with an eye to national-level visibility to work in video.

If you expect your work to be replayed locally on videocassette only, however, a careful off-line edited version may be more than adequate. Even quite elaborate documentaries that were edited off-line have been taken by cable or network television, and electronically "straightened out" by the reluctant engineering department. If your documentary goes that route, stay away from the engineers while they are doing it.

THE FIRST ASSEMBLY

Putting the material together for the first time is the most exciting part of editing. You should not worry at this stage about length or balance. In the film's paper edit, you have attempted to plan its themes and capitalize on your material. You can now put the material together as nearly as planned without agonizing over the consequences of what you are doing. Keep in mind that there is a strict limit to how much you can premeditate a film from knowledge of rushes just as there is a limit to how much planning you do before using a surfboard.

I think it is very important to *see the whole film as soon as possible in some long, loose form before doing any detailed work on any sections.* Once you have seen the whole ungainly epic, you can make far-reaching resolutions about its future development. Of course you will be longing to go to work on a favorite sequence, but fixing details would be avoiding the need to first assess the film's overall identity and purpose.

Leave everything long and do not worry about repetitiveness. You may need to see both men tell how the dam broke before you really know which to use or which to use most.

FIRST VIEWING: FINDING AN IDEAL LENGTH

That first viewing will yield some important realizations about the character, dramatic shape, and best length of the film. It may be that you have a particular length in mind. Television, for instance, usually has quite rigid specifications, with a 30-minute PBS or BBC "slot" requiring a film (including titles) of about 28:30 minutes to allow for announcements at either end. If your movie is to be shown on commercial television, it will have to be broken up into segments of perhaps five minutes with so-called natural breaks to allow for commercials. Thus the likely outlet for your film may determine both length and structure. Classroom films are normally 10 to 20 minutes while television uses 30-, 40-60-, and 90-minute slots. Short films that say a lot have an immeasurably better chance of acceptance everywhere.

Look to the content of your film itself for guidance. Films have a natural span according to the richness and significance of their content, but the hardest achievement in any art form is the confidence and ability to say a lot through a little. Most beginners' films are agonizingly long and slow so if you can recognize early that your film should be, say, 40 minutes at the very most, you can get tough with that 75-minute assembly and make some basic decisions. Most of all, you need a structure to make the movie as interesting and assimilable as any well-told tale. Bear in mind that a good plan does not guarantee a satisfying experience for an audience. Other criteria will come into play derived from the emotional changes and development an audience will actually experience.

DIAGNOSTIC QUESTIONING

To guess at a likely audience response, one has to begin by questioning oneself after the first viewing. At this point you are dealing with the film in its crudest form so the aim is to elicit your own dominant reactions methodically.

Does the film feel dramatically balanced? For instance, if you have a very moving and exciting sequence in the middle of the film, the rest of the film may seem anticlimactic. Or you may have a film that seems to circle around for a long while until suddenly it starts really moving.

When did you have the definite feeling of a story unfolding, and when did you not? This will help locate impediments in the film's development, and then you can analyze why the film stumbles.

Which parts of the film seem to work? Which drag? And why? Some of the participants may be more congenial or just better on camera than others. Of all the participants, who held your attention the most—and who the least?

Was there a satisfying alternation of types of material, or was similar material indigestibly clumped together? Where did you get effective contrasts and juxtapositions? Are there more to be found? Sometimes a sequence "does not work" because the ground has not been properly prepared or because there is insufficient contrast in mood with the previous sequence. Variety is as important in storytelling as it is in dining.

What kinds of metaphorical allusions did you notice your material making? Could it make more? This underlying statement is the way you imply your values and beliefs. That your tale carries a metaphorical charge is as important to your audience as the water table is to pasture.

ABOUT MATERIAL THAT DOESN'T WORK

A useful strategy after seeing an assembly is to list the memorable material and then, by referring to the paper edit sequence list, examine whatever else slipped through the cracks in your memory. The human memory discards quite purposefully what it doesn't find meaningful. All that good stuff you could not recall was forgotten because, whatever it was meant to do and whatever it looked like on paper, it simply did not work. This does not mean that it can never work, only that it is not doing so at present.

Why doesn't material deliver? There can be many reasons. You may have a series of sequences all making a similar point. Repetition does not advance a film argument in the way that escalation does so you need to make some choices and ditch the redundant. Alternatively the simple transposition of one or two sequences will sometimes work wonders. This can best be explained through the idea of a rising or falling emotional temperature: If your film is raising the "temperature" but inadvertently takes it down before the intended peak, the viewer's response is seriously impaired.

Failure also results when the viewer is set up by the preceding material to look for something other than what the sequence actually delivers. We read film by its context, and if the context gives misleading signals or fails to focus awareness in the right place, the material itself will seem flat.

THE DOCUMENTARY MAKER AS DRAMATIST

If all this questioning looks suspiciously like traditional drama analysis, that is precisely what it is. Like any playwright watching a first performance, you are using your instinctual nose for drama to sniff out faults and weaknesses. It is hard work because there aren't any objective measurements anyone can make. All you can do is dig for your own instincts through *feeling* the dramatic outcome of your material. If you are unsure, call in some people whose reactions and tastes you respect. You will probably find quite a bit of unanimity in what they tell you.

Where does the dramatic sense come from? My own feeling is that it comes from the collective unconscious and is one of the human constants. So far as anyone knows, it has been a human drive since antiquity. We have both a compulsion to tell stories and a hunger to hear them, sometimes over and over again. Think of the variations on the Arthurian legends that exist: The stories are products of the Middle Ages, yet they are still being adapted and updated and still giving pleasure after a thousand years!

In some ways, the documentary carries on the oral tradition; it is history personally felt and relayed. To be successful, it too must connect with the emotional and imaginative life of a contemporary audience. As a filmmaker, one must be concerned not just with self-expression, which is too often a narcissistic display of conscience or feelings, but also with the idea of serving one's society.

Like all entertainers, the filmmaker has a precarious economic existence and either gives her audience a sense of fulfillment or goes hungry. Robert Richardson, in his book *Literature into Film*,[1] argues convincingly that the vitality and optimism of the cinema in contrast to other twentieth-century art forms are due to its collaborative authorship and its dependency on public response. While it is absurd and cynical to claim that only the appreciation of the masses matters, the enduring presence of folk art—plays, poetry, music, architecture, and traditional tales—should alert us to the value of what we share with the untutored tastes of our forebears. The simple fact is that the "ordinary" person's tastes and instincts—yours and mine—are highly cultivated and accultured. But because we seldom discuss them in depth or consciously use them to make art statements, we lack confidence when it is time to live by them consciously. Making a documentary is exciting precisely because it challenges one to lay one's perceptions and judgments on the line.

---

1. Robert Richardson, *Literature into Film* (Bloomington: Indiana University Press, 1969), pp. 3–16.

MAKING THE VISIBLE SIGNIFICANT

Again in *Literature and Film,* Robert Richardson in Chapter 5 goes to the heart of the problem filmmakers face in comparison to writers: "Literature often has the problem of making the significant somehow visible, while film often finds itself trying to make the visible significant."[2]

It is difficult, as we have said before, to drive the audience's awareness beyond what is literally and materially in front of the camera. For instance, we may accept a scene in which a mother makes lunch for her children as simply that. So what? you might ask. Mothers make lunch for their kids all over the place. But there are nuances; one child has persistent difficulty choosing what she wants. The mother is trying to control her irritation. If one looks more closely, you can see that the child seems to be leading her mother a dance. With a little more insight, we could see that the question of food and eating has become their battleground. It is their frontier in a struggle for power. The mother's moral authority comes from telling her she must eat to stay healthy, while the child asserts her authority over her own body by a maddening noncompliance.

What we have here (and so often in film) is the problem of making the visible—a meal—significant as the metaphoric battleground it really is. Had we seen the child and her mother in some other, more overt conflict, we would probably read the scene correctly. There are a number of other ways, of course, in which our attention could be sensitized to the subtext of the scene. But without the proper structural support, the significance and universality of such a scene could go completely unappreciated. Naturally, what you the filmmaker can see happening will not necessarily strike even the most perceptive of first time viewers because they lack your behind-the-scenes knowledge and your repeated exposure in the cutting room to the same material, which on its own brings deeper insights. The only way to know what an audience is likely to pick up is to show your movie to a few people and ask them careful, nondirective questions.

THE FIRST ASSEMBLY: WHAT DO YOU REALLY HAVE?

The first assembly is when fundamental issues really begin to show. You may see, for instance, that you have a film with three endings—two false and one intended. Or that your favorite character makes no impact at all beside others who seem more spontaneous and alive. You may even painfully concede that a sequence in a dance hall, which was hell to shoot, has only one really good minute in it or that a woman you interviewed only for a minor opinion actually says some striking things and threatens to displace an "important" contributor.

The first assembly is really an audition for the best material and a departure point for a denser and more complex film. As a show, it is woefully inadequate because it is so long and crude, yet because of its very artlessness it can be both affecting and exciting.

---

2. Ibid., p. 68.

It is very important in the next stages to avoid trying to fix everything in one grandiose swipe. Deal only with the major needs of the film in each new round of changes you make. Grit your teeth and foreswear the pleasures of fine-tuning inessential details or you will soon be unable to see the forest for the trees.

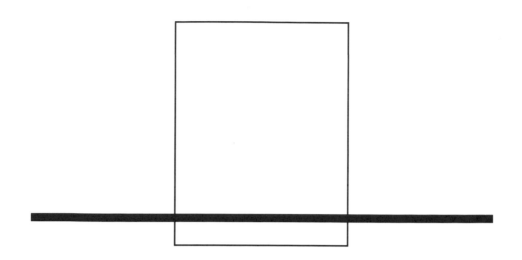

C•H•A•P•T•E•R 1•5

EDITING: THE PROCESS OF REFINEMENT

THE PROBLEM OF ACHIEVING A FLOW

After you have run your first assembly two or three times, it will strike you more and more as a series of clunky blocks of material with a dreadful lack of flow. First you may have some illustrative stuff, then several blocks of interview, then a montage of shots, then another block of something else, and so on. The film's sequences proceed like a series of floats in a parade, each quite different and perceptibly separate from its fellows. How does one achieve the effortless flow seen in other people's films? To explain that, I must first talk about the way human perception functions.

HOW EDITING MIMICS CONSCIOUSNESS

Take the commonly dramatized situation of two people having a conversation. When inexperienced players act such a scene, they invariably look into each other's eyes as they speak. This is the stereotyped idea of how people converse. But as always, reality is far more subtle and interesting, for if you observe yourself during normal conversations, you will find it unusual for either yourself or the other person to make eye contact more than fleetingly. The intensity of eye-to-eye contact is usually reserved for special moments either to search for additional information from the other person's expression or to check out what effect we are having. In both cases, we glance into the other person's face in search of information. We are either acting on or being acted upon; at crucial points, we search for facial or behavioral enlightenment. Much of the time a listener's gaze rests upon neutral objects as he scans in his mind's eye what is meant by his partner's words.

By paying attention to these shifts in eyeline and seeking the motivation behind the moments of change, we are getting close to a highly practical model for deciding both camera work and editing.

Now play the role of an interested observer and, being aware of how your eyeline shifts from person to person, watch two people talking. Notice how often you follow their shifts in eyeline by looking to see what they have noticed. As you watch, you will be conscious not only of a rhythm and motivation to their shifts of eyeline (controlled by the shifting contours of the conversation itself), but that *moment to moment your eyes make their own judgment over where to look*. Your center of attention will switch back and forth following the pair's action and reaction and their changes of eyeline. Notice that you often leave a speaker in mid sentence to monitor the effect on the listener. Unconsciously, *the observer "edits" according to his own developing insight, in order to extract the most significance from the scene*.

This little exercise sheds light on how and why editing developed as we know it. In my example, a film would have to relay three different points of view: one each for the participants and a third representing the perspective of the observing storyteller. This last is outside the enclosed consciousness of the two speakers and tends to show them in a more detached, authorial way. The audience, according to choices made in editing, can therefore identify with either one of the characters or with the more objective perspective of the invisible storyteller/observer. While character A talks, for instance, the film might allow the audience to look at either A or B in order to share the perspective of one on the other, or the film might allow the audience to look at both of them in long shot. This flexibility of viewpoint allows the director to structure not only what the spectator sees but also whose point of view he shares at any particular moment. This probing, analytic way of seeing is of course modeled upon the way we unconsciously delve into any event that interests us. *The film process thus mimics the interpretive quest that accompanies and directs human observation.*

EDITING RHYTHMS: AN ANALOGY IN MUSIC

Music makes a useful analogy here if we examine an edited version of a conversation between two people. We have two different but interlocked rhythms going: First there is the rhythmic pattern of their voices in a series of sentences that ebb and flow, speed up, slow down, halt, restart, fade, and so on. Set against this, and often taking a rhythmic cue from the sound rhythms, is the visual tempo set up by the complex interplay of cutting and camera composition and movement. The two streams, visual and aural, proceed independently yet are rhythmically related like the music and physical movements in a dance concert.

When you hear a speaker and you see his face as he talks, sound and vision are in an alliance like musical harmony. We could, however, break the literalness of always hearing and seeing the same thing (*harmony*) by making the transition from scene to scene into a temporary puzzle.

Here is an example: We are going to cut from a man talking about unemployment to a somber cityscape. We start with the speaker in picture and sound and then cut to the cityscape while he is still speaking, letting his remaining words play out over the cityscape. The effect is this: While our subject was talking to us about growing unemployment, we glanced out of the window to see all the houses spread out below us, and the empty parking lots and cold chimneys of closed factories. The film version mimics the instinctual glance of someone sitting there listening; the speaker's words are powerfully counterpointed by the image, and the image lets loose our imagination as we ponder the magnitude of the disruption, of what it is like to be one of the inhabitants of the houses.

This *counterpoint* of one kind of sound against another kind of image has its variations. One usage is simply to illustrate: we see taking place what the words are only able to describe.

Another usage exploits discrepancies. For instance, we hear a teacher describing an enlightened and attractive philosophy of teaching, but see the same man lecturing in a monotone, drowning his yawning students in a wash of irrelevant facts and stifling their discussion. This discrepancy, if we pursue the musical allusion, is a *dissonance*, spurring the viewer to crave a resolution. Comparing the man's beliefs to his practice, the viewer concludes that here is a man who does not know himself. It is interesting to note that this technique of ambiguous revelation is equally viable in documentary or in fiction film. Many an elegant contrapuntal sequence in a feature film is the work of an editor trying to raise the movie above a 1940s scriptwriting technique. Directing and editing documentaries has contributed importantly to the screen fluency of Robert Altman, Lindsay Anderson, Carroll Ballard, Werner Herzog, Louis Malle, Alain Resnais, Alain Tanner, and Haskell Wexler, to name but a few of the better-known fiction directors.

COUNTERPOINT IN PRACTICE: UNIFYING MATERIAL INTO A FLOW

Once a reasonable order for the material has been found, you will want to combine sound and action in a form that takes advantage of counterpoint techniques.

In practice this means bringing together the sound from one shot with the image from another, as we have said. To capitalize on the example in which a teacher with a superb teaching theory proved to have a poor performance, one could show this on the screen by shooting two sets of materials, one of relevantly structured interview, the other of the teacher droning away in class.

In editing, we bring these materials into juxtaposition. The conservative, first-assembly method would alternate segments as in Figure 15–1(A): a block of interview in which the man begins explaining his ideas, then a block of teaching, then another block of explanation, then another of teaching, and so on until the point is made. This is a common though clumsy way to accomplish the

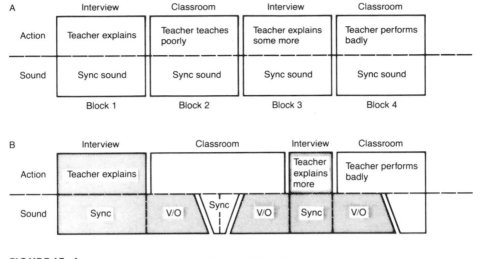

FIGURE 15–1

(A) First assembly of material through a block or "boxcar" approach compared to (B), an overlap edit, which allows a simultaneous counterpoint of idea and actuality.

objective, and after a few cuts, both the technique and the message are predictable. I call it boxcar cutting because each chunk goes by as regularly as do boxcars on a railroad.

Better would be to integrate the two sets of materials instead of playing them alternately as in Figure 15–1(B). Let us start him explaining his philosophy of teaching and then cut to the classroom sequence with its sound low and the interview voice continuing (this is called *voice-over*). When the voice has finished its sentence, we bring up the sound of the classroom sequence, and play the classroom at full level until the teacher resumes speaking. Here we lower classroom atmosphere and bring in the teacher's interview voice again. At the end of the classroom action, as he gets interesting, we cut to him in sync (now including his picture to go with his voice). At the end of what was Block 3 in (A) we continue his voice but cut—in picture only—back to the classroom, where we see the bored and mystified kids of Block 4. Now instead of having description and practice dealt with in separate blocks of material, description is laid against practice and ideas against reality in a much harder-hitting counterpoint.

The benefits are multiple. The total sequence is shorter and more sprightly. Talking-head material is kept to an interesting minimum while the behavioral material, the classroom evidence against which we measure his ideas, is now in the majority. The counterpointing of essentials allows an interview to be pared down, giving what is presented a muscular, spare quality usually lacking in unedited reminiscence. There is a much closer and more telling juxtaposition between vocalized theory and actual teaching behavior. The audience is challenged right away to reconcile the man's ideas with what he is actually doing.

Counterpoint editing cannot be worked out in the paper edit, but one can usually decide quite confidently which materials could effectively be intercut. The details will be worked out from the materials themselves.

THE AUDIENCE AS ACTIVE PARTICIPANTS

Significantly, this more demanding texture of word and image puts the spectator in a new relationship to the "evidence" presented. For it now encourages an active rather than just a passive participation. The contract is no longer just to absorb and be instructed. Instead the invitation is to interpret and weigh what is seen and heard. The film now sometimes uses action to illustrate, other times to contradict what has been set up and has seemed true. The viewer's independent judgment was invoked in the example of the teacher and the classroom above because the teacher's ideas acted as an interestingly unreliable narration instead of conventionally bland guidance.

But there are other ways for juxtaposition and counterpoint to stimulate imagination when the conventional coupling of sound and picture is changed. For instance, one might show a street shot in which a young couple go into a cafe. We presume they are lovers. They sit at a table in the window. We who remain outside are near an old couple talking about the price of fish, but the camera moves in close to the window, so that we can see the couple talking affectionately and energetically to each other. Though we see the young couple we hear the old couple arguing over the price of fish. The effect is to make an ironic contrast between two different states of intimacy; we see courtship but we hear ominously predictive middle-age concerns. With great economy of means and not a little humor, a cynical idea about marriage is set afloat—one that the rest of the film might ultimately dispel with a counterbalancing suggestion of alternatives.

By creating a texture of sound and picture that requires an interpretation, film is able to juxtapose two antithetical ideas with great economy of means and at the same time kindle the audience's involvement with the dialectical nature of life. Many people, faced with such a challenge in its more self-righteous forms, will turn away to more comfortable diversions. Documentaries must therefore aspire to be as funny, earthy and poignant as life itself if they wish to draw audiences into willing contemplation of the darker aspects of life.

The basic principle of counterpointing visual and aural impressions is only an extension of what was called *montage* early in film's history. Here the juxtaposition of two shots implies relatedness and continuity, but it is the audience's imagination that supplies the linkage between shots and between sequences. The use of contrapuntal sound came relatively late and was, I believe, developed by documentary makers. In fiction filmmaking, Robert Altman's films from *M*A*S*H* (1970) onward show the most inventiveness in producing a dense, layered counterpoint in their sound tracks. Altman's sound recordist even built a special 16-track location sound recorder, which could make individual recordings from up to 15 radio microphones.

THE OVERLAP CUT: DIALOGUE SEQUENCES

Another contrapuntal editing device useful to hide the seams between shots is called the overlap cut. It brings sound in earlier than picture, or vice versa, and thus avoids the jarring level cut, which results from the linear assemblage of material in blocks.

Look at Figure 15–2. There is a straight-cut version of a conversation between A and B in which whoever is speaking is on the screen. Predictable and boring after a while. You can alleviate this by slugging in some reaction shots (not shown). Now look at the same conversation using overlap cutting. A starts speaking, but when we hear B's voice, we wait a sentence before cutting to him. B is interrupted by A, and this time we hold on B's frustrated expression before cutting to A driving his point home. Before A has finished because we are now interested in B's rising anger, we cut back to him shaking his head. When A has finished, B caps the discussion, and we make a level cut to the next sequence. The three sections of integrated reaction are marked in Figure 15–2 as X, Y, and Z.

How do you decide when to make overlap cuts? It is a later stage of cutting usually, but we need a guiding theory. Let's return for a moment to my model for editing, human consciousness. Imagine you are witnessing a conversation between two people; you have to turn your head from one to the other. You will seldom turn at the right moment to catch the next speaker beginning—only an omniscient being could be so accurate. Inexperienced or downright bad editors almost invariably make neat, level cuts between speakers, and the results have a prepackaged, premeditated look that destroys the illusion of watching a spontaneous event.

For in real life one can seldom predict which person will speak next, and frequently it is the new voice that tells you where to look. So if a film or video editor is to convince us of the spontaneity of a dialogue sequence, he must

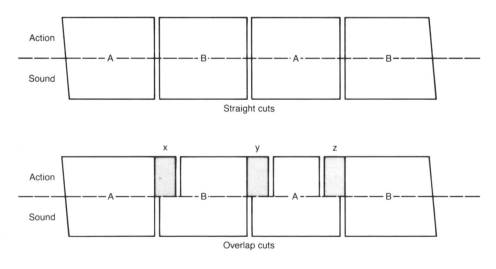

FIGURE 15–2

Intercutting two speakers to make use of overlap cutting. Overlaps X, Y, and Z function as listening, reacting shots. Use this technique to reduce the sound spaces between speakers with no apparent speed-up in pacing.

replicate the disjunctive shifts we unconsciously make as our eyes follow our hearing, or our hearing focuses in late upon something just seen.

The guideline to effective cutting is always to be found in the needs of the involved observer: Listening to a speaker, we often switch as he begins making his point to monitor the effect on his listener. Even as we ponder, that listener begins to reply. Unconsciously we are searching for visual clues in the facial expressions or the body language of the protagonists. A speaker's moment of forcefulness causes us to switch attention to the listener so without ceremony we glance away at him. The line of his mouth hardens, and we know he is disturbed. Here we are receiving two complementary impressions—the speaker through our hearing and the listener through our vision, the actor and the acted upon. When that situation reverses and our listener has begun his reply, we glance back to see how the original speaker is reacting.

The spectator is engaged not just in hearing and seeing each speaker as he speaks (which would be boring), but also in *interpreting what is going on inside each protagonist* through seeing key moments of action, reaction or subjective vision. In dramatic terms, this is the search for subtext.

For the film editor the message is clear: To be true to life and to implant in the audience the developing sensations of the critical observer, sound and picture changeover points must be staggered cuts more often than level ones. Overlap cuts achieve this important disjunction, allowing the film to cut from shot to shot independently of the "his turn, her turn, his turn" speech alternations in the sound track.

THE OVERLAP CUT: SEQUENCE TRANSITIONS

In the same way, a transition from one sequence to another may also be a staggered cut. For instance, imagine a boy and girl talking about going out together. The boy says he is worried that her mother will try to stop them. The girl says, "Oh don't worry about her, I can convince her." The next scene is of the mother closing the refrigerator with a bang and saying firmly, "Absolutely not!" to the aggrieved daughter.

A level cut would take us instantly from the boy/girl sequence to the mother/girl one following. But a more interesting way of leaving the boy/girl scene would be to cut to the mother at the refrigerator while the girl is still saying ". . . I can talk her round." As she finishes, the mother slams the fridge door shut and says her line, "Absolutely not!"

Another way to create an elision rather than present a scene change through a hard cut would be to hold on the boy and girl, have the mother's angry voice say "Absolutely not!" over the tail end of their shot, and use the surprise of the new voice to motivate cutting to the mother's picture as the scene continues.

Either of these devices serves to make the "joints" between one sequence and the next less noticeable. Sometimes one wants to bring a scene to a slow closure, perhaps with a fade-out, and then gently and slowly begin another, this time perhaps with a fade-in. More often, one simply wants to cut from one scene to the next and keep up the momentum. A level cut will often seem to jerk the viewer too rudely into a new place and time, and a dissolve seems necessary to integrate the two scenes. But dissolves insert a rest period between scenes, and the desired carry-over of momentum is lost.

The overlap cut is the answer, keeping the track alive and drawing the viewer after it, so the transition seems natural rather than forced. You have surely seen this done with sound effects. It might look like this: The factory worker rolls reluctantly out of bed, then as he shaves, and dresses, we hear the increasingly loud sound of machinery until we cut to him at work on the production line.

Here anticipatory sound dragged our attention forward to the next sequence. Because our curiosity demands an answer to the riddle of machine sounds in a bedroom, we do not feel the location switch is an arbitrary and theatrical shift from one act to the next.

Another overlap cutting technique would be to make sound work the other way; we cut from the man working on the assembly line to his getting food out of the refrigerator at home. The uproar of the factory subsides slowly and re-luctantly as he exhaustedly eats some left-overs.

In the first example, the aggressive factory sound draws him forward out of his bedroom; in the second, it lingers on even after he has got home. In both cases, the suggestion is that the sound exists in his head as the consciousness of how unpleasant his workplace is. At home he thinks of it and is sucked up by it; after work the din continues to haunt him. So here we have not just a way of softening transitions between locations, but also of suggesting subtext and point of view through suggesting the inner consciousness of a central character. We could play it the other way, and let the silence of the home trail out into the workplace, so that he is seen at work, and the bedroom radio continues to play softly before being swamped by the rising uproar of the factory. At the end of the day, the sounds of laughter on the television set could displace the factory noise and make us cut to him sitting at home relaxing with a sitcom.

By using sound and picture transitions creatively, we are better able to trans-port the viewer forward without the rather cumbersome (and expensive) device of optical effects such as dissolves, fades, and wipes, and we are also able to give important clues about the character's inner lives and imaginations.

These cutting techniques are probably hard to grasp from a book even though, as I have said, they mimic the way in which human awareness shifts. In the examples above, we have established that our consciousness can probe our sur-roundings either monodirectionally (eyes and ears on the same information source) or bidirectionally (eyes and ears on different sources). Our attention also moves forward or backward in time, and film re-creates all these aspects of conscious-ness to help the audience share the sensations of a character's shifting conscious-ness.

One welcome result from creative overlap cutting is that one can completely do away with the need for the fade or the dissolve.

HELP! I CAN'T UNDERSTAND!

If this is getting beyond you, don't worry. The best way to understand editing is to take a complex and interesting fiction sequence and, by running a shot or two at a time on a VCR, make a precise log of the relationship between the track elements and the visuals. Part III, Project 2: "Editing Analysis," is an editing self-education program with a list of editing techniques for you to track down and analyze. After some practice, try returning to this section, and it should all start to make sense.

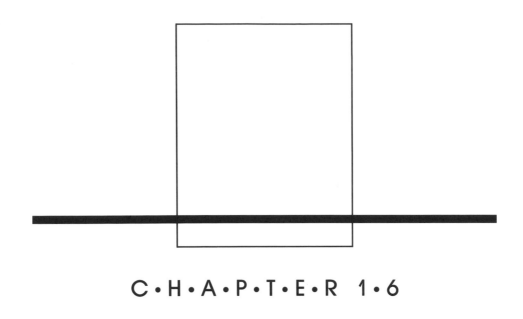

C·H·A·P·T·E·R 1·6

NARRATION

The question of whether narration is truly necessary is normally settled during editing. A film directed so that it will stand without narration usually succeeds in doing so, but if there is not an adequate story line in the available materials, the film's development may have to be helped. Narration is always available as a recourse and often neither a dishonorable or detrimental one at that. You may have intended to use it all along, or you may have directed a personal or anthropological film that quite properly needs your voice to provide links or to supply context. Whatever the reason for narration, the guidelines and the methods for producing it remain much the same.

NARRATION AS AN OPTION

Signs during the paper edit that your film may need some narration will be resolved during editing. A common problem is getting one's film started (its exposition, in the language of drama). Establishing the necessary factual background so the audience can enter the movie need not be complicated, but sometimes only a written narration can handle it succinctly. If you managed to elicit all relevant information from participants while the film was being shot, you probably know you can edit something together as an expository sequence, but you may be afraid it will be turgid and clumsy. Of course you should assemble the material and see if it stands on its own feet after all. Perhaps getting the film under way is not such an insuperable problem.

Your problem may not be in beginning the film but in keeping it moving. Perhaps you have good stories and good action, but getting from one sequence to the next takes too much explaining by the participants—explaining that could be accomplished in a fraction of the time with a few well-chosen words of narration.

Then again, it may happen that the best film you can produce persistently lacks a sense of resolution or closure because its evidence and argument never achieve a satisfying focus and articulation. Sure proof is when a trial audience expresses disappointment with the film's impact and then becomes enthusiastic when you add comments on the material. Obviously, a film cannot rely on its maker's presence to be effective, so the substance of what you supplied verbally needs to be built into the film. If it cannot be done through shot material, then you need to add some sort of narration.

Though narration can get you out of a number of tight spots, it does represent one more element to be shaped and controlled. Narration is so intrusive that if it isn't first-rate it will hamper rather than advance your movie.

DRAWBACKS AND ASSOCIATIONS OF NARRATION

Using a narrator poses certain problems. You may be opposed to it for the very good reason that a narrating voice is inevitably a mediating presence between audience and participants. For this reason alone, many directors rigorously avoid using a narrator, especially the authoritative male voice that steers the audience through so many commercials and factual films. That voice is of course the voice of *authority,* and its connotations are condescending and authoritarian. Television audiences are conditioned to wait wearily to find out what it wants to sell. Our relationship with such a film is essentially passive, for its contract dictates that we either accept *authority* or tune out altogether. Such films are not interested in engaging the viewer in a dialogue; they present take it-or-leave-it information. This is anathema to the intelligent documentary, which aims to involve the viewer's values and discrimination, not just to invade memory or colonize the subconscious.

In general, the narrator's voice is considered by the viewer to be *the voice of the film itself.* The audience makes judgments about the film's intelligence and biases based not only on what the narrator says but also on the quality and associations of the voice speaking. For this reason, finding a good narration voice is very hard. In effect, one is finding a voice that must by its words and its quality act as a surrogate for one's own attitude toward the subject.

POSITIVE ASPECTS OF NARRATION

In spite of narration's inauspicious associations, it can still be written and spoken in a manner neither condescending nor intrusive. Narration can be a lifesaver: It can, for instance, rapidly and effectively introduce a new character, summarize some intervening developments, or give a concise version of a few facts. When a film must fit into a limited time slot, time saved through narration's expositional economy is time won for additional "evidence" footage. Narration can also prepare the viewer to notice aspects of an upcoming situation whose significance will only emerge later.

The key to unobtrusive, effective narration lies in limiting it to the facts and avoiding all value judgments that are not fully supported by evidence in the footage. A good narration avoids predisposing the viewer in any direction but may justifiably draw attention to those aspects of the evidence—visual or verbal—whose significance might be overlooked if they are presented in a casual way. The goal is always to let the viewer make her own judgments from what evidence you can show.

Narration, then, is a viable option though not one devoid of problems. In making your paper edit and in reviewing your first assembly, keep it in mind as a shaping and accelerating resource. Well written, it can quickly and stylishly transport the audience to the next area of interest.

TWO WAYS OF CREATING NARRATION

There are basically two ways to create a narration: One is to write a script and have someone read it and the other is to arrive at it by some degree of improvisation. A written narration almost always sounds like someone reading a prepared announcement, no matter how careful you are in the writing and recording stages. A semi-improvised narration, however, can strike an attractively informal, "one-to-one" relationship with the audience.

Either way, you need to write or elicit simple and direct language that does not intrude between the viewer and the film. Because a film moves relentlessly forward in time, your audience either absorbs the narration the first time or it encounters obstacles to comprehension, which hinder emotional involvement. Unlike reading a book, there is no slowing down, no rereading to figure out what the filmmaker intended. Narration has to be readily assimilated, both as language and as the voice articulating that language. The commonest obstacle is the quality of the voice; it may be dull, condescending, egotistic, or just trying too hard. It can have associations that sidetrack the film's purpose in some way. Finding the right narrator and directing a good reading is one of the most difficult aspects of making documentaries. Just think how often narration alone makes a film unacceptably dull or "dated."

Let's consider the unconventional narration first.

CREATING THE IMPROVISED NARRATION

Under certain circumstances, a carefully improvised narration can be more effective than a written one. Examples are: when your narration should sound spoken and not read, when a documentary participant is to serve as narrator, or when your own voice in a "diary" type of film must sound spontaneous and not scripted.

Be warned that it is extremely hard to write spontaneous-sounding prose, and harder still for anyone to speak it effectively. Even professional actors are usually unable to read a commentary without giving it a premeditated quality.

Documentary participants are therefore even less likely to write or speak narration well. Expect instead the deadly self-consciousness familiar from small-town television advertising. This artificiality arises because a person reading aloud focuses her mind not on finding words to express an idea, as in everyday living, but in listening critically to her own voice speaking to an imagined audience.

Structured improvisation, however, evokes natural one-on-one conversation. The speaker's whole mind is engaged in finding words to act upon someone right there in front of her—a more normal process that elicits more normal speech. Here are some ways to create an improvised narration:

1. *Improvising from a rough script*. This method is relatively structured. Briefly show your narrator a rough script or list of ideas just before recording. She then paraphrases the sense, not having had the time to learn any lines. Finding the words to express the narration's content simulates what happens in life; we know what we want to say, but we have to find the words on the spot.

2. *Improvising from an identity*. This method develops a character or type of person for the narrator to "become." Together you go over what the narrator's character wants the audience to know. Then you "interview" that character, perhaps in character yourself, asking pertinent and leading questions. Replying from a defined identity helps the narrator lock into a focused relationship. This method might be used to create a historical character's voice-over.

3. *Simple interview*. This method is the most common. The director will interview the documentary's 'point of view' character carefully and extensively on audio tape during shooting. Out of this material a spontaneous-sounding narration can be found in the cutting room afterward. A variation is to shoot an extensive sync interview (that is, sound and picture) so you can cut to the speaker at critical moments. If you want to narrate your own film, get a competent friend to interview you.

All three methods produce an informal, spontaneous voice track that can be edited down, restructured, and purged of the interviewer's voice. The results will be fresh and strike a consistent relationship with the audience. Of course, this means vastly more editing than would a written narration, but the outcome is usually well worth the labor.

My film on baby expert Dr. Benjamin Spock (*Dr Spock*, "One Pair of Eyes" series, BBC) was covered by method 3. As the central, 'point of view' character in a television essay, Dr. Spock was expressing his vision of human aggression and its contribution to the American political scene during the turbulent 1960s. Shot all over the eastern United States, the film was due to be edited in England with no chance of return. In one, day-long session, I interviewed him widely to ensure I'd take home enough narration to cover every eventuality.

Recording and then fitting the improvised narration to picture during editing are procedures similar to those for the scripted narration so you should read the next section carefully and completely.

THE SCRIPTED NARRATION

WRITING

Every narrator needs a good text. One test of quality for any piece of writing—fact or fiction—is whether it can effectively be read aloud to a group of listeners. Good film narration uses the simple, basic English in which people habitually speak. As in poetry, the aim is to get the maximum meaning out of the fewest syllables, which puts a premium on finding just the right word for the job. Because narration, in common with poetry, is meant to be spoken, it must sound balanced and potent to the ear. This means axing the sonorous, ready-made phrase that jumps forward so readily when we go to write something. Use the active rather than the passive voice, and avoid all windy ornamentation and unnecessary jargon. As you edit and reedit your film, looking for the power of simplicity, so should you hone your prose, feeling a sense of accomplishment when you find a way to reduce a sentence by just one syllable.

Quite the best essay I know on writing is George Orwell's "Politics and the English Language." It is wonderfully acute about the way language is misused

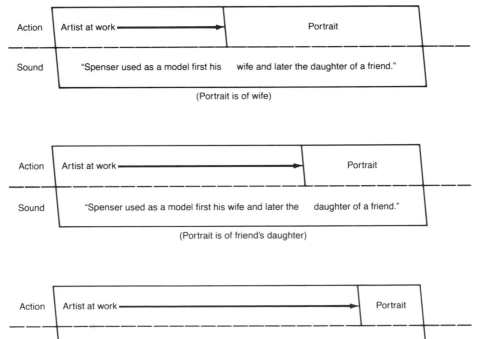

FIGURE 16–1

Three cutting points can convey three different meanings.

for obfuscation and personal gain, and because the author is Orwell, it is savagely funny. His analysis explains why communications made by government departments and academics are often so abysmal; neither can easily reverse their habitual rhetoric in favor of the plain dealing necessary in film.

THE TRYOUT

When you start writing narration, look at each section of the film carefully and write what you think necessary. Then try reading the section to film. You need to develop a feel for the rhythms of the outgoing and incoming sequences that are to be linked by narration. What you write has to sound good in relation to both old and new speakers, and it must be the right length though frequently the ends and beginnings of scenes can be tailored to accommodate narration.

ADJUSTING SYNTAX

Sometimes you have to invert conventional syntax in order to accommodate the impact of an incoming shot. For instance, if you have a shot of a big, rising sun with a small figure toiling across the landscape, the viewer notices the sun long before noticing the human being. You would probably write, "She goes out alone before anyone else is about." But this immediately sets the viewer looking for the "she." The rest of the sentence won't be assimilated because the viewer's mind is occupied in a search for the subject. If the sense is recast to accommodate the sequence of the viewer's perceptions (sun, landscape, woman), you would get something like this: "Early, before anyone else is about, she goes out alone." This complements the viewer's perceptions rather than confusing and interrupting them.

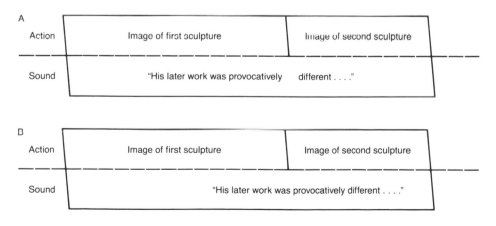

FIGURE 16–2

Shifting word position against image can shade meaning. In (A) the second sculpture will be seen as an example of departure in the artist's work while in (B) it is suggested more that the second sculpture (the "later work") had elicited an excited critical reaction.

ACCOMMODATING SOUND FEATURES

Another reason to alter phrasing or to break it up is when you have to make room for featured sound effects such as a car door closing noisily or a phone beginning to ring. Sound effects frequently create a powerful mood or drive the narrative forward compellingly, so you don't want to talk over them. Effects also help to reduce an overreliance on people talking, which is the curse of the documentary film.

THE POWER IN EACH FIRST WORD

One vital fact to keep in mind when writing narration is that the first word to fall on each new shot has a large influence on the audience's interpretation of that shot. For instance, we have two shots cut together; the outgoing is of a photo in which we see an artist at work at his easel, and the incoming shot shows a painting of a woman. The narration says, "Spencer used as a model first his wife and later the daughter of a friend."

Different juxtapositions of words and images actually yield quite different meanings, and the crux of the matter is the choice of word hitting the incoming shot as illustrated in Figure 16–1. A single, unchanged section of narration can actually identify the person in the portrait three different ways.

In another situation, illustrated in Figure 16–2, a simple shift in word positioning may alter only the emotional shading attached to an image rather than its basic identity. For instance, you see two shots, each of a piece of sculpture, and you hear the narrator say, "His later work was provocatively different."

Through altering the relationship of the picture cut to narration by only one word, the second sculpture can be made either just "different" or "*provocatively* different." Thus a combination of writing skill and sensitivity to positioning can create a subtle and effective tool of communication.

OPERATIVE WORDS

I have talked here about writing to images, but the reverse procedure is often the case—where pictures must be edited to narration or dialogue. In any piece of speech, there are strong places and weak places against which to make a picture cut. If you examine any spoken sentence, it usually indicates its dominant intention by stressed syllables. For instance: "I want you to wait right here and don't move. I'll talk to you later."

A number of readings, each suggesting a different subtext are possible, but a likely one is: "I want you to *wait* right here and *don't* move. I'll *talk* to you later."

Each of the stressed words represents an operative intention on the part of the speaker, and I think of such words as "operative words." If we were to write (using split-page format) images cut to this piece of dialogue, it might look like this:

Picture	Sound
Wide shot woman and son	"I want you to . . .
Close shot boy's mutinous face	wait right here and . . .
Close shot her hand on his shoulder	don't move. (pause) I'll . . .
Close shot mother's determined face	talk to you later."

This script specifies a cut to a new image on each operative word, and both the mother's determination and the boy's stubborn resistance are forcefully conveyed by the placing of the shots against strong, operative words.

COMPLEMENT, DON'T DUPLICATE

One temptation you should rigorously avoid while writing narration is to describe what can already be seen. Narration should add to the image, never describe the image's content. For example, one should neither say that the little girl in the shot is wearing a red raincoat (because it is blatantly evident) nor should one say that she is hesitant (because that is subtly evident). One might, however, say that she has just celebrated her sixth birthday because this is information additional to what we can see or infer.

TRYING IT OUT: THE SCRATCH RECORDING

After you have written your narration, it is a good idea to record a scratch (quick, trial) narration using any handy speaker or even your own voice. Transfer your cut of the film on to a spare cassette, mixing both tracks down to one (see Chapter 17, pages 250–251). On the remaining track, lay the scratch narration, and look dispassionately at the results three or four times. In all probability you will want to make some improvements in the wording, and you will begin to form definite ideas about the kind of voice you need and the pacing and emotional coloration you feel are appropriate. In some places, you may feel the narrator has to hurry to get the words in so here you may want to thin the narration out; elsewhere the narration may be too brief and perfunctory, and therefore, in need of developing. In either case, you may want to alter cutting points when the final narration is ready for laying.

Now you are ready to think about auditioning and recording the final narrator.

A SCRIPT FOR THE NARRATOR

The script prepared for the narrator should be a simple, double-spaced typescript, containing only what the narrator will read. Blocks of narration should be set apart and numbered for easy location. Try not to split a block across two pages, as this may lead to the narrator turning pages audibly during the recording. Where it is unavoidable, ask her to lay both pages down so no handling is required.

NARRATION: AUDITIONING AND RECORDING

Since choosing a narrator is in effect choosing a voice for the film itself, you will find yourself rejecting many types of voice on their associations alone. The convention at one time was to prefer the deep, authoritative male voice, but today that signals either a sales pitch or a deeply suspect paternalism. For these or other reasons, many of the voices available to you simply will not fit your particular film. Other voices you will want to audition. As with any situation of choice, you should record several, even when you believe you have stumbled on perfection.

VOICE AUDITIONS

In a scripted narration audition, you should let the person read something, then ask her to read it differently according to direction. You are interested in, first, native intelligence and the person's unguided ability. Second you want to see how the narrator responds to direction. One thing that happens is that some people can deal effectively with a new interpretation or an improvement but are unable to hold on to what was successful in the previous reading. Frequently this kind of reader is anxious to please and can carry out clear and restricted "orders" but does not have a grasp of the larger picture. This can be a real problem with actors whose only experience is in commercials.

When you have made an audition recording, thank the person and give her a date by which you will contact her. Even if you think this person is just right, do not tell her until you have listened carefully to the others. The reason for such caution is that listening afterward to the disembodied, recorded voice is often a greater or lesser experience than what you felt during the recording. Part of this may well be a natural sense of obligation toward a likable and very willing person. But it is only the voice that matters to an audience so your decision must be based on the voice alone.

RECORDING AND DIRECTING THE NARRATOR

A good voice recording will probably be made with the artist about a foot to two feet from the microphone. Surroundings should be acoustically dead (not enclosed or echoey), and there should be no distracting background noise. Listen through *good* headphones or through a speaker in another room. It is critically important to get the best out of your narrator's voice. Watch out for "popping" on certain sounds or distortion from overloading. Mike positioning and monitoring of sound decibel (dB) levels will cure each.

The narrator should read each block of narration and wait for a cue (a gentle tap on the shoulder or a cue light) before beginning the next. You will want to rehearse and give directions, which should be phrased positively and practically. A narrator should have seen the film and should know what it is all about, but during recording she needs to know how to say something rather than why. Stick to essentials like "Make the last part a little warmer" or "I'd like to hear that said a bit more formally." Try to name the quality you are after. Sometimes you will want to alter the word stressed in a sentence or change the amount of projection the speaker is using ("Could you give me the same intensity but use less voice?" or "Use more voice and keep it up at the ends of sentences"). Occasionally a narrator will have some insurmountable problem with phrasing. Invite her to reword it so the sense is retained, but be on guard if this starts happening a lot. Either your writing style needs revision or the reader is trying to write for you.

When you record narration, record with the picture running so the narrator is keyed into the rhythms and intonation of other voices in the film. Setting up equipment to do this is usually a pain to arrange, but the "cheapo" method of recording wild (without immediate regard for synchronization) is risky because you don't find out if the delivery was right until after the artist has been dismissed. The narrator should neither watch the picture (that is the job of the editor and director) nor be able to hear the accompanying track in- and outpoints, which would be distracting.

When all the narration has been recorded, play the whole film back and check that everything really works. If there are one or two doubtful readings, do several wild versions incorporating several different readings before letting the narrator go. These can be tried out later, and the best one chosen.

RECORDING THE PRESENCE TRACK

Whether you are recording a scripted or an improvised narration, you will need to record some of the recording studio or location atmosphere so you later have the right quality of "silence" if the editor wants to extend a pause or add to the head of a narration block. Presence track is also called buzz track or room tone, and no two are ever exactly alike, even in the same recording studio using the same mike. It should become an automatic act after recording a scene, an interview, or a narration to ask everyone to remain where they are and to record a couple minutes of silence *at the same sound level setting*. When this little ritual is overlooked it can cause the editor endless difficulties and frustration.

FITTING THE NARRATION

Fitting the narration (part of the sound preparation called track-laying) should be done carefully and experimentally so that operative words hit each new image to maximum effect. You may find you need to make small picture-cutting changes to accomplish this, though adding to or reducing the natural pauses in the narration can sometimes stretch or compress a section that is of unsuitable length. Be very careful, though, you do not noticeably disrupt the natural rhythms of the speaker. Paradoxically, the question of "manipulating" speakers seldom comes up unless there is visible or audible evidence of heavy-handed editing. Good editing (or good anything else) is the art that disguises art.

When you get a succession of sentences closely cut to changing images, it has the effect of driving the film along with a satisfying sense of inevitability. Because of the attention to operative words and their potential, you find that your pictures and your word patterns are responsive to each other and that the two are falling into mutually responsive patterns that are nothing less than musical in their relationship and in their effect on the viewer.

While this degree of adjustment is easy in film, where shots can be transposed and seconds added or subtracted, the linearity of videotape with its dependence on a cumulative building process makes it necessary to record the narration before the fine cut is complete or endure a duplication of effort.

USING MUSIC

Music must be used very discriminatingly since it is so often misused as a cheap dramatic crutch. Too often filmmakers reach for music as a reliable means of stirring emotion that should, but doesn't, arise out of content. Music should not be a substitute for anything; it should complement action and give us access to the inner, invisible life of a character or of the situation being portrayed.

Good music can initiate the emotional level at which the audience should investigate what is being shown. An example is in Godard's feature *Weekend* (1967), which starts with a girl dressed only in her underwear sitting on a psychiatrist's desk talking in a depressed monotone about her unhappiness and her husband. At first the scene is bizarre, then funny, then just as one is wondering where the sequence will lead, Godard slowly raises the level of a sombre orchestral piece for strings. The effect raises goose-bumps because it suddenly injects a poignancy, a tragical distancing to what seemed merely comic and eccentric. After a minute or two in which conversation is drowned and we are forced to look almost from a historical perspective at the girl and her doctor, the music recedes and we slide back into the present, with the girl still talking, talking. It is a masterly and highly cinematic use of music.

A film should provide its own clues about whether music is needed and where. It often seems natural during journeys and other bridging sequences—a montage of a character driving to a new home, for instance. Transitional sequences of any kind can benefit from music, especially if it lifts the film out of a prevailing mood. Music can highlight an emotional change when, for instance, an aspiring football player learns he can join the team or someone newly homeless lies down for the first night in a doorway.

Another use for music is to foreshadow an event and inject tension—a favorite function in B movies but of limited use in documentaries that usually do not allow for such an obvious storytelling "voice." Music can make a film modulate from realism to a more abstract point of view as in the Godard example above. It can also supply its own ironic comment or suggest alternative worlds as in Hans Eisler's score for Resnais' unforgettable holocaust documentary, *Night and Fog* (1955). Instead of picture-pointing deportation trains and captured human artifacts with tragic or poignant accompaniment, Eisler's score often plays a delicate, ghoulish dance or sustains a tense, unresolved question and answer between woodwind instruments.

In my examples, music doesn't merely illustrate, it gives voice to a point of view, either a character's or the storyteller's. It can function like a storyteller's aside that expresses an opinion or an alternative idea, imply what cannot be seen, or comment upon what can.

Be aware that film music, like debt, is easier started than stopped. Music is generally so addictive that we value it most keenly just when it is removed. Ending a music section painlessly can therefore be a real problem. The panacea is to give something in its place. This can either be a commanding effects track (a rich train-station atmosphere, for example) that is really a composition in its own right, or it can be a new scene's dialogue or some inciting moment of action when the spectator's attention has refocussed in a new dimension.

When you are using music not designed to fit your film, section ends can either be faded out or, better, come to a natural finish. In the latter mode, one would lay the music backward from the picture finish point and either fade it up at the picture start or adjust the scene length to make the picture fit the music from composer's start to composer's finish. When music is too long, one can frequently cut out a repeated phrase. Composers like to milk good musical ideas so most pieces are replete with repeated segments.

Often you will want to use commercially recorded music to go with your film. The best way to find an appropriate piece of music, if you are not knowledgeable yourself, is to enlist the advice of an enthusiast. However you generate choices, you will not know if a piece of music really works until you play it against the sequence in question. An informal arrangement using a cassette recorder can often solve this dilemma.

The copyright situation for music is complicated and may consist of fees and clearances from any or all of the following: composer, artist(s), publishers, and record company. Sometimes you can get agreement to use a specified piece of music for festivals and competitions only, at a relatively insignificant rate. If you then sell your film or receive rentals for showings, you may find yourself being sued. The alternative is to use original music, though many a low-budget film has been rendered lifeless by the meanderings of a banal score. It is better to use no music than bad music; good sound effects and atmosphere can in any case be a kind of musical composition that has great impact.

C·H·A·P·T·E·R 1·7

EDITING: THE END GAME

After considerable editing work on a film, a debilitating familiarity sets in. As you lose objectivity, you feel your ability to make judgments departing. Every alternative version looks similar, and all seem too long. This disability is particularly likely to hit director-editors who have lived with both the intentions and the footage since their inception.

Two steps are necessary. One is to make a flow chart, or block diagram of your film to gain an overview of its ideas and intentions, and the other is to show the working cut to a chosen few.

DIAGNOSIS: MAKING A FLOW CHART

Whenever one needs to better understand something, it helps to translate it into another form. Statisticians, for instance, know that the full implications of their figures are not evident until expressed as a graph, pie chart, or other proportional image.

In our case, we are dealing with the mesmerizing actuality of film, which, as we view it, concentrates our attention within its unfolding present to the exclusion of much sense of overview. But through a block diagram, one can gain a fresh and more objective perspective of one's work. An "Editing Diagnostic Form" is included in Appendix B to make this analysis easier.

To use it, run your film a sequence at a time, and after each sequence, write in the box a brief description of the sequence's characters and content. Next to the box write what the sequence contributes to the development of the film as a whole. It might contribute factual information; it might show a location or a relationship that will be developed later in the film; or it might contribute a special mood or feeling. Because each box leads to another box, the block diagram becomes a flow chart for your film.

Through articulating what each sequence is supposed to contribute, you tend to see dispassionately and functionally what is present for an audience. It is also helpful to give each sequence an impact rating. You might borrow from the newspaper reviewers and give each sequence up to five stars.

Now take a look at what your film looks like on paper. What does the progression of contributions add up to? As with the first assembly, you will find that it reveals some of the following:

- Nonlinear development of necessary information; holes or backtracking apparent in progression.

- Duplication or redundancy in information.

- The same kind of contribution made several ways; you need to choose the best and dump or possibly reposition the rest.

- A sequence or group of sequences that does not contribute to the thrust of the film and that does not belong. Be brave and dump it.

- The film's final determination emerges early and leaves the remainder of the film as an unnecessary recapitulation.

- The film appears to end before it actually does.

- Lack of early impact or an unnecessarily pedestrian opening so the film is a late starter (fatal for a television film).

- Type and frequency of impact poorly distributed over the film's length (resulting in poor dramatic development and progression).

Each ailment emerging from the analysis does in fact suggest its own cure. When you have put these into effect, you will feel the degree of improvement rather than be able to exactly account for it.

It is wise, after radical changes, to make a new flow chart to be sure housecleaning has not introduced other problems. I cannot overstress the seductions film practices upon its makers. You will certainly find more illogicalities and anomalies by repeating the process, even though it feels utterly unnecessary. Over a period of years, a lot of what emerges in this formal process will become second nature to you and will occur in the earlier stages of the cut. Even so, filmmakers of long standing invariably profit from subjecting their work to this formal scrutiny.

A FIRST SHOWING

Preparing a flow chart has an additional benefit. Having defined what every brick in your movie's edifice is supposed to accomplish, you are excellently prepared to test your intentions during a trial showing to a small audience. This audience should be half a dozen or so people whose tastes and interests you respect. The less they know of your aims, the better. You should, however, warn your audience that this is a work in progress and still technically raw. You may want to itemize the kinds of things that are missing, such as music, sound effects, and titles. Incidentally it is a good idea to cut in some sort of working title as this helps to focus the film's purpose or identity for the audience.

When you show the film, it is important to be able to control the sound levels without having to stand with one hand on the television monitor volume control. Even experienced film people can drastically misjudge a film whose sound elements are made inaudible or overbearing through level inequities. One way to overcome this is to feed the two tracks of the VCR into stereo equipment and use the balance and volume controls to unobtrusively adjust levels. Unless you are at some pains to present your film, you may get misleading negative responses.

SURVIVING YOUR CRITICS AND MAKING USE OF WHAT THEY SAY

After the viewing, you should ask for impressions of the film as a whole. If you do not focus and direct your viewers' attention, you may find yourself involved in a discussion quite peripheral to your needs. Asking for critical feedback needs to be handled carefully, or it can be rather a pointless exercise. On the one hand, you must listen very carefully, and on the other, you must retain your fundamental bearings toward the piece as a whole. It is very important to speak as little as possible. Avoid the temptation to explain the film and to explain what you intended. At this stage, explanations are in any case irrelevant and only serve to confuse and compromise the audience's own perceptions. After all, a film must eventually stand alone without explanations by its authors so you must concentrate your energy in listening to what your critics are really saying.

For many, listening to reactions and criticism of their work is an emotionally draining experience. It is quite usual to feel threatened, slighted, misunderstood, and unappreciated and to come out with a raging headache. It takes all the self-discipline one can muster to sit immobile and take notes.

Here is a suggested order of inquiry that moves from the large issues toward the component parts:

- What are the film's themes?
- What are the major issues in the film?
- Did the film feel the right length or was it too long?
- Which parts were unclear or puzzling?
- Which parts felt slow?
- Which parts were moving or otherwise successful?
- What did they feel about (name of character)?
- What did they end up knowing about (situation or issue)?

At this point, you are beginning to test what you wrote in the "what it contributes" description against each sequence. Depending on your trial audience's patience, you may only be able to test the dubious areas, or you may be able to get feedback on most of your film's parts and intentions.

Write anything and everything down, or make an audio recording to allow notes later. Subsequently you will be able to review the film and look at it with the eyes, say, of the three people in the audience who missed that the boy was the woman's son. You see that it is implied twice, but you find a way to put in an extra line where he calls her "Mom." Problem solved.

Dealing with criticism really means absorbing a lot of points of view and, when the dust settles, looking to see how these varying impressions are possible. You do, of course, have to take into account the number of people reporting a certain difficulty before rushing to fix anything. Where comments from different audience members cancel each other out, there may be no action called for. So far as you can, you must take into account the biases and subjectivity of some of your critics.

An irritation one must often suffer (especially in film schools) is the person who insists on talking about the film he would have made instead of the film you have just shown. This is a prime reason to diplomatically redirect the discussion.

On the whole, you should not make changes without careful reflection. Remember that when people are asked to give criticism, they tend to look for possible changes if only to make some sort of contributory mark on your work. *You will never under any circumstances be able to please everyone.* Nor should you be tempted to try.

Most important of all, never let your central intentions be lost. You should never revise these unless you find there are strong and positive reasons to do so. You should meanwhile *only act upon suggestions that support and further your central intentions.*

This is a dangerous time for the filmmaker or indeed for any artist. It is fatally easy to let go of your work's underlying identity and to lose your own sense of direction. So it is more important to keep listening than to act. Do not be tempted by strong emotions to carve into your film precipitously.

It is quite normal by now to feel that you have failed, that you have a piece of junk on your hands, that all is vanity. If this is so, take heart. You might have felt this during shooting, which is worse. And anyway, things are never so awful as one feels they are after showing a work print. For one thing, audiences are disproportionately alienated by a wrong sound balance here, a missed sound dissolve there, a shot or two that needs clipping, or a sequence that belongs earlier. These imbalances and rhythmic ineptitudes massively downgrade a film's impact to the nonspecialist viewer. The polish you will yet apply has a great influence over the film's reception.

THE USES OF PROCRASTINATION

Whether you are pleased or depressed about your film, it is always a good thing to stop working on it for a while and do something else. If this anxiety is new to you, take comfort: You are deep in the throes of the artist's experience. It is analogous to a long and painful labor before giving birth. When you pick up the film again after a lapse of days or months, its problems and their solutions will no longer seem complicated and overwhelming.

TRY, TRY AGAIN

With a film of some substance that requires a long evolution in the editing room, you should expect to try the film out on several new trial audiences. You may want to show the last cut to the original trial audience to see changes in what they report. While this is not reliable, you can sometimes get a real sense of the progress you have made during editing.

As a director with a lot of editing background, I am convinced that a film is really created in the editing process. Here magic and miracles are wrought out of the footage, yet even film crew members seldom know much about what really happens in the cutting room. It is a process unknown and unguessed by those who have not lived through it.

THE FINE CUT

The result of the evolutionary process described above is called the fine cut. With typical caution it is called fine rather final, for there may still be minor changes and accommodations. Some of these arise out of laying sound tracks in preparation to producing a master mixed track.

THE SOUND MIX

The culmination of the editing process, after the film has reached a fine cut, is to prepare and mix the component sound tracks. A whole book could be written on this subject alone, so what follows is no more than a list of essentials along with some useful tips.

At the point where you have finalized your film's content and have fitted music, recorded and laid narration, and laid sound effects and atmospheres, you are ready to make a mix-down of the tracks into one master track.

The mix procedure determines:

a. Comparative sound levels—say between a foreground track of an interview voice and a noisy factory scene it is played over.

b. Consistent quality—for example, two tracks from two angles on the same speaker, needing equalization ("tone control" adjustments) and level adjustment to make them sound similar.

c. Level changes—fade up, fade down, sound dissolves, level adjustments to accommodate new track elements such as narration, music, or dialogue.

d. Equalization—the filtering and profiling of individual tracks either to match others or to create maximum intelligibility, listener appeal, or "ear comfort." A voice track with a rumbly traffic background can, for instance, be much improved by "rolling off" the lower frequencies, leaving the voice range intact.

e. Sound processing—adding echo, reverberation, "telephone effect," and so forth.

f. Dynamic range—a compressor squeezes the broad dynamic range of a movie into the narrow range favored in television transmission; a limiter leaves the main range alone but limits peaks to a preset level.

g. Perspective—to some degree, equalization and level manipulation can mimic perspective changes, thus helping create a sense of space and dimensionality through sound.

h. Stereo channel distribution—if a stereo track is being compiled, different elements go to each side in order to create a sense of horizontal "spread."

i. Noise reduction—Dolby and other noise reduction systems help minimize the system hiss that would intrude on quiet passages.

The audience's intense, almost dream-like concentration on a good film is easily sabotaged by clumsy changes in sound level, quality, or content. Except for moments of legitimate shock, a film's sound should lead the audience's attention seamlessly from one plane of attention to the next.

The only way to make this technically possible is to alternate sound sections, checkerboard fashion, between two tracks as diagrammed in Figure 14-3. Without track splitting in film or video, you cannot make a sound segue (sound dissolve) or effectively match sound from one track to another. The reason is simple: changes at the mixerboard take some time and cannot be done instantaneously at a juncture between two tracks. An example in Figure 17–2 is the cut in Paul's dialogue scene between long and close shots at 1:36 (one minute, 36 seconds). The 15-second silence beforehand in track 1 allows the sound mixer to reset that channel's level and equalization before the next track section rides in. Each channel's blank sections are really adjustment periods and particularly vital to dialogue sequences as is explained below.

PREPARATION

Track elements are presented here in the conventional hierarchy of importance, though the order may vary; Music, for instance, might be faded up to the foreground and dialogue be played almost inaudibly low. When cutting and laying sound tracks, be careful not to cut off the barely audible tail of a decaying sound or to clip the attack. Sound cutting should be done at high volume so you hear everything that is there.

Laying film tracks is easier than it is in video because it follows a logic visible to the eye. Each track section is of brown magnetic stock, interspersed with different-colored spacing. Fine control is quick and easy since one can cut to the frame (1/24 second), and one's conception is aided by physically handling the

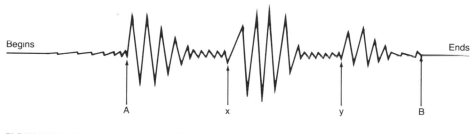

FIGURE 17–1

Diagram of sound attack and decay for a recording of footsteps: Points A and B are ideal in- and out-cutting points. Points X and Y are alternative in-points.

individual track one is cutting. Because videotape editing is accomplished by a transfer process, it is more of a remote-control situation, but the working principles remain identical.

Narration: The laying of narration has been described in detail previously. If narration is laid to a silent sequence, you will need to build up the gaps between narration sections with presence so the track remains live.

Dialogue tracks and the problem of inconsistencies: Dialogue tracks should have been checkerboarded during the editing stage (see chapter 14, "Equipment" section, pages 214–218). Each succeeding section is alternated between the recorder's two available tracks to allow prior mixing-board adjustments during the sections of silent or blank track. This allows the mixer to balance:

1. *Inconsistent backgrounds:* The ragged, truncated background is the badge of the poorly edited film, drawing attention away from the content to inadequacies of technique. Frequently when you cut between two speakers in the same location, the background to each is different in either level or quality because the mike was angled differently. Because one angle was recorded subsequent to the other, there may be a different amount of background activity. One shoots presence tracks on location so one can add to and *augment the lighter track to match its heavier counterpart.*

2. *Inconsistent voice qualities:* Varying location acoustical environments, different mikes, and different mike working distances all play havoc with the consistency of location voice recordings. Intelligent "doctoring" with sound filtering (equalization) at the mix stage can massively decrease the sense of strain and irritation arising from one's ear having to make constant adjustment to unmotivated and therefore irrational changes.

Music: Relatively easy to lay in, but remember to cut in just before the sound attack so one doesn't hear telltale studio atmosphere prior to the first chords (Figure 17–1). The arrow represents the ideal cut-in point; to the left of it is represented the studio presence or record surface hiss. Following the arrow A are three attacks in succession leading to a decay to silence at arrow B. All this is much as it would appear on an oscilloscope. Very much the same profile is forthcoming for many sound effects—footsteps, for instance—and the same editing strategy is used.

Spot sound effects: These are the effects that sync to something on-screen, such as a door closing, a coin placed on a table, or a phone ringing. They need to be carefully synchronized. Never assume that a sound effect listed in a library will sound the way you imagine or that it will work with your particular sequence until you have tried it. Sound effects, especially library or disc effects, often bring problematical backgrounds of their own. Again you can minimize this by cutting into the effect immediately before a sound's attack (Figure 17–1, arrow A) and immediately after its decay (arrow B), thus minimizing the unwanted background's intrusiveness. You can mask the existence of unwanted sound changes with another sound (position the unavoidable atmosphere change behind a doorbell ringing, for example). Sometimes you can get an alien background in and out unobtrusively by fading it in and out rather than letting it ride in as a cut. Bear in mind that *the ear registers a sound cut-in or a cut-out much more acutely than it does a graduated change.*

Atmospheres and background sound: One lays in an atmosphere either to create a mood (bird song over a morning shot of a wood, wood-saw effects over the exterior of a carpenter's shop) and to mask inconsistencies with something relevant but distracting. Always obey screen logic by laying atmospheres to cover the entire sequence, not just a part of it. If you want to create a sound dissolve, remember to lay the requisite amount for an overlap.

MIX CHART

Once tracks are laid to picture, you will need to make a mix chart. In Figure 17–2 you can see how each column represents an individual track and how track starts and finishes are marked with timings (or footages for a film mix). By reading down the chart you can see how individual tracks are playing against each other like instruments in a music score. A straight-line start or finish represents a cut (as at 1:21 and 1:41), while a chevron represents either a fade-in (track 3 at 2:04) or a fade-out (tracks 2 and 4 at 2:09). Here the timing refers to the beginning of a fade-in, or the end of a fade-out. A sound dissolve (as is happening between 2:04 and 2:09) is where one track fades in while another is fading out.

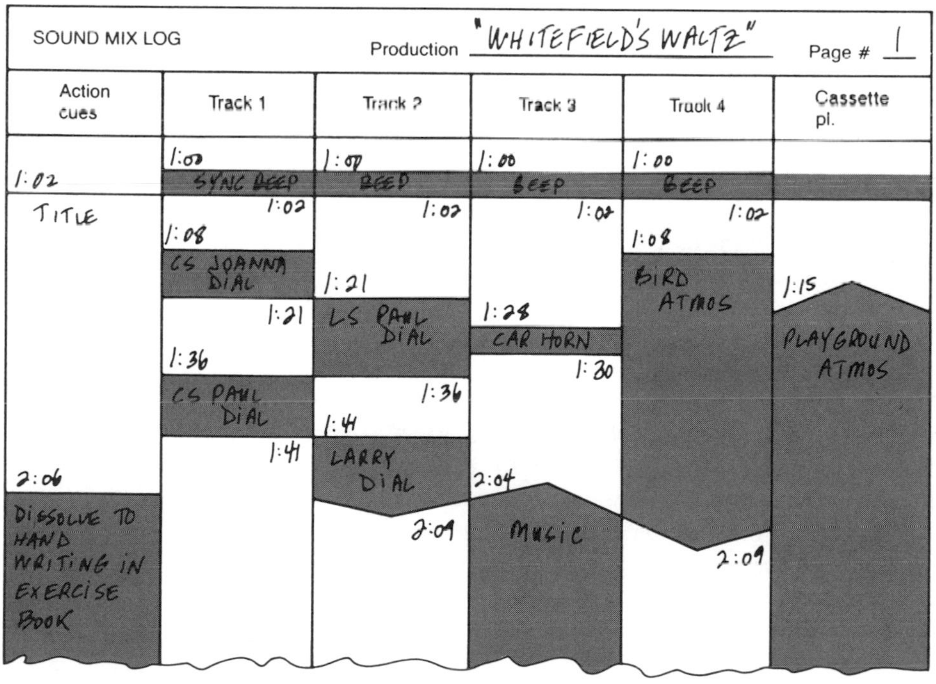

FIGURE 17–2

Part of a typical sound-mix chart.

Note that vertical space on the chart is seldom a linear representation of time since you might have seven minutes of talk with a very simple chart, then half a minute of industrial machinery montage with a profusion of individual tracks for each machine. To avoid either unwieldy or unduly crowded mix charts, allow no more vertical space than is necessary for clarity to the eye.

A blank sound-mix chart for you to photocopy and use appears among the forms in Appendix B.

SOUND-MIX STRATEGY

Premixing: One reel of a feature film may mix down from 40 or more tracks. Since one to four mixers work a board, it requires a sequence of premixes. The same is even true for the humble documentary, with its four- to eight-track mix, especially if the medium is videotape, where only two tracks at a time can be played off tape. It is vital you remember to *premix in an order that keeps control over the most important elements to the last.* If you were to premix dialogue and effects right away, a subsequent addition of more effects or music would uncontrollably augment and "thicken" the competition to the dialogue. Since the intelligibility of a dialogue film depends on dialogue being heard, you must retain control over dialogue-to-background level through the very last stage of mixing.

Though dialogue is not invariably the primary element, the order of premixes for video (two-track capability) might be:

1. Make dialogue premix from sync dialogue tracks.
2. Make FX premix of sound effects (abbreviated FX) and atmospheres.
3. Premix dialogue premix and music.
4. Amalgamate premixes 2 and 3, so you have dialogue, FX, and music.
5. Make final mix, narration (if there is one) with premix 4.

It is very important to remember that with nondigital recording each generation of sound transfer introduces an additional level of noise, or system hiss, most audible in quiet tracks such as a slow-speaking voice in a silent room or a very spare music track. The order of premixes may well be influenced by which tracks must be protected from repeated retransferring.

Using a wild (non-sync) source: To decrease premixing, it is not unusual to feed in non-sync atmospheres from a cassette player or other high-quality sound source (see Figure 14–3 in Chapter 14). The disadvantage is that sound must be faded in and out since frame-accurate cut-ins or cut-outs are impossible.

Rehearse, then record: Mixing is best accomplished through familiarizing oneself with the problems of a short section at a time and thus building sequence by sequence from convenient stopping points. Check your work as you go, and at the end, *check the whole mix without stopping.*

Tailoring: Many tracks played as laid will enter and exit abruptly, giving an unpleasingly ragged impression to the listener's ear. This badly affects how people unconsciously respond to your subject matter, so it is important to achieve a seamless effect whenever you are not deliberately disrupting attention. The trouble comes when you cut from a quiet to a noisy track or vice versa, and this can be greatly minimized by making a very quick fade-up or fade-down of the noisy track to meet the quiet track on its own terms. The effect on-screen is still of a cut, but one that no longer assaults the ear (Figure 17–3).

Comparative levels: err on the side of caution: It is common for mixing facilities to use expensive high-fidelity speakers. The results are misleading, because most television receivers have a miserably small, cheap speaker. Not only does the consumer lose frequency and dynamic ranges, he loses the separation between loud and soft. This means that foregrounds previously separate become swamped by backgrounds. If you are mixing a narration section with traffic background for a street scene, err on the conservative side and make a deliberately high separation by keeping the traffic lower than maximum. Many mix suites keep a "Granny's TV" speaker on hand to give the customer an idea of what the home viewer will actually hear.

Film mixes: The film medium, 16mm or 35 mm, is sprocketed so tracks or a premix are easily synced up to a leader start mark on the picture reel. The final mix will be transferred by a film laboratory onto an optical (photographic) track and photographically combined with the picture to produce a composite projection print. Oftentimes television will transmit "double system"; that is, picture and the magnetic mix will be loaded on separate but interlocked machines, and sound will be transmitted from the high-quality magnetic original instead of from the much-lower-quality photographic track.

Video mixes: Provided there are unbroken video control tracks, it is possible to transfer in absolute sync (using a sync start mark) from one tape to another (Figure 17–4). In practice this means that video mixing is done using copies

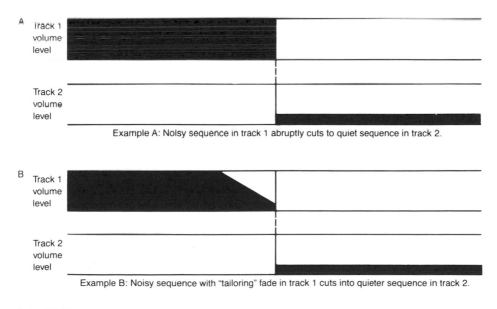

Example A: Noisy sequence in track 1 abruptly cuts to quiet sequence in track 2.

Example B: Noisy sequence with "tailoring" fade in track 1 cuts into quieter sequence in track 2.

FIGURE 17–3

A sound cut can (A) be a jarring transition or (B) tailored during the sound mix to be smooth.

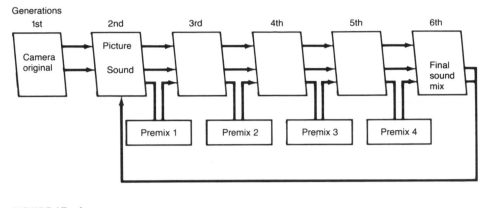

FIGURE 17–4

You can place a later-generation sound track (for instance, a sixth generation) against an earlier generation picture recording by wiping an audio track from the earlier generation video (combined picture and sound) tape, and replacing it with the sixth-generation sound mix, starting from a common sync point.

made from the master edit, and subsequently the master mix is dubbed back on to the master cut, which is only a second-generation picture. CAUTION: Since this means erasing original tracks to make way for the mix, always first experiment with copies to verify the procedure.

Keep a safety copy of the master mix: Because a mix is a long, painstaking procedure, it is professional practice to immediately make a safety or backup copy. This is stored safely away from the original "just in case," and copies are made from the master mix.

TITLES AND ACKNOWLEDGMENTS

Although every film has a working title, it is normal for the actual title to be the last thing decided. Often this is hard because it must epitomize the film's concerns and intentions. You should bear in mind that your film's title will be the only "advertising copy" most of your audience ever sees so the title must be informative and stimulate interest. Television listings and festival programs rarely have space to describe their offerings so the title is your particular label in the tray of hors d'oeuvres.

A sure sign of amateurism is a film accompanied by a grateful welter of credit titles. One four-minute film I saw recently had titles almost as long as the film itself, an indulgence greeted by the audience with sardonic clapping. The rule with titles is to keep them few in words and short in duration. The same name should not crop up egocentrically in different capacities, and acknowledgments should be brief. There are plenty of examples available on television as models, but here is a set of titles ready for an imaginary film:

Title card #	Title wording	Seconds on screen
1	(front title) HOW ARE YOU GOING TO KEEP THEM DOWN ON THE FARM?	7
	(end titles)	
2	Narration—Robin Ragg	4
3	Music—Graham Collier	4
4	Research—Maggie Hall	
	Camera—Tony Cummings	
	Sound—Rosalyn Mann	
	Sound mix—Daniel Richelet	
	Editing—Jacqueline Guinebault	13
5	Written and directed by Avril Lemoine	5
6	Thanks to: National Endowment for the Arts Illinois Humanities Council Agriculture Research Dept., Smith University, Illinois Mr. and Mrs. Mike Roy Joe and Lin Locker	10
7	Copyright Avril Lemoine © (1991)	3

Timings are assessed by reading the contents of each card (which represents one screen of titling) *one-and-a-half times out loud*. When you shoot the titles, be sure to shoot at least three times as much as you need. This will allow not only for a title to be extended if needed, but also for the all-important editing preroll.

White titles on a moving background are nice, but unless you have access to video superimposition technology, they are out of your reach, as will be dissolves and wipes. Plain titles on a colored background or with a still photo as a background, can be tasteful and effective.

Many favors are granted during filming merely for an acknowledgment in the titles, and of course promises must be carried out. Funding often comes with a contractual obligation to acknowledge the fund in a prescribed wording so this and all such obligations should be carefully checked before titles are specified.

Spelling should be carefully checked by at least two literate people, and the spelling of people's names should receive special care.

Titling work has to be done meticulously as even small inequities of proportion and straightness show up badly and make titles look amateurish. In general, a wide contrast ratio between lettering brightness and background brightness is best avoided in video, as the circuits that adjust for exposure tend to go haywire and give you out-of-focus lettering. Even using film, white titles are easy to overexpose, and this leads to a similar loss of definition.

Never assume that titles will be "all right on the night." They are often tricky to get right, especially if you are at all ambitious and want fancy effects. Titles, like troubles, are sent to try us, so give yourself plenty of time in case you must reshoot.

LOW-COST TITLING

If you are meticulous, quite professional-looking titles can be made up using press-stick lettering available from art shops and stationers. There is a bewildering choice of typefaces, and you should choose one that reflects the nature of your film. Keep in mind that spindly or ornate lettering may be illegible on the television screen. Lettering size can be adjusted by using either a loose or a tight framing, always assuming your layout permits the latter within the camera's frame, and assuming that your lens will focus close enough.

You can create black letters over a still frame by projecting a 35mm slide into a rear projection screen and placing the lettering on a clear plastic sheet (called an acetate sheet) over the screen. With rear projection (the slide is reversed so it reads the right way from the front) you must keep both slide projector and videotape camera on the same axis, so the lettering does not suffer from "keystone" distortion (Figure 17–5). You will, however, see the "grain" of the screen with any rear-projection work.

White lettering on a graphic background (a still photo or dark-toned painting, for example) can be achieved by using white lettering mounted on an acetate sheet, which can be laid over a choice of still background. The whole "sandwich" can be shot from the front. You can change white titles on a black ground to any color you want, simply by putting the appropriate filter gel in front of the camera lens or altering the camera's color balance.

If your camera has inverse video, you can change black letters on white to white letters on black at the flick of a switch.

A character generator is a computerized device that electronically produces lettering and symbols on the screen. It is useful for producing rapid, nicely spaced, centered and legible titling, but the low-priced ones are likely to have an "electronic" typeface, which is inappropriate for most films.

GETTING TITLES MADE COMMERCIALLY

Larger cities have companies that specialize in making up and shooting titles, and it may be a wise investment to give a good film professional-looking titles. Since the bulk of "optical house" work is for commercials, you should check prices carefully in advance, as titling can be vastly expensive. Be sure to meet with the person who will be making them up. One thing to check is what further charges you face for reshooting should you be dissatisfied.

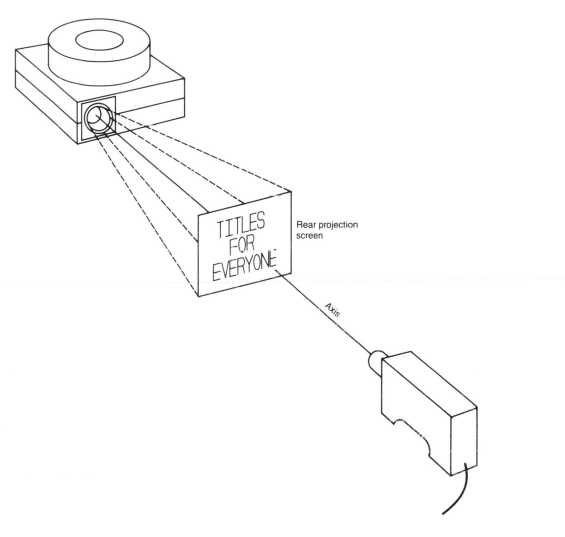

FIGURE 17–5

Rear projection only works if camera and slide projector are on the same axis.

POSTPRODUCTION SUMMARY

Editing

Think of it as mimicking the consciousness of an involved observer.

Film re-creates aspects of consciousness to help the audience share a character's (or storyteller's) shifting consciousness.

Remember that interesting discrepancies of information drive the audience into an active, problem-solving relationship with the film instead of the usual passive one.

Every call to imagination or judgment is an acknowledgment of equality with the audience and an invitation to participate in discovery.

The film's structure and authorial voice are developed during editing.

The editor comes to the film innocent of the director's hopes and experiences, seeing only what is in the material.

The editor needs to be patient, organized, experimental, and diplomatic.

A first-rate documentary editor is really a second director and should be willing to make subjective judgments.

The director is best advised to stay away from the cutting room while each new cut is evolving to preserve some objectivity.

Viewing rushes:

Note all ideas and transient impressions; they will be an important resource later.

Note moods and feelings evoked by scenes or individuals.

Avoid taking your attention away from the screen.

Listen to any discussion—you may learn something useful.

Set aside all former intentions; nothing outside the rushes is relevant to the film you can make.

Transcripts:

Remember that what's written takes no account of voice inflections so you cannot trust that anything written will stand alone on screen.

You can make a summary of topics and their location as an index to finding important material quickly.

Not making transcripts is "buy now, pay later."

Logging:

Time spent making a consistent, intelligent log is time liberated for creativity later.

Do not change systems in midfilm.

Selecting sections:

Make a photocopy of transcripts to use as follows:

During a viewing, draw a line against any good transcribed section.

Later bracket in- and out-points.

Put ID (cassette, character/scene, section number) in margin.

Also put a brief functional description in margin.

Preparing for a paper cut:

Make a photocopy of above marked transcript sheets to use as follows:

Cut selected transcript sections into slips.

Put name and origin of each action sequence on the slip of paper.

Structural considerations:

How is your film to be structured in time?

What basic, factual information must be passed over to the audience in order to make the unfolding film intelligible?

What other organizing features does it have that help you group material together?

How will your film reveal its purpose (the "contract" must not be long delayed)?

Are there dramatic advantages to be gained from disrupting the subject's natural advance in time?

Crosscutting between two stories allows time to be telescoped or stretched.

Crosscutting allows juxtaposition and aids comparison and irony.

How can you show development (which is so important)?

Above all, try to tell a good story.

Assembling the paper edit:

Do your best, but remember it is only marks on paper representing film.

Do not exclude anything workable if you are in doubt—leave the choice between alternatives for the cutting stage.

Make a simple blueprint and allow complexities to develop out of film, not within your head first.

First assembly:

Put a loose version of whole film together working on any detail. You cannot deal with embellishment until you first get a handle on the film's entire identity and purpose.

The order and juxtaposition of material has very potent consequences.

You are presenting pieces of evidence, one at a time, to build a case in the audience's mind.

Let your film speak to you and tell you what it wants you to do.

Rough cut:

Deal only with the film's major needs at every cutting stage (there will be many stages).

An early decision about maximum length can help you face the inevitability of jettisoning certain material.

It is easier to shorten a film than it is to pump substance back into one prematurely tightened.

Always try to see each new cut as an audience sees it, without prior conceptions and without any special knowledge.

If a cut is different from what you expected, see it again before commenting.

Where is the film dramatically unbalanced?

Does a graph of "dramatic temperature" make sense?

Where does it drag?

What remains in your memory, and what has left no trace?

Have you made the most of revealing contrasts?

Narration:

Try to make your film tell its own story without narration.

If narration is unavoidable, decide whether scripted or improvised narration will be best.

Narration, like all film language, must be assimilated by the audience the first time or not at all.

Narration must be in the simple, direct language of speech, not that of written language.

Never describe what can be seen in the shot. Add to the image with words, do not duplicate.

Be ready to invert syntax to fit film.

Leave spaces for featured sound effects.

The first (or "operative") word to fall on each new shot has a major consequence for the shot's interpretation.

Altering juxtaposition of words and shots can imply different meanings.

Use narration primarily to relay facts.

Avoid predisposing your audience to any particular attitude; they may resent it.

The intelligent narration helps audience members make their own value judgments.

Narration can accelerate your film's exposition and make brief, agile links between sequences.

Any narration, especially that badly written or poorly delivered, is an intrusion into the audience's relationship with the subject.

Narration can focus your audience on aspects of the material you want them to notice.

The audience looks upon the narrator as the voice of the film.

The narrator's voice quality and delivery must act as a surrogate for your own attitude to the subject.

Try a scratch narration before recording to be sure that it works and that you have covered all your bases.

Audition very cautiously, giving directions to see if narrator can respond.

Show the chosen narrator the film, and explain what characteristics must be embodied in the narration.

Give brief, positive, qualitative directions to a narrator.

The narrator studies the script, the director watches the picture while recording and listens through a speaker or headphones to assure that delivery is appropriate and correct tempo is.

Remember to record two minutes of studio presence track.

Music:

Music should not inject false emotion.

Choice of music should give access to the interior of character or subject.

Music can signal the emotional level at which audience should investigate what is being shown.

You cannot know if music choice really works until you try it against the picture.

Better to use no music than bad music.

Fine cut:

Use overlap cuts to smooth transitions and create interesting disjunctions between what is seen and what is heard.

Know the preset lengths for likely distribution so you can choose one.

Aim to say a lot through a little.

Good short films are welcome everywhere.

Most people are prejudiced against the long, well-meaning film unless it has a very high thematic density to repay the investment of patience it demands.

Evoking a trial audience response:

Remember, you can't please everyone!

Use sample audiences and the questions suggested in the text to make sure your film is functioning as intended.

In a trial showing, exert maximum control over sound—it affects audience responses disproportionately.

Direct audience attention to issues over which you need information, but ask open, nondirective questions, listening carefully for what people are really saying.

Is your audience getting the main underlying meanings? If not, why not?

Hang on to your fundamental intentions; do not let go of them without a very good reason.

Diagnostic methods:

Make a block diagram of the movie to spot invisible anomalies (see text for common ones).

After curing the latest round of difficulties, make another block diagram to see if the housecleaning was thorough.

Put the film aside for a week or two and see it again before deciding if the fine cut is final.

Track laying and mix chart:

Alternate ("checkerboard") dialogue tracks to facilitate equalization and level adjustments.

Use correct presence track to fill holes in dialogue, narration, or scene.

When presences are mismatched, lay in extra to bring the quieter up to balance louder.

Plan featured sound effects to go in dialogue gaps (or vice versa).

Sync spot FX carefully.

Mask unavoidable inconsistencies with a logical atmosphere track.

Cut into music or FX just before attack and just after complete decay to avoid hearing background.

Sound dissolves require an overlap of the tracks affected.

Make a fair-copy mix chart that the eye can easily follow.

Sound mix:

Premix so you retain control over the most important elements until last.

Rehearse each section before recording.

Soften ragged sound cuts by tailoring the louder to the quieter in a rapid fade up or fade down.

When mixing foreground speech with background (music, FX, atmos, and so on), err on the side of caution and separate foreground well from background.

Make a safety copy of the mix and store it somewhere separate and safe.

Titles and acknowledgments:

Use a working title until the film is fully edited.

Double-check spelling and contractual obligations for special wording.

Keep titles short and sweet.

Shoot plenty of title, just in case.

Hold each title card on-screen for one-and-a-half times as long as it takes to read it out loud.

Never assume titles can be done quickly and accurately.

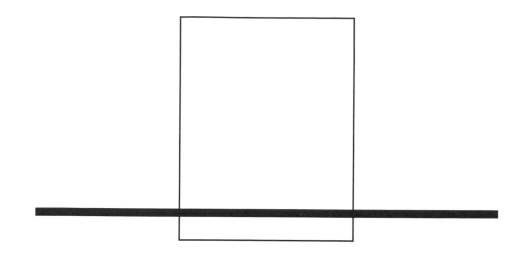

P·A·R·T I·X

PROJECTS: DEVELOPING SKILLS AS AN EDITOR

I·N·T·R·O·D·U·C·T·I·O·N

Of course, success in editing depends on the quality of the materials you start with. These editing projects are designed for use with the camera and authorship projects earlier in the book, but the italicized criteria can be applied as a rating system to much that the documentary editor is likely to handle, with the exception of compilation films that use many still photographs.

P·R·O·J·E·C·T 1·1

INTERVIEW, VARYING IMAGE SIZES

Appropriate materials for this project can come from Project 5 (section entitled "Tripod Interview: One Subject), or 6. First restructure the interview using transcripts and paper edit method if the interview is extensive. Like any story long or short, you must find a storytelling structure that has a beginning, a middle, and an end. Try to cut out the interviewer's voice so the interview stands alone. When editing, play sound loud so you don't inadvertently cut into the middle of any low breathing sounds—they are part of normal speech and usually should be left intact. Be careful to maintain the natural rhythms of the speaker's voice, and watch out that rising or falling inflections sound natural at the cutting points. Sometimes the least noticeable cut is one made after a sentence has begun. Using the null points between sentences, though logical, is often clumsy because it draws attention to technique instead of burying it in a flow of words and movement. Be careful that the speaker's head and body positions match as you cut from one image size to another. When this is a problem, remember that the more radical the change of image size, the less the audience will notice.

> *Interview is well structured*
> *Head and body positions are well matched at cutting points*
> *Speaker's rhythms sound natural*
> *Sound track is cleanly cut, no clipped breaths or sounds*
> *Sound levels are consistent throughout*
> *High overall impact as a piece of editing*

P·R·O·J·E·C·T 1·2

CONVERSATION, TWO OR MORE PERSONS

Materials for this assignment could come from Project 5 (section entitled "Tripod Coverage of Three-Person Conversation"), 7, or 8. All the comments in Project 11 concerning rhythms and matching also apply, but depending upon coverage and cutaways supplied, you can develop the reactions and inner life of the participant who is being acted on rather than the one who is speaking. You can also use motivated cut-ins or cutaways to give us more feeling of what the characters are seeing or thinking. (A cut-in is a magnified detail in an existing frame, while a cutaway is something beyond that frame.)

Conversation is well structured

Head and body positions are well matched at cutting points

Speakers' rhythms sound natural

Listeners' reactions are indicated through cutaways

Additional detail supplied in motivated cut-ins

Visual rhythm feels balanced throughout

Sound track is cleanly cut, no clipped breaths or sounds

Sound levels are consistent throughout

High overall impact as a piece of editing

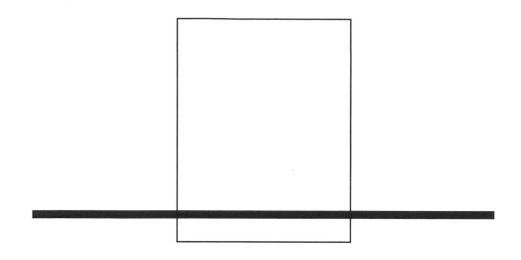

P·R·O·J·E·C·T 1·3

EDITING UNBROKEN COMPLEX TAKE

Materials for this assignment can come from Project 5 (section entitled "Hand-held Coverage of Complex Action"), 8, or 10. Often an editor is faced with an unbroken shot of a lengthy conversation or a process such as changing a car tire or planting a tree and must drastically shorten it. An alert camera operator will have shot reactions, cut-ins, and cutaways that can patch over ugly jump cuts. Even better, that operator will have covered the event from a number of logical angles. The editor can now compress essentials into a fraction of the original running time and has many options for maintaining "transparency"—that is, keeping up the illusion that one is seeing real life rather than an edited film.

But the unaware operator's rushes present difficulties. Starved of sufficient angle changes or cutaways, the hapless editor must use ingenuity or end up with a bumpy cut. The odd jump cut in an otherwise transparent sequence disrupts attention by intruding an inconsistent narrative style, but several bold jump cuts can be a tasteful way of signaling time shifts. If you cannot do dissolves and have no parallel storyline as a cutaway strand, there is another saving resource— sound. You can create the effect of an optical fade-out/fade-in by fading the outgoing scene to silence, then fading up the incoming one from the cut. Likewise if the two scenes have contrasting sound tracks, you can create the illusion of an optical dissolve by overlapping them and making one dissolve (or "segue") into the other. These sound strategies are classically simple and effective.

Solves the problem of compressing real time
Begins and ends appropriately

Each necessary stage of the action is shown or indicated
Those that can be inferred are left out
Each stage is onscreen for an appropriate time
Rhythms of actions and speech look natural
Process/conversation develops comprehensibly
Sequence uses narratively consistent screen language
Uses sound and sound transitions creatively
Uses available angles effectively
Makes cutaways and cut-ins look motivated
Length is appropriate
High overall impact as a piece of editing

P·R·O·J·E·C·T 1·4

COMPLEX EDITING PROJECT

Materials for this assignment might come from Project 5 (section entitled " 'Day-in-the-Life' Montage that Creates a Mood") or 9 or from a film of considerable complexity using a combination of materials and techniques. You would expect to see in such a film:

- Action match cutting
- Montage principles to render a mood, compress action, or create a sense of lyricism
- Cuts making use of movement either by subject or camera
- Intercutting between complementary shots
- Overlap cutting where sound precedes its accompanying picture
- Overlap cutting where sound continues over the next shot
- A sensitivity to inherent verbal, visual, and musical rhythms
- Use of cut-ins or cutaways as legitimate, motivated POV shots
- Development of subtextual hints and information
- Meaningful tension and counterpoint between words and images
- Use of figurative sound or visual devices to create foreshadowing, analogy, irony, metaphor, repetition.
- Music

Some of these points require explanation. Sound overlaps using simple video equipment often require that one transfer the overlap as a separate sound-only pass—either before transferring the sync segment or after it. So make the sync cut at a null point between words or sounds, or you will encounter sound-level difficulties when you add the sound overlap "tail."

Creating tension between words and images usually means looking at the available visuals for their figurative (as opposed to merely illustrative) content. A young man's voice saying it was a pleasure to leave home can take on different meanings: playing the voice over a shot of a cat looking through a window at the street carries different implications to playing it over a saucepan in a sink filling with water then overflowing. There is unlimited poetic force at your fingertips when you start placing ideas against the unexpected image, always providing that the image is organic to the world under scrutiny.

Successful exposition of facts and situations

Successful action match cuts

Uses subject motion to motivate cuts

Cuts make use of camera movement

Uses eyeline shifts or verbal cues to motivate cutaways

Successful overlap cuts, sound precedes its sync picture

Successful overlap cuts, track overhangs into next shot

Feeling for verbal rhythms

Feeling for visual rhythms

Feeling for musical rhythms

Creates factual and emotional perspective of characters

Visuals well used to create mood

Counterpoint and tension between words and images

Dialogue cutting and pacing make sound natural

Original and effective choice of music for mood

Length well judged

Premix sound checkerboarded

Sound mix well balanced and effective

High overall impact as editing

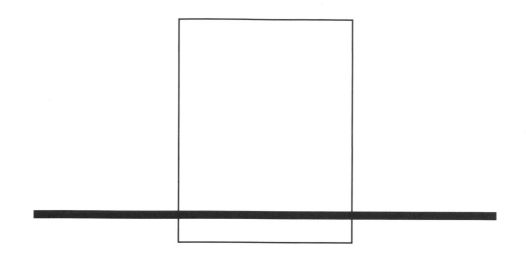

P·A·R·T X

AESTHETICS AND AUTHORSHIP

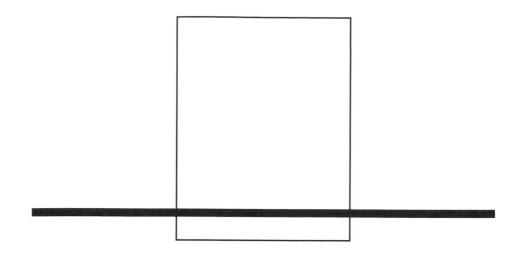

ELEMENTS OF THE DOCUMENTARY

SIZING UP THE INGREDIENTS

Though it seems impossible to come up with formulations into which all documentaries fit, the techniques and construction methods each uses are central to a film's aesthetic contours. It is interesting to realize how few are the ingredients from which all documentaries are made.

PICTURE

- Action footage—people doing things, carrying on their everyday activities, work, play and so on. We should also include shots of landscapes and inanimate things.

- Library footage—can be uncut archive material or material recycled from other films.

- People talking—to each other; the camera's presence is unobtrusive, perhaps it is even hidden.

- People talking—consciously contributing to the camera's portrait of themselves.

- Interviews—One or more people answering formal, structured questions although the questions themselves may be edited out. Interviewer may be on or off camera.

- Reenactments, factually accurate, of situations already past or that cannot be filmed for other valid reasons.

- Still photos, often shot by a camera that moves in, out, or across the still photo to enliven it.

- Documents, titles, headlines, cartoons, or other graphics.

- Blank screen—this causes us to reflect on what we have already seen or to give heightened attention to existing sound.

SOUND

- Voice-over—can be an audio-only interview, or it may be constructed from the sound track of a picture-and-sound interview with occasional segments of sync picture at salient points.

- Narration—can be a narrator, the voice of the author (for example, director Louis Malle in his *Phantom India* series) or commonly the voice of one of the participants.

- Synchronous sound—that is, accompanying sound shot while filming.

- Sound effects—can be spot (sync) sound effects or atmospheres.

- Music

- Silence—the temporary absence of sound can create a powerful change of mood or cause us to look with heightened awareness of what is happening in the picture.

All documents are permutations of some or all of these ingredients, but it is structure and point of view that give the ingredients shape and purpose.

POINT OF VIEW

We tend to think of point of view as an ideological slant, the kind of predictable viewpoint that philosophical or political systems bring to bear on any subject under scrutiny. But here I mean the sense of identity that emerges when we search for the vantage point from which a film's "story" is told. As in a literary work, a documentary's effectiveness and final "voice" are deeply affected by the point of view that is chosen. Most examples are not pure for they resort to varying points of view as need arises. Frequently the uniqueness and force of one viewpoint is best revealed by juxtaposing a countervailing one. Below are some categories and some mostly excellent films that exemplify them. With each, I have indicted possible strengths and weaknesses.

OMNISCIENT

The focus of this type of film moves freely around in time and space to suggest a multifaceted consciousness. Typically steered through a third person narration, it will express a collective rather than a more limited personal vision. Narration can, however, be implied or supplanted by subtitles and documents, and this avoids the imprimatur of a narrator's voice. The central organizing vision may simply be that of the filmmaker who makes no apology or explanation on screen.

For films of unassuming scope, the omniscient point of view often signifies an author's modest wish not to stand between the viewer and the subject. When, however, a subject is as complex and far reaching as war or race relations, it is probably beyond a legitimate, individual controlling point of view, and the omniscient point of view becomes inevitable. This can be troubling for, if patriotism is the last refuge of the scoundrel, omniscience is the last refuge of the propagandist. The unconfirmable nature of what is asserted and the undisclosed credentials of one's interpreters all should recommend caution.

Here are some films that tell their stories from an omniscient position. Joris Ivens' classic, *Rain* (1929), documents the timeless cycles of human behavior before, during, and after a rainstorm in a big city, Amsterdam. It creates a mood of attractive melancholy that evokes the intensity of childhood solitude. Jean Vigo's *A Propos de Nice* (1930) is a satirical montage by the revolutionary Vigo showing a privileged society whose degeneracy he saw as inviting its own overthrow. These are both silent films whose palpably musical atmosphere comes from their strong visual rhythms.

With the benefit of hindsight, we can see that Leni Riefenstahl's *Triumph of the Will* (1937) and *Olympiad* (1938) use objective-seeming language to present an intensely misleading view of Hitler and his Germany. Riefenstahl's masterly use of the documentary cinema, and the fact that she does it without narration, seem to ascribe power and inevitability to her subject. These works stand as a warning: All films seek to persuade, but films that mask their own subjectivity and that gloss over the paradoxes and conflicts of the real world instead of seeking them are attempting to condition more than communicate with their audience. These films also warn us what can lurk under cover of the "art for art's sake" banner.

Pare Lorentz's *The Plow that Broke the Plains* (1936) and *The River* (1937) each depend on a narration that turns the film into a long elegaic ballad, a folkform that underwrites the films' seemingly objective and egoless atmospheres. Their stark imagery (Figure 18–1) and ironic montage set up a haunting vision of a land plundered through ignorance and political opportunism.

Les Maîtres Fou (1957) is a famous and grisly Jean Rouch ethnographic record of a Ghanaian ceremony. Ordinary working men seclude themselves in the bush; go into a state of trance; and, foaming at the mouth, reenact aspects of their colonial masters. The film, which includes the killing and eating of a dog, is narrated from a stance of scientific objectivity that Rouch has since rethought.

Peter Watkins' *The War Game* (1966) appropriates the style of current affairs programs to posit the nuclear bombing of London. With grim impartiality, the film constructs an infernal, incontestable vision of nuclear war in all its slow finality. Passionately propagandistic, it holds us mesmerized by its air of veracity. By not heroizing individuals, it avoids the personalizing found so often in screen treatments of disaster and forces us to put ourselves and loved ones among the doomed.

Alan and Susan Raymond, who shot the deeply controversial *An American Family* PBS series in the early 1970s, went on to make *The Police Tapes* in 1977.

FIGURE 18–1 ————————————————————————————————————

The Plow That Broke the Plains, Pare Lorentz. Stark imagery and ironic montage are used to set up a haunting vision with an omniscient point of view. (Museum of Modern Art.)

Ostensibly the film watches the police doing their impossible work in one of New York's poorest and most violent areas, but soon the material polarizes our emotions and cries out for interpretation. The Raymonds try to balance the sensationalism of their material with the sociological insight of an astonishingly articulate police lieutenant, but one is left with a disturbing impression of an inhumane neutrality behind much of the shooting, as though the film is covertly revelling in its own toughness.

Television history series usually cover a vast amount of historical ground. They do so with the resources of a large corporation, and require an army of workers to produce. From all this, the omniscient point of view emerges as naturally as "we" from royalty. Thames Television's *The World at War* in the 1970s, WGBH's *Vietnam: A Television History* in the 1980s, and even Ken Burns' 1990 *The Civil War* all echo the history-book emphasis on facts. Laudable though this may be, the overwhelming size, impersonality, and apparent finality of such ventures makes one wonder if their real effect is to suffocate historical curiosity rather than awaken it. An openly critical film like Peter Davis' *Hearts and Minds* (1974) leaves one in no doubt that the film's purpose is to argue a position. Davis implies that certain threads in American culture merged inevitably to create the tragically mistaken U.S. involvement in southeast Asia. Because of this, the viewer is on a clearer footing and can engage with the film's propositions rather than submit to a deluge of information.

A CHARACTER WITHIN THE FILM

Here the film is seen through, and perhaps even narrated by, a main character. She may be a major or a minor participant in the events presented or a bystander or a protagonist, recounting or enacting events to form an autobiography.

Limitations of this mode include the inadequacy of using an individual point of view to represent a community or a class of persons. Another is that to locate experience normally social in nature in an individual may make that person seem egocentric or (more damagingly) imply that human destiny is experienced in isolation and is wholly open to individual control.

The seminal work is Robert Flaherty's *Nanook of the North* (1922), which avoids both these pitfalls. It takes as its central figure the Eskimo hunter struggling to survive amid the ultimate in hostile environments. Though silent, a sense of intimacy with Nanook and his family, of sharing their lives, emanates from the screen. As mentioned earlier, many scenes were reenacted for the camera's benefit, yet they seem so true to life and in good faith that one has no sense of artifice. In Flaherty's later work, particularly *Louisiana Story* (1948), the passion in Flaherty's storytelling is replaced by sentimentality and the contrivances in his filmmaking stand out embarrassingly naked.

The Maysles Brothers' *Salesman* (1969) stays at a distance from Paul Brennan's interior life while he tries to match his colleagues in selling bibles to people who do not really want them. Usually an audience is invited to identify with winners, but as the camera begins to single out Paul, one starts to identify with a loser. This compels us to question the nature of the competition, of the poignant human need to "do well" even when the race is so nakedly exploitative. Brennan's lack of introspection and perspective keeps him running, and as we witness his doomed struggles, we see our own fathers and mothers and know how we too can share their fate.

Werner Herzog's *Land of Silence and Darkness* (1971) focuses on the life story of a deaf-blind woman who lay in an institution for 30 years until she was taught the deaf-blind tactile language. She is seen traveling to locate others as isolated and despairing as she once was herself. As the film progresses, her eerie, prophetic simplicity shows us how elemental is the need for human contact, how devastating is its absence or loss. Fini Straubinger, handicapped though she is, becomes transformed under our gaze into a gauche angel personifying the love and nobility latent in the human spirit (Figure 18–2).

Jerry Bruck's *I.F. Stone's Weekly* (1973) is another kind of heroic tale connected with handicap. It tells the story of a feisty journalist who refused to be vanquished either by deafness or McCarthy blacklist makers. Stone published his own dissident newspaper from within Washington, relentlessly drawing attention to the anomolies and lies that tumble forth in a society of free governmental communications. His story, often told by himself, is one of exuberant anarchy, and he emerges as a real-life hero straight out of a Capra movie.

Robert Epstein's *The Times of Harvey Milk* (1984) is an unabashed idealization. Milk was a San Francisco gay activist who the film presents as a murdered folk-hero. Attractively energetic and iconoclastic, his career becomes that

FIGURE 18–2 ————————————————————————

Land of Silence and Darkness, Werner Herzog. This documentary, through its character-within-the-film point of view, shows that for the deaf-blind, contact with the rest of the world is by touch alone. (New Yorker Films.)

of a Christ figure crucified by jealousy and homophobia. The separation of good and bad, and the unwavering build the film makes to its climax, make one wonder uneasily how much the angularities of life have been straightened to fit the needs of drama—how much, in fact, the film recreates Milk in the image of hero.

MULTIPLE CHARACTERS WITHIN THE FILM

Unlike the previous category, this viewpoint is interested less in showing the heroic individual journey than it is in establishing the mechanisms of cause and effect experienced within a group or class of society. Each character usually represents a constituency in the social tapestry, the aim being to build a texture of different and often counterbalancing viewpoints to perhaps show both the social process and its outcome.

Basil Wright and Harry Watt's *Night Mail* (1936), fighting the image of the ordinary person's hardships of the 1930s, shows the teamwork and cameraderie behind the overnight mail journey from London to Scotland and celebrates an obscure group of men's pride in performing their intricately phased operation.

Marcel Ophuls' great study of how collaboration with the Nazi occupiers developed in wartime France, *The Sorrow and the Pity* (1970), necessarily pro-

FIGURE 18–3 ───

Harlan County, USA, Barbara Kopple. Music as part of protest adds to the many facets of the *multiple characters* point of view. (Krypton International Corporation.)

duces its testimony from a wide variety of people. But his *A Sense of Loss* (1972) applies the same type of net less successfully to a subject—the grinding drama of Northern Ireland—about which Ophuls has less knowledge and passion.

Peter Davis' *Hearts and Minds* (1974) is the story of that generation of young Americans who responded to the calls for patriotism and went off to fight in Vietnam. Then, like the soldiers of World War I, they became disillusioned and critical of their country's attitudes and government.

The Maysles Brothers' *Grey Gardens* (1975) deals with the life of a reclusive and eccentric mother and daughter duo living a *Waiting for Godot* existence in a dilapidated Long Island mansion. Without aligning itself with either protagonist, the film gives an alarming insight into the way the isolated improvise their own history and day-to-day reality.

Barbara Kopple's *Harlan County, USA* (1976) covers a strike by impoverished Kentucky coal miners (Figure 18–3). While there are prominent characters, there is no central point of view, for the film is about a grassroots conflict between workers and big business. There is a powerful aura of folktale and folkballad that makes the film live on in one's memory.

Connie Field's *The Life and Times of Rosie the Riveter* (1980) uses a carefully representative quartet of women to tell the stories of women who replaced the menfolk in industrial jobs during World War II. Through humor and a carefully structured argument, the film marshals an effectively feminist protest against their summary replacement when the soldiers came home.

Nick Broomfield's *Chicken Ranch* (1982) takes us into the seedy everyday life of a legal brothel in Nevada. As in *Soldier Girls* (1981), which he made with his cameraperson wife Joan Churchill, there is a gallery of individuals who help to define the main parts of the institution and its customers. Those with whom we become sympathetic are the suffering misfits. Both films uncover material for a strongly critical insight by slipping past those in power, and both subjects warrant the duplicity.

Claude Lanzmann's *Shoah* (1985) tackles the origins of the holocaust in a less obviously structured way. The film exposes us to more than nine hours of testimony presented not as fragments selected in a didactic thrust but as individual sustained encounters. The effect is of seeing raw evidence with all its disquieting implications left fresh and intact, rather than the convergent tidiness of an essay with a conclusive point of view.

Michael Apted's *28 Up* (1986) deals with an evolving sense of self in a cross-section of British children and is primarily interested in examining each individual's view of her- or himself. Apted begins with seven-year-olds and then returns every seven years like some biblical harbinger of judgment until his subjects are in their late twenties, sometimes pressing the very same issues. The questioning is empathetic yet neutral, cool but always incisive, and he manages to challenge even his wariest subjects to a deeper scrutiny of their life's hidden and most significant meanings. Marred only by some glib closing commentary, the film gives a poignant vision of young men and women struggling with their beliefs and their demons, each believing her or his destiny to have been freely chosen, yet each in conflict with some dimly perceived pattern of restraints no less detaining than the spider's web. A *35 Up* is promised.

PERSONAL

Here the point of view is unashamedly and subjectively that of the director, who may narrate the film herself. A director's surrogate may be in front of the camera as a "reporter" or catalyst, or the film may present its views in the form of a cinematic essay.

Paul Rotha's *The Life of Adolf Hitler* (1961) is a compilation film that nevertheless expresses a personally felt sense of threat and outrage. In the same mold is Alain Resnais' *Night and Fog* (1955) which uses a poetic, impassioned, and disciplined narration and a superb score. Through the imaginative use of these as well as compilation footage, Resnais exposes the foundations of the death camps within the psyche of those always ready to carry out orders that brutalize other human beings. This film is harrowing not only for what it shows (which has become relatively well known) but also for its spectral vision of the twentieth century.

Pierre Schoendoerffer's *Anderson Platoon* (1966) is the work of a French army cinematographer returning compulsively to Vietnam where Americans, instead of Frenchmen, are now fighting the unwinnable war. Schoendoerffer's laconic commentary and compassionate eye reveal the moral bankruptcy at the heart of this and most other warfare. It is most evident in the desperate companionship between soldiers and in the starkness of the human desire to hold on to life. This insight, one feels, is very much a product of Schoendoerffer's austere character.

FIGURE 18–4

Louis Malle's *Phantom India* is a good example of the personal point of view. (New Yorker Films.)

Louis Malle's *Phantom India* series (1968) shows Malle's perceptions while traveling through a continent whose values hardly correspond with his own at all (Figure 18–4). The series is like a travelogue except that Malle constantly evaluates what he sees, constantly tries to penetrate the surface of a tapestry of disturbingly alien and yet fascinating cultures.

Peter Watkins' *Munch* (1978) is superficially a cinema biography of the beleaguered artist, but the viewer is likely to feel a growing sense of Watkins' identification with his subject so that the profile has an eerie feeling of kinship amounting to displaced autobiography.

REFLEXIVE

"To be reflexive," says Jay Ruby, "is to structure a product in such a way that the audience assumes that the producer, the process of making, and the product are a coherent whole. Not only is the audience made aware of these relationships, but it is made to realize the necessity of that knowledge."[1] Ruby's main point is that reflexivity, by accidentally or deliberately subverting the pretence that we are watching life rather than a film, acknowledges that all films are "created,

---

[1]Jay Ruby, "The Image Mirrored: Reflexivity and the Documentary Film," in *New Challenges for Documentary,* Alan Rosenthal, ed. (Berkeley: University of California Press, 1988).

structured articulations of the filmmaker and not authentic, truthful, objective records."[2]

For a sophisticated audience, mere acknowledgment is unnecessary, but exposing the ambiguities of documentary exploration itself is quite another matter for it admits that a major question hangs over any documentary—how much of what we see is really the result of the filmmaking process itself? Ethnographic filmmaking is an obvious candidate for such examination, but so is any sphere of inquiry in which the audience is inexpert. Reflexivity permits the filmmaker to open windows on the conditions and paradoxes encountered during production and to share more of the process with the audience.

Separate from distortion issues are fascinating and more abstract questions about the medium's boundaries—what may or may not be ethical? How, when, and why do we suspend our disbelief? What deceptions does the medium practice upon its makers? and so on. This is to treat film as an art medium capable of infinite subtlety rather than to use it simplistically as a vehicle for a "subject."

Dziga Vertov, poet and film editor in 1920s Russia, is credited with the first radical investigation of documentary language. By seeking to show "life as it is," his Kino Eye theory was the precursor of the *cinéma vérité* movement 40 years later. Vertov's *The Man with the Movie Camera* (1929) presents city life as a teeming spectacle of dialectical opposites in which the camera, seemingly independent of human agency, exuberantly embraces the constants and contradictions of human life. The film implies that the inherent dynamic of camera and montage transcend human agency, and though we often see shots of the cameraman at work, he seems less the camera's operator than its servant, diabolically animated like the dancer in *The Red Shoes*. Vertov sought both to show the act of film authorship and yet for ideological reasons to deny it by making film truth seem objectively vested in the apparatus—trying to have his cake and eat it, so to speak.

In Bunuel's *Land Without Bread* (1932), there is a reflexive passage when the film shows a dying child and speaks of the crew examining her throat. Here the filmmakers' humane sympathies draw them temporarily into becoming participants instead of observers. This is an incidental reflexivity.

The ethnographer Jean Rouch's *Chronicle of a Summer* (1961) poses the people of Paris with a fundamental question, "Are you happy?" It evokes some stringent self-examination by both Rouch and his participants. By showing participants their footage, he invited them to amend or go deeper in what they had originally said. The resulting film reveals Rouch's radical curiosity, breadth of vision, and sympathy with the ordinary person's need to find meaning in life.

Michael Rubbo's *Sad Song of Yellow Skin* (1970) is a Canadian filmmaker's search to define Vietnam amid the flux of that country's impossible contradictions. By mostly confining his attention to city street people and the dissident Americans working with them, Rubbo makes us share his own paradoxical impressions of a peasant civilization rent asunder by a wealthy and technocratic occupying savior.

---

[2] Ibid.

Ira Wohl's *Best Boy* (1979) charts the progress the filmmaker makes in weaning his 52-year-old cousin Philly from parents reluctant to let their "boy" try a caring institution, in spite of the imminence of their own deaths. The experiment is a success. Plainly the film crew and the making of the document helped stabilize the family's decision-making by providing emotional continuity and, most importantly, a form of empathic witnessing.

Pierre Sauvage did not discover he was Jewish until he was 18 or that he had been born in the only haven area created by French villagers during the Nazi occupation. His *Weapons of the Spirit* (1986) is a return to Chambon to give thanks and to discover the minds and hearts of a community that had saved so many. A decade in the making, the film seeks to uncover the source of the community's convictions and spiritual toughness.

In *Dark Lullabies* (1986) Abbey Neidik and Irene Lillienheim Angelico, a husband and wife filmmaking team, set out to confront Irene's lifelong lacuna. The child of holocaust survivors who had never openly told her the painful truth, Irene was spurred into journeying from Canada to Israel and on to Germany itself after her father finally gave her an account of his journey to Dachau. The film implies that though the effort must be made, there are some truths too huge and terrible to encompass, especially concerning pain wreaked on our loved ones. The film is told in the first person by a woman on a metaphorical and actual journey of exorcism to Dachau.

Quite different is Michael Moore's murderously funny *Roger and Me* (1989). As the journalist offspring of Flint, Michigan, car workers, Moore uses his background as a springboard. Looking and acting like a factory worker, he lumbers through this, his first film, as an Everyman patiently searching for answers to the obvious questions about General Motors (GM) and the demise of his hometown. Feigning naïveté like a peasant seeking audience with the king, Moore seeks an interview with the elusive Roger Smith, GM's chairman, and eventually gets it. The movie's effectiveness lies in the way it piles irony on irony so that we laugh our way toward sharing Moore's political conclusions. Though not the first witty Marxist, Moore breaks new ground by infusing belly laughs and leftist views into a film genre often reputed to be gray and humorless.

Another funny documentary is Ross McElwee's *Sherman's March* (1986), its humor of a Woody Allen kind. Ostensibly setting out to make a film about General Sherman's destructive march from the South during the Civil War, McElwee demonstrates how to wrench a fresh and unexpected film from the jaws of cliché. Most often heard from behind the camera, but sometimes seen prowling in front of it, McElwee confesses that he has just lost his girlfriend and feels deeply depressed about ever maintaining a love relationship. Paralleling Sherman's destruction, McElwee journeys northward in a self-accusing and serendipitous voyage through a series of encounters with family, women friends, and marriageable southern women. The film becomes the vehicle for a modest, self-parodying man's relationship with others but is also a mask behind which he can hide. Through his camera he sees himself as he is seen by the women in his life. This film-as-hall-of-mirrors is both a delight, and in its own gentle, self-mocking way, endlessly surprising.

TIME, DEVELOPMENT, AND STRUCTURE

There are, of course, many possible elements that influence the structure of a film, but the handling of time must always be important. Documentaries often have trouble giving an adequate sense of development, so the ability to abridge time or to make comparisons between past and present is a vital part of demonstrating that some kind of change is taking place. In one BBC series, we tried in the planning stage to preempt this problem by building change and development into the series formula itself. Called "Breakaway," it concentrated upon individuals making a major change in their lives, and thus we set out to forestall making the frustrating and familiar film in which *nothing really happens.*

What follows are some common documentary structure types, each of which sets up a different expectation for the handling of time. The following categories and examples from among the classics are personal choices of mine and do not, as I warned earlier, represent any rigorous or complete classification system. Some of these films clearly belong in more than one grouping, and the list is mainly presented to demonstrate ways of looking at the relationship between content, structure, and form. One can easily add categories to this list; for instance, there is the *biographical film* (Peter Watkins' *Munch* [1978]; Ken Russell's many short films made in the 1960s for the BBC, notably *Elgar, Debussy,* and *Rousseau;* and recently the Kartemquin collective's *Golub* [1990] by Gordon Quinn and Jerry Blumenthal) and the *thesis film,* which assembles evidence to argue a case (all the socially conscious British documentaries of the 1930s; Julia Reichert and Jim Klein's *Union Maids* [1976] and *Seeing Red* [1983]). There is the *catalogue film* (many of the Les Blank films like *Garlic Is as Good as Ten Mothers* [1977], *In Heaven There Is No Beer* [1984], and the delightful *Gap-Toothed Women* [1987]), and Erroll Morris' contribution to stretching documentary form with *screwball world films* (*Vernon, Florida* [1982] and *Gates of Heaven* [1985]) and his superb *The Thin Blue Line* (1988), which gives us the *documentary noir* by stylistically linking the world of its participants to the appropriately dark and fatalistic fictional world of the *film noir*. Michael Moore's *Roger and Me* (1989) injects welcome humor by adding *documentary satire* to the possibilities of the form. There are, of course, many other "families" of films that could further diversify this list and amplify the possibilities for structural types.

THE EVENT-CENTERED FILM

Here the event is the backbone of the film. It might be the launching of a ship, a dairy show, or the capture of a notorious criminal. The event has its stages, and plugged into its forward movement may be sections of interview, pieces of relevant past, or even pieces of future such as the criminal telling what it was like to be surrounded by armed police. The event film may be one of the rare occasions when you do indeed need more than one camera. It often has its development and dynamics pegged out in advance by the shape of the event itself. Shooting them with multiple, mobile cameras take the kind of organization and timing usually reserved for military operations if the cameras are not to end up shooting each other.

Leni Riefenstahl's dark classic, *Olympia* (1936), shows the Olympic games in Berlin with extraordinary and seductive virtuosity with Adolf Hitler godlike at its center.

Peter Watkins' *The War Game* (1966) is about a fictitious event projected from real-life events after the holocaust bombings in Japan and Dresden. As a vision of what the nuclear bombing of London would do, it amounts to a deconstruction of society following the breakdown of civilized institutions.

Michael Wadleigh's *Woodstock* (1970) is a vast, sprawling, good-natured film that approvingly records Woodstock's mammoth rock concert, using many roving cameras and a constantly shifting montage technique.

Werner Herzog's *La Soufrière* (1976) centers on a volcano about to erupt and how the island people handle the imminent destruction of their home. Herzog and crew risked their lives to be there, but because the volcano elected not to explode, the film switches without batting an eyelid to meditating on the importance of taking risks and ends up making capital out of the documentarian's nightmare, a nonevent.

THE PROCESS FILM

This kind of film deals with the chain of events that add up to a significant process. Often it will show more than one strand of ongoing present, each serving as a cutaway from the others. Cutting among several parallel stories in this way allows each segment to be reduced to its essence. This technique further allows useful comparisons—ironic or otherwise—to be drawn between concurrent events.

Flaherty's *Nanook of the North* (1922) and the Maysles brothers' *Salesman* (1969) both define the process by which their protagonist competes to survive.

Riefenstahl's *Olympia* (1936) portrays the ritualized selection process by which winners distinguish themselves, presumably an underlying metaphor intended to legitimize Hitler's presence as head of the German state.

Humphrey Jenning's poetic *Fires Were Started* (1943) focuses on the unsung heroes of the National Fire Service in their nightly battles to contain London's erupting inferno during the Blitz.

Frederick Wiseman's *Titicut Follies* (1967) shows every stage, from induction to burial, at an institution designed to contain the criminally insane, including the attempts of one seemingly sane man to extricate himself from its nightmarish walls. The film's episodes, which lead the viewer progressively deeper into the lunatic logic of the institution's "treatment" and personnel, are organized as side departures from an ongoing show, the institution's annual review.

Not unlike *Titicut Follies* in its comprehensiveness and darkening mood is the Maysles brothers' *Gimme Shelter* (1970), which shows the evolution of the Rolling Stones' Altamont concert, beginning lightheartedly enough and culminating in a murder by Hell's Angels in the crowd.

Les Blank's *Burden of Dreams* (1982) follows Werner Herzog shooting *Fitzcarraldo* (1982), a feature about an opera impresario who contrived to bring a river steamer over the Peruvian Andes (Figure 18–5). Through Herzog's own struggle in the jungle to get a real steamer up a mountain side, Blank reveals without ever being judgmental the degree of Herzog's dictatorial obsessiveness and the risks to which he was ready to expose his workers. Blank turns the

FIGURE 18–5

Werner Herzog and the boat he hauls up a hillside in Les Blank's *Burden of Dreams* (Maureen Gosling)

crew's struggle with the boat into a central metaphor for filmmaking itself and all that realizing a film's vision may represent.

THE JOURNEY FILM

There is a belief in the feature film industry that no film taking place on a train has ever failed. The allure of the journey, with all its metaphorical overtones and in-built rhythms of movement, also applies to the documentary film.

Basil Wright and Harry Watt's *Night Mail* (1936) is the ideal journey film, having its beginning, middle, and end defined by the mail run and its rhythms set by the wheels, the steam locomotive's flailing pistons, and the hands of the sorters at work—all lending themselves to cinematic orchestration.

Pare Lorentz's *The River* (1937) also has a clearly defined beginning, middle, and end but with an inherent augmentation as, stage by stage, the film leads us from the beginning trickle all the way to the ocean. Henri Cartier Bresson's *Le Retour* (1946) chronicles a river of a different sort, the river of displaced humanity trudging the roads of Europe in search of home after World War II.

Werner Herzog's *Land of Silence and Darkness* (1971) follows, as we have said, a deaf and blind woman's mission to contact those like herself whose handicap, though consigning them to darkness and silence, should not leave them isolated from humanity. The film contains two kinds of journey; one (told retrospectively) is Fini Straubinger's journey through life, the other her ongoing travels, which take us into the lives of progressively more isolated men and women. The last person visited is a man whose functioning is on the level of an animal. By investigating increasingly circumscribed lives, the film compels the viewer to make an inward journey through a range of emotions that culminates in simple, boundless gratitude for one's own faculties and by implication for that easy access to other human beings that one formerly took so much for granted.

THE WALLED-CITY FILM

Societies and institutions tend to close in upon themselves and beget their own code of conduct. This code is revealing of the larger, host society. The "walled-city" film therefore uses a microcosm to imply criticism upon a much wider scale.

Buñuel's *Land Without Bread* (1932), by concentrating on starving villagers in a remote Spanish village and by defining the various forces that prevent them helping themselves, angrily exposes the pattern of cynical neglect imposed by church, state, and landowners.

Any of Frederick Wiseman's films qualify, notably *Titicut Follies* (1967), *High School* (1968), and *Hospital* (1969) (Figure 18–6). These films imply a strong criticism of our attitudes toward mental health and normality, toward preparing the young for democracy, and toward a society that condones violence both self-directed and visited upon others.

Allen King's *Warrendale* (1966), shot by Wiseman's cinematographer Bill Brayne, manages to say a great deal about failures in family life. It does this by showing the trauma suffered by children of inadequate homes and by showing the caring but controversial treatment developed as an antidote in this Canadian institution.

FIGURE 18–6

High School by Fred Wiseman. A "walled-city" film that looks at our attitudes toward preparing the young for democracy. (Zipporah Films, Inc.)

Two films by Nick Broomfield, *Soldier Girls* (1981) and *Chicken Ranch* (1982), also qualify as "walled city" films but differ significantly in approach from both the narrated and the direct cinema observational approach. One is about women soldiers doing basic training and the other about women and their customers in a brothel (Figure 18–7). Each shows how people are processed by an institution, and each gives us more than enough insight to feel knowledgeable and critical at the end. Neither film pretends to be neutral and unaffected by what it finds. By letting us, for example, see a discharged woman soldier embrace the camera operator or by including the brothel owner's harangue of the crew for filming what he wants kept confidential, both films allow us to see where the filmmakers' sympathies lie and to guess at the arrangements, liaisons, and even manipulation that developed during the shooting. The outcome is to imply some of the ethics and reasoning behind what the films show and to justify showing what authority would prefer kept hidden.

THE HISTORICAL FILM

To the degree that all films reproduce what is already past, all are historical. Consequently, film is inherently a good medium for bringing the past alive though

FIGURE 18–7

The ladies in Nick Broomfield's *Chicken Ranch* pose with their madame.

it functions very differently from written history. As Donald Watt and Jerry Kuehl's essays each reflect,[3] screen histories in the eyes of their makers have had only limited success. Accuracy can be fatally hampered when particular coverage is not available, and television executives' terror of making adult intellectual demands on the audience often means that programs play safe. The film medium itself, by its realism and ineluctable movement through time, discourages contemplation and hampers the making of any statement, particularly those that are abstract, that cannot be illustrated.

The fault lies partly in a general unwillingness to recognize that watching television is different from reading or attending an academic lecture, and it also lies in the grandiose desire to be comprehensive. Particularly when consortia are involved, the audience cannot tell what strings come with funding or to what degree television histories are shaped like modern buildings out of the corporate yearning for self-aggrandizing monuments. History, they say, is written by the winners so historical viewpoints can also founder as they do in school textbooks from trying to steer around controversy.

[3]Donald Watt and Jerry Kuehl, "History on the Public Screen I & II," in *New Challenges for Documentary*, Rosenthal, ed.

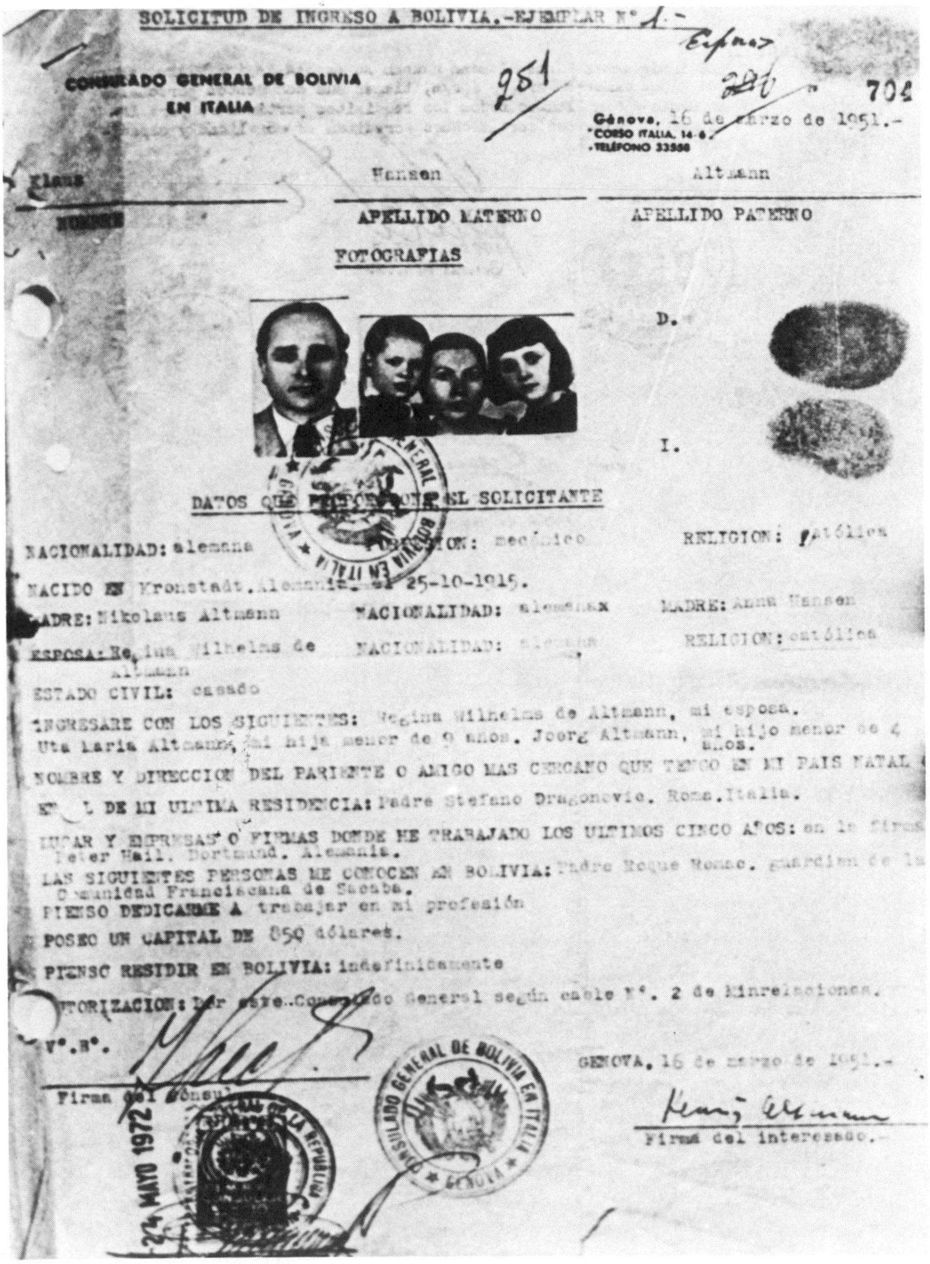

SOLICITUD DE INGRESO A BOLIVIA.-EJEMPLAR N° 1.-

CONSULADO GENERAL DE BOLIVIA
EN ITALIA

Génova, 16 de marzo de 1951.-
CORSO ITALIA, 14-6
TELÉFONO 33556

Klaus — Hansen — Altmann
NOMBRE — APELLIDO MATERNO — APELLIDO PATERNO

FOTOGRAFIAS

D.

I.

DATOS QUE PROPORCIONA EL SOLICITANTE

NACIONALIDAD: alemana PROFESION: mecánico RELIGION: católica
NACIDO EN Kronstadt, Alemania, el 25-10-1915.
PADRE: Nikolaus Altmann NACIONALIDAD: alemana MADRE: Anna Hansen
ESPOSA: Regina Wilhelms de Altmann NACIONALIDAD: alemana RELIGION: católica
ESTADO CIVIL: casado
INGRESARE CON LOS SIGUIENTES: Regina Wilhelms de Altmann, mi esposa. Uta Maria Altmann, mi hija menor de 9 años. Joerg Altmann, mi hijo menor de 4 años.
NOMBRE Y DIRECCION DEL PARIENTE O AMIGO MAS CERCANO QUE TENGO EN MI PAIS NATAL O EL DE MI ULTIMA RESIDENCIA: Padre Stefano Dragonovic. Roma, Italia.
LUGAR Y EMPRESAS O FIRMAS DONDE HE TRABAJADO LOS ULTIMOS CINCO AÑOS: en la firma Peter Hall. Dortmund. Alemania.
LAS SIGUIENTES PERSONAS ME CONOCEN EN BOLIVIA: Padre Roque Romac, guardián de la Comunidad Franciscana de Sacaba.
PIENSO DEDICARME A trabajar en mi profesión
POSEO UN CAPITAL DE 850 dólares.
PIENSO RESIDIR EN BOLIVIA: indefinidamente
AUTORIZACION: Por este Consulado General según cable N°. 2 de Minrelaciones.
V°.B°.

GENOVA, 16 de marzo de 1951.-

Firma del Consul

Firma del interesado.-

24 MAYO 1972

FIGURE 18–8

Incriminating document in *Hotel Terminus*—the false identity paper that allowed Klaus Barbie to enter Bolivia.

The British have produced some notable series (*The Great War, The World at War*), and America has produced its own blockbusters (*Vietnam: A Television History* and *The Civil War,* for example). Compressed and heavily mediated by narration, they function like encyclopedias by deluging the viewer with facts and concepts that require immense feats of memorization to keep straight. The viewer, as if back in kindergarten, constantly suffers a sense of inferiority at being unable to comprehend the lesson.

What one gains—a sense of virtue at surviving, a sense of atmosphere and mood, patches of vivid and clearly remembered drama—is clearly not the balanced and comprehensive understanding the producers imagined.

The incisive historical documentary, on the other hand, is not primarily concerned with conveying a balanced overall grasp. Its focus is probably a main issue or character, and it is likely to be more visibly fueled by a passion or smoldering sense of injustice. Good examples are extremely diverse both in purview and language.

Pare Lorentz's *The Plow that Broke the Plain* (1936) and *The River* (1937), both early ecology films, warn eloquently of the environmental and human disasters that follow in the wake of soil erosion and deforestation caused by opportunistic government action.

Alain Resnais' *Night and Fog* (1955) lead us to confront the implications of Auschwitz for the future. It resurrects the hellish life of the prisoners with concentrated imaginativeness and leaves us looking over our shoulders for those among us capable of administering another such system.

Paul Rotha's *The Life of Adolf Hitler* (1961) is a history of its subject from a personally felt perspective that indicts the German people for creating Hitler. Frederic Rossif's *To Die in Madrid* (1962) is less evidently personal, yet the prevailing impression is one of deepening tragedy as ill-armed and ill-prepared government troops during the Spanish Civil War try to put down an army rebellion backed by Hitler and Mussolini.

Since the 1960s, oral history for the screen has been gaining important ground. Its emphasis on personal experience sets clear and useful limits, for the history presented clearly arises from the particular experience of particular people and does not so obviously represent an invisibly contrived overview. Stephen Peet's "Yesterday's Witness" BBC series in England, which I helped start, made over a hundred films, but in the United States similar films have been made by independents—no doubt because of the political self-censorship that afflicts even the noncommercial PBS. Notable independent films are Reichert and Klein's *Union Maids* (1976) and *Seeing Red* (1983), Connie Field's *The Life and Times of Rosie the Riveter* (1981), and Lorraine Gray's *With Babies and Banners* (1979). In France, Marcel Ophuls' *Sorrow and the Pity* (1972) and *Hotel Terminus: The Life and Times of Klaus Barbie* (1988) and Claude Lanzmann's *Shoah* (1985) have concentrated on the workings of Fascism. With the collapse of communism in eastern Europe, we can expect to see a wealth of extraordinary individual stories in the future.

What distinguishes these films is that their authors do not approach history in a textbook way—as bygone events requiring closure by consensus pronouncement. They see it as a bright store of human experience awaiting use to illuminate contemporary predicaments.

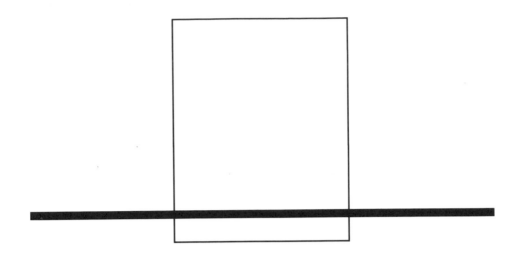

C·H·A·P·T·E·R 1·9

FORM, CONTROL, AND IDENTITY

In making the groupings outlined in Chapter 18, I wanted to arrive at a neat summary of optional aesthetic approaches to documentary-making, but I have been unable to produce reliably clear distinctions between types or families of films. I strongly suspect that any documentary film is only successful because someone has solved a particular problem: how to accommodate that unique footage into that particular narrative form. It means that good films are one of a kind and therefore not useful, in a narrow sense, as models.

It would be useful instead to work through some of the issues and contradictions in the documentarian's environment, ones that inevitably influence what film gets made. Some of the paradoxes lie in the medium, some in the framework of funding and audience interests, and some in the way filmmakers have so far used documentary. This chapter, concerned with form, control, and identity issues, looks at the relationship between subject and the chosen form, the difficulties of authorial control over a world meant to be spontaneous, how some topics themselves may be easy or difficult to film and the effect of this on the documentary's reputation, how documentaries must be justified to participants and funding sources, how ethics are bound up with this, how broadcasting handles the independent viewpoint, and how documentary language has influenced the fictional form but now needs revitalization.

CONTENT DICTATES FORM

Form must serve content in any successful artwork, so it is possible to claim that all successful artworks are unique and therefore unclassifiable. This is plainly a retreat from a common-sense necessity, but there are special difficulties in classifying the documentary, for it owes its credibility to acts, words, and images quite literally plucked from life and *lacking central authorship*. In almost every other area of expression, the creative artist has control over the form in which content is expressed, but in documentary, the filmmaker is in the position of a mosaic artist.

Evidently, freedom of expression is severely curtailed by the idiosyncratic nature of the given materials, even circumscribed by them. Like the graphic artist or sculptor who works with *objets trouvés,* the documentarian is to a great degree in the hands of the material, and the chosen narrative strategies must be those that elicit the most significance from available materials.

FICTION AND DOCUMENTARY: AUTHORIAL CONTROL

While the fiction filmmaker can mold and compress material during the writing stage to make the requisite inner qualities externally visible and appealing, the documentary director must make any such authorial statement in subtle and indirect ways. For the documentary genre compels one to work from behind the appearance of verisimilitude if one is not to devalue its coin.

The fiction director, drawing on traditions of form largely unavailable to the documentarian, can freely borrow from literary and theatrical conventions well understood by audiences. These help focus material and signal authorial intentions. The documentary, however, if it is to retain credibility, must somehow present tracts of autonomous, unfolding realism and simultaneously induce the spectator to put aside habits of passive acceptance if he is to rouse his imagination and pass beyond the looking glass of surface realism.

The documentary maker's central problem is therefore persuading his audience to look more deeply into appearances. Three aspects of filmmaking affect this:

1. How gripping and original is the film's subject.
2. How individual, flexible, and evident is the film's point of view.
3. How effectively film language and conventions are used.

Usually the director meets challenges in one or all of these areas, and the measure of a film's originality is the energy and freshness with which all three are tackled.

COMMON LIMITS ON THE RANGE OF SUBJECTS

All this difficulty in focusing attention on those fragile and transient moments of significance so easily accomplished by the writer and so difficult for the documentarian, means that documentary directors often play it safe by resorting to sensational subjects.

War, family violence, urban problems, eccentrics, deviants, demonstrations, revolts, and confrontations all offer the kind of material that promises something reliably heightened. Yet resorting to melodramatic subject matter is in the long run self-defeating. For by insistently promising the showdown, the genre must usually leave expectations unfulfilled. Further, by so often dealing in fashionable causes, the documentary becomes the "problem movie" and saddles itself with an obligation to preach solutions.

Documentaries, it must be concluded with regret, seldom penetrate to the heart of their subjects with that ease and precision we have come to expect of literature. For the true feel of small-town life or for the authentic claustrophobia of a middle-class family reunion, we look instinctively to fiction and not the documentary film.

There are difficulties at every level that produce this situation, not the least of which is raising money to budget a film about such "minor" subjects. One can blame those who administer the bidding system by which films are proposed, weeded out, and funded. Just imagine how many major works of literature would still exist if Jane Austen, Guy de Maupassant, Doris Lessing, John Updike, and other writers whose specialty is revealing the significance in unremarkable lives were forced to apply for huge sums of corporate money before writing a single word. Our libraries would turn into echoing vaults containing only supermarket novels.

But if filmmaking generally reflects its capitalistic foundations and thrives or fades according to audience figures, in the end it is futile and unproductive to complain about that fact. There are other obstacles that discourage working on a small canvas.

PARTICIPANTS' COOPERATION

Some of the problems in making the "ordinary-life" documentary arise from the participants themselves. One real problem is finding any suitable explanation to offer participants for wanting to film what they themselves consider to be the trivia of their lives. You are after all setting up intrusive equipment for a purpose that may at best seem spurious.

If you fail to justify your purposes to your human subjects, you also really fail to assure them of your underlying respect. To them, you may even be fulfilling some exploitative purpose. On the other hand, when you do make your interests clear and justifiable, many people will spontaneously set aside considerations of privacy because they feel your motives for making the film are overridingly important. A rape victim may volunteer to appear in a documentary because she urgently wants society to know not only about what she has experienced of rape and rapists but also about the way in which society processes the raped woman's legal case. Her choice, consciously made, is to sacrifice her privacy in order to raise public awareness.

RESISTANCE TO THE PERSONAL VIEWPOINT

Another obstacle to an openly personal choice of subject is the unwillingness of corporate television to countenance work that expresses personal politics or beliefs unless one's views just happen to attract large viewing figures. There are innately cautious and conservative prejudices at work here, for television is nervous about any original social criticism unless it can be safely yoked to a famous name or a widely approved movement. This serves a double purpose: It reliably attracts viewers, and it dissociates the television company from responsibility for the opinions expressed.

This pandering to audience figures can work in either direction; the Beatles were able to have quite silly work shown on national television because they were very popular, and at the other end of the scale, Louis Malle's thoughtful and critical *Phantom India* (1968) series might never have been shown in Britain had he not already made a reputation as a director of controversial fiction films. Malle, by the way, is an enigmatic figure who seems to have astutely kept himself in the public eye by making films about "forbidden" sexuality, escalating from adultery to incest and child prostitution as the public got harder to shock. Yet his documentary work is restrained and sensitive, and his feature film, *Lacombe, Lucien* (1974), about a boy unthinkingly joining the Nazi collaborators in Vichy France, is a provocative study of the way evil is rooted in ordinariness.

The documentary counterpart to Malle's *Lacombe, Lucien,* and possibly its inspiration, is Marcel Ophuls's remarkable *The Sorrow and the Pity* (1970). This reconstructs the roots of French participation in the Nazi occupation of France. It is a great film and decidedly the outcome of one man's obsessive desire to expose the way people rationalize seizing a short-term personal advantage when its consequences are likely to be evil.

DOCUMENTARY LANGUAGE

A colleague who made films in Africa took one back to show a remote tribe. They were entranced at seeing themselves until the film cut to close-ups when they turned to each other in confusion and amazement. Having no experience of jumping close to anyone in a single, invisible leap and having seen no film before, they stopped accepting what they saw as actuality when the close-ups appeared. Convention therefore plays a part in every audience's understanding.

Each medium communicates its subject to its audience by using an agreed language. Some art-form conventions are extremely stylized and nonrealistic—think of opera or Japanese theater. As with a spoken language, users slowly evolve and reinvigorate that language when current usage turns stale.

The documentary is by no means limited to *cinéma vérité* or compilation forms, nor need it be a slave to realism. Its only limitation is that it must present actuality (past, present, or even future) and take a critical approach to the fabric of social life.

It seems inescapable that the documentary director, like Flaherty with *Nanook,* is compelled to draw on storytelling techniques and narrative compression if he is to engage an audience. This is an uncomfortable fact of life for the ethnographer or *cinéma vérité* purist, either of whom may protest that this is unendurably manipulative especially after he has shot by available light and asked nothing of his subject beyond permission to record his activities. With the laudable intention of being nonmanipulative, Marxist filmmakers of the 1960s and 1970s attempted to achieve a more respectful presentation of participants by leaving what they said and did largely uncut. While this certainly makes a film look different (and seldom more coherent), it leaves the foundation of the documentary unchanged: *Whatever gets on the screen is the product of choices and relationships, and these unavoidably reflect the director's commitment to what is true and what needs to be said about those truths.*

Here we return to the idea that a film must imply a contract with its audience by the way it relays its subject. The film must remain consistent in this relationship and deliver what it promises. The relationship itself can only be derived from a comprehensive idea of the form and function of the particular subject you are handling.

This is one of the most difficult areas in which to obtain a sense of growth, since the director requires articulate, supportive criticism. Formal education in a good film school can vastly speed up one's evolution, for lacking ground rules, a good working theory, and committed critics, the novice is condemned to reinvent film history alone. Even the prickliest filmmaker, adamantly hostile to all teaching and tradition, must eventually concede that an audience's understanding is molded by historically formed conventions.

In the previous edition of this book I expressed profound dissatisfaction that documentary form had stagnated for so many years. The great films that followed in the wake of the *cinéma vérité* explosion of the 1960s such as Ophuls' *The Sorrow and the Pity* (1972), Kopple's *Harlan County, USA* (1976), and Wohl's *Best Boy* (1979) only broke new ground in humane subject matter and thoroughness, not in developing the language. After the novelty of spontaneously filmed actuality wore off, the documentary film settled into a complacent middle age. Innovation came in the area of narrative editing rather than in directing or camera usage.

Ironically it was the television commercial, always trying to cram a quart into a pint pot, that had done most to speed the evolution of film language. Though commercials themselves contributed nothing to film's grammar, they rapidly educated a mass audience and demonstrated that a taut narrative style is only a problem for conservative filmmakers.

But a renaissance in both audience interest and film language is at hand. Recent documentaries of significance all show a strong authorial point of view. Neidik and Angelico's reflexive *Dark Lullabies* (1986) is told in the first person as is Moore's *Roger and Me* (1989), which became the audience choice for favorite film at the Chicago International Film Festival. A *documentary* chosen over dozens of feature films? The subject is people losing their jobs, but the treatment is bitingly satirical.

Another popular success was Ross McElwee's long and playful autobiography of the heart, *Sherman's March* (1986). Following the success of Errol Morris' docudrama noir, *The Thin Blue Line* (1988), also shown in movie houses and on television, one can only rejoice that there's a change afoot.

In television too, there is an awareness of the change. With its *POV* series, PBS has begun regularly showing the work of single, often independently produced documentaries. Home Box Office (HBO) cable is also showing and even commissioning them, and some of the video stores now have a documentary shelf. Colleagues at other film schools report a rise of interest in documentary classes.

The message is obvious: There is a following for the right films, but conventional approaches must give way to fresh ones if the mainstream is to evolve. This means that the committees and panels by which public monies are dispensed must revise their habits and procedural expectations if they are to encourage products that rise above institutionalized pablum.

DOCUMENTARY, FICTION FILMS, AND THE FUTURE

Even when the documentary was marking time, it had cross-fertilized with the feature film. Ralph Rosenblum in *When the Shooting Stops* makes it clear how much of his approach to editing feature films, especially those with problems, was stimulated by first editing documentaries.[1] There are many editors like him.

The individuality characteristic of the documentary director is more visible in feature work since improvisational methods were revived by the French New Wave. After the innovative silent days, the film business became an industry in which the creative process lost most of its immediacy and flexibility. From the 1950s onward, lighter equipment made possible a return to more improvisatory methods. In America, Cassavetes and Altman were the pioneers, but the sustained subjective view of the handheld camera is nowadays standard in films with no intellectual pretensions whatsover such as *Star Wars* (1977) and *Halloween* (1978).

Experience in making documentaries has evidently allowed Alain Tanner, the Swiss documentarian and feature film director, to make *In the White City* (1984) through an informal, improvisatory relationship with his actors and without a conventional script. Mike Leigh, known for *High Hopes* (1989), is an English director who has arrived at similar working methods for the screen by way of theatre directing.

In a more general way, the *cinéma vérité* documentary has thrust into public consciousness a more demanding benchmark for screen realism, and I believe that this more than anything else has influenced directing relationships and styles of acting. Over the years these have become steadily more intimate and revealing of the actor's self.

It remains a mournful fact, however, that almost all network television directing is faceless and interchangeable, and this is particularly true for the politically explosive genre of documentary. Apparently the exception proves the rule; an obituary notice for the Hungarian emigré director Robert Vas conferred on him the distinction of having made some of the few BBC documentaries with a recognizable and individual style. Is standardization the inevitable cost of industrial timetables, union structures, and management conservatism? While industrialization is a sensible approach for processing news programs and soap opera, it is as disabling to documentaries as it would be to nature films. Sadly there is much self-censorship among filmmakers to help standardization evolve. Uncon-

---

[1]Ralph Rosenblum, *When The Shooting Stops . . . the Cutting Begins* (Boston: Focal Press, 1979).

scious and insidious, it represents the filmmaker's need to be acceptable to his paymaster and lifeline.

Much of value in the better network documentaries seems attributable to increasingly imaginative editing rather than to advances in the director's role as a catalyst. This could be because editors are permitted to function alone and along individual lines in an industrial system that otherwise looks upon individual vision as hazardous, indulgent, and not cost effective. Even the BBC in its best years (the late 1960s to early 1970s) made no attempt to schedule time for crews to see documentary rushes as this was considered a waste of resources.

The separation of the documentary from news journalism and its recent development as an individual voice could have far-reaching results. Because documentary can now be made inexpensively on the new miniature formats and because videomakers are no longer dependent on studios and production centers, we can expect to see authorship diversifying to regional centers. More experienced documentarians will eventually mean a mounting challenge to the Hollywood fiction manufacturing process with its reliance on animating a script. It is a matter of time before documentarians and experimental theater come together as Fassbinder made them do with the Munich *action-theater*, and as Mike Leigh (*High Hopes* [1989]) has done more recently in England. These possibilities are explored in my fiction directing book, *Directing: Film Techniques and Aesthetics*.[2]

---

[2]Michael Rabiger, *Directing: Film Techniques and Aesthetics* (Boston: Focal Press).

C·H·A·P·T·E·R 2·0

REENACTMENT, RECONSTRUCTION, AND DOCUDRAMA

An important aspect of the documentary remains to be discussed—that of reconstructing scenes from a person's life or even whole biographies of people no longer living. To take the less radical situation first, it sometimes happens when one is making a documentary that some important stage has been passed before you even arrived on the scene to begin filming. It might, for instance, be a crucial career interview for a job that one's main character has already begun.

If you get the participants to successfully reenact this scene, how important is it to be totally truthful with the audience? There is no easy answer to this question. Some filmmakers run a subtitle saying the scene is reenacted, but this seems unnecessarily dramatic if the scene is only part of the exposition needed to get the film under way, especially if one runs past-tense narration or voice-over to give the appropriate distancing. It would be dishonest in an evidence scene, however, to let the audience think it was seeing actuality instead of a reconstruction.

The dividing line seems to be one of good faith; there is nothing controversial about showing how a character got her job, if we know she got one. But if instead our character is asserting that the personnel manager used unfair interviewing techniques, then whether the audience sees the actual interview or only a reenactment from somebody's memory becomes extremely important, as everyone's integrity is at stake. Incidentally, you should encourage participants to approach a reenactment not as acting but rather as an exercise in reliving the spirit of what truly happened.

To summarize then: The reenactment of important scenes that cannot be shown any other way is a useful and valid way of stimulating the audience's imagination and of filling what would otherwise be significant gaps in your story. If, however, the audience will be misled into making formative judgments from the scene, it should be appropriately labeled either with a caption or by use of the voice track.

Large-scale reconstruction requires clear labeling. Here a scene, several scenes, or even a whole film is reconstructed from available sources. These might be eyewitness memories, documents, transcripts or hearsay. British television once showed an acted reconstruction directed by Stuart Hood of the trial of Sacco and Vanzetti. It was intelligent, restrained, austerely memorable, and had been put together from court transcripts of the famous anarchists' trial. Although all who appeared were actors, the piece was factually accurate and can really only be described as a documentary reenactment since there was no central authorship. By this, I mean that each of the participants—the actors portraying the two anarchists, the judge, and the legal representatives—all used the actual ideas and language preserved in the court records.

Similarly, Robert Kitt's BBC dramatized version of scenes from Mayhew's classic *London Labour and the London Poor* (1965) seems to qualify for inclusion with documentary because again the words, actions, and ideas are those of the people Henry Mayhew interviewed in the 1840s.

Even Peter Watkins *Culloden* (1964), a reconstruction of the 1746 Highlands battle in which Bonnie Prince Charlie's forces and the whole Stuart cause were brutally put down by the English, has been included with the documentary genre. Here historical accuracy must be debatable, and the words of the officers and foot soldiers who Watkins "interviewed" can only approximate what the actual participants might have said. Yet there is something in the attitude of the film itself to its subject that speaks of an overall respect and commitment not only to that distant historical actuality but also to understanding the human process by which such events recur throughout history. Although the film deals with power and politics, its true concern is with the subjugation of the crofter to his lord and with the manner in which the humble are appropriated as cannon fodder in the murderous ideological struggles of their masters.

Where then is the dividing line between documentary and fiction? A short answer is that nobody knows and that anyway the line is always being challenged. There is a yet more imaginative use of the real to be described, known as docudrama.

THE DOCUDRAMA

Two examples will suffice to explain this form, which, as its name signifies, is a hybrid straddling two worlds. One is an English dramatization of the plight of the homeless made in the 1960s, Jeremy Sandford's *Cathy Come Home* (1966). Working from case histories, Sandford and his wife constructed a "typical" blue-collar couple who overspend and encounter bad luck. The little family is evicted and becomes homeless, drifting rapidly down the remainder of the social scale until it is dismembered by the welfare state "for the good of the children."

Coming hard on the heels of the successful Conservative reelection slogan, "You never had it so good," the British public was at first stunned then appalled to find that the drama was in essence true to life in all its particulars. The force of public feeling even contributed to some amelioration in the law, a rare consequence indeed for a film of any kind. The effectiveness of the film was only partly because of its documentary basis; it was also superbly acted and presented.

Anthony Thomas's *Death of a Princess* (1980) is a more recent film that attempted to show how a member of the Saudi royalty could be publicly humiliated and executed for a sexual offense. From the highly critical reaction it raised on all sides, the film, which reconstructed the princess's life and death using actors, seems to have taken altogether too many risks—first with the truth, which was insufficiently determinable, then with the more general authenticity of its portrayal of Islamic culture and assumptions, which were outside the producer's own realm of experience. These uncertainties gave the film an unreal and speculative quality that made it successful neither as fiction drama nor as documentary.

Thus the premise upon which material is presented has a great deal of influence over the state of mind in which people assess and assimilate what is proffered as "true to life." If the premise seems unsupported or unsupportable, the film's pretensions to documentary authenticity are the first element to be rejected. It is interesting to compare Jack Gold's well-received reenactment of Ruth First's imprisonment in South Africa, *Ninety Days* (1966), with *Death of a Princess:* Since the part of Ruth First was played by herself, the program apparently raised no questions over its premise as a subjective and authentic account. If her account illuminated South African police-state methods, it also prompted an endorsement for she was afterward murdered in an act of brutally vindictive reprisal.

SUBJECTIVE RECONSTRUCTION

Several works of reconstruction deserve notice because their language is deliberately and successfully aimed at creating a heightened state of imaginative identification by the viewer with the subjects.

Volcano (1977) by the brilliant and quirky Canadian Donald Brittain reconstructs the life of Malcolm Lowry, author of the novel *Under the Volcano*. Lowry, like Brittain himself, was an alcoholic. After a life of tragicomic turmoil and self-destructiveness, he obsessively transmuted his own story into art and produced a novel of stunning depth. In telling Lowry's life, Brittain uses some of the standard apparatus of screen biography, but the film uses no film and few photos of Lowry himself, concentrating instead on creating place and atmosphere as a counterpoint to Lowry's own words and ideas. Afterward one seems to have lived through a destructive addiction oneself.

Erroll Morris' *The Thin Blue Line* (1988) investigates the indictment and trial of Randall Adams for the killing of a policeman many years earlier in Texas. Using minimalist music by Philip Glass and a camera that stares unblinkingly at a number of witnesses each composed and lit as if for a feature film, Morris's tale gathers force as a formal work of intricate detection. What really took place at the time of the shooting? Morris reenacts many versions according to each participant's testimony. The effect is like pondering a chess problem as Morris must have pondered the puzzle himself while groping for the truth. The outcome is haunting: a prisoner caught in a real-life *film noir* web whose story illustrates just how idiosyncratically and unjustly the law can be operated.

Each of PBS's poetry series, *Voices and Visions* (1988) attempts to take the viewer inside the life and work of an established American poet. Though made by a large team, the films weave together with fair consistency the usual mix of biographic materials—photos, film clips, voice recordings, artifacts, reconstruction, reenacted scenes, poems "illustrated," and so on. The films on Frost, Plath, Moore, and Dickinson are strong viewing experiences, and taken as a whole, the series is a veritable compendium of screen biography methodology. But whether because a series is inherently homogenizing or because the mannerisms of the quirkier literary critics have a disabling effect on one's concentration, the films are inconsistent in impact and try to cover too much ground. Even the best sometimes makes the viewer nauseous from sheer sensory overload.

Ken Burns' *Civil War* (1990) series, also a PBS venture, delivers another kind of surfeit, a factual overkill that muffles some of the fresh perspectives that might emerge. By using the authentic materials of photos, folk music, present day locations, and the words used by people of the time, however, Burns personalizes otherwise abstract issues like patriotism, racism, slavery, and ambition and shows the war as something arising from a multitude of individual wills. The cost is that, as in a Wiseman film, one retains the texture and some detail of the subject but almost none of its architecture.

C·H·A·P·T·E·R 2·1

ETHICS, AUTHORSHIP, AND DOCUMENTARY MISSION

Anyone who has directed documentary footage knows that the loyalties, obligations, and understandings that develop between oneself and participants sometimes pose difficult ethical dilemmas and that these are inseparable from the process of authorship. To take a simple example: You are making a film about the victims of a housing scam who you get to know and like. You also gain the confidence of the perpetrators and are offered hospitality by them. To refuse might expose your judgment of them so you go out with them, eat an expensive dinner, and laugh at their jokes. Now you feel like a whore when you next visit their victims.

How and why one works as a documentarian all belong on a moral continuum anchored deeply in one's sense of ethics and mission. As a beginning documentarian, even the smaller tasks demand self-examination. After a few years, particularly if you work in a news organization with older and cynical pros, there is a risk of becoming professional in the worst sense—that is, of using people to illustrate foregone views or of turning into a skeptical bystander. Having a camera, or belonging to a broadcasting corporation, makes it easy to acquire an exaggerated sense of one's own importance and to correspondingly undervalue those who trustingly let you into their lives.

Unlike the fiction filmmaker paying actors, the documentarian generally offers no financial compensation and can take no comfort from having paid to settle moral obligations. By publicly showing footage—though not necessarily by taking it—it is possible to harm someone's life irreparably.

Directing a documentary sometimes feels like being a doctor advising patients about the procedure, complications, and consequences of an irreversible operation. Some documentary participants are not attentive or sophisticated enough to absorb all the implications, and though the release form may discharge legal obligations, it doesn't meet those that are moral. An example: In America during the 1970s, the Loud family consented to have their lives filmed (*An American Family*, 1973, PBS, 12 hour-long episodes). Exposure to the camera and criticism afterward in the press as if the family were performers tore the family apart. They said afterward that the series' intentions were inadequately explained. In fact, the open-ended nature of the project made that virtually unavoidable.

Where do the filmmaker's responsibilities lie? When does one owe loyalty to the individual, when to larger truths? Is there an accepted code of ethics? How much can one say to participants before they become too alarmed to permit filming?

Regrettably none of these questions has a clear answer, so I will comment on what usually comes up at different stages of production.

APPROACHING PARTICIPANTS

At the time you ask someone to participate in a *cinéma vérité* project, you seldom have more than the sketchiest idea of who or what will be used in the film, what it will say, or how this individual will appear to the world. Given such a shadowy outcome, films can only be made on a basis of trust. Indeed one probably "casts" particular people because they are cooperative and of good will. Unfortunately documentarians have been known to abuse this trust. When I worked at the BBC, a woman factory worker spoke candidly and trustingly about sexual morals among her female coworkers. Outraged, they beat her up the day after the film was transmitted. The (male) film director apparently knew this was a risk and gambled with her safety for the sake of a more sensational film.

For most participants, there is nothing comparable at risk. To read them a standard list of possible consequences would scare the hell out of them for no good reason. In investigative filmmaking where one's film is bound to be critical of someone, the case is probably different. If you suspect someone runs an undeserved risk, you should explore the possibilities with the participant, taking particular care with everyone who is unused to being in the public eye. More often the problems lie in the other direction, and you will find yourself trying to convince someone that their fears are utterly unfounded.

Occasionally subterfuge is justified to get footage. Sometimes one's loyalty to the truth effortlessly overrides any scruples. If some maniacal dictator has just butchered 200 defenseless people, there is no moral dilemma about exposing the truth. You use any means necessary and expose an unequivocal evil. Of course, such clarity is rare; usually one is not dealing with black and white moral issues, but rather discriminating between shades of pale gray. This in fact requires more moral courage and energy than does the extreme case.

Occasionally the filmmaker, employing dubious practices that serve a larger purpose as Michael Moore found from making *Roger and Me* (1989), can discover his methods returning to haunt him. By simplifying and transposing cause and effect, Moore handed ammunition to his film's many enemies.

Since our profession exists only by virtue of the voluntary cooperation of participants, one should take every care to avoid unnecessary exploitation. The bottom line is to consider what it takes and what it will cost to do some good in the world and to decide whether it is worth it—a lonely calculation if ever there was one.

DIRECTING AND REFLEXIVITY

If it is true that "the unexamined life isn't worth living," the documentary is often justified solely for the examination and self-examination it brings one's participants. But this, especially when it is an unfamiliar activity, can serve to transform the very lives you wanted to record intact. This is a conundrum for the means can compromise, subvert, or conceivably even create the end result. In a genre that often purports to show life spontaneously unfolding, this is analogous to Cousteau showing deep sea fish shoals when the presence of a frogman wielding lights and camera amounted to an alien invasion. He got around it by reflexively making a feature of the sensation his men and equipment caused among the oceanic community. The developments of the 1980s show that reflexive acknowledgment like this is increasingly important.

Reflexivity can be so germane that it is designed into a film as in McElwee's *Sherman's March* (1986), or it can be accidental. A microphone lunging into shot or a participant suddenly questioning the camera operator, destroys a film's "transparency." Not only does it break our illusion of spying on spontaneous life but it probably gives us nothing of value in return. For ideological reasons in the 1960s and 1970s, some filmmakers would deliberately show crew members during a scene to "remind the audience they were watching a movie." But isolated Brechtian gestures toward "the process" generally break one's concentration and undermine the film's overall credibility. Today's audience, however, has become increasingly aware that filming is an artistic process and are also interested in what takes place behind the camera. In addition to curiosity about the authorship process itself, there is also a growing concern—maturity, one might say—about what the documentary process is doing to the situation under study. This can be interesting for the filmmaker but alarming to those whose techniques rely more on smoke and mirrors.

A film's validity as a truthful record is usually asserted in one of two ways. The traditional approach is to make a film that is honest to the spirit of one's best perceptions and to trust that the audience can infer how the filmmaking process has affected the outcome. Consciously or otherwise, spectators judge the film against their own instincts and knowledge of life. In the alternative approach, the director deliberately builds into the film whatever doubts and perceptions would be inadequately acknowledged through the material on its own. Such a film is reflexive. That is, it explores perception as well as what is perceived, and this usually means including some elements of self-portraiture by its makers. Louis Malle, in his *Phantom India* series (1968), often reflects on his relationship as a privileged westerner, alien in culture and economic resources to the crowds teeming past his camera for whom normality is often to be hungry. The conditions, attitudes, and peoples are so radically different that they should lead to a profound questioning of Malle's own values and assumptions. But because Malle's concerns are more rhetorical than substantive, his reflexivity sheds little light.

How one sees, how one connects with others while making a film, represent a Pandora's box that cannot be half opened.

SHOOTING PROCESS

The fear so many new directors express about "altering reality" is surely because they remain in awe of the objectivity affected by so much that appears on television. Leaving aside the invasiveness of cameras and equipment, it remains true that *every* set of relationships is changed according to who is present and observing. Even a family picnic is altered according to who arrives; a 10-year-old child will make a different impact and less change to the atmosphere than would, say, a man in sunglasses who silently takes photographs. If, however, the extra guest's appearance is mediated by a trusted member of the group who then explains the newcomer's interests or if the photographer himself first convinces the group that his interests are sympathetic and genuine, he will be trusted and welcomed.

Your presence cannot help altering an event, but the changes can be large or small according to who you film and how you handle the preparation. The documentary director must not only build bridges but he must also choose participants with care. Making a mistaken "casting" decision can mean waking up to find you have committed yourself to someone who resists, distorts, or even manipulates the process. To guard against this, defer decisions about who participates until the latest possible moment. The longer you give yourself to see people in action, the less likely you are to miscalculate. Avoid committing yourself even then about what makes it through the cutting room into the final film.

Other mishaps and twists of fortune will present both ethical and practical difficulties. Suppose the evidence you are getting does not support your hypothesis. Should you make a different film or simply stop shooting? Suppose somebody's basic situation changes—your lonely widow suddenly acquires a boyfriend, say. Do you collect materials to reconstruct the situation as it (interestingly) was, or do you alter your film to reflect the (less interesting) situation as it now is? The answers depend on what you have promised, what code of conduct you have set yourself, and what good story remains possible.

Here is another dilemma. You take an interviewee up to an important, perhaps unperceived, threshold in his life. In a revealing moment, the interviewee crosses into territory never before penetrated. We may see what Rouch calls a "privileged moment" where all notion of film as an artificial environment ceases for participant and audience alike. It is a wonderful moment, but it hinges on the revelation of some fact that should not become public. Do you afterward lean on the person to permit its inclusion in the film? Perhaps the participant is so trusting that you alone can make the decision whether it will damage him. Here wise and responsible co-workers can help you carry the burden of decision.

But if it is best to suppress the revelation, can you carry on with the film as though nothing new had taken place? Again the decision must be taken in the light of your values and circumstances.

Interviewing poses an ethical responsibility. For instance, the thrill of the righteous chase can delude one into unfairly demolishing a person's defenses. Though there is a second chance in the cutting room to recognize and prevent this situation becoming public, the damage to your relationship with your subject may remain.

There is also an ethical responsibility for causing change. As we have said, the documentary often alters its subjects' lives merely by exposing them to scrutiny—their own and others. This can develop imperceptibly. At first, participants will often maintain an "on the record" and an "off the record" relationship with the director. Then the line becomes blurred as a deepening trust or even emotional dependency develops. One day the director of a film finds she has become responsible for the direction of a life. In a single documentary class of mine at the time of writing, there are several projects where this is happening. One is about a man who, as a teenager, narrowly missed being the victim of a multiple sex murderer; another is about a middle-aged gang member who is dying and who sees the film about him as a posthumous message to his beloved daughter; another is about a young male prostitute whose activities are made possible by contempt for his own body; yet another concerns a *ménage à trois*. All the directors have repeatedly expressed anxieties about their responsibilities, and this has taken considerable class discussion time. Invariably they needed support for their decisions more than they need any radical advice.

Most films change the lives they record, and it is our responsibility to help make the chemistry a positive one. Conceivably while doing this, you may be told something that, were it to fall into the wrong hands, could lead to the injury or even killing of someone. This may be the time to stop the camera or even to destroy footage. Filmmakers who have broadcast revelations from people in danger in South Africa, Russia, and other benighted societies usually make absolutely certain that the individual knows the risks and is ready to take them.

A more usual level of responsibility is that of Loretta Smith, whose *Where Did You Get That Woman?* (1979) started from a chance encounter with an old lady in the cab that Loretta drove for a living. She remained a loyal friend of her film's subject for years after the film was finished—until Joan died in fact.

EDITING PROCESS

There are more than a few dubious editing practices. One that can happen inadvertently is to allow acted or reconstructed material to stand unidentified in a film made of otherwise original and authentic materials. If there is any doubt about how the audience will take it, identify the material's origin either by narration or subtitle.

Most documentary editing involves compression, and a long statement can be unfairly reduced to serve the film but misrepresent the speaker's original pronouncement. Any participant who runs his own audio recording while you film (as happened to me when I filmed the British Union of Fascists' leader Sir Oswald Mosley) may be preparing to challenge you on this score.

Apparent truths and bogus meanings can be manufactured by juxtaposing two unrelated events or statements. What has happened may be invisible or insignificant to a lay audience yet scandalize participants. Even the way you compress into three shots a long process such as buying a house may be attacked. You should be able to defend and justify every such device in your narrative flow.

Imagine that you must deal with a participant's fear-fantasy when, after weeks of anguish, she wants to retract some innocuous statement that is vital to your film. You have the legal right to use it, and you know it can bring no harm, but should you go ahead and override the participant's wish? Your good name and career may suffer, and at the very least your conscience will prick you for violating someone's trust. It is not unusual for a real risk to a participant to emerge only at the editing stage, and one must face up to the conflict between releasing a good film that causes pain and danger to someone and removing something important to the film's effectiveness, not to mention retarding one's career or even threatening one's survival as a filmmaker. Most real difficulties, however, do not lie in choosing between right and wrong, but rather between right and right.

Another ethical concern should be with the standard of arguments one puts forward. Evidence is always more persuasive than opinion. A documentary is always more powerful if its ideas arise out of a sustained life situation than it is when actuality has been plucked to illustrate a thesis. Interestingly the same principle applies to fiction films and makes the difference between "signifying" a situation instead of presenting it in the act of being. Once again, drama and the documentary share fundamentals.

Usually it is important to show that a point is wholly a participant's, not something one has contrived. In a film I made about an English country estate, *A Remnant of a Feudal Society* (BBC "Yesterday's Witness" series, 1970), a groom spontaneously held out his deformed hand to show what he thought eventually happened to horsemen after holding reins in all weathers at their master's pleasure. Because it was unclear what was wrong with his hand in the wide shot, the cameraman zoomed in so that the spontaneity of his action remained manifest. Cutting to the hand would have subtly changed the authenticity of his demonstration by looking more like my work. Demonstrating the origin and authenticity of evidence, and acknowledging ambiguity where it exists, all involve ethical decisions.

PUBLIC SHOWING

When should a participant have the prerogative to see and veto a cut? If you agreed that editing would involve feedback from participants, they obviously have such a prerogative. Offering participation may be the only way to overcome the kind of distrust that can poison relations between races, say, or between feminists and well-meaning males. With only a little grief, I filmed women's liberation militants in the 1960s under such an agreement. Indeed some film-makers feel they cannot adequately represent a constituency's wisdom and purpose except through some such democratic collaboration. Others regard such scruples as a luxury and believe they can ill afford the time and energy to persuade a group that particular fears and sensitivities are not shared by the general public.

You should only show your cut to participants after clearly explaining any limitation to their rights. If you are only willing to be advised, make this absolutely clear, or there will be much bad feeling.

Before a public showing, get legal opinion over anything that might land either you or your participants in trouble. Be aware that a lawyer's job is to look for snags and to err on the side of caution.

If you are showing your film when someone in the audience will feel betrayed by something critical in your film, you should probably prepare this person well in advance, so he does not feel ridiculous in the presence of family and friends. If you don't, that person may henceforward regard you as a traitor and all film people as frauds. While one avoids renegade behavior at all costs, participants invariably see their own impact on the screen with great subjectivity. To adjust over-sympathetically to this would be to abandon documentary work for public relations.

PHILOSOPHY AND MISSION

The two approaches outlined earlier—transparency and reflexivity—break down at their crudest into either directing the self to look outward at the world or employing the world as a lens through which to examine some aspect of self. This difference is supposed to distinguish the classicist temperament from the romantic, but either can be valid and fascinating so long as one recognizes at the outset one's real purpose and priorities. Of course in the long run, neither dimension is separable; there is no world without perception nor any perception without its object. Self and world are inextricably related as I have argued all along. The decision about which route to take should arise out of one's subject and what one wants to say about it. Often the approach chosen is simply a question of emphasis and of how one best functions as a storyteller.

Any philosophy of documentary filmmaking must still take into account the inevitable: that your human subjects will make some adaptations for you and your camera and that your audience will make its own assessment of your relationship to truthfulness—no matter whether you assist. The process of recording and interpreting needs to be justified, and the people making the record need to be liked and trusted. When the complexities of the relationship affect important truths they need to be acknowledged, either implicitly or explicitly if credibility or even truth itself is not be impaired.

These parameters put a lid on certain kinds of subjects, for the recording process is either too intrusive to document intimate occasions or will seem so to the audience.

Unlike other arts, documentary cannot be made in retreat from life but is created by moving within it—and by consciously and conscientiously living with the consequences. Because many issues and personalities remain unawakened and unresolved until the camera has made its mark, one must be ready to carry responsibility for change and criticism and to argue passionately for your freedom of speech when you are attacked for daring as one person to make an interpretive criticism.

Aesthetic and ethical decisions are seldom made from a position of cool intellectual neutrality; more often they are forged in discomfort and anxiety over conflicting obligations—to actual people who know and trust you on the one hand or to truths whose importance may transcend any individual's passing discomfort on the other.

One thought I keep in mind when making a documentary, one that I find both comforting and liberating: I remind myself that, even after my best efforts, my film is still only what the French call *"une tentative"*—an attempt, bid, or endeavor that is only one person's view at one moment in time. In the end, it is delusionary and productive of too much misery to saddle oneself with the responsibility for definitive truth. It is as irrational, as common, and humanly foolish as demanding that one's children be perfect.

If you and I each honestly take stock of ourselves, we see that we already carry the imprint of certain knowledge and certain convictions. To give this imprint full recognition is really to say to oneself, "This is the heart of that experience that I alone can pass on to others." If you also feel the need to communicate it, you have the drive for authorship and to make art—a human need no less enduring than the need for shelter or sex.

To some, the "transparent" documentarian busily finding and illuminating a subject ends up by negating his own importance as an author. For this kind of filmmaker often aims to present life on the screen so it exists with scarcely a trace of authorship. Almost certainly this filmmaker is engaging in displaced autobiography, for rather than expressing, say, "*I* have been the victim of a violent society, and look what has happened to *me*," she searches out others whose diversity and experience can give universality to what the filmmaker has already found in her own limited but deeply felt experience.

As a documentary maker, this is a way of putting your convictions to a test—by finding other people and other situations to convey what you want to say. As such, it is your *vision* you wish to share with the audience and not yourself as a subject. Your task is to identify the counterparts of your own experience floating unattached on life's stream and to catch and tether them in a structured statement that will faithfully mirror the deeply held truths that life has taught you.

Obviously this is neither scientific nor objective, but the restraints on indulging a display of ego and the fact that one's own most enduring preoccupations must be found freestanding outside oneself help to create a product with overtones of universality.

I must emphasize that a documentary of any vision and interest to others can only emerge from the kind of self-knowledge and self-acceptance that allows a director to look outward and away from the self. Only with this maturity can one identify the surrogates to one's own values and temperament and allow them to achieve a life of their own in a film. Naturally the discipline of such a process has its own rewards. Your work also alters the way you see the fundamentals of your own life—the very source from which your documentary process sprang. In this way, each film tends to lay the foundations for your next.

P·A·R·T X·I

CAREER TRACK

C·H·A·P·T·E·R 2·2

EDUCATION

PLANNING A CAREER

How does one get started in any kind of film- or videomaking? And where should one expect to be, say, after three years of professional work? These questions are asked all the time and deserve answers. The second, where one should expect to be after a given period of time, is the most immediately important because it indicates a perilous misunderstanding.

Filmmaking does not have a career ladder like banking or retail management with predictable promotion rates. It is a branch of show business: How far you get and how long it takes getting there depend on your ability, energy, luck, and persistence. If your primary loyalties are to home, children, family, community, and material well being, sustaining any commitment to filmmaking may be difficult because the industry is informally structured, unpredictable, and necessitates an unusual degree of initiative and autonomy in the individual.

On the other hand, if you are interested in people, social movements, and politics and you want to make your individual voice heard and if you are willing to invest a long, uphill, and impecunious struggle to gain recognition, you might really like the documentary filmmaker's way of life. Trying to tell the important truths publicly is a way of life, a mission. The life is insecure, but you never, never have to wonder like so many others why you go to work every day.

How do you get started? Oldtimers used to scorn any form of schooling, but that is changing as alumni from film schools achieve prominence. Although I received only on-the-job training myself, I believe ardently in the value of a good filmmaking education.

If that is out of the question, you can still do a great deal of self-preparation outside the available educational structures. The best education will always be that which one gives oneself. Schooling is and must be geared to the common denominator, and this institutionalization will be frustrating for those who learn rapidly or who are unusually motivated. On the other side of the coin, the "industry approach"—getting into some kind of ground-level apprenticeship program—can be fraught with its own kind of frustrations even though initially it looks very attractive.

In short, there are no sure routes, only intelligent traveling.

TO SCHOOL OR NOT TO SCHOOL

People ask skeptically whether a school can ever be the best place to learn film-making. Older people in the film and television industries may tell you that only on-the-job experience counts. Because such people tend to value procedural knowledge and professionalism (often deficiencies in recent graduates), they assume schooling fails. But a school cannot teach the consistency, tact, and reliability that are the hallmark of a professional attitude, nor should it drill students on the niceties of an industrial procedure.

Many holding down media jobs received no college-level education. They think that their own kind of education is "enough" and that college education only fills young people's heads with idealistic dreams that have no relation to "the business." This distorted view also exists among students, many of whom leave school prematurely when an industry job comes their way. This is almost always a terrible mistake.

To me, a good education gives a cultural and intellectual perspective on one's chosen medium, a historical knowledge of what one's role grows out of, and aspirations to use one's professional life to its fullest extent and for the widest good. Most of all by encouraging collaboration and unbridled individual vision, education should help one discover where one's talents, abilities, and energies truly lie.

As a slightly scarred survivor of the industry apprenticeship system myself, I very much want to stress the benefits of good formal education. One example should suffice: I regularly see students in my 15-week classes absorbing techniques and insight that took me 10 years on the job to discover for myself. Maybe I was unlucky or unobservant, but most of what I have heard confirms how isolated the apprentice usually is and how slowly she learns. The explanation is simple and stark: In the freelance world, know-how and experience are earning power so workers systematically *avoid* enlightening their juniors.

Thus the ill-prepared youngster, weary of "more school" and gratefully taking the first job that comes along, is apt to find herself still driving the company station wagon or answering the phones five years later. Most employers live pressurized lives and do not consider preparing the individual for more responsibility any part of their job. That individual is either *prepared through prior schooling* to assume more complex duties or must somehow devise an education for herself while serving as the company peon.

The communications school, however, exists solely to disseminate knowledge, build students' confidence, and systematically expose them to learning experiences. If the faculty knows its business, it can give the student a historical and conceptual purview as well as basic technical experience denied to most who presently earn their living by filmmaking. I for one only actually used a camera for *one* shot in the course of directing 20 films for television. Unfortunately trade union and pragmatic demarcation lines in people's working lives ensure that professionals develop mystiques about each other. In the long run, this discourages experiment and makes people overdeferential to the expertise claimed by others.

Only by going through all the stages of making a film—no matter how badly—can the aspiring director begin to truly see the faults or the strengths in her own (and other people's) work. To use film is to use such a dense and allusory language that a director is obliged to develop two separate kinds of ability. One is the slew of human and technical skills to put a well-exposed, well-composed series of shots on the screen and make them add up to a coherent statement. The other is much more profound: that of knowing oneself and of remaining true to oneself even when one's work comes under attack. The beginning filmmaker not only relives and reinvents the history of film during her early growth but also discovers with a shock how much of her personal identity and perceptions she has taken for granted and how precarious she feels putting her ideas and assumptions before an audience.

A good film school is an ideal place in which to have this experience; there is a structured program of learning, technical facilities, and enthusiastic expertise available and contemporaries with whom one may collaborate. Most important, in school one can experiment and afford failures. In a learning-level apprentice situation (if you can find one), unwise experiment spells professional suicide so the apprentice learns to be conservative and play safe, further slowing the learning process.

Schools are thus places in which to share enthusiasm, find peers, acquire the history of one's medium, and fly high on exhilarating theories of life and of film. An established school also represents the opportunity to make an informal network of contacts, each of whom tends to aid the others after they become established.

SEEKING A FORMAL EDUCATION

Many schools, colleges, and universities now have film courses. While no serious study of film is ever wasted, you should be careful and critical before committing yourself to any extended course of study. Many film departments are underequipped and underbudgeted. Often "film studies" is an offshoot of the English department, perhaps originally created to bolster sagging enrollments. While teaching in such a department may be enthusiastic, it will presumably come out of a literary sensibility, which has only a limited application to film. Ingmar Bergman says, "Film has nothing to do with literature; the character and substance of the two art forms are usually in conflict. . . . I would say there is no art form that has so much in common with film as music."[1]

---

[1] Ingmar Bergman, "Introduction," *Four Screenplays of Ingmar Bergman* (New York: Simon & Schuster, 1960).

If you intend to go into film or video production, avoid departments that seem lukewarm over production by their students. Film studies are good for sharpening the perceptions, but divorced from film production they become an end in themselves. The measure of a film school is what the students and the faculty produce (see Figure 22–1). If Bergman is right—and who would seriously question him?—the making of film is a musical rather than a literary pursuit so it makes more sense to study film at a music department than it does under English teachers. In fact, the literary and cerebral nature of much of what passes as film study makes a transition to filmmaking all but impossible. Quite simply, you will not get far learning to make films unless you study with filmmakers.

But—a further warning!—there are a number of people calling themselves film teachers whose own films are so far from the mainstream that they lack appeal for almost any audience. During the 1970s some of the more colorful experimentalists secured tenured positions in universities and art schools. School administrations welcomed them because they represented a buccaneering independence to students at the time and because they were ready to work with little equipment and small budgets.

Some experimental cinema achieves beautiful effects, and clearly there must

FIGURE 22–1

A unit of women from Columbia College Chicago shooting in a Chicago shelter for the homeless. (Jane Stevens.)

always be room for the inventive iconoclast in any art form. But what passes under the label "experimental film" is usually a product of the counterculture and by its very nature departs from or even despises the narrative form. Its advocates are thus equipped neither technically nor temperamentally to teach the conventions and nuances that created the modern film. Fine-art schools tend to undervalue craftsmanlike control of the medium and to overvalue "personal vision"; students work alone and compete for recognition like the painters and sculptors around them. This atmosphere tends to encourage gimmicky and self-centered production with poor basic control over the medium. The graduating student seldom leaves school with any work that film or television companies would take seriously although it must be said that music video presently has an appetite for extravagances of all kinds.

The opposite extreme is the trade school, which is more technically disciplined and infinitely less therapeutic. This kind of teaching is usually industry oriented and concerned with drilling students to carry out narrowly defined technical duties for a standardized industrial product. Union apprenticeship schemes tend to be along these lines—technically superb but intellectually arid. They do lead to jobs, unlike the hastily assembled "school of communications," which offers the illusion of a quick route to a television station job. For every occupation there is somewhere a diploma mill: In the television version, you should expect to find a private, unaffiliated facility with a primitive studio where students are run through the rudiments of equipment operation. Needless to say, it is doubtful whether any significant number ever find the work they hope for.

A good school should offer a broad balance of technical education with a strong foundation in conceptual, aesthetic, and historical course work. It should have defined tracks for specialization such as screenwriting, camera, sound, editing, directing, and production management. Animation is an advantage, but it is utterly separate from live-action filming and more akin to the graphic arts in its training. There should be a respectable contingent of professional-level equipment as well as enough basic cameras and editing equipment to support the beginning levels. Most important, a good school should be the center of an enthusiastic film-producing community in which students as a matter of course support and crew for each other (see Figure 22–2).

If that community has been in existence for a while, successful former students not only give visiting lectures but come back as teachers. In turn, they either employ or give vital references to the most promising students. This is "networking" where the lines that so often barricade a school from "real life" are being crossed in both directions. The school filmmaking community tapers off into the young (and not so young) professional community to mutual advantage. In the reverse flow, mentors not only give advice and steer projects but, more important, exemplify the way of life the student is trying to make her own. The film and video community, even in the largest cities, operates like a village in which personal recommendation is everything.

Much practical information can be gleaned from the periodically published *American Film Institute Guide to College Courses in Film and Television* (Princeton, N.J.: Peterson's Guides). Because it is so comprehensive, it allows one to make comparisons and to spot a department's emphasis. Even a promising statement of philosophy from a department of communications may be undercut

FIGURE 22–2 ——————————————————————————————————————

A mobile unit. Notice the handheld camera and gun mike. Weight, complexity, and interconnecting wires make separate equipment items cumbersome compared to a camcorder. (Jane Stevens.)

when you add up equipment holdings and examine course structure. Sometimes a department has evolved under the chairmanship of a journalist or radio specialist so film and television production may be public-relations orphans within an all-purpose "communications" mill.

Here are some approaches and questions you might try using to decide if a school's department fulfills your expectations:

a. How big is the department and what does its structure reveal? (Number of courses, number of students, what do the senior and most influential faculty actually teach?)

b. How long is the program? (See model syllabus.)

c. How much specialization is possible? How far do upper-level courses go?

d. How much equipment is there, and what kind? (This is a real giveaway.)

e. What kind of background do the faculty members have and what have they produced lately?

f. How much equipment and materials is supplied out of tuition and class fees, and how much is the student expected to supply along the way?

g. What does the department say about its attitudes and philosophy?

h. What does the place feel like? (Try to visit the facilities.)

i. What do the students think of the place? (Ask to speak to the senior students.)

j. How much of a specialty is documentary? What films have the people teaching documentary produced themselves?

A good way to locate good teaching is to go to student film festivals and note where the films you like are being made. A sure sign of energetic and productive teaching, even in a small facility, is when student work is receiving regular awards.

Below are some of the larger and well-recognized film/video schools, not all of which teach documentary at this time:

American Film Institute
AFI TV-Video
2021 N. Western
    Avenue
Los Angeles, CA 90027
(213) 856–7743

Australian Film and
    Television School
Box 126, North Ryde
NSW 2113,
    AUSTRALIA
(02) 805–6611

Brooks Institute
801 Alston Road
Santa Barbara,
    CA 93109
(805) 966–3888

California State
    University,
    Northridge
Department of Radio/
    TV/Film
18111 Nordhoff Street
Northridge, CA 91330
(818) 885–3192

California Institute of the
    Arts
Film School
24700 McBean
    Parkway
Valencia, CA 91355
(805) 253–7825

Columbia College
    Chicago
Film/Video Department
600 S. Michigan
    Avenue
Chicago, IL 60605
(312) 663–1600

Columbia University
Film Division
513 Dodge Hall
New York, NY 10027
(212) 854–2815

Deutsche Film- und
    Fernsehakademie
    Berlin GmbH
Pommeralle 1
1 Berlin 19
West Berlin,
    GERMANY

Dramatiska Institutet
    (The Swedish
    Media School)
Filmhuset
Borgvagen
Box 27090, S–102
51 Stockholm,
    SWEDEN

Emerson College
Mass Communications
    Division
100 Beacon Street
Boston, MA 02116
(617) 578–8832

Film and Television
    School of India
Law College Road
Poona 411 004, INDIA

Film and Television
    Institute of Tamil
    Nadu
Department of
    Information and
    Public Relations
Government of Tamil
    Nadu, Madras
Adyar, Madras–600
    020, INDIA

Hochschule fur Fernsehen
    und Film
Ohmstrasse 11
8000 Munchen 40,
    GERMANY

L'Institut des Hautes
    Etudes
    Cinematographiques
    (IDHEC)
4 Avenue de L'Europe
94360 Bry-sur-Marne,
    FRANCE

Ithaca College
    Roy H. Park School of
    Communications
Ithaca, NY 14850
    (607) 274–3895

London International
    Film School
24 Shelton Street
London WC2H 9HP,
    ENGLAND
071–240–0168

Loyola Marymount
    University
Communication Arts
    Department
Los Angeles, CA 90045
    (213) 338–3033

National Film and
    Television School
Beaconsfield Film
    Studios

Station Road,
    Beaconsfield,
Bucks HP9 1LG,
    ENGLAND
04946–71234

New School for Social
    Research
Media Studies
2 West 13th Street
New York, NY 10011
    (212) 741–8903

New York University
    Film Department
Tisch School of the
    Arts, Admissions
New York University,
    721 Broadway, 7th
    Floor
New York, NY 10003
    (212) 598–2416

Northwestern University
    NWU, Department of
    Radio-TV-Film
1905 Sheridan Road
Evanston, IL 60208
    (708) 491–7315

Ohio University
    School of Film
378 Lindley Hall
Athens, OH 45701
    (614) 593–1323

Panswowa Wyzsza Szkola
    Filmowa,
    Telwizyjna i
    Teatraina
im Leona Schillera, U1
Targowa 61/63
90–323 Lodz,
    POLAND

Penn State University
    Film and Video
    Program
201 Carnegie Building
University Park, PA
    16802
    (814) 865–0546

Pratt Institute
  Media Arts
      Department
  200 Willoughby
      Avenue
  Brooklyn, NY 11205
  (718) 636–3633

Rhode Island School of
      Design
  Film/Video Department
  2 College Street
  Providence, RI 02903
  (401) 331–3511

San Francisco Art
      Institute
  Filmmaking
      Department
  800 Chestnut Street
  San Francisco,
      CA 94133
  (415) 771–7020

School of Visual Arts,
      Inc.
  Film and Video
      Department
  209 East 23rd Street
  New York, NY 10010
  (212) 679–7350

Southern Illinois
      University
  Department of Cinema
      and Photography
  Carbondale, IL 62901
  (618) 453–2365

Stanford University
  Department of
      Communication
  McClatchy Hall
  Stanford, CA 94305–
      2050
  (415) 723–4700

Syracuse University
  Art Media Studies
  222 Smith Hall
  Syracuse, NY 13244–
      1180
  (315) 443–9199

Tel-Aviv University
  Department of Film
      and TV
  69978 Ramat–Aviv,
      ISRAEL
  972–03–5450412

Temple University
  Department of Radio-
      TV-Film
  Philadelphia, PA 19122
  (215) 787–1335

University of California,
      Los Angeles,
  Film and Television
      Department
  405 Hilgard
  Los Angeles,
      CA 90024–1622
  (213) 825–7891

University of Iowa
  Division of
      Broadcasting and
      Film
  105 Communication
      Studies
  Iowa City, IA 52242
  (319) 335–0575

University of Southern
      California
  School of Cinema-
      Television
  University Park
  Los Angeles, CA
      90089–2211
  (213) 743–3144

University of Texas at
      Austin
  Department of Radio,
      Television and
      Film
  School of
      Communications
  CMA6.118
  Austin, Texas
  (512) 471–4071

University of Toledo
  Department of Theatre,
    Film & Dance
  Film Division
  Toledo, OH 43606–
    3390
  (419) 537–2375

Vsesoyuzni
  Gosudarstvenni
  Institut
  Kinematografi Ulitsa
    Vilgelma Pika 3
  Moscow 129226,
    USSR

York University
  Film/Video Department
  4700 Keele Street
  North York,
  Ontario, M3J 1P3,
    CANADA
  (416) 736–5149

The *AFI Guide* and Jan Bone's *Opportunities in Film* list schools in Canada, Australia, New Zealand, and European countries. Many Americans assume that work and study abroad is easily arranged and will be an extension of conditions in the United States. The prospective student should be warned that many film schools have very competitive entry requirements and that self-support through part-time work in foreign countries is very hard to come by and usually illegal. To live and work professionally abroad, unless one is rich, is nowadays almost impossible since everywhere immigration policies exclude foreign workers when natives are underemployed. That situation changes only when you have special and unusual skills to offer. Check local conditions with the school's admissions officer and with the nearest consulate before committing yourself.

SELF-HELP AS A REALISTIC ALTERNATIVE

Since many can afford neither time nor money to go to school, they must find other means to acquire the necessary knowledge and experience. Werner Herzog has said that anyone who wants to make films should waste no more than a week learning film techniques. Given his flair for overstatement, this period would appear a little short, but fundamentally I share his attitude. Film and video is a practical subject and can be tackled by the intelligent do-it-yourselfer. This book is intended to encourage the reader to learn filmmaking by making films, to learn through doing, and, if absolutely necessary, through doing alone.

I have included a number of projects because I find most people are pragmatic and like to learn in a practical way. Projects are good because they are concrete and verifiable, and they leave knowledge organized memorably around a core of personal experience. Nobody should underestimate the importance of hobby magazines, with their "do-it-yourself" approach in the education of the world's doers.

Self-education in the arts, however, is different from self-education in a technology because the arts are not finite and calculable. Instead they are based on shared tastes and perceptions that at an early stage call for the criticism and participation of others. The painter, novelist, poet, photographer, or animator—

artists who usually create alone—is not complete in what she does until she submits her work for society's reactions. What seems like a career of pleasantly removed creation is really a long, isolated preparation to engage with the public for the final phase of closure.

PROS AND CONS OF COLLABORATION

If you use this book to begin active film-/videomaking, you will recognize that filmmaking is a social art, one stillborn if there is no spirit of collaboration. You will need other people as technicians to do any sophisticated shooting, and you will need to earn the interest of other people in your end product. If you are unused to working collaboratively—and sadly this is true of most students who are taught to compete for honors instead of cooperatively earning them—you have an inspirational experience ahead. Filmmaking by its nature is an intense, shared experience, and no relationship is left untouched. Lifelong friendships and partnerships develop out of it, but on the negative side, flaws emerge in one's own and other people's characters when pressures mount because of fatigue. If you want to rapidly become older and wiser, do not bother enlisting in any personal-growth classes—simply make a film!

Somewhere along the way you will want a mentor—someone to give reliable, knowledgeable, and reasonably objective criticism of your work and who can help solve the problems that arise. If none is in the offing right now, it is not important, for you can go far under your own steam. In any case, it is a law of nature that you only find the person you need when you really need her.

C·H·A·P·T·E·R 2·3

GETTING WORK

Let us suppose that you have acquired a good knowledge and experience in the field of film- or videomaking. How do you make the transition from student to paid worker in the medium? Film and television directing has traditionally been an area for the self-starter so, unless you are accepted by a going concern as a full-time employee, you and your friends must make cooperative efforts to get established. You may be lucky and straightaway direct work on commission. But it is more likely you will need to develop craft experience and contacts first. Plenty of people get work as a grip, an assistant editor, or a camera assistant straight out of school, but it happens only *if you have useful skills, professional discipline, and good references to prove it.*

The aspiring documentary maker will, initially and perhaps for a long time, have to use his skills to fulfill quite ordinary commercial needs. You may find yourself expending lots of imagination and effort crewing for industrial, training, or medical films or shooting conferences and weddings. Learning to do this reliably, well, and creatively will teach you a great deal. A training in industrials served Robert Altman and many another director well.

If, as a crew person or director, you do good work, on time, and within the projected cost, your reputation slowly spreads through the grapevine. Here everything I have said about reliability and realism in the whole film crew becomes a necessity, for employers are less interested in how you got the results than in the fact that you performed on time and on budget.

These requirements are not antithetical to first-rate work, but they do run contrary to undisciplined and immature personalities who are apt to imagine there is a place waiting for their "creativity" in the arts. Everything in this book surely demonstrates that shooting and structuring a film of any kind is a highly disciplined activity, and emphatically not something to be entrusted to unbridled instinct. The true creativity behind any film is structured and persistent, and the same industrious nature will undoubtedly be needed to get oneself established. There are no reliable shortcuts to recognition and reward. Filmmaking is a long, slow business: As a way of life, it can only in the end gratify those who value the process itself, and as such, it is just like any of the other arts.

Here the value of the school with professional ties becomes apparent; for if you do well, your teachers' opinions of you carry weight, and some may even be in a position to offer you a job or refer you to someone in search of a promising beginner. Well-established schools usually have an *internship system* with local media employers, and these temporary positions frequently lead to employment.

Unless you are fortunate enough to be wealthy, making a career in film-making will probably demand that you enter the marketplace as a freelancer. There are regional and national differences to the film and television industries, of course, but developing as a freelancer remains similar no matter where in the world you try to enter "the industry."

A degree is nice for it indicates you are serious, but more than anything you need a *portfolio* of your work to show prospective employers your skills. Here the teaching, equipment familiarization, and crewing in a film school can help you emerge with employment-level skills. If you have some original directing work, this will help you get interviews and even some commissioned work es-pecially if you have won some festival awards.

Most people starting out must first be willing to do anything in order to be in the right place at the right time when "something opens up." The aim is to make a living as a freelance technician and invest any spare time and cash in making films with contemporaries who are also struggling to gain experience and recognition. By investing in your own talent and developing it to a point where you have concrete, proven abilities, you then have something to offer an employer or a sponsor. Once you get a little work, you start building a track record and a reputation. It is this that recommends you for more interesting and demanding work.

All this emphasis on becoming known and fitting in may seem like the slip-way to destructive compromises. It doesn't have to be. After all, the films on which we were raised were produced for profit, and some were good art by any standards. Almost the entire history of cinema has its roots in commerce with each new work predicated on day-to-day ticket sales. If cinema and capitalism go hand in hand, one must also recognize a certain cantankerous democracy about the business of selling tickets, for they are votes from the wallet and ensure that the cinema cannot afford to be irrelevant or stray too far from the sensibil-ities of the common man.

Cinema and television descend to us by way of vaudeville, the fairground, the popular theater, and the music hall. They are modern inheritors of folk art traditions and do not encourage ivory tower creativity. There are Sunday paint-ers, but as yet no Sunday filmmakers. The cost and scale of film-/video-making, the long duration of the process, and the inescapably public, collective nature of the medium all compel the serious person wanting to live by filmmaking to be concerned with speaking to an audience.

FORM AND MARKETABILITY

The filmmaker must first find subjects interesting to a sizable audience, for people only pay to see what interests them. This need not be a cynically conceived or fixed commodity, however. For on the one hand, there is a subject, and on the other, there is *a way of seeing*. The innovative Swiss director Alain Tanner tells how idealistic young people used to come to him saying, "We hear you are a Marxist; we too want to change the world, and we want to use film to do it." He would answer, "Good, but first you must change film."

The implication is important: *How* a film sees is more important than *what* it sees. Tanner is saying that the world needs not new subjects but new ways of seeing. Or put another way, creativity in form may be more important than ingenuity at finding content.

To make a career for yourself you need not only find subjects of interest to an audience but also original and imaginative treatments of those subjects. I once saw a film about the plight of old people in Britain: not a particularly original or popular subject. The film, however, was extraordinary. The filmmaker had shot no talking heads but instead had asked each person to either look into the camera or to go through some piece of domestic routine. He had laid tape interviews (voice-over) against these lonely and inanimate shots, shots in which one listened to the person's thoughts while he stared at you, and the effect was devastating. For the unblinking stare was by turns resignation, loneliness, abandonment, boredom, or a human being waiting for death. The *form* of the film made what could have been a conventional film about "our responsibility" into a muted, accusatory confrontation with one's own bad dreams.

Fresh form invigorated this film, while stale form disables many another worthy effort. There has not yet been invented the range of forms for the documentary that exist for the fiction film, so documentaries tend to look alike. Much of your resourcefulness, therefore, should go to finding films with innovative forms.

THE SEARCH FOR SUBJECTS

By all means watch what other people are doing and what distributors seem to buy. Go through catalogues of available films, giving particular attention to your own areas of interest. If you make a list, you will certainly find gaps. Not only will you find significant holes in what is available, but also you will get an idea of what the distributors are offering and what presumably they are renting or even selling outright. By doing your own market study, you can decide where your interests might fit into the existing commercial structure. Bear in mind that there is a separation, by and large, between producers and distributors akin to that between authors and publishers. You cannot expect any money from a distributor until you have a product, and if the product proves to be marketable, you may then be able to go back and get an "advance" for your next film. At the time of writing, however, the distributors are in disarray. The market is changing rapidly as cable television and VCR rentals present a rapidly evolving set of new circumstances.

The real way to find subjects is to find something that deeply interests you, and the real way to get it into shape is to talk about it, argue it out, and discover all its possibilities, depths, and difficulties through conversations with filmmaking colleagues. Try your ideas on nonfilmmakers too; they need only be the kind of people for whom discussion of the world's affairs is a necessary part of living.

CONTINUING TO LEARN FROM OTHER PEOPLE'S WORK

It is possible to see other people's films and learn very little of use from them. The problem is that films, if at all good, fascinate us to the exclusion of our critical, analytical abilities. This is partly overcome by the change of perspective that comes automatically when one begins making films oneself, and that leads one to recognize the kinds of situations and approaches one has used, or considered using, oneself. A more active solution is to set up some kind of analytical exercise with a VCR so that you make yourself observe methodically and absorb whatever could be useful for the future.

Here is a suggested study program, actually an abbreviated version of Project 2: "Editing Analysis," in Part III.

1. First see the whole film through without interruption and experience it as an audience does, not allowing your expertise to make you reflect on technique.

2. Write down your dominant impressions of the film, especially what it conveys to you in the way of knowledge and attitude about its subject. Most important, what does it leave you *feeling?*

3. Run the film a sequence at a time. This means stopping and making a note each time it changes time or location and begins a new block of content. You will end up with a block diagram of the whole movie.

4. Run the movie again, this time analyzing each sequence for its contribution to the whole.

5. Analyze also what special technique each sequence uses to achieve its ends, and assign a value to the language or *form* chosen. Was it appropriate? Could you see a better way of reaching the same communicative ends?

From this analysis you will learn an immense amount about the way a movie affects people and about the art used to create certain kinds of impressions. One valuable outcome of an analysis is the ability to intelligently question the makers of the film if they happen to appear in your area. Documentary is a small and select world, and documentary makers are disproportionately pleased to meet someone who not only knows their work but has a few penetrating questions to ask about its genesis and intentions.

Out of such conversations, links are formed. Informal though they are, contacts of this nature frequently lead to work of some sort. If you genuinely admire someone's work, it is not unlikely that he or she will take very seriously your desire to work and learn. Film work is irregular and unpredictable; it is not unusual to suddenly need a gofer or to have room for an observer. Anyone who values that position by working in a dedicated way is someone everyone will remember. Work most often goes to those who have earned a warm spot in everyone's heart.

THE DOCUMENTARY PROPOSAL

When you have films of your own to show, you are in a better position to approach the various funds. Many funding organizations will grant up to 50 percent or even more of a budget if the proposal is well written, unusually interesting, and businesslike. Naturally the competition for funds is keen, but you would be surprised how poorly most prospective filmmakers represent themselves on paper.

It is an irony of filmmaking that only those who write good proposals get funded. Filmmaking is not an escape from the need for logic and literacy as many a college student has discovered to his chagrin. The ability to write or speak fluently about one's ideas and intentions is all the more necessary to the beginner who has yet to thoroughly prove himself on the screen. Few people write adequate proposals for their documentaries; far too many read like puff pieces for the *TV Guide* and are quite useless to committee members who must decide from words on paper whether Applicant A rather than Applicant B deserves the funding.

To produce a coherent documentary, as we have so often said, *you must have a working hypothesis*. It might say, for instance, that "the Moral Majority is a movement believing that authoritarian moral pressure can take America back to morality, goodness, godliness, and burgeoning wealth, just as it 'used to be.' " The hypothesis might also set out to show as definitively as possible "that no such America ever existed outside the frame of a Norman Rockwell picture."

You should, during *research*, have tested this hypothesis by locating likely people, doing initial interviews on cassette, and analyzing them for common denominators, common threads, and repeated idioms. You should check out whether there are figures, anecdotes, reports, film clips, or studies that either support or refute the Moral Majority's contention. Search out the Moral Majority's proponents and opponents so you can use their views and evidence. Plan to make your points through filmed action and behavior rather than through discussion and interview. Make sure that opposing people or points of view are brought together on the screen and are led to some form of *confrontation*.

When you have the parts of the *conflict* you wish to choreograph on the screen, you are ready to sit down and write. You know what you want to say through your film, and now you have to think of the best way to say it. What sequences will you shoot *(content)*? In what special way will you elicit and shoot each sequence *(form)*? In what order will you probably show your material, and what is to be the film's major organizing factor *(structure)*?

If you are shooting a deer hunt and are setting out to show man as a technological killer, the *time sequence* of a particular hunt with all its ritual will be your major organizing factor. If your film is about the connection between street violence and special weather conditions, you will have to set your own best linear structure since you do not have a clear process organized in time.

See Part II, Preproduction, for help with writing your proposal, which should be written and rewritten until it is pared down to the *shortest, clearest piece of writing you can possibly produce.*

Show you are realistic when you write about the audience you want to reach, and do not ever write "Everyone!!!." Say why you really think your film will appeal to a wide audience, and show you are practical. Show you have done your homework, and *include quotes and figures where they will supply essential detail* for your reader. Use direct and appropriately colorful language to describe people and situations. It helps to establish your sharp eye for telling detail, your intelligence, wit, and sense of irony. You are not a government sociologist when you make a documentary, and you are not a social scientist with an obligation to be impersonal and objective. You are much more like a good journalist who builds a case by marshaling compelling evidence.

Don't ever label your film "An Inquiry into. . . ." By the time you propose a film, you should not only have made your inquiry, but you should also have a lot to say. To be sure, you will learn more while you are shooting, but nobody starts an inquiry while directing a film unit, and specialized readers on a funding panel know it. You need your ingredients and your strategy already mapped out, and you need to firmly demonstrate it. Make sure your proposal reflects your knowledge and is purposeful about how you are going to project it into the viewer's mind. Don't use hype or public relations dramatics. That is for gullible viewers, not professional media people.

Be brief, structured, and businesslike in your writing. Have it checked by a couple of good readers for logic, comprehensiveness, brevity, accurate math, spelling, and so on. Be ready to rewrite and retype it several times because with film proposals, *you are what you write.*

Experienced people consider someone who cannot write clearly and interestingly, who does not bother to spell correctly, or whose figures do not add up neither the kind of person to deal accurately with facts and truth nor one likely to carry an expensive and painstaking project like a film.

With thorough research and a good proposal under your belt, you should have all the arguments you need at your fingertips. Writing the proposal not only clarifies your thinking, it also serves as a self-administered briefing that prepares you, when it is necessary, to *talk* knowledgeably and persuasively about the project. This may later be a vital factor in confirming your credibility and competence.

FUNDS, JOBS, AND TRAINING SCHEMES

In the United States, there is a complex and shifting system of *federal, state, and private funding agencies.* Each has guidelines and a track record in funding some special area. Usually only local organizations will fund first films. Fund money is good money because you usually are not required to pay it back, so making use of local or national funds is an important means of financing documentary filmmaking. As a general rule, private grant funds prefer to give completion money to films that are shot and may be viewed, while government agencies are a little more likely to fund research and preproduction. Needless to say, all arts funding shrank under the Reagan administration and continues to shrink under the Bush administration.

If your track record is slender (perhaps a short film that has won a festival award), and you are seeking either preproduction, production, or completion money, you should investigate your *state or city arts council,* which is probably affiliated with the *National Endowment for the Arts.* If it doesn't fund film- or videomaking, its officers usually know about the other local sources of funding. As with all research, use one expert's knowledge to get to the others. The national organization's guidelines can be obtained by writing to: Grants Office, National Endowment for the Arts, 2401 E Street, N.W., Washington, D.C. 20506.

Each state has a *state humanities committee,* which works in association with the *National Endowment for the Humanities.* This agency works to fund groups of accredited individuals (usually academics) producing work in the humanities. National guidelines can be obtained from: The National Endowment for the Humanities, 806 15th Street, N.W., MS 256, Washington, D.C. 20506.

Many states and big cities have a *film commission or bureau* that exists to encourage and facilitate filmmaking. A full list can be obtained through the American Film Institute or through *Opportunities in Film* (both listed below). These film bureau offices develop formal and informal relationships with the whole local filmmaking community and can be an excellent source of information on all aspects of local production.

Specifically for funding documentaries, there is the *Independent Documentary Fund,* which is administered by the Corporation for Public Broadcasting (CPB). The CPB also runs a program fund for financing independent films. Information and guidelines are available from: Television Activities, Corporation for Public Broadcasting, 1111 16th Street, N.W., Washington, D.C. 20036.

The American Film Institute (AFI) administers funds and also serves as an intermediary; for anyone looking for internships, funding, or special information, membership in the AFI is imperative. The institute publishes a range of informational materials called Factfiles; those of special interest here include:

No. 1 Film and Television Periodicals in English
No. 2 Careers in Film and Television
No. 3 Film/Video Festivals and Awards
No. 6 Independent Film and Video
No. 11 Film/Television: A Research Guide
No. 12 Film/Television: Grants, Scholarships, Special Programs

The AFI administers the Academy of Motion Picture Arts and Sciences annual Internship Program, in which successful applicants spend time observing on shoots by well-known directors. It has held drama-directing workshops specifically for women, and it has a center for advanced film studies, with entry very competitive. Contact: American Film Institute, 2021 North Western Avenue, Los Angeles, Calif. 90027.

A good move is to take out a subscription to *American Cinematographer,* a monthly publication that keeps one abreast of the latest technical innovations and also includes news, interviews, and a great deal of useful "who's doing what" information. Contact: *American Cinematographer,* American Society of Cinematographers, Inc., P.O. Box 2230, Hollywood, Calif. 90028.

The Independent Television Service has been authorized by Congress to oversee the distribution of $6 million to independent producers and to encourage innovative programming for underserved audiences, in particular minorities and children. For information and guidelines, contact: Independent Television Service, PO Box 65797, Saint Paul, MN 55165.

The International Documentary Association (IDA) is based in Los Angeles and has a strong program of events in that area. It publishes an excellent quarterly journal, *International Documentary* with featured articles on new films, filmmakers, trends, festivals, and technology. The IDA also publishes a *Membership Directory and Survival Guide* and a newsletter. Contact: International Documentary Association, 1551 S. Robertson Boulevard, Los Angeles, CA 90035.

The following books contain a vast amount of interlocking information on the structure of the film/video industry, job descriptions, pay scales, funding agencies, proposals, grants, budgeting, contracts, and distribution:

Mollie Gregory, *Making Films Your Business* (New York: Schocken, 1979).

Jan Bone, *Opportunities in Film* (Lincolnwood, Ill.: VGM Career Horizons, 1983).

Michael Wiese, *The Independent Film and Videomaker's Guide* (Boston: Focal Press, 1984).

Michael Wiese, *Film and Video Budgets* (Boston: Focal Press, 1984).

All these works give case histories and examples; collectively they represent a mine of information. Wiese's *The Independent Film and Videomaker's Guide*, dealing as it does specifically with documentaries, is particularly valuable. He corrects the commonly held notion that any worthy film can be sold to the PBS and shows through his own experience how Byzantine this sprawling, decentralized organization is. "If you have the idea that PBS is a benevolent network serving public and education interests," warns Wiese in an earlier version of the book, "a renewed study is suggested." You can get an Independent Producer's Kit by writing to: PBS Development Office, 609 Fifth Avenue, New York, N.Y. 10017.

There are survey organizations to help you find the appropriate private fund or charity to approach. For instance, Chicago has the Donors Forum (208 North LaSalle Street, Chicago, Ill. 60601), a clearinghouse that publishes local information periodically, and in New York, there is the Foundation Center (888 Seventh Avenue, New York, NY 10106), which serves as a center for nationwide reference collections for study by those wishing to approach donors and donor organizations.

PRESENTING YOURSELF

Naturally a good resume is important when you seek work, but quite the best reference, apart from letters of recommendation from established filmmakers, is awards won at festivals. The IDA and AFI list upcoming festivals, and you should enter your work in as many as you can afford. Most film and video competition entries are abysmal, so if you do good work, it is realistic to hope to win. Prizes

are inordinately important in swinging votes during a funding application process or in securing an interview. It is said that nothing succeeds like success, and
people with judgmental responsibilities often seem most impressed by prizes and
honors they know nothing about, preferring to add to one person's honors rather
than take a chance on an outsider.

Whomever you approach and for whatever reason, make full inquiries first.
Take the trouble to learn all you can about the business of the individual or
organization you are approaching. People accustomed to dealing with a volume
of job seekers learn to distinguish rapidly between those who are realistic and
those who are adrift in alien seas. This judgment is made not on who you are
(only your mother knows that) but on how you present yourself, either on paper
or in person. You can only do this well if you first do your homework, through
resourceful reading and networking on the telephone.

When you send your resume to an individual or company, send a brief,
carefully composed, *individual* cover letter that describes your goals and how
you think you might best contribute to the organization. Call up after a few
days and ask if you might have a brief chat with someone in case a position
opens up in the future. If you are called for an interview, dress appropriately,
be punctual, know what you want, and show you are willing to do any kind of
work to get there. Let the interviewer ask the questions, and when you reply, be
brief and to the point. Tell the interviewer concisely what skills and qualities
you think you have to offer. This is where you can demonstrate your knowledge
of (and therefore commitment to) his business. Interviewers often ask if you have
any questions; here too you can demonstrate the level of your involvement by
having several good questions ready.

If you know that shyness is going to hold you back, do something about it
now. If you need assertiveness training, get it. If no such thing is available, join
a theater group and force yourself to act, preferably in improvisational material.
You alone can make the moves to start believing in yourself.

MAKING A JOB FOR YOURSELF

I don't remember ever seeing an advertisement for a documentary filmmaker,
but this does not mean there are no jobs. It simply means that one must find or
create a job rather than expect one ready made. I heard of one person who took
the elevator to the top of an office highrise and knocked on every door on his
way down. By the time he got to the bottom, he had enough work to get started.

The aspiring director must one way or another create a "portfolio" of work,
samples that show what he can do. Selling one's services is initially a grisly
business, and rejections hurt. But they help make you better at what's unavoidable: talking people into letting you use their money to make your films.

Some interesting facts emerged from a colloquium given at Columbia College
Chicago by former film students who had "made it" in various capacities in the
industry. One was that everyone seemed to take about the same (long) time to
get established and to begin to earn a reasonable amount of money. Another
was that everybody had moved up the ladder of responsibility at roughly the
same (slow) pace. Everyone reported that greater responsibility came suddenly

and without warning, and when it came all were scared stiff, feeling they were conning their way into an area beyond their competence. All felt they had grown into their new levels of responsibility, and all loved their work and said they felt privileged to be working in such an important area of public life.

WHY YOU AND I MATTER

For anyone who wants to help create a mirror of contemporary life, filmmaking is a wonderful and fulfilling medium. To me, the value of the documentary process is that it affirms the importance of imagination and empathy when probing the depths of real life for its meanings. It is a learning process that makes one feel truly alive. Part of its reward for me is the knowledge that, unlike the generations of ordinary people before me, I shall not pass silently out of life taking my human testimony with me. It's astonishing and tragic that we the common people know virtually nothing firsthand about the thought and aspirations of our ancestors. Apart from their songs and tales they left nothing because they owned nothing and could leave no personal record. Their history, practically the only one we have, was instead written for them by their masters.

Documentary filmmaking now allows the common man not only to publicly argue his case but to leave a highly sophisticated record of his mind, surroundings, and vision. I like to think that future historians will find the documentarian's record of man and woman no less important than those of the chroniclers and diarists of old.

P·A·R·T X·I·I

APPENDIXES, GLOSSARY,
AND ANNOTATED
BIBLIOGRAPHY

A·P·P·E·N·D·I·X A

SAMPLE OF QUESTIONS USED IN AN INTERVIEW

These are the questions I mapped out for myself when I was interviewing Alexandra Tolstoy about her famous father. They are included to show how specific and directive questioning can be, and how often questions are a form of prompting based on research or prior conversation. What answers were actually elicited and how these answers were structured into long sections of apparently spontaneous talk, may be seen in the resulting film (*Tolstoy Remembered by His Daughter,* "Yesterday's Witness" series, BBC).

The interview is structured chronologically with the exception of the last question, which deals with the profound effect upon her of discovering in childhood that she had been an unwanted baby and that her mother had tried to abort her.

All the questions are designed either to elicit factual answers or to call on what she saw and felt as a surviving witness.

1. Could you tell us who your father was and which of his many children you are?
2. What are your earliest memories of Tolstoy?
3. You write that he could reach you children, each of you in your own way. Tell us about this and about his other qualities as a father.
4. Tell us about the game your father called "The Charge of the Numidian Cavalry."
5. His study was the holy of holies; do you remember going for one of his talks—what you call "a great and exciting event"?

6. The price of fame was that people brought your father all manner of personal problems, some of them rather crazy. Could you talk about this?

7. Tolstoy wrote in his diary that each of his daughters "cherished a fanatic belief in him." What was yours, and when did you first become aware of it?

8. When and how did you start becoming aware of the rift between your parents?

9. Tell us about the famous and the humble people who used to come and see your father.

10. Tell us briefly how Tolstoy antagonized the Russian Orthodox church, how he was excommunicated, and how on the day it happened your household was reunited in an almost holiday atmosphere.

11. Tell us what now increasingly separated your parents, and how this showed as time went by [mother's anxiety over property, need for guards, etc.].

12. You are described as understanding Tolstoy's loneliness and isolation better than anyone else. How was that?

13. Did you ever feel in an awkward position, copying out your father's diaries, which contained his sometimes bitter reflections on your mother?

14. At 17 or 18 you had difficulty in following your father's convictions concerning possessions and property. How did he perceive this, and how did he try and help you?

15. Your family history is made tragic by the frequent illnesses and the deaths that occurred, particularly of Vanichka and Masha. Their deaths greatly affected the family but had special meanings for Tolstoy, didn't they?

16. Your father was singularly unimpressed by technological progress, but he did make use of a present from Thomas Edison. Tell us about the present and its first trial.

17. Your mother had become increasingly ill. She was terribly jealous of your father's closest friend, Chertkov. Chertkov had his photograph taken with Tolstoy, and this triggered off a tremendous scene between your mother and Tolstoy, didn't it?

18. Later, when your father was very sick, your mother's jealousy of Chertkov reached such a pitch that you literally had to guard Tolstoy's door.

19. Simmons writes of "gnawing dissatisfactions Tolstoy felt over the disparity between the life around him and that which he wanted to lead." Why did he so prolong this state?

20. Tolstoy was a great diarist: These diaries were central to the tension between Sophia and Tolstoy, weren't they? [her fear of the image he was creating, who should have custody of them, etc.].

21. The question of leaving home to find peace and solitude was ever on Tolstoy's mind. Tell us how it finally happened.

22. What were your father's last words, and what did you find especially significant in them?

23. Of all your father's teachings, what has been of supreme significance to you in your long life?

24. This may be too personal a question: How did you feel in later years when you learned the joyless circumstances of your coming into the world?

A·P·P·E·N·D·I·X B

USEFUL FORMS

BUDGET

Note that two figures are entered, the highest and lowest likely. These correspond with optimistic and pessimistic approaches and keep the filmmaker from a painful underestimation. A contingency percentage is always added at the end of a film budget to cover the unforeseen, such as bad-weather delays, reshoots, additions, or substitutions.

SHORT BUDGET FORM

Production Details

Working Title:..................................... Length: .... min.

Personnel:

    Director: ....Tel.: ....(h) ....(w)

        Address: ....,,,...............

              ....

    Cinematographer: ....

    Sound: ....

    Prod. Mgr.: ....

Format (circle all that apply):

    Video: Beta/VHS/¾"/1"/Hi8/Betacam

    Film: B&W/color negative/reversal 8mm/16mm/35mm

Project is at stage of (circle one): Preproduction/Production/Postproduction

Schedule at present is:

    Preproduction from...............to ....

    Production   ....

    Postproduction   ....

Brief description of subject:

Working hypothesis of film is:

Preproduction Costs

	Low	High
Travel	$	$.....
Phone	....	.....
Photocopying	....	.....
Food, accommodations	....	.....
Tests	....	.....
Total	....	.....

Crew

Director   for . . ./. . . days at $. . . . . per day   . . .   . . .
Camera   " . . ./. . . " "   . . . . . " "   . . .   . . .
Sound   " . . ./. . . " "   . . . . . " "   . . .   . . .
Gaffer   " . . ./. . . " "   . . . . . " "   . . .   . . .
Grip   " . . ./. . . " "   . . . . . " "   . . .   . . .
Prod. Mgr.   " . . ./. . . " "   . . . . . " "   . . .   . . .

Equipment

Camera (film/video) . . . . . . .for $. . ./. . . days at $. . . . . per day   . . .   . . .
Magazines (film). . . . . " . . ./. . . " "   . . . . . . " "   . . .   . . .
Changing bag (film) . . . . " . . ./. . . " "   . . . . . . " "   . . .   . . .
Clapper board (film) . . . . " . . ./. . . " "   . . . . . . " "   . . .   . . .
Nagra recorder (film) . . . . . . " . . ./. . . " "   . . . . . . " "   . . .   . . .
Video recorder. . . . . " . . ./. . . " "   . . . . . . " "   . . .   . . .
Lenses. . . . . " . . ./. . . " "   . . . . . . " " . . .   . . .
Filter kit. . . . . " . . ./. . . " "   . . . . . . " " . . .   . . .
Exposure meter. . . . . " . . ./. . . " "   . . . . . . " "   . . .   . . .
Color-temperature meter. . . " . . ./. . . " "   . . . . . . " "   . . .   . . .
Camera supports: tripod . . . " . . ./. . . " "   . . . . . . " "   . . .   . . .
                 baby legs " . . ./. . . " "   . . . . . . " "   . . .   . . .
                 hi-hat . . . " . . ./. . . " "   . . . . . . " "   . . .   . . .
Tilt head. . . . . " . . ./. . . " "   . . . . . . " " . . .   . . .
Spreader. . . . . " . . ./. . . " "   . . . . . . " "   . . .   . . .
Video monitor. . . . . " . . ./. . . " "   . . . . . . " "   . . .   . . .
Headphones . . . . " . . ./. . . " "   . . . . . . " "   . . .   . . .
Mike boom. . . . . " . . ./. . . " "   . . . . . . " "   . . .   . . .
Mikes: gun . . . . " . . ./. . . " "   . . . . . . " "   . . .   . . .
       omni. . . . . " . . ./. . . " "   . . . . . . " "   . . .   . . .
       cardioid . . . . " . . ./. . . " "   . . . . . . " "   . . .   . . .
       lavalier. . . . . " . . ./. . . " "   . . . . . . " "   . . .   . . .
       extension cords . . . . " . . ./. . . " "   . . . . . . " "   . . .   . . .
       mixer . . . . " . . ./. . . " "   . . . . . . " "   . . .   . . .
Batteries. . . . . " . . ./. . . " "   . . . . . . " " . . .   . . .
Sun gun. . . . . " . . ./. . . " "   . . . . . . " " . . .   . . .
Open-face quartz kit(s) . . . . " . . ./. . . " "   . . . . . . " "   . . .   . . .
Softlight(s). . . . . " . . ./. . . " "   . . . . . . " " . . .   . . .
Spotlight kit(s)   " . . ./. . . " "   . . . . . . " "   . . .   . . .
Extension cords. . . . . " . . ./. . . " "   . . . . . . " "   . . .   . . .
Tie-in cables . . . . " . . ./. . . " "   . . . . . . " " . . .   . . .

Materials

Camera raw stock. . ./. . . rolls of type . . . . @ $. . . . per roll (film)   . . .   . . .
Nagra tape   . . ./. . . "   "   "   @ $. . . . "   "   "   . . .   . . .
Develop . . ./. . . ft of cam. orig @ $. . . . . per ft.   "   . . .   . . .
Print . . ./. . . ft of work print @ $. . . . . per ft.   "   . . .   . . .
Sound transfer . . . . hrs. @ $. . . . . per hr.   "   . . .   . . .
Sound stock (8mm/16mm/35mm) . . . ft. @ $. . . . per ft.   "   . . .   . . .
Videocassettes . . ./. . . required of type . . . . . . @ $. . . . . . each   . . .   . . .

Other

Transport . . ./. . . days @ $. . . . . per day
Food . . ./. . .   person days @ $. . . . . per person per day   . . .   . . .
Accommodations . . ./. . .   "   "   " $. . . . . . "   "   "   "   . . .   . . .
Location or other fees   . . .   . . .

                                                      Total   . . .   . . .

Postproduction Costs

Editor ... ./... days @ $...... per day	... ...
Editing equipment ... ./... " " $...... " "	... ...
Time coding ... ./... hrs. @ $...... at $...... per hr.	... ...
Window dub ... ./... hrs. @ $...... at $...... per hr.	... ...
Narrator ... ./... hrs. @ $...... per hr.	... ...
Music	... ...
Titles	... ...
Sound mix ... ./... hrs. @ $...... per hour	... ...
Transfer mag master to optical ... ./... ft. @ $...... per ft. (film)	... ...
Conform cam. original to work print ... ./... hrs. @ $...... per hr. (film)	....
Make first answer print ... ./... ft. @ $...... per ft. (film)	... ...
Make first release print ... ./... ft. @ $...... per ft. (film)	... ...
On-line edit, timebase correction, etc. ... ./... hr. @ $...... per hr.	... ...
Legal	... ...
Production office	... ...
Miscellaneous:	
....	... ...
....	... ...
....	... ...
Total	... ...

Summary:

Preproduction total	$ ... ...
Production total	$ ... ...
Postproduction total...................................	$ ... ...
Subtotal..	$ ... ...
Contingency addition (12% of total)................................	$ ... ...
GRAND TOTAL	$ ... ...

SHOOTING LOG

SHOOTING LOG	Title _____ Page ____

Camera operator _____ Camera _____ Date __/__19__
Roll# _____ Location _____

Digital reading	Scene Description	Remarks

Signed: _____

RELEASE FORM

Asking people to sign a release form is always a slightly awkward moment, and the more "legal" the form looks, the more people are apt to wonder if one is doing something underhanded. The release here is a simple, nonthreatening one, but a more thorough one can be found in any work on media law or in Kris Malkiewicz's *Cinematography* (New York: Van Nostrand Reinhold, 1973). For a release to be binding, there must be an exchange of money. Usually it will be the $1 token payment. Minors must get the consent of their parent or legal guardian.

Personal Release Form

For the $_____ consideration received, I give _____
Productions, its successors and assigns, my unrestricted permission to distribute and sell all still photographs, motion-picture film, video recordings and sound recordings taken of me for the screen production tentatively titled __.

Signed _____
Name (please print) _____
Address _____
_____
Date _____

Signature of parent or guardian _____
Witnessed by _____
Date _____

EDIT LOG

| EDIT LOG | Production _____ Page _____ |

| Editor _____ Date __/__/____ Cassette # _____ |

Digital Reading	Time	Scene Description Sound on Track: 1 2			Remarks
	:				
	:				
	:				
	:				
	:				
	:				
	:				
	:				
	:				
	:				
	:				
	:				
	:				
	:				
	:				
	:				
	:				
	:				
	:				
	:				
	:				
	:				
	:				
	:				
	:				
	:				
	:				
	:				
	:				
	:				
	:				
	:				
	:				
	:				
	:				
	:				
	:				
	:				
	:				

SOUND MIX LOG

SOUND MIX LOG	Production _____ Page # ____				
Action Cues	Track 1	Track 2	Track 3	Track 4	Cassette/Disc

EDITING DIAGNOSTIC FORM

EDITING DIAGNOSTIC FORM   Page _____

Production title _____ Length _____

Editor _____ Date __/__/____

Sequence Defined by Brief Line Title	Sequence's Contribution to Film's Developing "Argument"
Seq. #____	Contributes: ....
Ends:__' __"	Length:__' __"
Seq. #____	Contributes: ....
Ends:__' __"	Length:__' __"
Seq. #____	Contributes: ....
Ends:__' __"	Length:__' __"
Seq. #____	Contributes: ....
Ends:__' __"	Length:__' __"
Seq. #____	Contributes: ....
Ends:__' __"	Length:__' __"

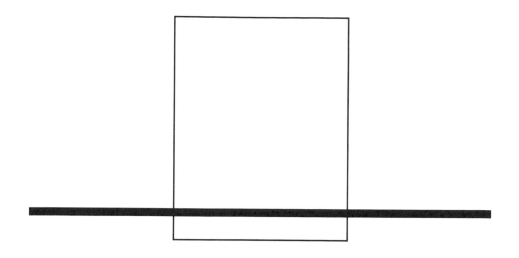

FILMOGRAPHY OF DIRECTOR MICHAEL RABIGER

1968   **AU PAIR TO PARIS** (30 min., Great Britain and France, BBC "Breakaway" series). Shows a young London girl breaking with home for first time to go and work in a Paris suburb where her assumptions and her schoolgirl French are tested.

   KIBBUTZNIKS (30 min., Great Britain and Israel, BBC "Breakaway" series). Follows a London working-class Jewish family emigrating to a kibbutz in the euphoria immediately following the Six-Day War where they begin adjusting to a new life.

   GERARD ET REGINE (30 min., France and Austria, BBC "Faces of Paris" series). A *Paris-Match* photojournalist and his much younger girlfriend set off to cover pre-Olympic ski trials. The alternating periods of waiting and frenetic work put their unequal relationship under stress. We see their partnership disintegrating amid a sense of confusion and regret.

1969   **CESAR** (30 min., France, BBC "Faces of Paris" series). Follows the sculptor Cesar in his habitual wanderings through the streets of Paris. Relates his working-class background and his ideas of artistic and sexual freedom to his free-form experiments with liquid plastics.

   PRISONERS OF CONSCIENCE (2 × 30 min., Great Britain, BBC "Yesterday's Witness" series). Eyewitness accounts by survivors of those who refused to fight in World War I. Includes interviews with four conscientious objectors who had their death sentences read out to them. Shows moral power of passive resistance to government and military edicts, and ends on interviews with American anti-Vietnam War counselors, indicating the historical parallel between the two episodes.

THE CRAMLINGTON TRAIN WRECKERS (30 min., Great Britain, BBC "Yesterday's Witness" series). Account by four participating miners of how they derailed a train during the 1926 General Strike in England, of the bad conditions that impelled them to this desperate act, and of the savage official reaction.

BREAKING THE SILENCE (30 min., Great Britain, BBC "Yesterday's Witness" series). Pioneers of radio communication in Britain tell how, from about 1902 onward, engineers and kitchen-table amateurs worked together to make the first magical connections through the ether.

DR. SPOCK (45 min., USA, BBC "One Pair of Eyes" series). The famous baby doctor travels the campuses speaking out for civil disobedience to help end the Vietnam War. Demonstrates his ideas on the mechanisms of human aggression, particularly in connection with anti-Communism paranoia. Includes biographical material and sequences revealing his disharmony with current ideas on the women's liberation movement.

TOLSTOY REMEMBERED BY HIS DAUGHTER (30 min., USA, BBC "Yesterday's Witness" series). Memorable and poignant account by Alexandra Tolstoy of her father's last years, of the unhappy relationship between her parents, of Tolstoy's final journey to escape his wife, which ended ironically with his death in a stationmaster's cottage.

1970   **OUR TIME IS COMING NOW** (30 min., Great Britain, BBC "Voices of the Seventies" series). The first film about the modern women's movement becoming organized and articulate in England as seen by proponent Selma James, who contends that women have been written out of history.

THE BATTLE OF CABLE STREET (45 min., Great Britain, BBC "Yesterday's Witness" series). Accounts from partisan eyewitnesses and protagonists of the classic 1936 London street battle when Mosley's British Union of Fascists tried to march through the Jewish East End. A quarter-million people turned out to stop the Blackshirts. Includes interviews with Mosley and Communist organizers, and a segment shows contemporary neo-fascist activity. Film accurately prophesied that the old fascist xenophobia was again on the rise.

A REMNANT OF A FEUDAL SOCIETY (30 min., Great Britain, BBC "Yesterday's Witness" series). Reconstruction, through interviews with old retainers and Lord and Lady Digby, of the atmosphere and relationships on a lordly estate still run on feudal lines into the 1930s. Using Digby film archives, the film documents a highly structured "upstairs, downstairs" society held together by economic need and complex emotional ties running up and down the social pyramid.

PREJUDICE: ON THE FACE OF IT (45 min., Great Britain, BBC "Cameron Country" series). Veteran journalist James Cameron elicits from West Indians what it's like to be "in the lion's mouth," what being a black in London feels like. Memorable confrontation in black actors' workshop in which Cameron is accused of manipulating them to entertain a television audience. Film expresses pessimism over race relations especially as shown in police behavior.

1971   **PATRIOTISM** (45 min., Great Britain, BBC "Cameron Country" series). James Cameron traveled the length of Britain in search of patriotic feelings on the eve of Britain joining the Common Market. He found an exaggerated fear that British autonomy, identity, and even the Royal Family were in danger of extinction.

THE DREAMWALKERS (45 min., Great Britain, BBC "One Pair of Eyes" series). Well-known Sufi writer and translator Idries Shah looks at western society and suggest ways in which psychological restrictions cause us to operate below potential.

CAN YOU LIVE LIKE THAT? (45 min., Great Britain, independently produced for Krishnamurti Foundation). Famous philosophical teacher Jiddu Krishnamurti in conversation with young people over self-image and authority. Filmed at the foundation's school in England, it includes an interview with Krishnamurti interpreting his interaction with the students.

LEONARDO RICCI: CITIES OF THE FUTURE (45 min., Italy/Sicily, BBC "One Pair of Eyes" series). Ricci, dean of the School of Architecture, University of Florence, makes an impassioned tour of Renaissance landmark buildings in Florence to show their community-building properties. Demonstrates how he borrowed their principles in his attractive modern building complexes. Finishes with a visionary model for a city of the future.

1972 **RONALD FRASER** (30 min., Great Britain, BBC "In the Limelight" series). Noted character actor Ronald Fraser returns to the kind of theater in which his career began, a company of dedicated amateurs. The film follows the inception of an Agatha Christie thriller, complete with butler, corpse, and French window. The diverse parts and the people who play them emerge in counterpoint as jobs in life are interwoven with the play's characterizations.

BARRY TOOK (30 min., Great Britain, BBC "In the Limelight" series). "Laugh-In" comedy writer and comedian Barry Took returns to the scene of his education as a comic—the gritty working men's clubs of industrial Yorkshire. Through the medium of a black Yorkshireman's comedy act, he demonstrates how humor is a safety valve for collective anxieties—in this case, sexual and racial tensions.

A CAUSE WORTH FIGHTING FOR (45 min., Great Britain, BBC "Yesterday's Witness" series). Through eyewitnesses, film, and volunteers, the film reconstructs the atmosphere in which British workers and intellectuals joined the International Brigade to fight fascism in Spain in the 1930s. Still bitter at the nonintervention policy of France, Britain, and the United States, they contend it allowed Hitler and Mussolini to use Spain as a rehearsal for the bigger war to come.

1973 **CHARLIE SMITH AT 131** (30 min., USA, BBC "Yesterday's Witness" series). America's oldest inhabitant, born in 19th-century Liberia, recalls coming to America on a slave ship. Brought up with a white rancher's family in Texas, he remembers the Civil War and his later career as a cowboy.

1974 **GRAVITY IS THE THERAPIST** (53 min., USA, independently produced for Rolf Foundation). Dr. Ida Rolf demonstrates the physical therapy she pioneered. The film weaves exposition of principles, three ongoing treatments, and reports by former patients of successful physical and psychological changes.

1975 **THE MEMORIAL DAY MASSACRE** (20 min., USA, independently produced for Illinois Labor History Society). Chicago police in 1937 slaughtered workers picketing outside United Steel. Makes extensive use of news footage subsequently used to discredit the police version of events. Commenting and analyzing is Sam Evett, who took part as a young man.

1978 **THE TEMPTATION OF CHARLES C. CHARLEY** (26 min., USA, fiction pilot). Adaptation of a Grace Paley short story about a small-town air conditioner repairman who cheerfully enters a relationship with a headstrong teenager 20 years his junior.

1981   **BISHOP HILL CELEBRATES** (30 min., USA, made for DePaul University Sociology Department's "Festivals of Illinois" series). Bishop Hill, an Illinois village founded by Swedish immigrants in the 1840s as a religious commune, has been lovingly restored by descendents of the original settlers. As a living museum, it epitomizes the way ordinary people have recently begun reconstructing and presenting their own history.

1982   **PORTRAIT OF A DIRECTOR** (30 min., USA, Columbia College). Shows the evolution of a play in a suburban community theater, concentrating on the process of directing by filmmaker Tony Loeb. Shot as a videotape editing exercise, its secondary educational purpose was to reveal the interdependency of actors and director, and the process of mutual artistic accommodation in pursuit of the production's final identity.

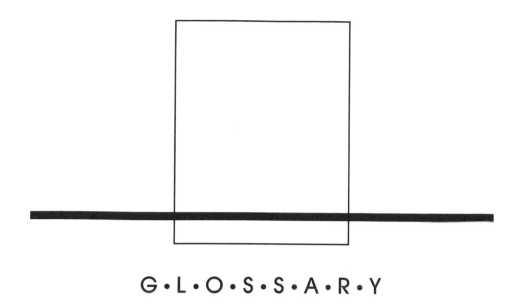

G·L·O·S·S·A·R·Y

Terms are grouped in production order and by family rather than in alphabetical order. For further help, see the Index.

SCRIPT AND EDITING TERMINOLOGY

Describing location: Each new location should be headed with the following information: scene number, interior or exterior, its name and the time of day. Examples:

    20.   EXT. PAUL'S GAS STATION, NIGHT.
    23.   INT. PIPPA'S STUDIO, MORNING.

Describing shot by size: Shots are named according to their relative size and their content, for example, "MS Arnie filling cup." Standard abbreviations and their meanings are:

WS   Wide shot, shot showing the most space.
WA   Wide angle, sometimes taken with wide-angle lens.
LS   Long shot, sometimes taken with telephoto lens.
Master   Wide shot containing complete version of the action.
Estab. shot   Wide shot that establishes a scene's geography.
XLS   Extra long shot.
MLS   Medium long shot.
MS   Medium shot.
MCS   Medium close shot.
CS   Close shot.
CU   Close-up.
BCU   Big close-up.
Insert or cut-in   Close-up detail to be inserted in longer shot.
Cutaway   Shot that enables cutting away from main action.

2S Two-shot (two people in shot).
3S Three-shot (three people in shot).
Single Single-person shot (only noted when among group shots).
O/S Over-shoulder (over one person's shoulder on to the other).
Complementary A shot that complements the foregoing shot (the other over-shoulder shot, for instance).

Describing shot by angle: Unless the camera is at eye level, its position will be described according to its height and angle of view.

LA Low angle, camera looking up at subject.
HA High angle, camera looking down on subject.
HD High down, camera looking down on subject.
Dutch angle Camera shooting so horizontals slope to one side.
Aerial shot Shot taken from the air.

Describing shot by camera movement: The camera can be moved in any direction relative to the camera-subject axis. This can mean toward/away from, sideways or "crabbing" motion, and up/down. The camera can also be swiveled at its point of mounting, either up/down or from side to side.

Pan Swivel camera sideways to show a horizontal panorama.
Whip pan Very fast pan, often used as illusory transition.
Tilt Swivel camera upward or downward (for example, to show flagpole).
Dolly in Move camera on wheeled dolly toward subject.
Dolly out Move camera on wheeled dolly away from subject.
Tracking L–R Move camera on tracks left to right.
Trucking R–L Same meaning, right to left, on "truck."
Craning down Camera height lowering.
Craning up Camera height ascending.
Zoom in Use zoom lens to give illusion of going closer.
Zoom out Use zoom lens to give illusion of backing away.
Crash zoom Very fast zoom, often used for shock effect.

Transitional devices: These can include simple or complex cutting techniques, optical effects, and compositional teasers.

CUTS

Cut Simply switching to another image, possibly in another scene.
Match cut Joining two different-sized shots of same scene to give the illusion of continuity.
Action match cut A match cut made on a movement that flows across the cut. Editors always prefer to cut on a movement if it is practical.
Jump cut Cut in a scene that usually signals that a piece of time has been taken out—useful in jumping a narrative forward in time or for signaling the elision of nonessentials. Unplanned jump cuts appear in World War I footage where a

broken negative has been joined—marching men suddenly jump forward half a pace.

OPTICAL EFFECTS

F/O Fade out image to black.
F/I Fade in image from black.
Fade to white Fade image up to white.
Fade from white Fade from white to image.
Dissolve Merging by overlap of one image into another.
Lap dissolve Same as above.
Wipe One image replaces another progressively as a line travels across the screen.
Iris wipe One image replaces another beginning from a point in the center of the screen like the iris of a camera lens expanding or contracting.
S/I Superimposition, or superimposed image, usually titles.

Describing screen direction: Movement on the screen is described by its direction, which is crucial in suggesting a sense of continuity from one shot to the next. Screen direction also suggests relationship. For instance, cutting back and forth between two characters both walking in the same screen direction suggests one is following the other, but cutting back and forth between two characters going in opposite directions would be likely to suggest they were going to meet or even that they were walking away from each other, depending on the context. Because the film image is a two-dimensional image of a three-dimensional world, there is ample scope for confusion, so only the simplest of screen movements are normally abbreviated:

Train L–R Train moves from left to right of screen.

Other movements are likely to be more fully described, thus:

Bird flies from top to bottom of screen (or downscreen).
Bird flies from bottom to top of screen (or upscreen).
Bird flies to cam = flies toward camera.
Bird flies to F/G = flies toward foreground (same as above).
Bird flies away from cam = away from camera.
Bird flies to B/G = away toward background (same as above).

A character talking to the camera will often have his or her eyeline offset, thus:

Jo, full face but eyeline L–R = Jo looking just to the left of camera.
Jo, full face but eyeline R–L = Jo looking just to the right of camera.
Jo, looking slightly above camera.
Jo, looking below camera.

Entry or exit points are often described in relation to framing, thus:

> Penny enters frame top left.
>
> Penny enters frame bottom right.
>
> Penny rises from bottom center screen.
>
> Penny descends from left of center, top of screen.

These specifications can be both clumsy and redundant in a screenplay but may be vital when making a lighting plan or briefing the art director for a fiction film. When a lot of very tight planning takes place, directors usually communicate through the story board, which, like a comic strip, is a series of key frames.

Sound terminology: This covers dialogue, music, and effects that have been mixed together from their component parts.

Sync dialogue   Dialogue that is seen being spoken synchronously.
Wild dialogue   Dialogue that does not sync with a visible speaker.
Wild track   Any nonsync track, usually of speech.
V/O   Voice-over, for example, a voice speaking contents of a letter being read silently by a character onscreen.
MOS   Silent, or as German directors in Hollywood once said, "mit out sound."
Narr   narration.
Comm   Commentary.
FX   Sound-effects track.
Atmos   Sound atmosphere track (for example, birds, traffic, wind).
Mus   Music track.
FT   Footstep track specially recorded (fiction films only).
Sound dissolve   One track blending into another.
Segue   One track blending into another (pronounced "seg-way").
Mix to . . .   Different way of saying segue or dissolve to.
Fade down   Fade to lower overall level.
F/O   Fade out (to silence).
F/I   Fade in (from silence).
Fade up   Raise overall level.
Perspective   Distance perceived through sound as in a close-up voice quality, or a long-shot voice quality. Only worth noting when sound and picture perspectives are deliberately mismatched.

CAMERA TERMINOLOGY

LENSES

Angle of acceptance   Angle of a lens' intake expressed in degrees.
Focal length   Lens rating: distance (in millimeters) from optical center of lens to focal plane when lens focused upon distant object ("infinity").
Focal plane   Point in space behind lens where image is in sharp focus.
Focal distance   Distance from focal plane to point of focus in composition.
Depth of field   Amount of image depth that is acceptably in focus. It varies according to aperture and focal length of lens in use.

Wide angle   Lens having a wider angle of acceptance than does a standard lens.
Standard   Lens reproducing perspective as perceived by the human eye.
Telephoto   Lens with narrower, or telescopic, angle of acceptance.
Zoom   Lens adjustable between a wide and a telescopic setting.
Zoom ratio   Telescopic end (in millimeters) divided by wide angle (in millimeters) of lens.
f-stop   An increment of lens iris size. To "open up by one stop" means to double the lens' light transmission.
Aperture   Size of lens iris opening expressed in f-stops.
Lens speed   Widest aperture of lens (the bigger, the "faster" the lens in low-light situations).
C-mount   Standard screw mount for 16mm film and video lenses.
Bayonet mount   Quick mount for interchangeable lenses (several standards).
Lens turret   Rotatable plate with several lenses for fast lens substitution.
Halation   Excess light diffusing in camera or optics, which degrades image.
Lens hood   Device to prevent unwanted light hitting front lens element.

CAMERA

Intermittent motion   The stop-go movement of film through camera, which allows a rapid succession of still images to be recorded.
Shutter   Rotating blade that blocks the image from reaching the film plane while unexposed film is moved into position.
Claw   The mechanism that rapidly moves each new film frame into the gate.
Film gate   Area in which image strikes film plane, including aperture and pressure plate.
Aperture   Precisely shaped opening in camera body through which the image is projected onto film.
Pressure plate   Plate holding film firmly against aperture.
Magazine   Removable container holding fresh or exposed film.
Turret   Rotatable plate allowing a choice of lenses to be rapidly swung into position.
Reflex viewing   Viewfinder sees through the taking lens.
Color temperature   A method of rating (in degrees Kelvin) the color bias of a light source.
Color correction   Optical or electronic color balancing. The usual object in cinematography is to make flesh tones look natural.
CC filter   Color conversion filter. Alters color temperature.
ND filter   Neutral-density filter. Cuts overall quantity of light without altering color temperature.
Baby legs   Camera support, a miniature tripod.
Hi-hat   Lowest practicable camera support, shaped like a top hat.
Body pod   Camera support, fitting operator's body.
Steadicam   A complex and expensive camera mount that allows steady shooting from a camera attached to an operator's body.
Shoulder brace   Camera support, fitting operator's body.
Dolly   Camera support on wheeled platform.
Crab dolly   Dolly whose wheels allow it to roll in any direction.
Crane   Camera support on boom allowing camera to rise or fall.
Battery belt   Belt containing rechargeable camera battery.

Battery pack   Battery power source for camera or other location equipment.
Battery eliminator   AC power source producing DC for camera, and so on.

SOUND RECORDING TERMINOLOGY

Boom   Long extending mike support, usually on floor stand.
Fishpole   Short extending mike support, handheld.
Windscreen   Porous cover protecting mike diaphragm from air currents.
Shock mount   Shock absorbing mike mount that isolates mike from handling noise.
Electret mic   Electrostatic mike of small construction.
Dynamic mic   Electrodynamic mike, relatively large but rugged.
Crystal mic   Piezo mike, now outdated.
Wireless/Radio mic   Cordless mike transmitting its output to a recorder via a receiver.
Omnidirectional mic   Mike that picks up sound from all directions equally.
Cardioid mic   Mike with heart-shaped pick-up pattern favoring mike's axis.
Ultra-directional mic   Mike with very narrow pickup pattern.
Gun mic   Mike with very narrow pickup pattern.
Lavalier mic   Any mike designed to be worn on the chest.
Noise canceling mic   Mike designed to cancel ambient noise.
Balanced line   A cable system designed to cancel interference (three wire connection).
Unbalanced line   A cable system without interference canceling (two wire connection).
Ambient noise   Background, or sound inherent to the location.
Room tone/Buzz track/Presence   Recorded presence track to fill sound gaps in editing.
Signal to noise ratio   Ratio of audio to unwanted system noise.
Reverberation   Reflected sound with disorganized delay pattern.
Echo   Reflected sound with consistent delay pattern.
Live acoustics   Recording situation with inherent reverberation.
Dry acoustics   Recording situation relatively free of reverberation.
V/U meter   Volume units meter to monitor against overloading.
dB/Decibel   Unit of sound loudness measurement.
Compressor   Electronic device that squeezes loudness range into a preset range.
Limiter   Automatic level reduction at overload point.
Mixer   Circuitry capable of mixing two or more sound inputs to one output.
RF   Radio frequency interference.
Audio sweetening   Making final mix consistent and seamless through level and equalization adjustments.

VIDEO TERMINOLOGY

CAMERA

White balance   Electronic adjustments to render a white object as white on screen.
Image lag   Afterimage left on screen, usually of bright objects.

Tube burn   Image left "burnt" into picture pickup element.
Bleeding   Areas of bright light spilling into adjacent image area.
RGB   Red/Green/Blue—primary colors.
Single-tube camera   Camera with combined RGB pickup element.
Three-tube camera   Camera with separate RGB pickup elements.
CCD pickup   Charge-coupled device (solid state picture pickup element).
Registration   Process of aligning three separate pickups.
Color bars   Color test pattern generated by camera circuitry.
Gain   Electronic compensation for low-light situation, achieved at some loss of picture quality.

RECORDER

Tracking control   Linear adjustment to align record/pickup heads.
Skew   Rake or skew adjustment of pickup heads.
Noise   Any interference that degrades picture quality.
Video gain   Adjustment to control picture recording level.
Sound gain   Adjustment to control sound recording level.
Mic/line input   Switchable input for low-level (mike) or high-level (amplified) signal.
Line in   Input socket for amplified signal (say from mixerboard).
Line out   Amplified signal output to other machine or amplifier.
RF out   Radio frequency (composite sound and image) output.
Roll-off   Audio frequence cutoff, usually bass, to assist in rumbly recording situations such as heavy traffic.
Tune code generator   Built-in devise that generates an identifying code number for each recorded video frame.

MONITOR

Saturation control   Adjustment controlling color intensity in an image.
Hue control   Color fidelity controls, adjusted to color bars.
RF input   Radio frequency (composite sound and image) input.
Line in   Sound input socket for recorder/playback deck.
Video   Video input socket for recorder/playback deck.

VIDEO EDITING

On-line edit   Editing using computerized location and assembly process.
Off-line edit   Editing using manually operated control and location.
Time code numbering   Cumulative time reference invisibly recorded upon master cassettes and showing up in a window dub copy as a time identification system.
Window dub   Copy made from time-coded camera originals that displays each frame's time code in a "window" at bottom of frame.
Control track   Picture information sync signal usually generated by camera.
Video black   Black recording with control track ready to accept edit.
Preroll   Editing machines' run-up time prior to recording.
Insert edit   Edit sections inserted against a prerecorded control track.
Assemble edit   Edit sections assembled each with its own control track.
Audio sweetening   Audio level and equalization process.

Timebase corrector Signal processing device that electronically stabilizes recorded picture information.

Waveform monitor Video signal information display.

LIGHTING TERMINOLOGY

TYPES OF LIGHTING STYLE

High-key picture Shot looks overall bright with small areas of shadow (for example, exterior day shot).

Low-key picture Shot looks overall dark with few highlight areas (for example, basement at night with a shaft of light penetrating from a streetlamp).

Graduated tonality Shot would have neither very bright highlights nor deep shadow but would instead consist mainly of midtones if viewed without color (for example, fog scene or rainy landscape).

CONTRAST

High-contrast picture Shot may be lit either high key or low key, but there is a big difference in illumination level between highlight and shadow area. (Either of the examples above—the day exterior if it is sunny or the generally dark basement scene—could be high contrast and so would a moonlight shot.)

Low-contrast picture Shot would probably be high key but with high shadow area illumination (for example, a bright, overcast day but *not* a sunny day with its areas of deep shadow and brilliant sunlight).

LIGHT: QUALITY

Hard light Any light source that creates hard-edged shadows (for example, sun, studio spotlight, candle flame).

Soft light Any light source that creates soft-edged shadows (for example, fluorescent tubes, sunlight reflecting off matte-finish wall, light from overcast sky, studio softlight).

Diffused light Same as soft light.

LIGHT: COLOR TEMPERATURE

This refers to a scientific measurement of light in degrees Kelvin (or °K), which rates it according to the output of a theoretical blackbody heated to different temperatures and emitting light in ascending order through the spectrum, thus:

Invisible	Ultraviolet	
Visible	Violet	
|	Indigo	"Hot" end
|	Blue	
|	Green	
|	Yellow	
|	Orange	
Visible	Red	"Cool" end
Invisible	Infrared	

Note that, in the Kelvin scale, blue is hotter than red, quite different from the everyday associations of colors. Rather confusingly, cinematographers also use "cool" and "hot" to indicate brightness ("That sky is too hot") and speak of a "warm" or a "cool" print. A cool print looks bluish while a warm one will be more orange.

3200° K Color temperature of standard tungsten-filament movie lights.
5400° K Color temperature of average noonday sunlight. At its rising and setting, sunlight is much "cooler"—that is, more inclined to include red light.

Color-temperature meters are available that give a direct numerical readout.

LIGHT: MEASUREMENT

Practical light measurement is concerned with two different but related factors: the quantity of *incident light* (light falling on the subject) and the quantity of *reflected light* given off by the object. The amount of light reflected back by any surface depends upon its texture (shiny = directionally reflective, matte = light-scattering and apparently less reflective) as well as its tone. Light tones reflect much light, dark tones absorb rather than reflect light. Although in video what you see is what you get, it helps to understand light properties and light measurement. The standard light measurement units are:

Foot-candle (candela) Unit of light intensity (1 standard candle power at 1-foot distance). Measured with *incident light meter*.
Foot-lambert (candles per square foot) Unit of brightness of a reflective area. Measured with *reflective light meter*.

Note that two different kinds of meter are used for the two kinds of measurement, although one instrument commonly combines both.

NAMES OF PRINCIPAL LIGHTING SOURCES

Key light Not necessarily an artificial source, for it can be the sun. It is the light that creates intended shadows in the shot, and these in turn reveal the angle and position of the supposed source light.
Fill light The light used to raise illumination in a shadow area. For interiors it will probably be soft light thrown from the direction of the camera to avoid creating an additional set of shadows. Fill light, especially in exteriors, is often provided from reflectors.
Back light Light thrown on the subject from behind and often from above as well; a favorite way of putting a rim of light around a subject's head and shoulders, thus creating a separation between subject and background.
Practical Any light source that appears in frame as part of the scene (for example, table lamp, overhead fluorescent, candle).

TYPES OF LIGHTING SETUPS

Frontal Key light very close to camera so shadows are all thrown backward out of camera's view (for example, a snapshot taken with a flash, or an interrogation scene in which the victim sits in a merciless frontal glare).

Broad   Key light is some way to the side, so a broad area of a human subject's face would be highlighted (for example, through windshield onto a person sitting in parked car at night with illumination supposedly provided by a streetlamp from the side of car).

Narrow   Key light is to the side of the subject or even beyond, so that only a narrow portion of the human subject's face would receive highlight (for example, the same person in a parked car but with the streetlamp a little to the rear of the car).

Back   Key light coming from somewhere behind the subject (for example, exterior of a house on a moonlit night; someone opens a door. We dimly see features, but most of the light streams out around the person from the lighted room).

Silhouette   A backlit shot in which the subject is seen in outline and reflects virtually no light at all.

Day for night   A night effect can be produced by shooting in hard sunlight, with a clear sky and then underexposing the picture and filtering it blue (if it is in color). Day for night usually uses a low sunlight coming from the rear of the subject so there are long shadows in the foreground.

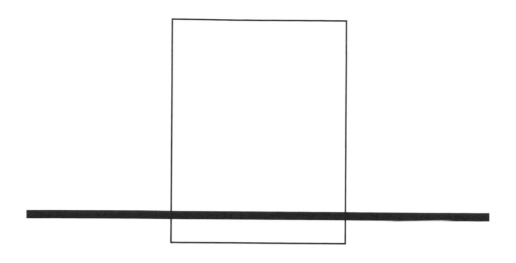

A·N·N·O·T·A·T·E·D
B·I·B·L·I·O·G·R·A·P·H·Y

LIGHTING

Carlson, Verne and Sylvia. *Professional Lighting Handbook*. Boston: Focal Press, 1985. Professional lighting methods and hardware.

Millerson, Gerald. *The Technique of Lighting for Television and Motion Pictures*. Boston: Focal Press, 1982. Thorough, but good for beginners.

Ritsko, Alan J. *Lighting for Location Motion Pictures*. New York: Van Nostrand Reinhold, 1979. Covers every aspect of the lighting and rigging problems that beset the film made on location—presumes no advance knowledge.

Samuelson, David W. *Motion Picture Camera and Lighting Equipment: Choice and Technique*. Boston: Focal Press, 1986. Specifics and use of a wide range of equipment; discusses special situations.

Sylvania Corporation. *Lighting Handbook for Television, Theatre and Professional Photography*. Danvers, Mass.: GTE Sylvania, 1984. Manufacturer's handbook detailing many lamp types but also containing articles on light, light measurement, electricity, and lighting setups.

VIDEO CAMERAS AND RECORDING

Cheshire, David. *The Video Manual*. New York: Van Nostrand Reinhold, 1982. Good for explaining principles to beginners.

Fuller, B., et al. *Single-Camera Video Production*. Englewood Cliffs, N.J.: Prentice-Hall, 1982. Comprehensive production techniques manual that explains principles.

Mathias, Harry and Richard Patterson. *Electronic Cinematography: Achieving Photographic Control over the Video Image*. Belmont, Calif.: Wadsworth, 1985. Advanced video techniques.

Millerson, Gerald. *Video Camera Techniques*. Boston: Focal Press, 1983. Handling, operation, and use of video cameras.

Robinson, J.F. and P.H. Beards. *Using Videotape*. Boston: Focal Press, 1981. Operation, principles, and care of videotape recording machines.

Robinson, Richard. *The Video Primer*. New York: Perigee, 1983. Field production techniques and concepts of video, the latter both in overview and in depth.

MOTION PICTURE TECHNIQUES

Arijon, Daniel. *Grammar of the Film Language*. Boston: Focal Press, 1976. Useful for understanding the mysteries of camera placement and framing to ensure smooth editing. Quantities of inexplicably nude figures.

Carlson, Verne and Sylvia. *Professional Cameraman's Handbook*. Boston: Focal Press, 1983. This handbook is made to accompany cameramen wherever they are working, giving them on-the-spot technical information.

Clarke, Charles G., ed. *American Cinematographer's Handbook*. Los Angeles: A.S.C. Reprinted regularly, this is the cinematographer's bible and contains an incredible breadth of professional-level information compactly presented. Surprisingly accessible to the beginner.

Eastman Kodak Co. *Cinematographer's Field Guide*. Rochester, N.Y.: Kodak, 1978. Hip-pocket guide to using Kodak motion picture products.

Happe, L. Bernard. *Basic Motion Picture Technology*. Boston: Focal Press, 1978. Good at explaining working principles.

Malkiewicz, J. Kris. *Cinematography: A Guide for Film Makers and Film Teachers*. New York: Van Nostrand Reinhold, 1973. A preferred text for intermediate filmmaking that extends from cameras, filters, lighting, and sound recording through editing and production.

Pincus, Edward and Steven Ascher. *The Filmmakers Handbook*. New York: Plume, 1984. Accessible to the beginner, lots of information both technical and conceptual.

Samuelson, David W. *Motion Picture Camera Techniques*. Boston: Focal Press, 1979. Information on a wide range of camera-related topics clearly presented.

MICROPHONE, RECORDING, AND SOUND MIXING TECHNIQUES

Clifford, Martin. *Microphones: How They Work and How to Use Them*. Blue Ridge Summit, Pa.: Tab Books, 1977. Thorough and user-friendly for a relatively technical work.

Nisbett, Alec. *The Technique of the Sound Studio*. Boston: Focal Press, 1979. Useful for understanding possibilities of sound mixing.

———. *The Use of Microphones*. Boston: Focal Press, 1983. Well-presented audio engineer theory and practice.

EDITING

Browne, Steven E. *Videotape Editing: A Postproduction Primer*. Boston: Focal Press, 1989. Very detailed manual of technical operations in a variety of video formats and situations.

Burder, John. *The Technique of Editing 16mm Films*. Boston: Focal Press, 1979. Practical introduction to tools and concepts.

Hollyn, Norman. *The Film Editing Handbook*. New York: Arco, 1984. Deals with feature film editing but very good on organization and method in the cutting room.

Reisz, Karel and Gavin Millar. *The Technique of Film Editing*. Boston: Focal Press, 1968. The standard work for the concepts of editing, but although full of good information, it has cramped layout and oppressively dated examples.

Rosenblum, Ralph. *When the Shooting Stops . . . the Cutting Begins*. New York: Penguin, 1980. Excellent and personable account of the professional editor's way of life.

Walter, Ernest. *The Technique of the Film Cutting Room*. Boston: Focal Press, 1982. An A to Z of the physical process of the cutting room.

WRITING AND DIRECTING

Rabiger, Michael. *Directing: Film Techniques and Aesthetics,* Boston: Focal Press, 1989. Fictional counterpart to this book, and also a practical guide to fiction writing, directing, and postproduction that supplies a range of projects to develop necessary skills. The approach values documentary-maker awareness and abilities as a means of experimental development for low-budget feature work.

Rosenthal, Alan. *Writing, Directing and Producing Documentary Films*. Carbondale; Southern Illinois University Press, 1990. Concentrates on the conceptual and human relations side of making documentaries, and stresses importance of preproduction work. Excellent on how to propose and negotiate as an independent to make factual films for clients or television corporations. The book is unnecessarily daunting to use, lacking illustrations, bibliography, and even a general index.

DOCUMENTARY THEORY, HISTORY, CRITICISM, AND SOURCES

Barnouw, Eric. *Documentary: A History of the Non-Fiction Film*. London: Oxford University Press, 1974. Clearest, warmest, and most readable critical history. Bibliography but no filmography.

Barsam, Richard Meran. *Nonfiction Film: A Critical History*. New York: Dutton, 1973. Scholarly but rather dry overview of documentary's development from 1920 to 1970. Includes useful filmography with year and length for each work (information that is often annoyingly hard to find), Academy award winners, and select bibliography.

———. *Nonfiction Film Theory and Criticism*. New York: Dutton, 1976. A useful anthology of earlier writings about documentary and documentarians. Select bibliography but no index.

Burton, Julianne, ed. *The Social Documentary in Latin America*. Pittsburgh: University of Pittsburgh Press, 1990. Collection of essays dealing with history, social purposes, and methods of representation used in Latin American documentary cinema.

Jacobs, Lewis. *The Documentary Tradition: From Nanook to Woodstock*. New York: Norton, 1971. Very full anthology of essays both by and about documentarians and their work between 1922 and 1970. The book is divided into five periods with a useful selection of documentaries suggested for each. Includes selected bibliography.

Levin, G. Roy. *Documentary Explorations: Fifteen Interviews with Filmmakers*. Garden City, N.Y.: Doubleday, 1971. Brief history plus interviews with filmmakers from four countries. Selected bibliography.

Peyton, Patricia, ed. *Reel Change: A Guide to Social Issue Films*. San Francisco: Film Fund, 1979. Superb guide to both fictional and documentary films treating social issues.

Rosenthal, Alan. *The Documentary Conscience: A Casebook in Filmmaking*. Berkeley; California: University of California Press, 1980. TV documentaries and trends as well as important individual filmmakers and their statments. As always with transcribed interviews, the reader must put in a lot of work to gain much enlightenment.

———. *New Challenges for Documentary*. Berkeley: University of California Press, 1988. Required reading. Excellent anthology of contemporary essays on theory, shape, and form of documentaries, ethics, ethnography, the documentary on television, the documentary treatment of history, and documentary treatment of contemporary issues—and much more besides. Inevitably with an anthology that includes academic theorists, the writing is sometimes obscure and turgid. Rosenthal's link pieces and commentary are always clear and helpful.

———. *The New Documentary in Action*. Berkeley: University of California Press, 1971. Interviews with Maysles Brothers, McClaren, Pennebaker, Watkins, Wiseman.

Rotha, Paul. *Documentary Film*. London: Faber & Faber, 1939. A director's provocative view of the possibilities, history, and potential of the medium during its most influential period.

FINANCE AND DISTRIBUTION

Goodell, Gregory. *Independent Feature Film Production*. New York: St. Martin's Press, 1982. A manual for feature film producers giving a comprehensive overview of the film industry's legal, financial, and partnership structures and information on distribution and marketing.

Gregory, Mollie, *Making Films Your Business*. New York: Schocken, 1979. Survival qualities, writing skills, budgeting, the law, financing, distribution, contracts; specific section for documentaries.

Wiese, Michael. *Film and Video Marketing*. Boston: Focal Press, 1989. Covers independent feature films and original home video programs. Much of what goes into marketing fiction films is the same for selling a large budget documentary.

————. *The Independent Film and Videomaker's Guide*. London: Focal, 1984. About finding investors, preparing the prospectus, researching the market, and producing and distributing. Specifically for short and documentary films.

EDUCATION AND CAREER POSSIBILITIES

American Film Institute Guide to College Courses in Film and Television. Princeton, N.J.: Peterson's Guides (Dept. 7591, P.O. Box 978, Edison, N.J. 08817), 1986. Comprehensive listing of institutions, their faculty, philosophy, equipment, and core courses.

Bone, Jan. *Opportunities in Film*. Lincolnwood, Ill.: VGM Career Horizons, 1983. Organization of the film industry, workshops, seminars, conventions, unions, job hunting, schooling abroad. Feature-film oriented, but contains much useful information.

Draigh, David. *Behind the Screen: The American Museum of the Moving Image Guide to Who Does What in Motion Pictures and Television*. New York: Abbeville Press, 1988. Definition and history of production roles in all aspects of screen production, down to "pyrotechnic specialist," including union affiliations.

Videomaker (P.O. Box 558, Mt. Morris, Ill. 61054). Excellent chatty monthly magazine that explains basic principles as well as reviewing equipment and career possibilities for the semiprofessional.

I·N·D·E·X